The Elections in Israel 1992

Edited by
ASHER ARIAN
and
MICHAL SHAMIR

STATE UNIVERSITY OF NEW YORK PRESS

Published by
State University of New York Press, Albany

For information, address State University of New York Press,
State University Plaza, Albany, N.Y., 12246

Production by Cathleen Collins
Marketing by Nancy Farrell

Library of Congress Cataloging in Publication Data

The Elections in Israel 1992 / edited by Asher Arian and Michal
    Shamir.
        p.   cm. — (SUNY series in Israeli studies.)
    Includes bibliographical references and index.
    ISBN 0-7914-2175-9 (hard). — ISBN 0-7914-2176-7 (pbk.)
    1. Israel. Knesset—Elections, 1992. 2. Israel—Politics and
government. I. Arian, Asher. II. Shamir, Michal, 1951– .
III. Series.
JQ1825.P365E448 1994
324.95694'054—dc20   93-49761
                                                                CIP

10 9 8 7 6 5 4 3 2 1

Contents

List of Tables

List of Figures

Introduction

MICHAL SHAMIR AND ASHER ARIAN

I

The 1992 elections have been widely seen as ushering in a new era in Israeli politics, and in many senses that depiction is accurate. Fifteen years after the defeat of 1977, and eight years after the stalemate of 1984, Labor returned to power in a dramatic manner. It was no longer necessary to share power with the Likud, as had happened after the 1984 and 1988 elections. Yitzhak Rabin returned to the prime ministry he had left in 1977, with his two principal nemeses—Yitzhak Shamir of the Likud and Shimon Peres of Labor—relegated to leader of the opposition and foreign minister, respectively, after Rabin's moment of victory.

There was no denying the sense of change in the country following the victory won by Rabin's Labor Party in 1992. His party's 44 seats were far and away the largest of the Knesset's ten factions, with the defeated Likud's next at 32 (see table I.1). Along with the left-wing Meretz (12 seats), the support of the ultraorthodox Shas (6 seats) and the backing of 5 members of Arab lists, Rabin's quickly formed government commanded a working majority in the 120-member Knesset, while Labor made efforts to coax other parties into joining. Based on this majority, Rabin's colleagues could try to implement their campaign promises to change national priorities, to be more flexible in the peace talks with Arab countries, to reduce the amount of money channeled to settlements in the territories, to restore good relations with the United States, to attend to the economy and the high rate of unemployment, to better absorb immigrants, and to prepare for future waves of immigration. It could not be predicted from the vote that the historic breakthrough with the PLO in the summer of 1993 would come about, but once it in fact occurred, it was clear that the 1992 election results had made that development possible.

We wish to thank Rinat Philosof and Dorit Tene for their help in data collection.

1

Table I.1. Results of the 1992 Knesset Elections

	Valid Votes	% of Valid Votes	No. of Knesset Seats
Labor	906,810	34.6	44
Likud	651,229	24.9	32
Meretz	250,667	9.6	12
Tzomet	166,366	6.4	8
National Religious	129,663	5.0	6
Shas	129,347	4.9	6
United Torah Jewry	86,167	3.3	4
Moledet	62,269	2.4	3
Hadash (DFPE)	62,546	2.4	3
Democratic Arab	40,788	1.6	2
Tehiya	31,957	1.2	0
Progressive List for Peace	24,181	0.9	0
New Liberal Party	16,669	0.6	0
Geulat Israel	12,851	0.5	0
Democracy and Immigration	11,697	0.4	0
Pensioners	8,327	0.3	0
Mortgage Victims	5,962	0.2	0
Pikanti	3,750	0.1	0
Torah and Land	3,708	0.1	0
On Wheels	3,355	0.1	0
Women	2,886	0.1	0
Hope	2,053	—[a]	0
Law of Nature	1,734	—[a]	0
Tali	1,336	—[a]	0
Zipor	523	—[a]	0
TOTAL	2,616,841	99.6[b]	120

Source: Central Bureau of Statistics. The participation rate was 77.4 percent. There were 3,409,015 eligible voters, of whom 2,637,943 actually voted. 21,102 votes were not valid.

[a] Less than 0.1 percent of the vote.

[b] The total is less than 100 percent due to rounding.

After fifteen years of drift to the right, sometimes stalemated by political paralysis, the election was indeed dramatic. Observers could point to the smooth transfer of power, highlighting the vitality of Israeli democracy. Depending on the political point of view, some were joyous while others wept. But there could be no doubt that something important had happened. Just how important would be clear later in 1993 when the agreement of joint recognition between Israel and the Palestine Liberation Organization was signed.

The 1992 reversal was the second turnover in government in the forty-four years of Israel's political history, or in more than sixty years if one also considers the politics of the Jewish Yishuv period before independence under the British mandate. The first reversal occurred in 1977, when the dominant Labor Party, which had always won, suddenly crumbled. The second turnover in government occurred on June 23, 1992. 1977 was a political earthquake; 1992 was nearly as dramatic.

The 1992 results can be fully appreciated by comparison to 1988: Likud went from forty to thirty-two Knesset seats; Labor added five members of Knesset over the thirty-nine won in the 1988 election. As is often the case when turnovers occur, the setback of the party in power had more impact than did the increase of the opposition. In 1977, for example, Likud increased its representation in the Knesset by only four seats, but Labor lost nineteen! These comparisons and others are expanded on in the article by Arian and Shamir. They contend that the 1992 reversal was founded on ideological division reflecting divisions regarding the territories more strongly than the ethnic cleavage in the society, while the 1977 election was influenced by both.

The 1992 victory was very much Yitzhak Rabin's. He not only won the election and emerged as prime minister but also came out of the election with an open mandate and with a hopeful electorate. He came back as Labor's leader following his party's primaries, in which he defeated his long-time foe—Shimon Peres. He returned to a second term as premier, picking up the reins of government from the Likud, to which his party lost power in 1977, shortly after Rabin withdrew as head of his list over an illegal foreign bank account. He starred in the election campaign, running as though this were a direct personal election for prime minister. And when Labor won, he thought this had indeed been the case, only to find out through the coalition negotiations and first months in office that things had changed less than he had hoped.

Another indication of the disparity between the perception and reality of the degree of change achieved by the 1992 elections—as well as a sign of the prospects for change in political culture and policy—has to do with the Knesset members elected in 1992. The results of the innovative Labor primaries for the selection of its list, the personalized campaign of Yitzhak Rabin, and the emergence of many new faces in the Knesset gave rise to the impression of a major change. However, as seen in figure I.1, the actual number of new members was not very different from that in past years. As in the past, about a third of the incoming Knesset members were new. For the first elections in 1949, all members were necessarily new; for the July 1961

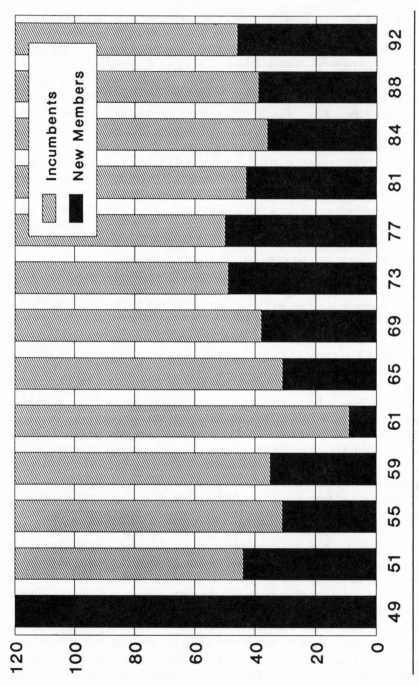

Figure I.1. New Knesset Members, 1949–1992

elections to the Fifth Knesset, held less than two years after the November 1959 for the Fourth Knesset and decided upon months earlier, only 9 new members entered. Besides those two unusual years, the range of new members in the 120-member Knesset was between 30 (1955) and 50 (1977); the average for those eleven elections (excluding 1949 and 1959) was 40.2 new Knesset members.[1]

The 1992 election results magnified comparatively modest changes in electoral behavior into shifts with tremendous potential for substantial policy change, in particular in relations with the Arabs and Palestinians. Whether those will materialize remains to be seen. If they do, it is possible that the country will embark on a new course and that the momentum of the 1992 elections will strengthen Labor and the left, just as the elections of 1977 ushered in the Likud era. Like the wave that grows as it becomes more distant from its source, the shift in 1992 may prove enormous. On the other hand 1992 might be a benchmark in that it will signal the beginning of an era in Israeli democracy with much more electoral volatility and more turnover between the major parties, increased voter efficacy, and growing party accountability.

II

The 1992 elections marked more than the defeat of the Likud; they also signalled, at least temporarily, the weakening of the bloc of parties on the right in Israeli politics and the breakdown of the coalition of the right bloc with religious parties. Israeli coalition politics have historically been conducted within the following blocs: (1) the left bloc, including Labor and the smaller Jewish and Arab left-wing parties, (2) the right bloc, including the Likud and smaller right-wing parties, and (3) the religious parties. Until the first reversal in 1977, religious parties tended to coalesce with Labor. Since 1977, the religious parties have gone with the Likud and the right; their policy positions in foreign and security affairs as well as their vision of the state of Israel have been much closer to Likud than to Labor, and their followers have also been more right- than left-wingers. The parliamentary balance between the left and right/religious was 61:59 in favor of the left in 1992; in 1988, it had been 55:65. This result enabled a Labor dominated coalition in 1992, as the left had a blocking majority that could prevent a right-religious coalition from emerging even if the left-bloc could form the coalition among the constituent parties with difficulty.

The results also served as a reminder that what is labelled "right" in Israeli politics is not as clear-cut as what is labelled "left" and that the religious parties have interests that vary depending on the election results. Religious parties often displayed no convincing ideological reluctance to join the stronger bloc, whichever it proved to be. Despite the election campaign rhetoric, which emphasized their being part of the "right," all religious parties entered into coalition negotiations with Labor after the election victory.

Numerically, Likud's defeat was much greater than was the decline of the right block of parties; yet the picture was more complicated. Within the right bloc, the major beneficiary of the public's disappointment with the Likud was the secular Tzomet Party, whose roots can be traced to the Labor movement. Tzomet increased its delegation to the Knesset fourfold: from two to eight seats. However, the other small right-wing parties fared much more poorly. The more extreme Moledet, contrary to expectations, increased its delegation only by one (from two to three MKs). Tehiya, which had three representatives in the Twelfth Knesset, did not achieve the minimum 1.5 percent needed for representation and lost all parliamentary representation. Two other right-wing lists obtained less than 1 percent of the vote: one was headed by Rabbi Moshe Levinger, a major figure among the Jewish settlers in Judea and Samaria, and the other was headed by Eliezer Mizrahi, who was a member in the outgoing Knesset from Agudat Israel, but ran on his own in 1992. These results, and in particular the disappearance of Tehiya, indicate the weakening appeal of the Greater Israel movement, the focus on settlements in the territories as an overriding issue, and the breakdown of the combination of religious and secular forces within the right camp.

III

To what extent were the elections a referendum on peace and territories, as some observers have suggested? The political and international context in which the elections were held sets the stage for such an interpretation. The 1992 elections took place eighteen months after the Gulf War and nine months after the beginning of the peace talks in Madrid in October 1991. These talks between Israel and neighboring Arab states, with the Palestinians being part of the Jordanian delegation, seemed to have stalled before the elections. All sides were eager to see how Shamir's Likud would do in the June elections and how George Bush would do in his effort to be reelected president of the United States in November 1992.

The 1992 election was held about four and one-half years into the intifada, the Arab uprising in the territories held by Israel since the 1967 Six Days war. Analyses of the 1988 election, which was held about a year after the intifada had started, suggested that the Arab uprising had significant effect on the voters despite the fact that the aggregate results did not differ much from the past. In 1992 an aggregate electoral shift was discernable, and it brought about the turnover in government. The contributions in this volume by Arian and Shamir and by Shachar and Shamir suggest that the dilemmas relating to the Israeli-Arab conflict, the territories, and the intifada were a major source of the electoral change.

Voter performance evaluations of Likud and Labor in terms of security and foreign affairs, and in particular with regard to prospects of peace and putting an end to the intifada, were most important factors in explaining the election results. They were the most important of the voters' considerations, and they were also the major source of the turnover between 1988 and 1992. Voters' images of the two major parties in these respects had changed dramatically to the detriment of the Likud. Voters' policy positions on these issues were another important factor; they became a more significant consideration in the voting decision at the same time as attitudes in the electorate moved in a dovish direction.

The election campaign—in contrast to that of 1988—avoided taking on these difficult policy dilemmas. Labor's strategy in particular was to address them in valence terms by attacking the Likud for its distorted priorities and as being responsible for the deteriorating sense of personal security. Labor avoided attacking the issue on the merits of retaining or returning the territories; instead it denounced the Likud's settlement policy in the territories because it allocated too much of Israel's limited resources to the wrong target and because that policy complicated relations with the United States over the proposed loan guarantee of $10 billion for absorbing immigrants. Issue positions were cardinal for the general electorate. Labor's strategy of emphasizing a different order of priorities seems to have been in tune with public sentiment, and it seems to have paid off, Arian and Shamir argue.

Yitzhak Shamir characterized Labor's victory as an accident, but this seems to be the minority view. Not many observers concurred, including other Likud leaders. Only 18 percent of a sample of Jewish voters, interviewed shortly after the election, agreed with him; 74 percent disagreed.[2] Many more respondents thought that the elections signified that the general public did not subscribe to the notion of Greater Israel and was more willing to return territories and compromise with the Palestinians.

About a month before the elections, a young high school girl, Helena Rapp, was murdered in Bat-Yam by a Palestinian terrorist from Gaza. The city erupted into violent anti-Arab demonstrations and riots including calls for lynching Arabs in which radical right groups played a leading role. But unlike past elections in which such terrorist attacks were generally perceived as benefitting the right, the Bat-Yam tragedy was used by Labor and the left as well. This time, all parties tried to exploit the events, and it was not at all clear who gained at the polls from this and other such acts of terrorism.

Security policy and the future of the territories were clearly important in 1992, but there were other factors behind the electoral turnover. There was widespread disappointment with the ruling Likud, similar in nature to the upset with Labor in 1977. Internal party strife and examples of ineptitude abounded. Corruption by Likud officials was not only charged; just before election day, the much-respected state comptroller issued a report that substantiated many of the claims being made by the opposition. Unemployment reached levels that were regarded as unacceptable in other times, the absorption of the mass immigration from the former Soviet Union was faltering, and the American loan guarantees were denied because of the government's settlement policy. Also, the personal popularity of the candidates had an impact on the final results.

Keeping in mind social and economic concerns is important in understanding the 1992 elections; these entered the campaign mainly as valence issues. The two major parties contested with each other over the image of who was best able to conduct the economy, to help create jobs and sustain economic growth, to fight unemployment, and to absorb the new immigrants. Shachar and Shamir found that these considerations were significant parts of the general electorate's calculus.

IV

Elections are the results of individual behavior often mediated by the groups to which these individuals belong. Herzog places the public behavior of politically impoverished groups into a theoretical perspective by comparing cooptation practices used in relation to these groups. Her analysis enlightens Yishai's treatment of one of the recurring anomalies of Israeli political life— the failure of the gender issue to generate substantial difference in political behavior or political results. There is a very committed kernel dedicated to women's issues, but on the whole their achievements have been less substantial than their numbers in the population would suggest. Yishai's analysis focuses on the gender gap in Israel.

The religious cleavage—a major one among Israeli Jews—has become more and more related to the territorial issue over the 1980s, but in the 1992 election, issues stemming from it seem to have regained their independent place, at least in the election campaign, crosscutting to some extent the territorial cleavage. A particularly good case in point was offered by Tzomet, the extreme right-wing surprise of the election, which emphasized in its campaign issues such as the military draft of Orthodox religious Jews. Shas, the Sephardi-Orthodox party, able to retain its six Knesset seats despite police investigations of several of its key members, is discussed in Willis's paper. He analyzes the Shas phenomenon as a social movement, combining both ethnic and religious elements.

Arab groups, like women's groups and unlike the religious groups, win a smaller fraction of their share of power than expected, if simple percentage of the population compared to percent of the vote is used as the index of political power. The maneuverings and calculations of these Arab political groups are presented by Al-Haj. His contention is that there is a disparity between the politicized leadership of this community and the behavior of the masses of Arab voters.

Fein's article shows the important role that the two hundred thousand or so voters who recently immigrated from the former Soviet Union played in returning Labor to power. Capable of electing ten percent of the Knesset, they abandoned the notion of supporting a party of immigrants, and half of them ultimately voted for Labor.

Like any other political system, that of the Israeli elections is affected not only by those who vote but also by those who do not vote. Participation rates are one reflection of this. Another is the behavior of influential nonvoting constituencies. The articles by Frisch and Rubin analyze these intangibles, Frisch for the Palestinian Liberation Organization (PLO), and Rubin for the United States. In the Israeli elections of 1992, both of these were extremely significant; the PLO involved in decisions of negotiations and terror; the US in matters of loan guarantees and monetary aid. Both Frisch and Rubin conclude that even if preferences exist, control does not. Both groups are actors in the play; their impact on the voters must not be ignored. The postelection developments show just how important and surprising an impact these two groups had. As the peace accords in 1993 were prepared, the PLO became a major actor, and the United States a host and onlooker.

V

In the public mind, the word used to describe the 1992 elections was *mahapach*, "reversal" or "turnabout." This word was used widely on television the night of the election and in newspaper coverage in the following days. It is ironic then that the election campaign was often criticized for avoiding the major policy issues and that the public was portrayed as indifferent and uninterested. This offers a good reminder that the meaning of elections goes beyond the election campaign and the themes it raises. Election campaigns are targeted to very specific audiences (mainly different types of undecided voters), and they are the result of political-party concerns and constraints. Thus they can be very far from most voters' and the country's policy agenda. Mendilow's and Wolsfeld's articles analyze these and other aspects of the election campaign and the public's discomfort with it.

We should also be careful with our indicators for political interest. The turnout rate of 77.4 percent was a bit lower, but not very different from that of elections in the 1980s: it had been 79.7 percent in 1988, 78.8 percent in 1984, and 78.5 percent in 1981. Some of those elections—especially 1981's—

were very turbulent. Style is not necessarily substance, and the fact that fewer voters participated in political meetings and rallies and only few watched the parties' television ads regularly is an indication that the expression of public involvement in election campaigns has probably changed over time. Weimann's analysis of the polls over time provides another indication of the change in the political culture of Israel.

When voters went to the polls, issue concerns were high on their mind, despite the fact that the political parties did much to hide them. Moreover, the electorate seems to have come out of the campaign with a strong sense of electoral efficacy. During the election campaign Labor nurtured this theme in its attempts to lure Likud loyalists. One of its slogans read "Government is like a shirt: if you don't change it, it starts to stink." After the reversal, this interpretation gained momentum. In the postelection poll cited, 86 percent supported the statement that the 1992 election showed that the electorate today is not the property of any political party and that if the party in government does not satisfy the concerns of voters, they may very well switch to the opposition in the next election.

VI

Historians are likely to view the 1992 elections as transitional. For all of the tension and promise that surrounded them, the next elections will probably be held using different electoral rules. Although the 1992 election followed older electoral law, the Knesset had already decided that in future elections the voters would directly elect the prime minister rather than have him or her selected by the Knesset after the elections. This would undoubtedly alter the nature of coalition formation and party maneuvering. In the 1992 elections, this development was already foreshadowed. Primaries were used to select the leadership of Labor, the campaign was run as if the new electoral law were already in place, and a reversal occurred. For better or worse, the future is likely to be different.

Reform was a major theme of the 1992 elections, and the beginning of constitutional transformation of the system may be dated from the "dirty trick" of 1990, the name given by Yitzhak Rabin to the failed attempt by Shimon Peres to replace the Likud-led National Unity government with a Labor-led coalition. The background of the story was a peace initiative put forth by Israel. It gained support in Washington and Cairo, but when United States Secretary of State James Baker pressed the Israeli government to be more flexible regarding details, Prime Minister Yitzhak Shamir recoiled. The Knesset expressed no-confidence in its government for the first time in Israeli history, and the Unity government fell.

Yitzhak Modai, minister of finance, and his group of four other Knesset members (former members of the Liberal faction of the Likud), for a total of five votes, demanded recognition as an independent Knesset faction in return for their support of Shamir's position. The approval of their demand was granted just before the vote of no confidence. On 15 March 1990, the government fell by a vote of sixty to fifty-five, based on a coalition of Labor, the Arabs, the left, and ultraorthodox Agudat Israel. The key to the "victory" of Peres and Labor was the fact that five of the six Knesset members of the ultraorthodox Shas Party absented themselves from the vote.

With the fall of the government, Shimon Peres was appointed by President Chaim Herzog to form a government. Peres had to placate his own party, made up of hawks and doves, and to fashion a government of religious parties and the extreme left. He needed the votes of Arab parties too, but he could not plan on negotiating away territory if their support was seen as pivotal. To succeed, Peres had to find Knesset members of the other camp willing to desert to the Labor side. Israeli constitutional practice did not prohibit the Knesset member from switching allegiance. The three most promising turncoat candidates had all been placed on the Likud list in deals cut to solve previous coalition crises. One was Yigael Horowitz, leader of Ometz (two seats), who had left the Labor Party years before; another was Aharon Abu-Hatzeira, former head of the Tami list; finally, there was the Modai group, with five seats, recently liberated from the Likud and now recognized as an independent Knesset faction.

Things went poorly for Peres. Aguda, an ultraorthodox party, agreed not to participate in a Likud government and to support a Labor government without formally joining it. On the other hand, the deciding rabbinical council of the Sephardi, ultraorthodox, non-Zionist Shas, decided to back a government headed by Shamir. Charlie Bitton, of the Communist list (Rakah), was wooed to Labor's ranks. Avraham Sharir, one of Modai's group who felt that Prime Minister Shamir had slighted him in the past, seemed to be leaning to Labor, and Modai was also reportedly wavering. It was a seller's market. Peres and Labor agreed to appoint Sharir minister of transportation and to give him a sure place on the Labor list for the next two elections.

Meanwhile, the Likud was busy trying to block Peres's attempt and prenegotiating their own government. Shamir met with Modai; the Likud promised him an important ministry (foreign, defense, or treasury), another for one of his colleagues, five certain places in the next Likud election list, and a $10 million security deposit to guarantee these pledges. After petitions to the judicial system, and a massive demonstration calling for constitutional reform, Modai backed down from his demand for a cash deposit and agreed to make do with the signatures of all of the Likud ministers backing the agreement with him. When four of them refused to go along, Modai reopened negotiations with Labor.

Peres planned to present his government to the Knesset on the day that his twenty-one-day mandate ended. By adding Sharir to the sixty votes that had brought down the Unity government, Peres thought that he had enough votes. But his plans unraveled when two of the Aguda supporters bolted, despite the discipline with which Aguda Knesset members had always followed the dictates of their party's Council of Torah Sages. Verdiger and Mizrahi chose to disobey party dictates rather than to allow the creation of a government headed by Peres. The president gave Peres a fifteen-day extension to form the government. The Aguda lined up Verdiger, one of its two wayward Knesset members, after extracting a promise from Peres that new elections would be held before any territory was returned. Mizrahi was to be tried before a rabbinical tribunal for breaking his promise to follow the dictates of the Council of Torah Sages. Ultimately, he resigned from the Aguda and set up his own one-member faction in the Knesset (to run unsuccessfully in 1992).

The uncertainty grew. After a meeting with David Levy, Sharir seemed ready to shift his support back to the Likud. The deal with Modai's group drew sharp criticism; many Herut members were incensed that much of the next Likud list was being given away. Once Peres failed, it was Shamir's turn, and he had troubles of his own. He won the support of Mizrahi of the Aguda list and turned a Labor Knesset member, Ephraim Gur. With them, the Likud could count on sixty-two Knesset members. Both were rewarded with appointments as deputy ministers, and Gur was given a promise of a secure place on the Likud list for the next Knesset.

Reform followed. In February 1991, the Knesset reacted to this unseemly chain of events by passing legislation that was intended to change basic parliamentary norms. The legislation stipulated that a Knesset member who resigned from the party on whose list he or she was elected, or who voted noconfidence against the decision of the party on whose list elected, would be penalized. The offending Knesset member would not be recognized as being a member of any other party-grouping within the Knesset, would not be allowed to run in the next elections on a list represented in the current Knesset, would not be allowed to serve as a minister or a deputy minister during the term of the Knesset in which the prohibited act occurred, and would not be entitled to party financing from the public treasury.

Reform and its various meanings are discussed in the articles by Hermann and by Doron and Kay. Both articles consider the reforms as they emerged and provide a picture of a complex political process responding to a generalized feeling of discomfort with the then-existing situation. Hermann's article uses theories of mass political participation to assess their introduction and impact, while Doron and Kay's article scrutinizes the reforms in terms of general principles of electoral reform. Electoral reform, although discussed endlessly in the pre-election period, was thwarted. The opposition was so intense that the idea of electoral reform was soon replaced with the idea of governmental reform, as much to protect the incumbent parliamentarians (the cynics said) as to increase governmental efficiency. The Knesset passed two amendments to the electoral law. The more important one established direct election of the prime minister, similar to that in presidential systems, as an addition to the parliamentary elections. Labor supported this change, mainly out of short-term electoral considerations; Likud made no clear-cut decision, although Prime Minister Shamir explicitly and publicly opposed it. The Knesset passed this legislation before the 1992 election of the Thirteenth Knesset, but decided to postpone its implementation until the election to the Fourteenth Knesset. Thus, even though this important amendment was passed, it was formally irrelevant to the 1992 election. In effect, though, Labor conducted its election campaign as though these were direct elections for the prime minister, placing Rabin firmly at the center of its campaign[3] and exploiting the themes of change and Likud's opposition to reform. As if in anticipation of the direct election for the prime minister that had been promulgated for the next elections, the Labor Party went so far as to officially call itself "The Labor Party Headed by Rabin."

The other amendment increased the minimum a list had to obtain in order to be represented in the 120-member Knesset from 1 percent to 1.5 percent. While minor, this change reacted to the public's feeling that something had to be done about the small delegations that seemed to have inordinate influence on the formation of coalitions. This reform in effect eliminated the single-member Knesset delegation in 1992. The number of parties represented also decreased, from fifteen in 1988 to ten in 1992. The increased threshhold amount was the compromise result of different political interests; at the time of its passage, it seemed trivial and went almost unnoticed. Ultimately, it proved to be of consequence, as it excluded from the Knesset the extreme right-wing party Tehiya, which would have entered under the old minimum rule.

Another important reform occurred within the Labor Party in its internal candidate selection procedures. Democratization was the codeword and primaries were the tool. The party opened up to its 160 thousand registered members and let them choose the party's candidate for prime minister as well as its candidates for the Knesset. The Labor primaries stood in stark contrast to the selection process in the Likud, which in the past was hailed as a major move toward democratization. In 1992, with its deals, power struggles, faction infighting, and ethnic undertones, the Likud seemed to epitomize the dirty politics that the public wanted to hear no more of.

The reform movement and the actual reforms passed and executed are relevant to the 1992 election in a deeper sense. They express aversion with the way politics were being conducted, distrust in politicians, and a deep yearning for change. Hermann discusses these aspects in her article with reference to the reform movement, and she attributes the success of the reform movement to its ability to impart a sense of empowerment to the electorate. Many of these feelings are not unique to Israel; they characterize many postindustrial societies.

Notes

1. Of the total of 571 individuals who served in the Knesset through the 1992 election, most (about 65 percent) served more than 1 term. The average number of terms served was 2.74, or about eleven years; the median was 2 terms, or about eight years.

2. These data are from a survey carried out by Modiin Ezrahi in September 1992 among a representative sample of the adult Jewish population of Israel, not including kibbutzim and settlements in the territories ($N = 685$). This survey is part of a larger research project on the dyanmics of Israeli public opinion directed by Jacob and Michal Shamir, supported by the Israel Foundation Trustees, the Israel Academy of Sciences and Humanities and the Tami Steinmetz Center for Peace Research at Tel Aviv University. The figures reported in the text do not sum to 100 percent due to the middle "not sure" category.

3. In 1988, Labor had put much emphasis in its election campaign on its then-unsuccessful candidate for prime minister, Shimon Peres.

PART I

Political Turnover

CHAPTER 1

Two Reversals: Why 1992 Was Not 1977

ASHER ARIAN
City University of New York and University of Haifa
and
MICHAL SHAMIR
Tel Aviv University

I. Introduction

Israeli voters have only twice changed the party in power at the polls, once in 1977 and again in 1992. The first time, the dominant Labor Party lost power to the Likud as Labor hemorrhaged from self-inflicted wounds and lost votes to the reformist Democratic Movement for Change, on the one hand, and to the Likud, on the other.[1] In 1992, the shift was less complex and numerically smaller, but the potential political impact was just as large, as the Likud lost its fifteen-year lease on power to Labor.

Motifs of the 1992 elections had been encountered before: an enormous number of new voters were added to the rolls through immigration, this time from the former Soviet Union; the party in power engineered for itself an electoral loss of major proportions, and Yitzhak Rabin became prime minister again after his first appointment in 1974, as Labor came back to power. In both 1977 and 1992, the combination of a ruling party in retreat and social and economic turmoil set the stage for the transfer of power. In both cases a significant number of voters abandoned the party in power; and

Our thanks to Arthur Goldberg, Carol Gordon, Zeev Maoz, and Alan Zuckerman for very useful comments.

A version of this article appeared in *Electoral Studies* 12, no. 4 (December, 1993): 315–41.

these votes were dispersed to other parties on the same side of the political divide or to parties in the other camp.

We shall specify the factors that accompanied these transitions. Like others who have attempted to account for electoral change, we shall focus on "evolving social and attitudinal structures" (Franklin et al., 1992). The comparison of 1992 with 1977 will provide a temporal base for assessing the meaning of the 1992 election; in the concluding section, these results will be considered in a broader comparative and theoretical perspective.

II. The Arithmetic of Reversal

The arithmetic of the elections indicates that there were some 330,000 valid votes more in 1992 than in 1988, an increase of 14.6 percent (see table 1.1). Although there was a large increase in the number of voters, the Likud vote decreased in both the relative and the absolute senses. Compared with that of 1988, the 1992 Likud vote decreased by 8 percent, from 709,305 to 651,229, reducing the party's parliamentary delegation from 40 seats in 1988 to 32 seats in 1992. Labor's delegation, on the other hand, grew from 39 to 44 seats, as its vote total swelled by a third, from 685,363 votes in 1988 to 906,810 votes in 1992. Labor's percentage of the vote grew faster than the electorate, as its percentage of the vote grew by fifteen points between 1988 and 1992. The left-wing Meretz vote grew handsomely by almost 30 percent, and its Knesset representation increased from ten to twelve members. The total increase of votes for religious parties was only 3.2 percent, since these parties were unable to make inroads with the new, secular immigrant voting stock. Tzomet, on the right, registered an amazing 265 percent increase compared with 1988 and had its delegation to the Knesset grow from two to eight seats.

On the whole, the parties of the left outdid the parties of the right. Voters for left-wing parties (Labor, Meretz, and the Arab lists) totalled 1,284,992 voters. Parties of the right (Likud, Tzomet, Moledet, and three parties of the right that did not achieve the minimum 1.5 percent needed for representation) won 928,380 votes. Including in the right the National Religious Party (first and foremost a religious party, but which positioned itself to the right of the Likud), the total for the right would be 1,058,043 votes. Adding to this total the two ultraorthodox parties, we obtain 1,273,557 for the right-wing religious bloc combined, very close to the total left vote. More votes for parties that failed to win representation were registered for the right wing than for the left wing.

In terms of seats won, the left bloc had a slight edge of 61:59 over the right-wing/religious bloc. This hardly qualified as a landslide for the left, or for Labor. The previous Knesset, elected in 1988, split 55:65 along these lines. Labor with its 44 seats of 120 in 1992 was as large as it was in 1984 and

Table 1.1. Votes and Seats for Labor and Likud, 1988–1992

	Valid Votes	Labor	Likud
1988	2,283,123	685,363	709,305
1992	2,616,841	906,810	651,229
Increase over 1988 (%)	14.6	32.3	-8.2
	Labor seats		Likud seats
1988	39		40
1992	44		32
Increase over 1988 (%)	12.8		-20.0

Note: See note 1 at the end of this chapter.

Table 1.2. Votes and Seats for Labor and Likud, 1973–1977

	Valid Votes	Labor	Likud
1973	1,566,855	621,183	473,309
1977	1,747,820	430,023	583,968
Increase over 1973 (%)	11.5	-30.8	23.4
	Labor seats		Likud seats
1973	51		39
1977	32		43
Increase over 1973 (%)	-37.3		10.3

Note: See note 1 at the end of this chapter.

3 seats smaller than its 1981 strength. Furthermore, more Israeli Jews voted for the right-wing/religious bloc than for the left bloc. The total of the parties of the left was bigger than the right and religious only in conjunction with the votes of Israeli Arabs.

In 1977, the Democratic Movement for Change (DMC) took away so many votes from Labor that the Likud emerged as the largest party, ushering in an era dominated by Menachem Begin and Yitzhak Shamir that lasted until 1992. Labor's loss of votes in 1977 (more than 30 percent of its 1973 total) was even larger than was the Likud loss in 1992 (see table 1.2). The Likud in 1977 increased its total vote over 1973 by almost a quarter. When the growth of the electorate is factored in, the Likud increased its proportion of the vote by 10 percent, while Labor's decreased by almost 40 percent.

Table 1.3 reveals the patterns of voting in 1992 based on the 1988 vote of the respondents.[2] In total, some 68 percent of the sample reported stable voting between the two time periods. This rate was similar to the 1973 elections, higher than the 50 percent rate in 1977, but lower than the usual rate of 75 percent in Israeli elections recorded in 1969, 1981, 1984, and 1988, as discussed by Arian (1989) and Zuckerman (1990). Table 1.3 reflects the grim performance of the Likud: in the prevote poll, a third of the sample reported voting for Likud in 1988, but only a quarter reported that they were committed to doing so in 1992. Moreover, of those who reported voting for the Likud in 1988, only about 60 percent (19 percent of 32 percent) said they would do so again in 1992.

Labor did better, jumping from 23 percent to 30 percent for the vote totals and retaining 84 percent (19 percent of 23 percent) of its 1988 contingent. Not only was Labor's retention rate much more impressive, the percentage that had yet to decide about 1992 among former Likud voters was much higher (15 percent) than for Labor (7 percent). Likud lost large shares to Labor and to the parties of the right, while Labor lost much smaller fractions to the left and to the right and almost nothing to the Likud.

Based on these data, Labor won about half of its increased support from new voters and half from Likud voters. Of the votes that the Likud lost, about half went to Labor and half to parties of the right. It is reasonable to estimate that Labor won one hundred thousand votes from new immigrants and other first-time voters and another hundred thousand votes from people who had voted Likud in 1988. Anticipating the analysis that will follow, we can note that sixty-five thousand of the former Likud voters were Sephardim! The key to Labor's 1992 electoral success was in prying enough of these voters away from the Likud, after failing to do so throughout the 1980s. To this important topic we shall return.

In 1977 the rate of voting turnover was even higher. Most of the change was among those who had supported the Labor-Mapam Alignment in 1973 (see table 1.4). The Alignment was the 1973 choice of 37 percent of the 1977 sample, but fell to less than 20 percent. Of those who reported voting Alignment in 1973, only 40 percent (15 percent of 37 percent) reported that they would repeat in 1977. More than a third of former Alignment voters had yet to decide on their 1977 vote or were not about to tell a pollster whom they had just met their party of choice; about 10 percent said they would vote Likud; and another 10 percent, the DMC. Based on a postelection survey described in Arian (1989, 163), we know that the DMC received two-thirds of its voters who had participated in the 1973 elections from the Alignment, and the Likud almost 30 percent of its 1977 vote from that source. The 1973 Likud voters remained more loyal, with some 15 percent undecided, another 13 percent supporting the DMC, and about 10 percent switching to the Labor Alignment.

First-time voters just coming of age and new immigrants are potential spoilers in electoral contests. Although they are only segments of larger

Table 1.3. The 1992 Vote Choice by the 1988 Vote

1988	Left	Labor	Religious	Likud	Right	No answer	Row Total
			1992				
Left							
Count (*n*)	72	15		1	1	8	97
Row (%)	74.2	15.5		1.0	1.0	8.2	8.2
Column (%)	55.8	4.2		.3	.7	4.5	
Total (%)	*6.0*	1.3		.1	.1	.7	
Labor							
Count (*n*)	17	227		3	7	18	272
Row (%)	6.3	83.5		1.1	2.6	6.6	22.8
Column (%)	13.2	63.4		1.0	4.7	10.2	
Total (%)	1.4	*19.0*		.3	.6	1.5	
Religious							
Count (*n*)		2	52	10	7	9	80
Row (%)		2.5	65.0	12.5	8.8	11.3	6.8
Column (%)		.6	64.2	3.3	4.7	5.1	
Total (%)		.2	*4.4*	.8	.6	.8	
Likud							
Count (*n*)	6	44	10	227	40	56	383
Row (%)	1.6	11.5	2.6	59.3	10.4	14.6	32.1
Column (%)	4.7	12.3	12.3	75.9	27.0	31.6	
Total (%)	.5	3.7	.8	*19.0*	3.4	4.7	
Right							
Count (*n*)	2	7	2	11	48	6	76
Row (%)	2.6	9.2	2.6	14.5	63.2	7.9	6.4
Column (%)	1.6	2.0	2.5	3.7	32.4	3.4	
Total (%)	.2	.6	.2	.9	*4.0*	.5	
No vote							
Count (*n*)	30	57	16	41	44	48	236
Row (%)	12.7	24.2	6.8	17.4	18.6	20.3	19.7
Column (%)	23.3	15.9	19.8	13.7	29.7	27.1	
Total (%)	2.5	4.8	1.3	3.4	3.7	4.0	
No answer							
Count (*n*)	2	6	1	6	1	32	48
Row (%)	4.2	12.5	2.1	12.5	2.1	66.7	4.1
Column (%)	1.6	1.7	1.2	2.0	.7	18.1	
Total (%)	.2	.5	.1	.5	.1	2.7	
Column	129	358	81	299	148	177	1192
Total	10.8	30.1	6.8	25.0	12.5	14.9	100.1[a]

Note: Based on preelection June 1992 survey; stable choices set italics.

[a] Total does not equal 100 percent due to rounding

Table 1.4. The 1977 Vote Choice by the 1973 Vote

1973	1977						
	Likud	Labor	DMC	Religious	Other	No answer	Row Total
Likud							
Count (*n*)	59	9	13	2	1	16	100
Row (%)	59.0	9.0	13.0	2.0	1.0	16.0	20.7
Column (%)	56.2	9.4	26.0	5.6	5.9	8.8	
Total (%)	*12.2*	1.9	2.7	.4	.2	3.3	
Labor							
Count (*n*)	21	73	18		4	65	181
Row (%)	11.6	40.3	9.9		2.2	35.9	37.3
Column (%)	20.0	76.0	36.0		23.5	35.9	
Total (%)	9.3	*15.1*	3.7		.8	13.4	
Religious							
Count (*n*)	3			29		5	37
Row (%)	8.1			78.4		13.5	7.6
Column (%)	2.9			80.6		2.8	
Total (%)	.6			*6.0*		1.0	
Other							
Count (*n*)	2	6	10	2	10	10	40
Row (%)	5.0	15.0	25.0	5.0	25.0	25.0	8.3
Column (%)	1.9	6.3	20.0	5.6	58.8	5.5	
Total (%)	.4	1.2.	2.1	.4	*2.1*	2.1	
No vote							
Count (*n*)	17	8	8	2	2	35	72
Row (%)	23.6	11.1	11.1	2.8	2.8	48.6	14.7
Column (%)	16.2	8.3	16.0	5.6	11.8	19.3	
Total (%)	3.5	1.6	1.6	.4	.4	7.2	
No answer							
Count (*n*)	3		1	1		50	55
Row (%)	5.5		1.8	1.8		90.9	11.3
Column (%)	2.9		2.0	2.8		27.6	
Total (%)	.6		.2	.2		*10.3*	
Column	105	96	50	36	17	181	485
Total	21.6	19.8	10.3	7.4	3.5	37.3	99.9[a]

Note: Based on preelection May 1977 survey; stable votes set italics.

[a] Total does not equal 100 percent due to rounding.

samples, the differences between the findings of tables 1.3 and 1.4 regarding the new voters are indicative of larger differences between these elections. The general impression from the 1992 results (see table 1.3) is how similar the behavior of the new voters was to the overall pattern followed by veteran voters. Those who reported not voting in 1988 made up a fifth of the sample, and as a group they supported Labor more heavily than the Likud, and the right more strongly than the left. Adding Labor and left together and Likud and right together provided an almost even split; they were only slightly more undecided or reticent in answering questions about voting preferences than was the sample as a whole.

These results hide differences between the group of young first-time voters and the new immigrants. The immigrants were much more likely to prefer Labor over Likud, whereas the youngsters split more evenly among them. The young first-time voters who were not immigrants voted much more than did the new immigrants for the small—left and right—parties. The immigrants split about equally between these left and right parties, while the first-time voters who were not immigrants favored the small right over the small left parties. Adding Likud with right-wing parties on the one hand, and Labor with left on the other, the results show that the right had a small advantage among the nonimmigrant first-time voters, and the left had a big advantage among the immigrants. But a comparison of the electoral preferences of the young first-time voters in 1992 with their counterparts in the 1970s and 1980s shows change in the same direction as the aggregate results. As was the case with other voters, the rate of support for the Likud dropped for nonimmigrant first-time voters, and their preference for right over left decreased as well. The new immigrants accentuated these trends, but in effect they reflected more than created them.

The 1977 picture was very different (see table 1.4). An astounding half of the new voters (mostly nonimmigrants) did not answer the voting question. New voters who did reply supported the Likud more strongly than did the total sample, and they went for Labor at a rate only half as large as the general population. About a quarter of those who did not vote in 1973 supported the Likud in 1977, with 10 percent or more each going to the DMC and Labor. New voters led the reversal in 1977; in 1992 they were part of it along with many others.

III. Issues and Demography

When we move beyond the arithmetic of reversals and probe the sources of electoral change, attention turns to issues and sociodemographic factors (Franklin et al. 1992; Dalton et al. 1984). In order to get a broader perspective of the changes that have occurred, we will examine these factors since the 1969 elections—the first election after the Six Days war of 1967—and not only for 1977 and 1992.

Political homogeneity of groups in the Israeli population increased from the 1970s through 1984 in terms of ethnicity, social-class indicators, and religiosity, and this process was interpreted as an indication of a realignment process in the electorate (Shamir 1986, 272–75). This same analysis also established the growing electoral importance of the territories issue over time. Extending the analysis to the 1988 and 1992 elections seems to indicate that the role of demographic factors has receded since 1984 while the role of issues has continued to be high.

Table 1.5 presents the correlations between the Labor/Likud vote and various demographic and issue variables.[3] Inspecting table 1.4 along the columns, it is apparent that the twin issues of God and nationalism, always good predictors of the vote, have become more powerful over the years. For these issues, 1977 and 1992 do not stand out as critical years in the time series. On the state/religion issue, the trend of increasing correlations is smooth over time. The identification of Labor as an anticlerical party has strengthened, while the Likud has played to the traditional sympathies of much of its voting base, even though the origins and ideology of the Likud are very secular, as Liebman and Don-Yehiya (1983) showed.

On the territories issue, the trend of growing correlations is less smooth, with the critical election being 1984, the one following the war in Lebanon and the first one with Shamir replacing Begin as the head of the Likud. Since 1984, the correlations of the territories issue with the vote have been very high and of similar magnitude.[4] Over time, Labor has more unambiguously identified itself as the territories-for-peace party, and the platform of Labor has become less vague on this issue. The public perception of the difference between these two parties on the territories issue did not change much; almost two-thirds of the respondents in the 1981, 1984, and 1992 surveys thought that these differences were big or very big. Yet 1992 was different from previous elections in that many more voters said that the territories would be an important consideration in their voting decision. Of our 1992 sample, 52 percent said that the issue of the territories would very greatly influence their vote; less than a third said this in previous elections. Adding the next category of response, 81 percent said in 1992 that it would influence them greatly or very greatly; 63 percent responded thus in previous elections.

The correlations between the vote and the classical economic cleavage between capitalism and socialism do not follow a clear pattern over time. They were strongest in 1984 and 1988. In 1992 there was no relationship whatsoever between voters' position on this question and their preference for Likud or Labor. We will return to this point shortly.

Table 1.5. Correlations between Likud/Labor Vote and Demographic Variables and Issues, 1969–1992

| | | Demographic Data | | | | | | | Issues | | |
Survey[a]	(N)	Age	Gender	Density	Education	Income	Religion	Ethnicity	Territories[b]	Capitalist/ Socialist[c]	State/ Religion[d]
Oct. 1969	1,017	.17	(.05)	.07	(.00)	(-.04)	.08	.13	-.15	.23	.12
May 1973	1,062	.27	(.01)	.15	(-.02)	(-.01)	(.04)	.13	-.23	.17	
Mar. 1977	620	.29	(-.03)	.18	(.01)	(.06)	.18	.32	-.28	.22	.17
Mar. 1981	798	.13	(.06)	.07	.09	(.00)	.19	.23	-.27	.16	.20
July 1984	807	.20	(-.03)	.25	.22	.08	.37	.53	-.57	.32	
Oct. 1988	532	.16	(.04)	.09	.15	(.01)	.27	.27	-.61	.30	.24
June 1992	657	.10	(.07)	.13	.24	(-.02)	.40	.35	-.57	(.05)	.29

Notes: Pearson correlations, significant above the .05 level, except those in parentheses. See note 3.

The coding for these correlations was Likud = 1, Labor = 2. Low scores for the other variables indicate young age, female, sephardi, high density, low income, low education, high religiosity, willingness to concede territories for peace, favoring capitalism over socialism, and favoring public life in accordance with Jewish religious law, respectively.

[a] Preelection surveys used. In years for which multiple surveys were available, the one that contained the most variables used in the table was chosen.

[b] Before 1984, a question concerning the maximum amount of territory Israel should give up in order to achieve a peace settlement. In 1984 and after, constructed from two questions, the first asking preference between return of territories for peace, annexation, or status quo, and a follow-up question forcing a choice of those who chose the "status quo" option. See note 4, and Arian 1992.

[c] The question asked about preference for the socialist or capitalist approach. The 1973 question asked if the Histadrut labor union should see to it that public life in Israel be conducted according to the Jewish religious tradition.

[d] The question asked whether the government should see to it that public life in Israel be conducted according to the Jewish religious tradition.

Focusing now on 1977 and 1992, we note that the correlations in table 1.5 provide important clues as to the nature of these two electoral reversals. Age has had a consistent relationship with vote, with the young somewhat more likely to vote Likud and the old, Labor. This relationship has been generally regarded as indicating generation rather than life-cycle effects (Abramson 1990). Yet it is important to note that this correlation peaked in 1977 (and 1973) and reached its recorded nadir in 1992. The 1977 reversal was lead by the young: youth abandoned Labor for the promises of the Likud or the DMC. In 1992 the Likud was forsaken by both the young and the old. Even though young voters were more attracted by the right (see table 1.5), it is also true that Labor was more successful than in the past in attracting voters across generations.

Gender has never been related to vote choice in Israeli surveys, and it played no role in either of the two electoral reversals. Class differences mattered to a degree, although the correlations were not consistent, and not very strong. There was usually no relationship between the Likud/Labor vote and income, but the income variable is not the best measure of class in Israel, as it is the kind of topic an Israeli is unlikely to discuss in an open manner with an interviewer-stranger. Two other measures of class, living density (the number of persons per room) and education, tell a different story.

Class differences appeared with the reversal of 1977, with lower-class voters abandoning Labor in favor of the Likud. Voters' education level gained in importance after 1981, with the return to Labor of more highly educated voters who had deserted for the DMC in 1977. This process of class stratification continued in the 1980s and was still in evidence in 1992, although over time the education variable was stronger than the living-density indicator. But based on the nonconsistent and not too strong correlations of the vote with class indicators, combined with the pattern of correlations between the vote and the socialist versus capitalistic views, the class cleavage does not seem to be the driving force behind electoral choice and change in Israel. Note that in 1992 there was virtually no relationship between voters' preferences as to the structure of the economy and their vote, and in 1977 the correlation was of the same magnitude as throughout the seventies. Moreover, we read the responses to this question more as an indicator of whether or not a voter belongs to the camp of socialism-Zionism socially, politically and culturally, than as one of ideological commitment. And class is not the most potent correlate of the vote in Israel.

Ethnicity and religiosity are much stronger correlates of the vote. For both, 1977 was the critical election year. Before 1977, both dimensions barely distinguished Labor voters from Likud voters. In 1977, they both became important. Religiosity gained in importance over time, reaching an all-time high in the 1992 election. The relationship between ethnicity and the vote reached its highest point in the 1984 election, and it has receded since.

For the two reversal elections, 1977 and 1992, both sociodemographic factors and issue concerns were important, but their impact was very different. To summarize their respective roles, we calculated multiple regressions for each year to explain the Likud/Labor vote with blocs of explanatory variables of sociodemographics and of issues (all appearing in table 1.5).[5] We used stepwise regression in the following way: We defined two blocs of variables, one including the sociodemographic variables, the other including the three issue variables. We then computed two stepwise regressions, entering once the sociodemographic bloc first, and once the issue bloc first.

We were better able to account for the vote in 1992 than in 1977 with these variables (the total R^2 for 1992 was .37, and for 1977 it was .22). But more importantly, issues were dominant in the explanation of the 1992 vote to a much greater degree than were the sociodemographic characteristics of the voters. When coming first in the regression, issues "explained" 30 percent of the variance of the vote in 1992; sociodemographics accounted for 18 percent when they came first. In the full regression, the territories question had the strongest impact as measured by beta (.46); the other variables that achieved statistical significance were age, ethnic background, religiosity, and whether the respondent supported socialism or capitalism, with betas that ranged between .09 and .19.

The 1977 results were exactly the opposite: the R^2 for the bloc of sociodemographics alone was .18, compared to .11 for issues alone. In 1977 demography carried the weight, although the additional effect of the territories issue cannot be denied. In the full 1977 regression, three variables were statistically significant, with age, territories, and ethnicity each having betas around .20.

Ethnicity has been a very important theme of the first two generations of Israeli independence and has occupied a major place in social science studies of Israeli society and politics (see Shamir and Arian 1982; Smooha 1987; Diskin 1991). The 1977 reversal and the ascent of the Likud and the right in Israeli politics have been attributed by many to the ethnic cleavage. We therefore wish to expand somewhat on this theme.

The social and political tension between Ashkenazim and Sephardim referred to as the "ethnic issue" emerged from the imbalances occasioned by the dominant community of European background in new-born Israel absorbing hundreds of thousands of immigrants from Asia and Africa in the years after independence in 1948. The terms themselves are related to different ritual practices and usage adopted by scattered Jewish communities, but they have been used to distinguish Jews of European origin from those stemming from North Africa and the Middle East. The Ashkenazi/Sephardi terms are very problematic and imprecise. Thus, for example, many Jewish communities of southern Europe were sephardim, while communities in the eastern Mediterranean, India, Yemen, and Ethiopia could not appropriately be put in either category. Especially in the last half of the twentieth century, flourishing Sephardi communities have been established in the Americas and conspicuously in France. On the other hand, Ashkenazim lived in Egypt and China. Regardless of the misleading impression incorporated in the terms, this Sephardi/Ashkenazi division became part of the political reality of Israel and has emerged as a major theme in Israeli politics.

The theme, however, while still important, has changed. To begin with, the proportions of the groups in the population have changed over time. In 1977, the majority (53 percent) of the electorate was Ashkenazi, 43 percent were Sephardi, and 4 percent were Israeli born with fathers also born in Israel. In the 1988 election, for the first time the Jews of Sephardi background outnumbered the Jews of Ashkenazi background in the electorate. In 1992, with the addition of many Ashkenazi voters in the mass immigration from the former Soviet Union, the proportions were 48 percent Ashkenazim, 44 percent Sephardim and 8 percent Israeli born whose fathers were also born in Israel.[6] As a larger percentage of Israeli Jews were native born, this cleavage became more distant. Consider as indicators that a majority of Israeli Jewish voters and 90 percent of Jewish children in Israeli elementary schools at the beginning of the 1990s were native born. They were exposed to a culture that downplayed—if it did not successfully alleviate—the disparities of these ethnic distinctions. The rate at which a member of one group married a member of the other group was a high and constant 20 percent. The number of children from these "mixed marriages" grew with the blurring of the terms heightened.

Beyond the label is the question of social and political meaning. While fading, the labels are still of enormous importance. The major political parties vied to recruit politicians who could be presented as authentic leaders of these groups, and by 1992, the lists of both Labor and the Likud featured impressive and almost equal numbers of Sephardi politicians. And yet, in spite of significant headway achieved by Sephardim in and through politics, equality in terms of actual power was not achieved.

Two telling incidents involving the ethnic theme occurred during the 1992 campaign. One involved David Levy, then foreign minister in the Likud government. When the convention of his party determined their candidates for the Knesset and their positions on the Likud list, Levy did poorly in this preelection politicking. He attributed this to ethnic discrimination and threatened to withdraw from the Likud and run on a separate list which would appeal to Likud voters of Moroccan descent. He was ultimately placated by being granted various concessions and promises, and he remained on the Likud list, but the incident rekindled the animosities common to Israeli politics in the 1980s and raised the question whether ethnicity had faded as an issue.

The second episode took place in the non-Zionist ultraorthodox Haredi community. A venerated spiritual leader well into his nineties, Rabbi Eliezer Shach, pronounced that it was desirable to vote for the haredi-Ashkenazi United Torah list rather than for the haredi-Sephardi Shas list, because Sephardi leaders had not yet developed sufficient maturity to be entrusted with political power. Incensed, many of the devout Sephardi followers abandoned their rabbi and voted Shas, a list which met their desire to vote for an ultraorthodox party and satisfied their desire to identify with their slurred ethnic group. Perhaps Rabbi Shach had a correct theological point to make; his understanding of the social psychological correlates of electoral behavior in Israel—or most places—however, was imperfect.

Ethnicity matters in Israeli politics, just as it does in social spheres. Politicians of Sephardi background are more obvious in both big parties, although often in places lower on the electoral lists submitted by the parties, not in top positions. Ashkenazim still dominate much of the economy and bureaucracy, and while Sephardim are abundant in numbers, on the whole they are in positions of lower status. Stubborn facts of the reality of Israel in the early 1990s are that Ashkenazim continue to dominate in the two major parties, in the smaller parties of both right and left, and, more broadly, in other social institutions such as the media, the armed forces, and the universities, while Jews in Israeli jails are still overwhelmingly Sephardi, mostly North African, and especially Moroccans.

The ethnic cleavage manifested itself in voting behavior dramatically in the 1977 election when many voters abandoned their long-standing practice of supporting Labor. But they shifted largely along ethnic lines. Sephardim gravitated to the Likud, and Ashkenazim to the DMC. These two defections so weakened Labor that the Likud could take over the reins of power, resulting in the beginning of the Likud era of Israeli politics. In 1981 and 1984 many of the Ashkenazim were back with Labor; the campaigns were especially bitter and focused on the feelings of exploitation toward labor felt by may Sephardim. The ethnic vote was most pronounced in the 1984 elections, although the 1981 election campaign was most taken up with the ethnic cleavage.

As the proportion of Sephardim grew in the electorate, it was clear that Labor would always have an uphill battle regaining power until it could increase its share of the Sephardi vote. That shift occurred in 1992. The trend was not overwhelming, but the movement of Sephardim to Labor was substantial enough to provide the bounce that Labor needed to regain power. This transformation worked only because it occurred in conjunction with two other things: the movement of other former supporters away from the Likud to parties of the right and the impetus given Labor by the new Soviet immigrants who supported it.

The ethnic bounce that Labor received is depicted in table 1.6. Of those born in Asia and Africa or whose fathers were born there, 26 percent reported that they had decided to vote Labor in 1992. This was slightly lower than the 1977 rate (29 percent), but the sheer numerical increase of the sephardi population made the net electoral increase dramatic. At the same time, the Likud's share of this group fell from 53 percent to 41 percent. So while it is accurate to report that the Likud still did much better among Sephardim than Labor did, the relative and absolute successes of Labor within this group must be considered to attain a complete picture. If we consider only Likud and Labor voters, Labor's share of the two-party vote was higher in 1992 than in 1977. Moreover, the comparison between 1977 and 1992 is incomplete in another sense as well. In all the elections since 1977 the share of the Labor vote among Sephardim continually decreased; only in 1992 did this share increase.

The group born in Israel whose fathers were also born in Israel is another important indicator of the fortunes of the parties. Likud was twenty percentage points less successful with these voters in 1992 than it was in 1977, while Labor's draw was nine points higher. To calculate the political signifi-cance of these figures, recall that the size of this group in the sample doubled in the course of these fifteen years. Labor in 1992 did best among the shrink-ing group of Ashkenazim (those who were born or whose fathers were born in Europe and America) at the rate of 47 percent of their vote, but Likud's support was minuscule at 16 percent.

Looked at the other way, by considering the contribution of each group to the electoral fortunes of the parties (see table 1.6), a fascinating picture emerges. Likud was more heavily Sephardi in 1992 than in 1977, with two-thirds of its votes coming from that group in 1992 compared with about one-half in 1977; Labor was much more balanced, with half of its voters Ashkenazim, one-third Sephardim, and the rest second-generation Israelis. The Likud came close to being left with only the hard core of its supporters, while Labor in 1992 was able to enlarge the circle of its voters.

The conclusions regarding other parties confirm many of the trends discussed above. Meretz did more than three times better among Ashkenazim and second-generation Israelis than among Sephardim, and the parties of the right were twice as popular among Sephardim than they were among Ashkenazim. The religious parties drew equally from all ethnic groups in 1992, very different from their 1977 pattern, which showed strong support among ashkenazim.

Table 1.6. Ethnicity and Voting Behavior, 1977 and 1992

	Election	Birthplace of Respondent or Father		
		Asia or Africa	Europe or America	Both in Israel
Likud	1977	53*	20	44
	1992	41	16	24
Labor	1977	29	40	26
	1992	26	47	37
DMC	1977	12	26	20
Meretz	1992	6	20	18
Right-wing parties	1992	19	10	13
Religious parties	1977	5	11	9
	1992	8	8	8

* Percentage of ethnic group reported to vote for each party; other vote choices not reported.

Table 1.7. Ethnic Composition of Parties, 1977 and 1992

	Election	N	Birthplace of Respondent or Father		
			Asia or Africa	Europe or America	Both in Israel
Likud	1977	305	52*	38	10
	1992	297	68	21	11
Labor	1977	337	26	69	5
	1992	356	35	50	15
DMC	1977	202	18	75	6
Meretz	1992	129	23	57	19
Right-wing parties	1992	148	64	24	12
Religious parties	1977	83	17	76	7
	1992	81	51	36	14

* The percentage of the party's vote received from that ethnic group; percents sum horizontally.

Most of Meretz's support came from Ashkenazim; this was similar to the rate of support for the DMC, for which three of every four voters were from that group. Two-thirds of the voters for the parties of the right in 1992 were Sephardim. The most notable shift was for the religious parties. They successfully adapted to the demographic shifts in Israel after 1977. From a situation in which three quarters of their vote came from Ashkenazim, in 1992 half their vote was Sephardi, one-third was Ashkenazi, and one in seven was a second-generation Israeli. The pattern of their support was almost identical to the distribution in the general population. This is a political achievement of enormous magnitude; had one of the large parties been able to achieve that distribution of appeal at a high level, its electoral victory would have been massive.

IV. Who Went Where?

An important determinant of the 1992 election result was the blunting of the high degree of support that Sephardim gave the Likud. As seen in table 1.5, the correlation between ethnicity and the Likud/Labor vote was still high in 1992 at .35, although lower than the peak 1984 correlation of .54. It was enough for certain slippage to take place; coupled with the flow of Likud supporters to the right and the influx of Labor supporters from the new immigrants, the added support for Labor was sufficient. The correlations reported in table 1.5 provide the cross-sectional picture; we can explore the dynamics of these elections by analyzing the patterns of respondents who switched. For example, we shall focus on the Likud voters in 1988 and ask: How did they vote in 1992? Among them, who remained loyal and who deserted? In which direction did they go? What was their demographic profile? What position did they hold regarding the territories and the PLO? What influenced their vote? In parallel fashion, we ask the same questions for respondents who supported Labor in 1993; How did they vote in 1977? Who stayed with Labor and who left it? Where did they go? What was their attitude about the territories and the PLO? What effected their vote?

The analysis considers only those respondents who reported voting for Likud in 1988 and who said that they would vote for the right, the Likud, or Labor in 1992 (see table 1.8) and those who had voted Labor in 1973 and said they would vote for the Likud, Labor, or the DMC in 1977 (see table 1.9). Those who had not made up their minds or gave no answer to the vote intention question were not included in these analyses.[7]

When we examine the sociodemographic profiles of the three 1992 groups, it is clear that the predominant distinction among them is along the religiosity dimension. It is also the only statistically significant distinction. The largest differences both between 1992 Likud and Labor voters (34 percent to 14 percent) and among the three groups of voters are in the percent religious. Moving from the 1992 right voters through the 1992 Likud group to the 1992 Labor voters, the chances decrease that a respondent is religiously observant (45 percent to 34 percent to 14 percent).

In 1992, all three groups of 1988 Likud voters were overwhelmingly Sephardim, explaining why there is no statistical difference among them. The figures range from 78 percent for those who shifted to the right,

Table 1.8. Profile of 1988 Likud Voters by Their 1992 Vote

	1992 vote		
	Right	Likud	Labor
N = 310	40	226	44
Of 1988 Likud voters:			
Demographic data			
% religious	45	34	14
% Sephardim[a]	(78	70	64)
% under 30	(46	32	32)
% female	(60	52	43)
Attitudes			
% opposed to returning territories[b]	67	66	24
% opposed to negotiating with PLO[c]	85	72	61
% for Jewish religious law			
in Israeli public life[d]	38	41	21
% considered security/peace to be			
most important issue	(59	54	41)
% preferred capitalism[e]	(60	58	59)
Vote motivation (%)			
party	22	43	23
candidate	17	12	20
issues	(61	45	57)
Effect on vote choice			
economic stand of parties	48	25	55
territories stand of parties	(65	50	55)

Using the chi-square test, differences are statistically significant above .05 level except for those in parentheses.

[a] Respondent or father born in (1) Asia-Africa (here labeled "Sephardim"), contrasted to (2) those born in Europe or America or both born in Israel.

[b] Question described in table 1.5, note b.

[c] Based on a yes-no question on whether Israel should be willing to conduct negotiations with the PLO.

[d] Question described in table 1.5, note d.

[e] Question described in table 1.5, note c.

through 70 percent of those that stayed with the Likud, to 64 percent for those who shifted to Labor. Winning this nucleus of Sephardim away from the Likud was crucial for Labor to succeed in 1992. Although Labor attracted them at lower rates than did the right or those who stayed with the Likud, the fact that Labor did it at all shows that the party was at least partially successful in changing its image from a party of Ashkenazim with antipathy toward Sephardim. Labor managed to retain Sephardim in its ranks while simultaneously drawing away others from the Likud.[8]

The three groups of voters differed also on the other variables, but these differences were generally much smaller. This result is consistent with the high correlation between religiosity and the vote for all Likud and Labor voters in table 1.5—the highest among the sociodemographic variables.

Regarding age the differences are not statistically significant, and it is interesting to note that there was no difference in the percent under the age of thirty between the Likud loyalists and the 1992 Labor voters (32 percent); in the past Likud was much more often the party of the young than was Labor. Taken together with the small difference (6 percent) in the ethnic composition of these two groups of voters, we see the curbing of the two factors that were crucial in the 1977 turnabout and in voting patterns since. Age and ethnicity were still meaningful in distinguishing between Labor and Likud supporters, as the 1992 cross-sectional correlations in table 1.5 showed, but their discriminating power was diminishing. The group that moved from the Likud to parties of the right had a much higher percentage of people under the age of thirty than did the other two groups (46 percent compared to 32 percent). The higher preference of the young for the right—a pattern long established—continued in 1992. It is only in the comparison of the Likud loyalists with 1988 Likud voters who switched to Labor in 1992 that this relationship no longer holds.

The differences among the three groups of voters in their attitude toward the territories are the largest in table 1.8. The group that shifted to Labor was much more conciliatory regarding the future of the territories than were the other groups. Those who shifted from the Likud to the right were as likely as Likud loyalists to oppose returning territories, but they were much more likely to oppose negotiations with the PLO.

On the question of state end religion, there were also clear differences: about 40 percent of the right and Likud groups supported the position that the government should see to it that public life be conducted according to religious tradition; this was true of only 21 percent of those who switched to Labor. On the economic cleavage of capitalism and socialism there was no difference among the three groups of voters.

How different was the 1977 picture? Labor in 1977 lost a greater percentage of its previous vote than did the Likud of 1992, and many more of the 1973 Labor respondents were undecided or refused to tell how they would vote in 1977. The number of voters that selected Labor in 1973 and Likud in 1977 was almost twice as large as the number that went to the DMC (see table 1.9). The 1992 shift was less along ethnic lines and more along issues, whereas the voters in 1977 who had chosen Labor in 1973 split by both ethnicity and policy. Most of those who left Labor for Likud in 1977 were Sephardim (56 percent), while those who stayed with Labor and those who shifted to the DMC were predominantly Ashkenazim (only 25 and 15 percent Sephardi, respectively). Also the age and gender differences among the groups were more pronounced in 1977 compared to 1992, as seen by their size and statistical significance. Those who moved either to the Likud or to the DMC in 1977 were more likely to be young and more likely to be female than those who remained with Labor.

The ones who moved from Labor to Likud were clearly different from those who stayed and from those who shifted to the DMC in their more hawkish policy stand regarding the territories and their greater affinity to religious observance (also in their preference for Jewish religious law in Israeli public life, although these differences were not statistically significant). The majority of all groups opposed dealing with the PLO, although this was much more prevalent among those who eventually voted Likud than for those who went for the DMC. The switchers to the DMC supported capitalism more strongly; those who remained with Labor clung stubbornly to their socialism.

In 1977 the dynamic was driven much more by social factors, as judged by the size of differences among the three groups of voters, and in particular between Likud and Labor voters. Of the sociodemographic factors, ethnicity was the most important. Issues mattered as well. By 1992, the edge of the ethnic sword was deflected, while the ideological blade remained keen. Actually, of the demographic factors only religion remained a meaningful distinction in 1992, and the issue of the territories gained in strength over 1977. In 1977, the difference in the ethnic profile between Labor loyalists and deserters to the Likud was 31 percent; the difference between these two groups in their attitude toward the territories was 26 percent. In 1992, the comparable figures were 6 percent and 42 percent!

It is fascinating to note how similar the 1977 and 1992 patterns were for the samples when survey subjects were asked what factors determined their vote: identification with a certain party, the stands that a party takes on issues, the candidates offered, or whether a party is in government or in the opposition. In both cases, the parties' stands on issues were credited with determining the vote much more than were the others. This choice was followed by party identification, and then the candidates; the opposition option was negligible. For those who were loyal to the same party in both periods, however, the rate of choosing the ideological factor was lowest compared to the other groups. Almost as high as the platform for the loyalists in both time periods was identification with the party. Ideology was flaunted by the changers; whether this was real or an artifact of the political culture was immaterial, what mattered was that the norm was to report that change of party tended to be driven by ideological reasons.

Table 1.9. Profile of 1973 Labor Voters by Their 1977 Vote

	1977 vote		
	Likud	Labor	DMC
N = 382	77	265	40
Of 1973 Labor voters:			
Demographic data			
% religious	33	17	10
% Sephardim[a]	56	25	15
% under 30	35	14	30
% female	63	43	53
Attitudes			
% opposed to returning territories[b]	53	27	27
% opposed to negotiating with PLO[c]	67	59	51
% for Jewish religious law			
in Israeli public life[d]	(57	43	34)
% considered security/peace as			
most important issue	38	49	32
% preferred capitalism[e]	25	15	36
Vote motivation (%)			
Party	(30	41	24)
Candidate	(19	15	19)
Iissues	51	44	57
Effect on vote choice			
Economic stand of parties	33	20	50
Territories stand of parties	40	25	22
Corruption	44	16	62

Note: Using the chi-square test, differences are statistically significant above .05 level except for those in parentheses.

[a] Based on the background of whether respondent or father were born in (1) Asia-Africa (here labeled "Sephardim"; or (2) Europe or America, or both born in Israel.

[b] Question described in table 1.5, note b.

[c] Based on a yes-no question on whether Israel should be willing to conduct negotiations with the PLO.

[d] Question described in table 1.5, note d.

[e] Question described in table 1.5, note c.

This finding is fortified by considering the answers to the questions in the two periods about whether various issues will effect the vote decision of the respondents. Stands of parties on the territories or the economic issue were least important for the stayers and most important for the strayers. In 1992, territories was important for at least half of each voting group, but they were least important for the loyalists. Economics in 1992 was much more important for those who left the Likud than for those who stayed with it. In 1977 a different dynamic was at work: the Likud voters who left Labor reported that they were affected by the territories issue, and the DMC voters by the economic one.

The different dynamics of the two elections become clearer when one considers the correlations of the vote with demographic variables and the policy issues, as was presented in table 1.5 for all Likud/Labor voters in the elections between 1969 and 1992. In table 1.10, we present the correlations for the voting groups discussed above. We can assess which variables discriminated among the 1988 Likud voters as they decided how to vote in 1992, and among 1973 Labor voters as they approached 1977. The sociodemographic variables of education, ethnicity, and social class (density and income) were related to that choice in 1977 for the three groups; these factors, however, lost their efficacy when applied to the three groups of 1988 Likud voters in 1992. Religiosity retained its potency in both periods, and the state-religion relations issue became more relevant to vote choice in 1992. The territories issue became sharper between 1977 and 1992. Interestingly, the classic social-economic ideological cleavage of socialism-capitalism had no significance at all for the 1988 Likud voters when deciding for whom to vote in 1992. This contrasts to the 1973 Labor voters in 1977; for them this issue was associated with the vote—yet in the opposite direction than some Marxists would expect: those who shifted to the Likud, and who were of lower income, lower education, and lower standard of living, tended to support the capitalistic point of view more strongly compared to those who remained loyal to Labor. As we suggested before, this pattern is related to whether or not a voter belonged to the socialist-Zionist camp socially, politically, and culturally more than ideological commitment either to socialism or capitalism.

In order to assess the relative importance of sociodemographics and issues when considered jointly, we performed a similar multivariate analysis as we did for the full sample, with the vote variable defined as in table 1.10. The results complement the correlation analysis and are similar to those for the full sample: demographic characteristics were dominant in 1977, issues more important in 1992. In the stepwise regressions for 1977, the bloc of sociodemographics accounted for 12 percent of the variance alone; issues added only 2 percent more when added next. By themselves, issues explained 6 percent of the vote variance when coming first in the regression. In 1992, issues and demographics "explained" together 10 percent of the variance, issues alone 8 percent, sociodemographics alone 5 percent. The only variable that was statistically significant in the full 1992 regression was the question of whether or not to return the territories. In the full 1977 regression equation, three variables were statistically significant: education,

Table 1.10. Correlations among Voting Types, Demographic Variables, and Issues, 1977 and 1992

	Demographic Data							Issues[a]		
Survey	Age	Gender	Density	Education	Income	Religion	Ethnicity	Territories	Capitalism/ Society	State/ Religion
Mar. 1977	(−.03)	(−.02)	.15	.28	.12	.16	.24	−.12	−.20	.10
June 1992	(.09)	(.09)	(.04)	(.01)	(.04)	.18	(.08)	−.29	(.02)	.16

Notes: For 1977, N = 382; for 1992, N = 309.

Pearson correlations, significant above the .05 level, except those in parentheses.

Voters were divided into three categories: for 1992, respondents who had voted Likud in 1988 were categorized as either having switched to the right = 1, remained with the Likud = 2, or shifted to Labor = 3. For 1977, respondents who had voted for the Labor Alignment in 1973 were categorized as shifting to the Likud = 1, remaining with Labor = 2, or switching to the Democratic Movement for Change = 3.

The coding for these correlations was: low scores indicate young age, female, sephardi, high density, low income, low education, high religiosity, willingness to concede territories for peace, favoring capitalism over socialism, and favoring public life in accordance with Jewish religious law, respectively.

[a] See Table 1.5, notes b, c, and d.

ethnic background, and the socialist/capitalist question. Recalling our interpretation of this last variable as an indication of a rather broad affiliation to
the Labor camp—not only or even mainly ideological—the results reiterate
our interpretation of 1977 as a realignment grounded in demographics and
establishing new and enduring election groupings. The 1992 election was
predominantly issue based, with the question of the territories looming
large. We turn now to a further consideration of the effect of issues in 1992.

V. Wedge Issues

Issues have been classified as valence or position, the former related to high
levels of agreement, the latter to conflict (Stokes 1963). Peace and unemployment are classic valence issues: all agree that it is good to have the former,
bad to have the latter. Elections are sometimes portrayed as a contest over
position issues, and the 1992 election is a good example. It was seen by many
observers as a referendum over the future of the territories, and its results as
a rebuttal of the not-one-inch position of the Greater Israel ideology. But
party strategists prefer to stress valence issues so as not to alienate important
segments of the electorate. In such cases the contest is over images, over
which party or leader is perceived to be better able to achieve the desired
value such as peace or prosperity. Labor clearly chose this strategy in 1992.

Beyond the question of whether to stress valence or position issues,
party strategists are anxious to find issues—wedge issues—that will split the
opposing camp and make at least some former supporters of the other side
amenable to appeals to change their vote. Such wedge issues may be crosscutting position issues that split the opponent's supporters, an example of
which would be the relations between state and religion in Israeli politics.
Labor did not choose this approach in 1992, but Tzomet did. Wedge issues
may also be valence issues, such as the corruption charges levelled against
Labor in 1977 and against the Likud in 1992. Whether using position or
valence issues, the tactic is to place the issue high on the public agenda so
that it overrides other concerns for at least some of the opponent's voters.

Another strategy of wedge-issue campaigning—and perhaps a more
interesting one—relates to priorities. One may try to lure voters on the basis
of a different priority set rather than a different issue position or party image.
Labor took this tack in 1992 by emphasizing its different order of priorities,
denouncing the Likud's settlement policy in the territories on the basis of
allocating too much of Israel's limited resources to the wrong target, rather
than attacking the merits of retaining the territories. Contrasting its program
with the Likud's policies of pouring resources into the West Bank and Gaza
settlements, Labor promised to invest in infrastructure, education, welfare,
and job creation within Israel. This line of argument could appeal not only

to Likud voters with more conciliatory attitudes toward the territories, but also to hard-line voters who were not willing to give up territories but felt that their direct concerns of employment and opportunity were being neglected because of the Likud government's order of priorities.

Wedge issues may be defined by differences in electoral behavior, in the direction and intensity of attitudes for different voting groups. We shall look at different aspects of this question. First we examine whether respondents claimed that a series of items did or did not affect their vote decision.[9] The items are reported in table 1.11 in descending order for the total sample, and then for four groups of voters: those who voted for Labor in both 1988 and 1992, those who chose Likud in 1988 and Labor in 1992, Likud twice, and Likud in 1988 to parties of the right in 1992. Of the eight issues, the differences among the voting groups were statistically significant only for three. On the party related items, all six had significant differences.

Wedge issues appeal disproportionately to one group but not to others. Those who voted for the Likud in 1988 but switched to Labor in 1992 mentioned the Likud's settlement policy and the intifada more often as a factor in their vote decision than did the other groups of voters. These were major wedge issues in terms of Labor's campaign strategy. The intifada was dealt with indirectly, in valence terms, by reference to "personal security," which under the Likud had seemed to deteriorate. The settlements too were attacked not directly but rather in terms of the Likud's distorted order of priorities. Regardless of Labor's strategy to frame these themes in terms of a valence issue or in terms of priorities, the position element could not be taken out. On the basis of the question reported in table 1.11 we cannot distinguish among these various aspects. The intifada and the settlements issues worked on both position and valence levels. All Jewish Israelis wanted to see an end to the intifada, and they wanted more money spent on such things as education, health, and jobs within Israel. Yet by the very mention of these motifs, one was likely to elicit a position preference as well regarding the territories.

Displeasure with immigrant absorption and with relations with the United States were two other valence issues of the campaign. Yet on the basis of the importance attached to them by the different voting groups, they probably should not be considered wedge issues in 1992. About 70 percent of the sample said that the question of immigrant absorption had an effect on their vote, but there were almost no differences among the voting groups. As to the state of the relations with the United States, the picture was somewhat more complex. Shamir and the Likud had refused American requests to halt settlement construction in the territories, and Washington countered by refusing to grant guarantees for the $10-billion loans that Israel wished to take for the absorption of the Soviet immigrants. This item discriminated

Table 1.11. Influence on the Vote Decision for Selected Voting Groups, 1992 (in Percentages)

	Total Population	Labor 1988 Labor 1992	Likud 1988 Labor 1992	Likud 1988 Likud 1992	Likud 1988 Right 1992	1–2 Spread
			(1)	(2)		
N	1,192	227	44	227	40	
Issue-related influences						
Intifada	86	(90	96	85	94)	11
Unemployment	81	(86	84	81	78)	3
Handling of peace talks	78	(84	84	83	86)	1
Beginning of peace talks	74	(80	73	83	83)	–10
Corruption	74	81	91	68	61	23
Likud settlement policy	72	79	84	67	72	17
Immigrant absorption	69	(76	68	69	72)	–1
Relations with USA	62	74	63	59	39	4
Party-related influences						
Shamir head of Likud	48	31	48	73	48	–25
Rabin head of Labor	47	69	80	32	23	48
Labor list	46	80	66	28	28	38
Likud list	45	26	50	70	58	–20
Labor party primaries	36	65	51	20	20	31
Likud selection procedures	34	31	40	48	30	–8

Note: Using the chi-square test, differences are statistically significant above .05 level except for those in parentheses.

best among former Likud voters who went to the right—for whom the issue was not important—and other former Likud voters. It was most important for loyal Labor voters. The issue was not at all potent in luring Likud supporters to Labor; it did not distinguish between 1988 Likud voters who stayed with Likud and those who moved to Labor.

Corruption was the best example of a wedge issue in the 1992 election, if we judge it by the size of the difference in importance attached to it. Generally speaking, the corruption issue operates in this manner in elections in many countries and is a wedge issue that the opposition tries to use against the party in government. Before the 1992 elections, the state controller issued a series of scathing attacks on government ministries, and the corruption issue played a prominent role in the campaign against the Likud. Two-• thirds of those who voted Likud in 1988 and chose Likud again as well as 61 percent who moved to the right in 1992 said that the corruption issue influenced their choice. But for those who moved from Likud to Labor, 91 percent mentioned corruption as an influence, compared with 81 percent who chose Labor both times. The differential between Likud loyalists and voters who switched to Labor on this item is the largest (23 points). The corruption issue was significant in prying voters away from the Likud and to Labor, according to their own account. This is an echo of the 1977 race in which a very high 62 percent of DMC voters who had voted Labor in 1973 as well as 44 percent of the 1977 Likud voters who chose Labor in 1993 said that corruption affected their choice; this was true of only 16 percent among Labor loyalists (see table 1.9).

The data in table 1.11 do not provide information on the direction of preference and do not allow us to distinguish between valence or position or priority considerations. To do these things, we asked respondents another series of questions. We inquired about each of several topics whether the government should spend more, less, or about the same as it does.[10] For two of the most important areas of the Likud coalition—religious institutions and yeshivot, and the settlements in the territories—the expenditures were seen as undesirable (see table 1.12). Jobs, education, and health on the other hand were very popular. The public wanted a new ordering of priorities, which Labor represented well in its campaign strategy.

It is clear from table 1.12 that the settlements were the major wedge issue of the 1992 elections. The differential score of 75 is huge, and this is the only issue area on which one side (1992 Labor voters) as a group wanted less spending and the other side (1992 Likud/right voters) wanted more spending. This trade-off between spending in the territories and spending on other domestic matters was raised by Labor and the left in previous elections, but not as a major theme. It caught fire only in the 1992 campaign, and it did make a difference. Recalling that the disparity in the position issue of

Table 1.12. Differences between "Spend More" and "Spend Less" for Voting Groups

	Total Population	Labor 1988 Labor 1992	Likud 1988 Labor 1992	Likud 1988 Likud 1992	Likud 1988 Right 1992	1–2 Spread
		(1)		(2)		
N	1,192	227	44	227	40	
New Jobs	89	(90	96	88	86)	8
Education	83	90	82	75	75	7
Health	75	81	84	76	60	8
Security	60	(61	73	70	70)	3
Immigrant absorption	34	(40	34	21	39)	13
Unemployed	33	22	36	41	34	−5
Ecology	20	42	11	−3	10	14
Settlements	−29	−70	−59	16	25	−75
Religious institutions and yeshivot	−61	−87	−84	−44	−50	−40

Notes: Those surveyed were asked, "For each of the following, should the state spend more, spend less, or about the same as now?" The numbers reported are obtained by subtracting the percent saying "spend more" from the percent saying "spend less." The statistical significance of the differences was tested using the chi-square test on the basic crosstabulations. Differences were statistically significant above .05 level except for those in parentheses. The spread is the gap between these results for groups (1) and (2).

territorial concessions between 1992 Labor and Likud voters who voted Likud in 1988 was 42 points (see table 1.8), it would seem that the practical matter of expenditures in the territories made a difference beyond the position issue of the territories. We tested this notion in our sample using the same method introduced before to assess the relative impact of issues and sociodemographics. We ran two stepwise regressions on the Likud/Labor vote using as predictors positions on the territories and desirable level of expenditure for the settlements.[11] Using both the R^2s and the beta measures from the regression with both predictors, we find that policy positions were clearly more important than the priorities question in the total population, although priorities made a significant additional contribution. Among 1988 Likud voters, both variables had a similar effect on the vote. These results support the supposition that the question of expenditures on settlements mattered beyond the issue of the future of the territories and operated as a wedge issue in the 1992 election.

Expenditures for religious institutions and yeshivot were found to be another wedge issue in 1992. The differential score of 40 points was also very high. Using the same stepwise regression analysis described above, the expenditures and the policy questions had similar-sized effects on the vote in the general sample, with the former somewhat stronger. Among Likud voters, level of expenditure for religious institutions was more important than the attitude on the issue.[12]

VI. More on the 1992 Election

Issue concerns were central to the 1992 turnover, in particular the issue of the territories. We have shown the relevance of issue positions and the additional potency of priorities relating to these positions. Another influential aspect in the 1992 election involved prospective evaluations of the competing parties—the answer to the question, Who can deliver? (see Miller and Wattenberg 1985; Fiorina 1981). We asked respondents to evaluate which political party (Labor or Likud) would best be able to achieve different goals. Such questions are of course heavily loaded with party identification and can be meaningfully analyzed only in multivariate analysis or comparatively across groups of voters and across items, as we did for the results of tables 1.11 and 1.12. Comparing the four groups of voters, we found that the largest differences in prospective party evaluations involved who can bring an end to the intifada and who will lead to true peace with the Arabs. Next came immigrant absorption, sustaining democracy, curtailing unemployment, and maintaining good relations with the United States. The evaluations relating to the intifada and the prospects for peace were also the ones that have changed the most since 1988, to the detriment of the Likud.

Prospective evaluations have been found to be most important in explaining both the 1992 and 1988 election results in other multivariate analyses (Shachar and Shamir in this volume; Shamir and Arian 1990). The analysis of the 1988 elections sorted out short-term (intifada related) from long-term (the future of the territories) aspects and pointed to the latter as the more potent one for voting behavior. The analysis regarding 1992 distinguished between the security aspect and the economic one and showed the former as the crucial one. Taking all these analyses together, it is clear that the images of the parties in terms of their ability to achieve goals that are generally favored by the electorate are significant factors in voting behavior. The dimension that mattered related to the Israeli-Arab conflict and the future of the territories, as seen by the items of putting an end to the intifada and striving for peace. Prospective evaluations—primarily but not only in areas relating to the future of the territories—were a significant factor in the 1992 voting patterns. They complemented other issue considerations such as the positions held by voters on whether or not to compromise on the territories and on their priorities in budget allocations in the territories rather than within Israel. All these concerns taken together present a picture of an electorate that was very much issue driven.

Another question is that of the effect of the selection procedures and candidates of the parties on the voters. There was much speculation about the electoral effect of the new primaries system Labor introduced and its choice of Rabin over Peres to head its list, on the one hand, and of the internal fights within the Likud during its selection of candidates, on the other.

Referring again to table 1.11, we see that the items regarding candidates, party lists, and selection procedures were cited as influential by far fewer respondents than were issues. Fewer than half of the respondents in the total sample said that these considerations affected their vote decision. Yet they had the highest capability of discriminating among the groups of voters we considered, and all differences were statistically significant. The most important item for understanding the switchers was Rabin as the head of Labor's list. This item had the highest spread of all: 80 percent of those who left Likud for Labor said that it influenced their vote choice! The other items tell more about what mattered to the loyalists. Shamir being head of the Likud list impacted on Likud voters but not greatly on others. The Labor list itself was influential especially for Labor loyalists, just as the Likud list was most important for those who voted for the Likud twice. The vaunted first-time primaries of the Labor party were important for those loyal to that party, less so to those who came to Labor from the Likud, and least to the other groups. The much-attacked selection process of the Likud was considered of relevance to relatively few voters in all groups. To Likud voters who switched to Labor, this was the least important item.

We get additional clues about the effect of candidates, and especially of Rabin at the head of Labor, from scores generated by love/hate thermometers for Rabin, Shamir, and Peres (see table 1.13). Peres was included because he had been head of Labor for fifteen years, had been prime minister, and had run a hard battle against Rabin for the top spot on the 1992 Labor list. Peres headed the 1977 list after Rabin relinquished his position as head of the list following the allegations that his wife had illegally maintained a foreign bank account in the United States. For the next fifteen years Rabin struggled to win back the first place on the list; he did so only in 1992 in a first-ever primary of all Labor party members. The opinion was expressed that the public felt such animosity toward Peres that Labor would never be able to regain power under his leadership.

In the total sample, the love/hate scores ranged from 5.8 for Rabin, through 5.3 for Shamir, to 4.7 for Peres. Within the voting groups the patterns were more distinct. Labor loyalists accepted Rabin at a slightly higher level than Peres, and they decidedly rejected Shamir. Labor voters who came from Likud were attracted to Rabin (as they explicitly told us in response to our question reported in table 1.11 about the effect of Rabin's nomination on their vote); they were much less sympathetic to Peres and even less so to Shamir. This finding gives credence to the speculation that Rabin rather than Peres at the head of Labor's list made a difference in the Labor victory (see also Shachar and Shamir in this volume). Peres was greatly detested by Likud and right parties voters who voted for the Likud in 1988; Rabin got neutral marks, but lower for loyal Likud voters. Shamir was attractive to voters who twice supported the Likud, and he was less so for those who switched to the right.

VII. Conclusion

We have analyzed the 1992 election by comparing it to 1977, the only other turnover election in Israel. One major conclusion was that the grasp of social allegiance on voting patterns weakened, while the weight of issues in general and of the divisive issue of the territories as a factor in voting further increased. It is instructive to place these results regarding electoral behavior in the broader perspective of postindustrial societies. The same two processes we identified in Israel characterize these other polities: a general decline in the importance of social cleavages for electoral behavior, and the simultaneous increase in issue voting (e.g., Rose and McAllister 1986; Dalton 1988; Bartolini and Mair 1990; Franklin et al. 1992). Franklin et al. regard this as a developmental process, taking place in some countries later than in others.

Franklin et al. (1992) also claim that the decline in the structuring properties of the traditional social cleavages has not been balanced by

Table 1.13. Mean Attraction Scores for Parties and Leaders

	Total Population	Labor 1988 Labor 1992	Likud 1988 Labor 1992	Likud 1988 Likud 1992	Likud 1988 Right 1992	1–2 Spread
			(1)	(2)		
N	1,192	227	44	227	40	
Likud	5.6	3.5	4.2	8.3	7.0	−4.1
Labor	5.4	7.8	7.0	3.5	3.6	3.5
Rabin	5.8	7.6	7.4	4.4	5.1	3.0
Shamir	5.3	3.2	4.4	8.1	6.4	−3.7
Peres	4.7	7.2	5.5	2.8	2.6	2.7

Note: Ten point scale; 1 = rejection/hate; 10 = support/love. All differences (including 1–2 spreads) statistically significant at $p < .001$ using the F test.

increases in the structuring properties of new cleavages (chaps. 19 and 20). In most countries covered in their book, the amount of the vote variance explained by social structure and attitudinal variables has been reduced from the 1960s through the 1980s. This has not been the case in Israel. The difference lies in the nature of the issues that have captured the agenda. In most Western countries, issues involving postbourgeois versus materialist values, gender issues, public versus private consumption, and state employment have gained ascendancy. While important, these issues energize certain publics and not others; and they are not as central, critical, and engulfing as the major issue dimension in Israeli politics, that of the territories and the Israeli-Arab conflict. No wonder then that voting in Israel has become more structured and that this issue has become a more important determinant of it over time.

The atomizing influences of advanced industrial societies are used to explain these changes and to suggest that the bases for electoral politics are changing. As a result of these processes, groups' cultural distinctiveness, social homogeneity, and organizational density are weakening, using Bartolini and Mair's (1990, chap. 9) terms. The more highly organized into exclusive and overlapping networks and associations whose internal structures are personalistic and hierarchical, the greater the group's political cohesion (Zuckerman 1982). As Zuckerman points out, such conditions are usually not prevalent, and postindustrial societies are even less likely to produce these conditions. With increasing levels of urbanization, social and geographic mobility, growing heterogeneity, secularization, and embourgeoisement, the revolutions in the mass media, in education and cognitive mobilization, changing organizational structures and ties, and the emergence of values and issues that are only weakly linked to specific demographic groups, issues, and social bases are likely to become less coordinated.

Yet it is important to emphasize that the type of issue may generate different degrees and types of group loyalty. Some issues may be only weakly related to specific social groupings, as the postindustrial literature argues, but others can connect and can reinforce existing cleavage structures by providing new reasons for the same people and groups to support the same parties (Franklin et al. 1992, 402). Ethnic grievances may have partly operated in this way in Israel in the 1980s. The complex issue of state-religion relations, which Israel has not yet resolved, is a good example of one that has gained in importance over time simultaneously with the social demographic characteristic of religiosity. Here we see a mutual reinforcement process between the issue and the groups, groups that are still quite clearly defined and are both socially and politically cohesive (in particular on the religious side). Thus the extent to which vote is related to sociodemographic characteristics of voters depends also on the nature of the issues on the agenda.

Greater individual and aggregate level volatility in the vote have been attributed to the changing bases of electoral behavior (Dalton, Flanagan, and Beck 1984; Bartolini and Mair 1990). And as Franklin suggests, "a natural concomitant of this liberation (where it has occurred), is that the fortunes of individual political parties have become much less certain, and are dependent more largely on variations in leadership skills and other contingencies" (Franklin et al. 1992, 403). We found this to be the case in the 1992 election in Israel. It seemed to empower the electorate and called upon Labor to perform for this term, with the implicit threat that they too could be replaced in future elections. The reversal—as is often the case—stemmed from the failings of the party in power and the rejection of that party by a significant number of former supporters. Labor was able to attract voters disappointed with the Likud by blunting the ethnic issue, by placing Rabin instead of Peres at the head of its list, and by highlighting the wedge issue of the Likud investing heavily in the settlements in the territories. Pursuing the priority of supporting the settlements in spite of the clear displeasure of the United States, at a time of very high unemployment, and of difficulties in absorbing the huge wave of immigrants from the Soviet Union, tipped the scales in favor of Labor among this group of voters. Scales are notoriously unstable, and the few extra grains of sand that were added to Labor's side could quickly be scattered in the winds of the Middle East; alternatively, those few grains may form the nucleus of something more stable—for a while.

Notes

1. Labor ran alone in 1992, but in previous years the list had other names. In 1965, Mapai and Ahdut Haavoda ran on a joint list called the Alignment. In 1968, Mapai, Ahdut Haavoda, and Rafi merged to form Labor. Between 1969 and 1984 Labor and Mapam put up a joint list called the "Alignment." In 1988, Labor and Mapam each offered separate lists. In 1992, Labor ran alone, while Mapam joined with the Civil Rights Movement and Shinui to form Meretz. The Likud was formed in 1973 and was a joint list of Herut, the Liberal party, La'am, and others.

2. Surveys reported in this article were composed of representative samples of the adult Jewish population of Israel, excluding individuals from kibbutzim and from the territories. Questionnaires were composed and data analyzed by the authors; fieldwork was conducted by the Guttman Institute for Applied Social Research until 1981 and by the Dahaf Research Institute since then. Surveys were funded by many sources, including the National Security and Public Opinion Project of the Jaffee Center for Strategic Studies and the Sapir Center for Development, both at Tel Aviv University, and by the Department of Political Science of the University of Haifa.

Vote frequencies as reported in the surveys do not always coincide with the actual vote results. There are several reasons for this: as stated, the samples do not include Israeli Arabs, settlers in the territories, and kibbutz members. Also, the surveys are preelection surveys, and respondents may change their decision; and, more importantly, many do not report vote choice. Discrepancies were larger up to and including 1977, while Labor was dominant; in 1992, the divergence was minor. For pollsters whose goal is prediction, this state of affairs presents a major obstacle, hopefully overcome by various weighting and other data manipulation schemes. Since our goal is explaining the vote and the turnover, and our focus is on certain categories of voters and on relations, these discrepancies present less of a problem, and weighting does not change the results of the analysis.

3. The relations between the issues and demographic variables were measured with Pearson correlations.

(*a*) Since the vote variable is dichotomous (Labor/Likud), there is an upper bound on the size of the correlations which is less than one (Cohen 1983).

(*b*) Correlations indicate how far and in what direction two variables covary. In other words, how much of the fact that some voters preferred Likud, and others preferred Labor, "was due" to variations in the explanatory variables (for example, to age differences among them). Since we do not assume that the "true model" is bivariate, r measures association, not the structural effect of X on Y. For relevant discussions of the meaning and use of standardized measures, see Achen 1982; King 1986; Luskin 1991.

(*c*) When comparing correlations (or other standardized measures) across samples, one must check variances of the variables involved, because the correlations are affected by this variance in addition to the relationship in which one is interested. For most sociodemographic variables, the standard deviations across the samples changed very little. The standard deviation of ethnicity has increased slightly since the 1981 survey and has been constant since. This does not interfere with the pattern of correlations obtained. The standard deviation on the religious issue decreased in 1988 and 1992, meaning that the pattern of increasing relations indicated by the correlations could only be more pronounced. The standard deviation of the socialism-capitalism issue changed but in no specific direction and not in any consistent way with the correlations. The standard deviation of the territories questions is much higher for 1984 and on, compared to the earlier elections, about 1.5–1.7 times higher. This means that there are two reasons why the correlations have increased; first, there is more polarization and variance on this issue compared to before and, second, the relationship has increased. The standard deviation of the dependent vote variable is quite constant, although it has increased by about 10 percent since the 1977 election, again, not interfering with our interpretation of the correlation pattern in table 1.5.

4. As explained in note b of table 1.5, we used one territories question through 1981 and another one since 1984. Luckily the 1984 and 1988 questionnaires contained both question formats. The correlations for the early question (not given in table 1.5) were of similar magnitude as those presented in the table: .53 in 1984, and .47 in 1988; this compares to correlations in the .20 range in the earlier elections. There can be no doubt then that a real change occurred in 1984 and that the correlation is not simply a methodological artifact.

5. The application of regression analysis to a dichotomous dependent variable is not straightforward, yet, given certain assumptions that we were willing to make, it is appropriate. The results of a parallel discriminant analysis are of course equivalent. See also note 3(c), which is also relevant to the use of R^2.

6. These figures are based on the Central Bureau of Statistics data, pertaining to the Jewish population over the age of twenty. The specific sources are: *Demographic Characteristics of the Israeli Population, 1977, 1978*, Special Report 634 (Jerusalem, 1980), table 9, pp. 14–15; *Statistical Abstract of Israel—1992*, 43 (Jerusalem, 1992), table 2.27, pp. 94–95.

7. These are sizeable groups, comprising 15 percent of the 1988 Likud voters in 1992 and 36 percent of the 1973 Labor voters in 1977. By leaving them out, we implicitly assume that they were similar to those who decided earlier, and we regard this assumption as plausible. Although others may not agree with this assumption, in the absence of additional data, this is the only way we can treat these respondents.

8. It is interesting to note that the profile of young first-time voters is broadly the same as the general patterns in table 1.8 for 1988 Likud voters. In terms of ethnicity, a third of the Likud and right voters were Sephardi, compared to 22 percent of Labor voters. The major difference among these groups was with regard to their attitude regarding the future of the territories.

9. Since many voters said that everything had an effect on them, the only way to read the results is comparatively: compare the items in terms of relative importance to voters and compare voters with different voting records as to how different items influenced decisions.

10. In order to minimize the chances for a response set of "spend more" on all items, we asked first whether the respondent supported a tax increase, which would mean paying more taxes. Even though 72 percent opposed paying more taxes, on six of the nine items, majorities wanted to spend more, and for seven of them the quotient (found by subtracting the percent that wanted less expenditure from the percent wanting more) was positive (see table 1.12). The results should be compared across issues and across voting groups.

11. We looked at Likud/Labor voters as they are the most interesting and most relevant for our discussion of wedge issues. See note 5 on the use of regression with a dichotomous dependent variable.

12. In both regressions reported here, the two variables had weaker effects on the vote among the 1988 Likud voters than in the total population.

References

Abramson, Paul. 1990. "Demographic Change and Partisan Support." In *The Elections in Israel—1988*, Asher Arian and Michal Shamir. Boulder: Westview Press.

Achen, Christopher H. 1982. *Interpreting and Using Regression*. Quantitative Applications in the Social Sciences 07–029. Beverly Hills: Sage.

Arian, Asher. 1989. *Politics in Israel: The Second Generation*. 2nd ed. Chatham, N.J.: Chatham House.

———. 1992. "Security and Political Attitudes in Israel: 1986–1991." *Public Opinion Quarterly* 56, no. 1 (Spring): 116–28.

Bartolini, Stefano, and Peter Mair. 1990. *Identity, Competition and Electoral Availability: The Stabilisation of European Electorates 1885 1985*. Cambridge: Cambridge University Press.

Cohen, J. 1983. "The Cost of Dichotomization." *Applied Psychological Measurement* 7, no. 3: 249–53.

Dalton, Russell J. 1988. *Citizen Politics in Western Democracies*. Chatham, N.J.: Chatham House.

Dalton, Russell J., Scott C. Flanagan, and Paul Allen Beck. 1984. *Electoral Change in Advanced Industrial Democracies: Realignment or Dealignment?* Princeton: Princeton University Press.

Diskin, Abraham. 1991. *Elections and Voters in Israel*. New York: Praeger.

Fiorina, Morris. 1981. *Retrospective Voting in American National Elections*. New Haven: Yale University Press.

Franklin, Mark N., et al. 1992. *Electoral Change: Responses to Evolving Social and Attitudinal Structures in Western Countries*. Cambridge: Cambridge University Press.

King, Gary. 1986. "How Not to Lie with Statistics: Avoiding Common Mistakes in Quantitative Political Science." *American Journal of Political Science* 30, no. 3 (August): 666–87.

Liebman, Charles S., and Eliezer Don-Yehiya. 1983. *Civil Religion in Israel*. Berkeley and Los Angeles: University of California Press.

Luskin, Robert C. 1991. "Abusus Non Tollit Usum: Standardized Coefficients, Correlations and R^2s." *American Journal of Political Science*, 35, no. 4 (November): 1032–46.

Miller, Arthur H., and Martin P. Wattenberg. 1985. "Throwing the Rascals Out: Policy and Performance Evaluations of Presidential Candidates, 1952–1980." *American Political Science Review* 79, no. 2 (June): 359–72.

Rose, Richard, and Ian McAllister. 1986. *Voters Begin to Choose.* Beverly Hills: Sage.

Shachar, Ron, and Michal Shamir. 1994. "Modelling Victory in the 1992 Election. In *The Elections in Israel—1992*, ed. Asher Arian and Michal Shamir. Albany: SUNY Press.

Shamir, Michal. 1986. "Realignment in the Israeli Party System." In *The Elections in Israel—1984*, ed. Asher Arian and Michal Shamir. New Brunswick, N.J.: Transaction.

Shamir, Michal, and Asher Arian. 1982. "Ethnicity in the 1981 Elections in Israel," *Electoral Studies* 1, no. 3 (December): 315–32.

———. 1990. "The Intifada and Israeli Voters: Policy Preferences and Performance Evaluations." In *The Elections in Israel—1988*, ed. Asher Arian and Michal Shamir. Boulder: Westview Press.

Smooha, Sammy. 1987. *Social Research on Jewish Ethnicity in Israel, 1948–1986.* Haifa: Haifa University Press.

Stokes, Donald E. 1963. "Spatial Models of Party Competition." *American Political Science Review* 57, no. 2 (June): 368–77.

Zuckerman, Alan. 1982. "New Approaches to Political Cleavages." *Comparative Political Studies* 15: 131–44.

———. 1990. "The Flow of the Vote in Israel: A Reconsideration of Stability and Change." In *The Elections in Israel—1988*, ed. Asher Arian and Michal Shamir. Boulder: Westview Press.

CHAPTER 2

Modelling Victory in the 1992 Election

RON SHACHAR
Tel Aviv University and Yale University
and
MICHAL SHAMIR
Tel Aviv University

I. Introduction

When do parties win and when do they lose? No questions are more important to the practitioner and student of politics. It is clear from the vast literature on the subject that the major components of the answer and their
relative importance vary across elections and that the issues are multifaceted.
Take, for example, performance evaluations of the major contenders. It
seems clear that performance evaluations were very important in 1992 to
many Israeli voters regarding security affairs and to many American and
British voters regarding domestic affairs. But were these matters also of significance in bringing about the electoral turnover in the first two countries
mentioned and in retaining the party in power in the third? This article
focuses on Israel, and we shall show that these performance evaluations also
had the most effect on the dispersion of the predicted vote probabilities and
hence played a role in bringing about the electoral turnover. The difference
between Likud and Labor on performance evaluation was small, however,
and therefore its overall impact was not very large.

In order to provide a full account of the 1992 election, we shall address the
following four questions (see Miller and Shanks 1982; Shanks and Miller 1990;
Markus 1988; Denk and Finkel 1992; and Achen 1982, for a general discussion):

Our thanks to Asher Arian, Zvi Eckstein and Alan Zuckerman for the helpful comments.

1. What was important to individual voters in terms of their vote decision?
2. What was the contribution of different factors to the aggregate outcome of the elections: to the left bloc's victory and to the right's defeat? What factors gave the winner its advantage?
3. What factors were important in terms of dispersing or polarizing the votes in an aggregate sense? What was effective in separating voters?
4. What brought about the electoral turnover? Which factors brought down one party and elevated the other compared with past elections?

II. Elements of the Model: Factors in the 1992 Election

Building on a combination of the sociological model (Berelson, Lazarsfeld, and McPhee 1954; Rose 1974) and a more rational choice oriented Michigan model (Campbell et al. 1960; Downs 1957; Fiorina 1981), we include the relevant sociodemographic characteristics and attitudinal variables representing party identification, candidate evaluations, issue positions, and (prospective/retrospective) performance evaluations. After introducing these factors as they manifested themselves in the 23 June, 1992 election in Israel, we shall delineate the model in detail in the next section.

Candidates

Israel's electoral system comes close to a pure proportional representation system, with party lists competing and the whole country making up one constituency. Compared to presidential systems and to systems with multiple constituencies, Israel's system does not emphasize candidates. Still, recent studies of parliamentary systems have argued that party leaders are increasingly influential factors in voters' considerations (e.g., Graetz and McAllister 1987; Bean and Mughan 1989), and similar arguments may apply in Israel.

Before the 1992 election, the Knesset passed two amendments to the electoral law. The more important for this discussion provided for *direct* elections for the prime minister, in addition to the parliamentary elections, but postponed its enactment until the next election.[1] Nonetheless, Labor conducted its election campaign as though these were direct elections for the prime minister, placing Yitzhak Rabin at the center of the stage.[2]

That was one reason why there was so much interest and speculation about the role of the candidates in this election. The second—and more important—reason was the fact that Rabin replaced his long-time foe, Shimon Peres, at the head of the list. Many, in particular Labor adherents, pondered whether this change made the important difference and brought victory to Labor.

The Likud's candidate for prime minister was the outgoing premier, Yitzhak Shamir, who had led the Likud since Menachem Begin's resignation in 1983. Shamir was perceived by voters as stronger and much more able to resist pressure than Rabin.[3] Rabin was seen as more creative and innovative and as having more leadership ability. Respondents perceived no difference between them regarding the likelihood that each would prefer their party's needs over those of the state, their negotiation skills, or their decisiveness and their trustworthiness. Rabin was better liked than Shamir, and Peres was least liked (see Arian and Shamir in this volume, table 1.13). The same rank order was also obtained in 1988. We shall explore whether these candidate evaluations made a difference in the voters' electoral decision and on the electoral outcome.[4]

Issues

The Israeli electorate is relatively knowledgeable about politics and aware of political issues and events (e.g., Shamir and Sullivan 1983, 915). When asked about considerations they use in determining how to vote, issues always come out in first place (followed by party identification, with candidates being in third place). In 1992, a record 55 percent said that issues were the major factor structuring their vote, 28 percent mentioned party identification, and only 12 percent said candidates. These results may be an accurate description of the vote calculus, but they may also just be a reflection of the political norms prevailing in Israel (Arian 1973, 1989).

We also asked more specifically whether the issue of the territories occupied by Israel since 1967 and whether economic issues would affect their vote. That majorities answered these questions in the positive is not surprising; they always have since such questions have been asked.[5] In the past, consistently 60 to 67 percent have answered both questions affirmatively. In 1992, however, 81 percent said that the issue of the territories would influence their vote greatly or to a certain extent, and 72 percent said so with regard to economic issues. Considering these numbers in comparison to past levels suggests that issues may have been especially important in electoral behavior in the 1992 election. In the analyses that follow we will focus on two questions: the role of issues versus other factors in the vote, and the relative impact of different issues.

Three issues are considered (Gutmann 1977); first, the question of the territories, which epitomizes the realm of security and foreign affairs. In contrast to other countries in which domestic issues dominate, security issues are generally considered the major cleavage dimension in Israeli politics (Ventura and Shamir 1992; Shamir 1986; Galnoor 1980). Second is the matter of religion and state relations, which in Israel are complex and intertwined. The specific issue we will consider is the degree of government involvement in assuring that public life in Israel be conducted according to Jewish religious tradition.

The third issue is the socioeconomic cleavage, the classic issue dividing left and right. We operationalize this in terms of support for a socialist versus a capitalistic approach to the economy. The trend here over time is in favor of capitalism, and in the course of the 1980s the socialist-oriented majority lost its grip over the public, and today a majority prefer capitalism.[6]

Performance Evaluations

In addition to issues, voters take into account how effective contenders were and are likely to be in realizing goals, that is retrospective and prospective evaluations (Fiorina 1981; Abramson, Aldrich, and Rohde 1982; Miller and Wattenberg 1985; Shamir and Arian 1990). These evaluations are contaminated by voters' party identification, but comparing them across years and evaluation dimensions is revealing.

Respondents in the 1988 and 1992 surveys were asked to evaluate the performance of Likud versus Labor along various dimensions.[7] In 1988 the Likud held an edge over Labor on all items (Shamir and Arian 1990). By 1992 the picture had changed. The two biggest changes in image were on cardinal dimensions. Regarding which party would restore order in the territories, 48 percent said the Likud in 1988, and only 24 percent Labor. From this ratio of 2:1 in favor of the Likud, the images in 1992 shifted to an equal split: 32 percent thought Likud would do better, 31 percent Labor. On the question of who would lead to real peace with the Arabs, the ratio changed from 41:29 in favor of the Likud to 33:37 in favor of Labor. In order to appreciate these changes and not attribute them to changing vote intentions, it is important to note that changes on other dimensions were all smaller and went different ways. Some were in the same direction, but smaller (who will assure democracy), some went in the other direction, that is, in favor of the Likud (securing a Jewish majority), and on some dimensions there was no change at all (on images relating to ethnic issues, on who will stand firm in peace negotiations). In 1992 there were also a few items not asked in 1988: which party would best know to reduce unemployment, absorb immigration, and keep good relations with the U.S. On all of these, Labor was perceived as better able to deliver (the Likud\Labor ratios were 22:38; 28:32; and 23:46, respectively).

The summary items tell the same story. In 1988, 45 percent thought that the Likud team would be better able to deal with the economic problems, and 34 percent Labor. As to security and foreign affairs issues, 48 percent said the Likud team would do better, and 33 percent Labor. By 1992,

Labor had the upper hand in the economic sphere (the comparable figures were 33:41), and in the security and foreign affairs realm there was an equal split (41:42).

Party Attachment

Party attachment as a factor in voting decisions has not been a major focus of research in Israeli voting studies, despite the clear effect of the Michigan school on such studies (e.g., Arian 1973). Conceptualizing the decision as a habituation process, Shachar and Eckstein (1992) reaffirmed its importance. While not the focus of their paper, Shamir and Arian (1990) obtained similar results in their analysis of the 1988 election.

The idea of party attachment as a standing partisan decision is widely accepted in voting behavior studies, even though its content and sources are not. The original Michigan school's notion conceived of party identification as a psychological attachment to a party distinct from the vote (Campbell et al. 1960). Non-American accounts have disputed this notion, with much of the debate centered on the degree of independence between party identification and the actual vote (e.g., Budge, Crewe, and Farlie 1976; Richardson 1991). It is well established that party attachments are developed at an early age, often much before other political learning occurs, and that parents are the primary socialization agent in transmitting these. Electoral experience often strengthens party attachment in a reinforcement or habituation process (Converse 1976; Page and Jones 1979; Markus and Converse 1979; Shachar 1992). Party attachments have also been found to be more stable than other political attitudes (Jennings and Niemi 1981; Inglehart 1990; Arian, Shamir, and Ventura 1992).

We operationalize party attachment as past vote in our analysis of the 1992 election. Past vote captures the basic understanding of a standing partisan decision, while avoiding the debate over the substance and measurement of party attachment.[8] In our survey, 43 percent stated they had voted in 1988 for the Likud bloc, 35 percent for the Labor bloc, and 21 percent did not vote (those were young voters, new immigrants, or eligible voters who had abstained).

The Social Basis of the Vote

Like most elections research, Israeli voting studies have focused heavily on the sociodemographic basis of voting patterns. Among those, the ethnic factor has received most attention (e.g., Diskin 1991, Shamir and Arian 1982), referring to the distinction between Ashkenazim and Sephardim.[9] It is well established that Sephardi voters tend more to the Likud and to the right, whereas Ashkenazim tend more to Labor and to left parties. In relation to the 1992 election campaign, two important questions were how the new immigrants from the former Soviet Union (most of whom were Ashkenazi) were going to vote and whether Labor would succeed in luring Sephardi Likud voters.

In addition to ethnic background we include in the analysis religiosity, age, education, income, and gender.[10] The last two have been found in past research to be only weakly, if at all, related to vote. Higher education and older age are associated with vote for Labor and the left. Level of religiosity among Jews has been found to be strongly correlated with the vote, gaining in strength over time, with the more secular tending toward Labor and the left (Arian and Shamir in this volume).

III. The Model

We adopt here the model suggested by Shachar (1992) to describe voting behavior.[11]

Assume the political system contains two parties: M and L. The individual decides in each period which party to vote for in the elections. The dichotomous variable d_t is equal to unity if the voter votes for party M in period t and equal to zero if he/she votes for party L.

Suppose the utility function is given by:

$$U_t = -a \cdot (X_t - X_t^\gamma)' \cdot (X_t - X_t^\gamma) + b \cdot EF_t + ML(Y_t, d_{t-1}, \ldots, d_1, u_t) \cdot (2d_t - 1)$$

$$ML(\cdot) = M(Y_t) + \sum_{j=1}^{t-1} \delta^j \cdot (2d_{t-j} - 1) + u_t$$

$$a > 0, \ b > 0, \ \delta > 0.$$

The variables are defined as follows: $X_t = \{X_t^L$ or $X_t^M\}$ is a vector of n-policies (e.g., policy with respect to the Arab-Israeli conflict) that are carried out by the party in power at period t, where the L or M superscript indicates which party is in power; the vector X_t^γ represents the voter's view of the optimal n-policies (e.g., the voter's view of the ideal solution to the Israeli-Arab conflict). $EF_t = \{EF_t^L$ or $EF_t^M\}$ represents the incumbent's competence to govern the country. In a party system such as the Israeli one, this term covers both party and candidate's evaluations. Here are included party performance evaluations on the major policy dimensions and the party leader's attributes such as integrity, reliability, personality, and charisma, considered desirable by all voters. The superscript indicates again which party is the incumbent; Y_t is a vector of k socioeconomic and demographic characteristics of the voter in period t.

u_t is an independent random variable which represents random shifts in the individual's preferences over the parties in period t. It is known to the individual at time t, but it is unobservable to the researcher. For example, the preferences of an individual who had a bad business connection with M may have changed against this party. It is assumed that u_t is distributed normally with mean zero and variance σ_u^2.

The first expression in the utility function implies that the individuals' welfare decreases as the policy followed by the incumbent is further away from their preferred policy. Utility is a positive function of the incumbent party and leader's performance.

Voting for the party the individual sympathizes yields direct satisfaction, while voting for the other party yields displeasure, according to the third term in the utility. $ML(\bullet)$ represents the individual's relative sympathy for M versus L. These preferences depend on three factors: (*a*) socioeconomic and demographic characteristics, (*b*) previous voting decisions, and (*c*) a temporal and personal random effect. If $ML(\bullet)$ is equal to zero, the individual does not like either one of the parties. If he/she likes M (L), $ML(\bullet)$ is positive (negative). This means that if the individual likes M and votes for it (L), the third term in the utility is positive (negative) and if he/she likes L and votes for M (L), this term is negative (positive).

The voter has a subjective probability that party j will win the elections in period t - P_t^j, conditional on his/her decision not to vote for it; ϵ is the subjective influence of the voter on the election results, as it is in Ledyard (1984), for example. It is obvious that $P_t^M + P_t^L + \epsilon = 1$. It is also assumed that the cost of voting is zero.

Under these assumptions the decision rule at t is

$$d_t = 1 \text{ if } u_t > 0.5 \bullet \epsilon \bullet (-a \bullet \langle (X_t^L - X_t^i)^2 - (X_t^M - X_t^i)^2 \rangle + b \bullet \langle EF_t^L - EF_t^M \rangle)$$

$$- M(Y_t) - \delta \bullet K_{t-1} = u_t^* (K_{t-1}, \Theta_t)$$

$$d_t = 0, \text{ otherwise}$$

$$K_t = \sum_{j=0}^{t-1} \delta^j \bullet (2 \bullet d_{t-j} - 1)$$

The state space Θ_t includes the policy distance between the individual and the parties, their assessment and her or his socioeconomic and demographic characteristics.

It is also clear that the higher stock of past votes for M, K_{t-1}, the higher the probability that the individual will vote for M. This means that voting for one of the parties today increases the sympathy with this party and the probability of voting for it in the future. The higher the party and its leader's evaluation by the voter, the higher the probability of voting for it. The higher the sensitivity of utility with respect to these assessments (*b* is higher) and the higher one's subjective sense of influence on elections results (ε is higher), the higher the influence of changes in the party and candidate's evaluations on the voting probability. The lower the policy distance of a voter from a party, the higher the probability of voting for it. The higher the sensitivity of utility with respect to the policy distance (*a* is higher) and the higher the voter's subjective sense of influence on elections results (ε is higher), the higher the influence of changes in policy distance on the voting probability.

IV. Empirical Results

In a multiparty system such as that in Israel, the definition of the dependent vote variable is not straightforward. Our choice—not the only one possible[12]—is dividing the political parties into left and right blocs. The left bloc includes Labor and the small Jewish and Arab left-wing parties. The right bloc includes Likud, the small right-wing parties, and the religious parties that before the election presented themselves to the voters as belonging to the right.[13] The rationale for this decision is both substantive and technical. First of all, these two blocs are well defined in Israel, and they are meaningful politically. For example, irrespective of the relative fortunes of Likud and Labor in the election, the major question for coalition building was the size of the blocs. Moreover, we can use all the valid cases—most of the sample, an important consideration with the sample sizes we are working with. In terms of the analysis, it is important then to clarify what we are and what we are not explaining. Our analysis refers to vote and change in vote for the Likud and Labor blocs. Because of our definition of the dependent variable, we cannot explain vote and change in vote inside blocs; for example, our results do not pertain to 1988 Likud voters who switched in this election to small right-wing or religious parties compared to those who remained loyal to the Likud, as they all remained within the right bloc (on this see Arian and Shamir in this volume).

To begin with we estimated the full probit model with all specified predictors.[14] Those included the sociodemographic variables (ethnic background, religiosity, age, education, income, and gender), past vote, a summary comparative candidate evaluation measure (Rabin vs. Shamir), three issue positions (on territories, on state-religion relations, on socioeconomic viewpoint), two Likud versus Labor performance evaluations (one in the social and economic sphere and one on security and foreign affairs) and a Likud versus Labor comparative corruption measure.[15] The last item was included in the questionnaire and in our model as charges of corruption were high on the agenda during the election campaign, following reports of the state comptroller.[16]

Several of the variables had *t* values of less than 1, and the final model presented in table 2.1 leaves them out. Before moving to the table, it is instructive to briefly examine those variables. *All* of the sociodemographic variables fall into this group. This means, that the *American Voter* (Campbell et al., 1960) funnel of causality is an appropriate model in terms of the integration of sociological and attitudinal influences on the vote. The social and demographic characteristics of the voters may of course have an effect on the vote through the different political orientations of the individuals (specified in our model) but no additional direct impact.[17]

In addition to the sociodemographic variables, two of the issue variables were statistically insignificant in the full model. One was people's orientation toward capitalism versus socialism; even its zero-order correlation with the vote was close to zero and not statistically significant. The classic socioeconomic cleavage was totally unrelated to the vote in Israel in 1992. The question of state-religion relations also did not have a significant independent effect in the model. But it is important to emphasize that unlike the socioeconomic issue, its zero-order correlation with vote is quite meaningful, in the .3 range. Thus the religious dimension is related to bloc voting patterns, but when considering all the other factors, it washes out. Of the three issue areas we examined, only one then, that of foreign and security affairs, was found to have an independent effect on the vote, and an important one, as we shall see.

The candidate evaluation measure was at the borderline of commonly accepted statistical significance ($p = .07$) and was left in the final model for theoretical and election-specific reasons. Of the factors in the model, it was the least important one (coefficient of .35).

We pursue the analysis along the four questions we raised in the introduction as to what decided the election outcome.

Utility Parameters—Importance for the Individual Voter

Table 2.1 presents the final probit model. All independent variables were rescaled so as to be between −1 to +1, with 0 representing the neutral point.[18] Thus we can easily and meaningfully compare the size of their coefficients.

The first column in the table presents the probit coefficients, indicating the sensitivity or importance attached by voters to the different factors. Here we look at variation at the individual level, accounting for differences between voters for the two competing blocs. Most influential is the Likud versus Labor performance evaluation in the area of security and foreign affairs. Although the different elements of this scale are closely related, it is

Table 2.1. 1992 Bloc Vote—Probit Estimates

Variable[a]	Coefficient[b]	(S.E.)	t	Mean
Performance evaluation (security and foreign affairs)	1.58	(.24)	6.73	.04
1988 bloc vote	.77	(.12)	6.61	−.08
Territories issue	−.67	(.11)	−6.04	−.20
Corruption	−.66	(.18)	−3.69	−.05
Performance evaluation (social/economic sphere)	.54	(.21)	2.64	.13
Candidate evaluation	−.35	(.19)	−1.82	−.03
Constant	−.18	(.10)	−1.78	

Notes:
$N = 970$
Log Likelihood = −128.1.
Chi-square (6) = 1088.6 ; $p < .0001$.
[a] The dependent variable is coded as 0—right bloc; 1—left bloc.
All independent variables are scaled between −1 and +1, with the higher score denoting past vote for left, evaluation in favor of Shamir, performance evaluations in favor of Labor, evaluation of Labor as corrupt and hawkish position on the territories.
[b] All coefficients significant at $p < .01$, except for candidate evaluation ($p = .07$) and constant ($p = .08$).

still worthwhile to note that among them, the most decisive elements are those of leading to real peace with the Arabs and putting an end to the intifada in the territories.[19] This general evaluation dimension is by far the most important consideration in the voters' mind. The other dimension of performance evaluation, in the social and economic spheres, has also an effect on the vote, but it is of much lesser magnitude (compare 1.58 to .54). Taking together both factors, it is clear that a consideration of which party (as the head of a bloc coalition) will be better able to cope with the country's problems and challenges is a primary factor in the voters' calculus. Similar results were obtained in an analysis of the 1988 election (Shamir and Arian 1990). One of the major differences between 1988 and 1992 was a change in those evaluations to the detriment of the Likud. We will have more to say about this shortly.

The cleavage dimension defined narrowly by the territories occupied by Israel following the Six Day war, and more broadly by views on the Arab-Israeli conflict is most dominant in voters' decisions in another respect as well: the position itself. We have seen that the assessment of which party will be better able "to deliver" the valence dimension of ending or containing the conflict is the primary factor in the voters' calculus. In addition, the third factor in terms of importance for the voters is the issue of the territories (.67). The question we asked referred to willingness to give up territories for peace; people's position on it is found to be a major determinant of their vote, with hawkish voters tending to vote for the Likud bloc, and doves for the Labor bloc. If we consider in combination issue positions and performance evaluations in the security and foreign affairs area, these results corroborate the respondents' self-reports as to the importance of issues and of these specific issues among their vote concerns.

Past vote is the second factor in importance; we regard it as an indicator for voters' standing partisan decision, and as such its influence is great, considering all the other current attitudes of the voters (coefficient of .77).[20] In the conclusion, we will refer to its role in vote persistence.

The issue of corruption is also found to have been of relevance to voters' calculus, of similar magnitude to the territorial issue. The candidates' assessments were less influential, but still of importance. Our measure here was a comparative summary evaluation of Shamir and Rabin's leadership qualities, in personal terms. As it is impossible to totally separate the images of candidate and party, it is of course possible that the party performance evaluations also have some component of the leaders' performance evaluations in the areas we asked about. But it is interesting to note that the candidate factor comes out as less important in the voters' calculus than issues and party (indicated by past vote), just as the sample respondents have told us when asked directly.

Vote Probabilities: Party Blocs' Sources of Advantage

The next two perspectives on the relative importance of the various factors can be obtained from table 2.2. Here the focus is on the aggregate electoral result: what contributed to Labor's success, which factors worked to its advantage? We look at the probability of voting for the Labor bloc under various assumptions. Assuming past vote makes no difference (and taking it out from the predictive equation), we compute the predicted vote probability for the Labor bloc (first column). It is 52.02 percent, compared to just more than 50 percent (50.34) when past vote is included. The difference between those two estimated probabilities gives us the advantage of the Likud bloc over the Labor bloc due to the specific factor in question (third column in table). This measure incorporates both the importance attached to each factor by the voters (as estimated by the model in table 2.1) and where they stand on it. The fact that the voting decision is in part a standing decision, reinforced by past vote, and given the population's past vote, increased the probability of voting for the right in this election by 1.68 points, to the detriment of the left.

All the other factors make less of a difference in this sense, and they all work in the favor of the Labor bloc. Thus, were it not for people's partisan attachment, the left's chances for victory would have been greater. Although performance evaluation in security and foreign affairs had the strongest impact on voters in terms of differentiating between voters for the left and for the right, the fact is that on the aggregate there was almost no difference between Likud and Labor evaluations (mean of .04). Therefore, the impact of this factor on the election results is small. On the other hand, attitudes on the issue of the territories turn out to have had more of an impact on the elections (difference of 1.00 percent in probability), due to a combination of the dovish position of the electorate and the importance attached to it by the voters. The issue of corruption, which has a coefficient of similar size as the territories issue, had only a very small impact on the election results, because again, overall, the parties are not perceived as being very different on it. The candidates' leadership qualities appear to have had a minuscule effect in the elections, as a result of a combination of a very small difference between the candidates and the relatively little impact this factor has on the vote.

Dispersion of Vote Probabilities

The last column in Table 2.2 gives us the third measure of impact on the election outcome, in terms of the dispersion of vote probabilities. A higher score on this measure means that the factor had more of an effect on the dispersion of the predicted vote probabilities and that it contributed more heavily to polarization in vote intentions.

Again assuming past vote makes no difference (and taking it out from the predictive equation), we look at the standard deviation of the predicted vote probability (second column in table). It is .4364, compared to .4581 when past vote is incorporated. The difference between those two figures, as a proportion of the full model standard deviation, tells us by how much the dispersion of the vote probabilities in the population decreased when past vote is not considered, when it is not included in the model. The answer is 4.7 percent, which is the second highest figure in this column. The factor with most impact in this sense is that of performance evaluations in the security and foreign affairs area. When it was neutralized, the dispersion of the vote probabilities decreased by 11.6 percent. The other factors had much less of an impact on this dispersion.

Table 2.2. Vote Probabilities (for Left Bloc) under Various Assumptions

Variable Neutralized	Predicted Vote Probability		Difference in	
	Mean	SD	Mean[a]	SD[b] (%)
Full Model	.5034	.4581		
1988 bloc vote	.5202	.4364	+1.68	−4.7
Territories issue	.4934	.4461	−1.00	−2.6
Performance evaluation (social/economic sphere)	.4962	.4472	−0.72	−2.4
Performance evaluation (security and foreign affairs)	.5009	.4050	−0.25	−11.6
Corruption	.5011	.4548	−0.23	−0.7
Candidate evaluation	.5025	.4517	−0.09	−1.4

[a] The difference in the probability of voting for the Left bloc between full model, and model in which one variable at a time is missing (e.g., +1.68 = 52.02 − 50.34).

[b] The difference in the standard deviation of the voting probability proportionwise between full model and model in which one variable at time is taken out (e.g., −4.7 = (.4364 − .4581)/.4581 * 100).

The Sources of Electoral Turnover: 1992 versus 1988

Table 2.3 provides measures for the fourth perspective on the "importance" of the different factors, also on the aggregate level. Here we are looking at the sources of the electoral turnover: What brought about the change between 1988 and 1992? What brought down the Likud and the right, what elevated Labor and its left bloc?

The measure presented in the last column is dynamic and compares the 1992 election to the previous one (1988).[21] For each election we compute the mathematical product of the estimated parameter by the mean for each predictor. By combining measures for where the public stands on each factor with its influence on the vote, we get a measure of impact of that factor in the election. Our final measure is simply the difference between these products for the two elections.[22]

The answer as to the sources of the 1992 turnover is very clear. Between the 1988 and 1992 elections the images of the major parties as to "who can deliver" changed dramatically, mainly in the area of security and foreign affairs, but also, additionally, in social and economic matters. As can be seen from a comparison of the coefficients for the two elections, the importance of these factors for the voters remained fairly constant, but their perceptions of the parties changed significantly, as indicated by the means. We have discussed these changes earlier: the Likud's image greatly deteriorated, and Labor's image improved. In 1988 the two dimensions of performance evaluations worked strongly in favor of the Likud bloc; by 1992 the two factors favored Labor, though to a lesser extent than they had advantaged the Likud bloc in 1988.

Second in importance in explaining the electoral turnover comes the issue of the territories. Here we note two changes. The territories became more influential in voters' considerations (the probit coefficient increased from -.37 to -.66),[23] *and* between 1988 and 1992 voters moved further toward dovish positions (the mean changed from -.09 to -.20).

Candidates were instrumental in the electoral turnover, but less so than the other factors. One needs though to allow for the possibility that the replacement of Peres by Rabin may have had an effect through the party performance image in the areas we asked about, in particular in the area of security and foreign affairs. It is also worthwhile noting that the mean of zero from 1988, suggesting that on the average the public was almost indifferent between Shamir and Peres, changed to an advantage of Rabin over Shamir (although not a big one).[24] The influence of candidate evaluations on voters' decisions increased between 1988 and 1992 (compare .42 and .67). This result may be attributed to one or all of the following: Rabin's candidacy, Labor's campaign strategy which put Rabin in the center, or the highly publicized legislative amendment that established direct elections for the prime minister in the next elections.

Corruption charges were not an issue in the 1988 elections, and there were no questions about it in the 1988 questionnaire. If we assume that the difference between Likud and Labor corruption images was zero and/or that this question was irrelevant in the elections in the sense that it was no consideration in the voters' mind in 1988, we can take the 1992 figure from the first column in table 2.3 as an estimate of the corruption issue contribution to the 1992 turnover. As such it was very small.

Partisan allegiance or habit (measured here by past vote) was no factor in explaining the change between 1988 and 1992. In both elections it operated in favor of the right. Somewhat surprising is the finding that its importance in voters' considerations (once we control for current attitudes and evaluations) was higher in 1992 than in 1988 (coefficients of .78 vs. .52). With respect to 1992 it means that partisan loyalty has not weakened and that if it were not for such loyalty, the right's loss would have been even greater. This result is contrary to many interpretations of the 1992 election and, on the face of it, is not consistent with the aggregate results, which in 1988 showed little change and in 1992 brought about a reversal in government. However in 1992 most of those who shifted blocs moved from the Likud bloc to the

Table 2.3. Sources of Electoral Turnover

Variables	Coefficient × Mean		1992–1988 Difference
	1992	1988	
Performance evaluation (security and foreign affairs)	+.0702 [1.61 × .04]	−.2902 [1.44 × (−.20)]	+.3604
Performance evaluation (social/economic sphere)	+.0779 [.60 × .13]	−.0875 [.65 × (−.13)]	+.1674
Territories issue	+.1301 [(−.66) × (−.20)]	+.0305 [(−.37) × (−.09)]	+.0996
Candidate evaluation[a]	+.0555 [.67 × .08]	−.0036 [.42 × (−.01)]	+.0591
Corruption	+.0292 [(−.62) × (−.05)]		
Past bloc vote	−.0625 [.78 × (−.08)]	−.0443 [.52 × (−.08)]	−.0182
N	970	663	

[a] For this analysis we used thermometer questions referring to Shamir and Peres in 1988 and to Shamir and Rabin in 1992.

Labor bloc. In 1988 people moved in both directions, and thus on the aggregate most of these shifts canceled out. But the question of persistence and change in vote is not only a question of direction of shift but it is also a question of the sources of persistence in vote, on which we will comment briefly in the conclusion.

V. Summary and Conclusion

Why then did Labor win and Likud lose in the 1992 elections? If we put together the information from the four measures we suggested (tables 2.1 through 2.3), our answer is multifaceted.

We definitely start with performance evaluations in foreign and security affairs. These were by far the most important consideration of the individual voter and the strongest factor in bringing about the electoral turnover. These performance evaluations also had the most effect on the dispersion of the predicted vote probabilities, that is, on polarization in vote intentions. But in terms of the advantage given by this factor to each of the party blocs, it was among the least important, because the difference between Likud and Labor on it was small.

The issue of the territories was of much significance in determining the election outcome, but along different dimensions. Voters' stand on this issue was an important consideration in their mind. It was third in importance in this sense and also in explaining the turnover between 1988 and 1992. But it was the most potent factor working to the advantage of the Labor bloc over the Likud bloc in the election!

Social and economic concerns were not central to voters. Basic socioeconomic principles did not relate at all to electoral choices. Performance evaluations in the social and economic spheres were relevant, but they were usually secondary to performance evaluations in security and foreign affairs. The electorate was not most sensitive to this dimension but sensitive enough. Thus in combination with the size of the difference between the Likud and Labor evaluations, this dimension was second in importance among the factors operating to the advantage of the Labor bloc over the Likud bloc. It was also second among the turnover factors, as the change in those evaluations between 1988 and 1992 was among the largest.

Candidate evaluations and the corruption issue were found to be unimportant on most measures. As to corruption, it is not the case that the public is not sensitive to it. But the image of the two major parties along this dimension is not much different, and therefore it was not significant in deciding the election outcome. Candidate evaluations appear to be of relatively little importance on all counts; one should allow though for the possibility that some of the candidates' effect was represented through the party performance evaluations.

Past vote was found to be the second most powerful factor in terms of voters' sensitivity, and it was most significant in giving an edge to the Likud bloc over the Labor bloc in the 1992 election. It was actually the only factor working in favor of the Likud bloc in this election.

Our analysis illustrates that when seeking explanations for electoral turnovers and electoral outcomes more generally, one needs to phrase the questions very precisely. An explicit voting decision model facilitates the task by pointing to statistical measures through which one can answer the questions. We referred to voters' sensitivity to various considerations, to the electoral advantage to the parties of each of the factors, to the effect of each factor on the dispersion of vote probabilities, and to the contribution of each factor to the change from the previous election. Different factors were important in these different respects, and therefore it is impossible to explain the election results in any simple terms and unequivocally.

When a turnover occurs, focus is on change. Yet, there is always also persistence in voting patterns. Vote persistence is generally high in most countries, and it was also high in Israel in 1992. Elsewhere we have decomposed it and shown that its sources are partisan attachment reinforced by people's voting record and, even more so, continuity in political attitudes and evaluations. A priori fixed preferences exist and are relevant, but they have little impact on vote persistence (Shachar and Shamir 1993). This means that unless people's acquired partisan preferences are supported by political experience that reinforces repeated voting for the same party, and continuity in political attitudes, they lose their grip.

Electoral persistence as well as electoral change are thus brought about to a significant extent by political attitudes and evaluations. Attitude change on the aggregate can be the result of individual level change or of demographic change—that is, entry of new groups (young voters, new immigrants) into the population. In Israel both processes occurred. They produced enough change, mainly along the security and foreign affairs dimension, that turnover resulted.

Notes

1. The other amendment increased the minimum a list has to obtain in order to be represented in the 120-member Knesset from 1 percent to 1.5 percent. This change was the compromise result of different political interests, and at the time of its passage, it seemed trivial and went almost unnoticed. It proved to be of consequence, though, as it prevented the extreme right-wing Techiya from winning representation.

2. Also in 1988, with no relationship to this electoral initiative, Labor put much emphasis in its election campaign on Shimon Peres, who was then its candidate for prime minister.

3. The analyses in this paper are based on two preelection surveys conducted in October 1988 ($N = 873$) and in June 1992 ($N = 1192$). Both samples are representative of the adult Jewish population of Israel, excluding those on kibbutzim and settlements in the territories. The surveys were directed by Michal Shamir and Asher Arian, and the data were collected by the Dahaf Research Institute.

4. Candidate evaluations were measured by a series of eight questions. The respondents were asked to indicate whether each of eight qualities better fit Shamir, Rabin, both of them, or neither of them. The qualities asked about were: leadership ability or charisma; toughness; trustworthiness; decisiveness; negotiation skills; preference of country's needs over those of their party; initiative and creativity; ability to resist pressure. These items were combined into a summary comparative candidate evaluation measure of Rabin versus Shamir (eight-item scale, coefficient alpha = .93).

5. These questions have been asked in Israeli election surveys, conducted by Asher Arian, since 1973. Whenever reference is made in the paper to survey results before 1988, they are based on these election surveys.

6. Position on the territories (Judea, Samaria, and the Gaza Strip) was measured by first asking the respondent to choose among the following three alternatives:

(*a*) the return of most of the territories as part of a peace agreement
(*b*) the annexation of the territories to Israel
(*c*) status quo

Respondents who chose (*c*) were then asked to decide between the first two options. Out of these two questions we created one (five-category) variable. The state-religion relations question read: "In your opinion, should the government of Israel, or should it not, see to it that public life in the state be conducted according to the Jewish religious tradition?"

(*a*) the government should definitely see to it
(*b*) perhaps the government should do so
(*c*) I don't think the government should do so
(*d*) the government should definitely not do so

Socioeconomic viewpoint was measured by "As to the economic structure in Israel, do you support more a socialist approach or a capitalist approach?", with four options from definitely capitalist to definitely socialist. This question indicates a rather broad affiliation to sociopolitical camps, beyond ideological orientation.

7. The question was, "Which of the two major parties does each of these attributes fit better?" The response categories were Likud, Labor, both parties the same, and neither party.

Performance evaluations in the social and economic sphere were measured by items asking which party would know how to absorb immigration and reduce unemployment, and which team would be better able to deal with the economic problems of the country. These produced a three-item scale, with an alpha coefficient of .86.

Performance evaluations in security and foreign affairs were measured by items asking which party would know how to restore law and order to the territories, lead to real peace with the Arabs, stand firm in negotiations on territories and peace, keep good relations with the U.S., and be better able to deal with the security and foreign affairs problems of the country. These produced a five-item scale; coefficient alpha = .89.

8. Another advantage of using past vote is the fact that it is a standard question in public opinion surveys, available across time and countries. The

problem of retrospective bias in the use of this question can be dealt with statistically (Shachar and Eckstein 1992).

9. Ethnic background is indicated here, as in most other studies, by country of origin of the respondent and his/her father. The answers were dichotomized, with one category including African and Asian origin (of respondent or father) versus all others.

10. Religiosity was measured by a four-point subjective scale in which respondents were asked to report the extent to which they keep the religious tradition. Income was indicated by a five-point subjective scale in which respondents were asked whether their monthly expenditures were average, above average, or below average.

11. This is a static version of that model in the sense that it ignores the influence of the current decisions on future choices.

12. Another option, used quite often, is Likud versus Labor vote. The major drawback of this definition is that is leaves out all the voters for the other parties, which in 1992 amounted to more than a third of the electorate. The sample *N* is seriously reduced, and the explanation does not cover those voters. Another alternative is building a (four- or five-point) ordinal (assumed to be interval) measure of vote, defining the parties from extreme right ot extreme left. There is no consensus on such an order, and in each election there are several parties that are hard to order (in particular the religious parties are problematic in this respect).

13. The haredi parties (Shas and Yahadut HaTorah) as well as the Russian parties and the new Liberal Party, lead by Modai, were not included, as they could not be easily defined as left or right. Voters for these parties in our sample total about 5 percent.

14. In the estimation process we replace the relative policy distance of the voters from the parties by their policy positions, due to lack of data. This of course means that we build in a fixed perception of party positions. All party performance evaluations and candidate assessments are comparative, that is, differential scores. Previous vote decisions are represented by vote in the 1988 elections only. Also, as explained in the previous paragraph, party blocs replace parties *M* and *L* in the model.

15. Several of our predictors refer to a comparison of Likud versus Labor (candidates, corruption, the two performance evaluation measures). They are indeed related more closely to the dichotomy between Labor and Likud voters than to the bloc dichotomy, but only very marginally. Basically, the Israeli party system consists of two blocs, each of which is composed of one major party and its satellites. Thus voters for the smaller parties can take into consideration the evaluations of their associated parties and their leaders.

16. The corruption question was asked in the same format as the performance evaluation items: Which political party, Labor or Likud, is characterized by corruption (either one, both, or neither)?

17. Similar results were obtained in the analysis of the 1988 elections (Shamir and Arian 1990) and in another recent study based on data from 1991 (Shachar and Eckstein 1992). In the latter study education was the only sociodemographic variable coming close to achieving commonly accepted statistical significance.

18. Past vote was 1 for respondents who indicated they had voted for left bloc in 1988 elections ($N = 342$), -1 for respondents who had voted for the right bloc in 1988 ($N = 420$), and 0 for respondents who had not voted in the 1988 elections ($N = 208$). Those were mainly first-time voters and new immigrants. This approach to past vote captures well our understanding of it as an indicator of a standing decision, which reinforces itself when activated. Of course, using this procedure allows us not to lose 1992 voters who did not vote in 1988. We also performed the analysis without respondents who had not voted in 1988, and the results were virtually the same.

19. The first evaluation is clearly a long-term concern, with peace being a major goal of Israel's foreign policy and a high priority in Israelis' value system (see Shamir and Arian 1994). The latter evaluation is more of a short-term considerateion. Our analysis does not differentiate between the effects of short- and long-term concerns. In a study of the 1988 election in Israel, it was found that the long-term concerns were more important in terms of the vote than the short-term concerns (Shamir and Arian 1990; but see Barzilai 1990, for a different interpretation). The eminence of movement toward peace and of curtailing the intifada among the dimensions of security and foreign affairs is indicated by several measures. These two items have the highest correlations with the general assessment question of the parties' performance in security and foreign affairs as well as with vote; their removal from the scale also most reduces its alpha coefficient.

20. The estimated coefficient is probably somewhat biased (upwards), due to the problem of retrospective bias. We estimate this bias to be between 10 and 20 percent, based on Schachar and Eckstein (1992) and Zuckerman (1990).

21. (a) For this analysis, we had to use another measure for candidate evaluations because there were no items on candidates' leadership qualities in the 1988 questionnaire. The estimates for the 1992 model obtained using the thermometer questions are very similar to those presented in table 2.1, with the only difference being a somewhat higher (and statistically significant at $p < .01$) coefficient for the candidates variable, of similar magnitude to that of the territories issue (.67).

(b) The estimates of the parameters of the 1988 model in comparison to 1992 were similar for the two performance evaluations; for past vote, the territories issue and candidate evaluations they were smaller in 1988. There was no corruption item in 1988. The two evaluation measures had the highest coefficients, followed by past vote, candidate evaluation, and the territories issue.

22. If we had panel data we could estimate change at the individual level, and aggregation based on it would be more precise, as also Denk and Finkel (1992) suggest. The source of the inaccuracy of our measure is the fact that the probabilities are not a linear function. We do not use the method Denk and Finkel propose, for two major reasons. First, their procedure requires the assumption of fixed parameters across time—which we find untenable in theory and reject in practice. Second, for the case of cross-sectional data, they suggest making assumptions about how the independent variables change, which we find hard to apply.

23. This increase in the importance of the territories issue in the voters' calculus was also indicated by the direct question, described above.

24. Recall that for the comparison of 1992 to 1988 we use thermometer questions rather than the series of items on leadership qualities. Rabin had a slight edge over Shamir on this scale, and he had an even larger advantage on the thermometer (love-hate) question.

References

Abramson, Paul R., John H. Aldrich, and R. W. Rohde. 1982. *Change and Continuity in the 1980 Elections.* Washington D.C.: Congressional Quarterly Press.

Achen, Christopher H. 1982. *Interpreting and Using Regression.* Beverly Hills: Sage.

Arian, Asher. 1973. *The Choosing People: Voting Behavior in Israel.* Cleveland: Press of Case Western Reserve University.

———. 1989. *Politics in Israel: The Second Generation.* 2nd edition, Chatham, N.J.: Chatham House.

Arian, Asher, and Michal Shamir. 1994. "Two Reversals: Why 1992 Was Not 1977." In *The Elections in Israel—1992*, ed. Asher Arian and Michal Shamir. Albany: SUNY Press.

Arian, Asher, Michal Shamir, and Raphael Ventura. 1992. "Public Opinion and Political Change: Israel and the Intifada." *Comparative Politics* 24 no. 3: (April): 317–34.

Barzilai, Gad. 1990. "National Security Crises and Voting Behavior: The Intifada and the 1988 Elections." In *The Elections in Israel—1988*, ed. Asher Arian and Michal Shamir. Boulder: Westview Press.

Bean, Clive, and Anthony Mughan. 1989. "Leadership Effects in Parliamentary Elections in Australia and Britain." *American Political Science Review* 83 no. 4 (December): 1165–79.

Berelson, Bernard R., Paul F. Lazarsfeld, and William N. McPhee. 1954. *Voting.* Chicago: University of Chicago Press.

Budge, Ian, Ivor Crewe, and Dennis Farlie. 1976. *Party Identification and Beyond.* London: Wiley.

Campbell, Angus, Philip. E. Converse, Warren E. Miller, and Donald E. Stokes. 1960. *The American Voter.* New York: Wiley.

Converse, Philip E. 1976. *The Dynamic of Party Support.* Beverly Hills: Sage.

Denk, Charles E., and Steven E. Finkel. 1992. "The Aggregate Impact of Explanatory Variables in Logit and Linear Probability Models." *American Journal of Political Science* 36 no. 3: 785–804.

Diskin, Avraham. 1991. *Elections and Voters in Israel.* New York: Praeger.

Downs, Anthony. 1957. *An Economic Theory of Democracy.* New York: Harper & Row.

Fiorina, M. 1981. *Retrospective Voting in American National Elections.* New Haven: Yale University Press.

Galnoor, Itzhak. 1980. "Transformation in the Israeli Political System since the Yom Kippur War." In *The Elections in Israel—1977,* ed. A. Arian. Jerusalem: Jerusalem Academic Press.

Graetz, Brian, and Ian McAllister. 1987. "Party Leaders and Election Outcomes in Britain 1974–1983." *Comparative Political Studies* 19: 484–507.

Gutmann, Emanuel. 1977. "Political Parties and Groups: Stability and Change." In *The Israeli Political System,* ed. Moshe Lissak and Emanuel Gutmann. Tel Aviv: Am Oved.

Inglehart, Ronald. 1990. *Culture Shift in Advanced Industrial Society.* Princeton: Princeton University Press.

Jennings, M. Kent, and Richard G. Niemi. 1981. *Generations and Politics.* Princeton: Princeton University Press.

Ledyard, John O. 1984. "The Pure Theory of Larg Two-Candidate Elections." *Public Choice* 44: 7–41.

Markus, Gregory B. 1979. "The Political Environment and the Dynamics of Public Attitudes: A Panel Study." *American Journal of Political Science* 23 no. 2: 338–59.

———. 1988. "The Impact of Personal and National Economic Conditions on the Presidential Vote: A Pooled Cross-sectional Analysis." *American Journal of Political Science* 32 no. 1: 137–54.

Markus, Gregory B., and Philip E. Converse. 1979. "A Dynamic Simultaneous Equation Model of Electoral Choice." *American Political Science Review* 73 no. 4: 1055–70.

Miller, Warren E., and J. Merrill Shanks. 1982. "Policy Directions and Presidential Leadership: Alternative Interpretations of the 1980 Presidential Election." *British Journal of Political Science* 12: 299–356.

Miller, Arthur H., and Martin P. Wattenberg. 1985. "Throwing the Rascals Out: Policy and Performance Evaluations of Presidential Candidates, 1952–1980." *American Political Science Review* 79 no. 2: (June): 359–72.

Page, Benjamin I., and Calvin C. Jones. 1979. "Reciprocal Effects of Policy Preferences, Party Loyalties and the Vote." *American Political Science Review* 73 no. 2: 1071–89.

Richardson, Bradley M. 1991. "European Party Loyalties Revisited." *American Political Science Review* 85 no. 3: (September): 751–75.

Rose, Richard, ed. 1974. *Electoral Behavior: A Comparative Handbook.* New York: Free Press.

Shachar, Ron. 1992. "Party Identification as an Habituation Process in a Dynamic Vote Model: Theory and Empirical Findings." Ph.D. diss., Tel Aviv University.

Shachar, Ron, and Zvi Eckstein. 1992. "Party Identification as an Habituation Process in Israel" (in Hebrew). Discussion Paper 5–92. Pinhas Sapir Center for Development, Tel Aviv University.

Shachar, Ron, and Michal Shamir. 1993. "Modelling the 1992 Electoral Victory in Israel." Working paper.

Shamir, Michal. 1986. "Realignment in the Israeli Party System." In *The Elections in Israel—1984*, ed. Asher Arian and Michal Shamir. New Brunswick, N.J.: Transaction.

Shamir, Michal, and Asher Arian. 1982. "Ethnicity in the 1981 Elections in Israel." *Electoral Studies* 1 no. 3: (December): 315–32.

———. 1990. "The Intifada and Israeli Voters: Policy Preferences and Performance Evaluations." In *The Elections in Israel—1988*, ed. Asher Arian and Michal Shamir. Boulder: Westview Press.

———. 1994. "Competing Values and Policy Choices: Israeli Public Opinion on Foreign and Security Affairs." *British Journal of Political Science* 24: 249–71.

Shamir, Michal, and John L. Sullivan. 1983. "The Political Context of Tolerance: The United States and Israel." *American Political Science Review* 77 no. 4: (December): 911–28.

Shanks, J. Merrill, and Warren E. Miller. 1990. "Policy Directions and Performance Evaluation: Complementay Explanations of the Reagan Elections." *British Journal of Political Science* 20 no. 2: (April): 143–235.

Ventura, Raphael, and Michal Shamir. 1992. "Left and Right in Israeli Politics" (in Hebrew). *State, Government and International Relations* 35 (fall–winter): 21–50.

Zuckerman, Alan S. 1990. "The Flow of the Vote in Israel: A Reconsideration of Stability and Change" in Asher Arian and Michal Shamir (eds.) *The Elections in Israel—1988.* Boulder: Westview.

PART II

Group Influences

CHAPTER 3

Penetrating the System:
The Politics of Collective Identities

HANNA HERZOG
Tel Aviv University

This chapter deals with parties based on collective identity: religious, ethnic, Arab, and women's parties. Collective identity has the potential to be an efficient and thrifty resource for political mobilization and organization, all the more so when social affiliation is a major cause for social interests and/or social deprivation in a given society. In practice two major factors affect the ability to convert it to political mobilization: organizational efficiency and symbolic recognition. Each of the factors is necessary but not sufficient. This chapter highlights the symbolic dimension and claims that winning and/or preserving legitimacy for collective identity is an inseparable part of political competition. The legitimacy of collective identity is struggled over through a process of meaning construction, and negotiations over its symbolic value, in Hall's terms through the "politics of signification" (Hall 1982). In the following, religious, ethnic, Arab, and women's parties are examined in historical perspective in light of the politics of signification of their social identity. The basic claim is that the way these four social categories are framed and signified in Israeli political culture determines the course of their inclusion and/or exclusion in the political arena. On the structural level all four are regarded as differentiated social categories, yet on the symbolic level only the religious parties have gained legitimacy. The ascriptive identity (of Jewish ethnic groups, Arab, and women) as a basis for independent political

I would like to thank Dafna Israeli and Silvie Fogiel-Bijaoui for helpful comments on an earlier draft of this article.

organization has been decried and delegitimized. Although the same basic mechanisms shaped the political destiny of the three ascriptive groups, because different options were open to them they each developed different political behavior.

I. Religious Parties

Although most democratic societies separate religion from the state, in Israel there is no such separation. The religious community, although constituting a numerical minority of 30 percent, was never defined as a minority group. Originally the Zionist movement was secular and challenged the traditional Jewish life, but the religious parties have been an integral part of Israeli political system since its beginning (Schiff 1977; Liebman and Don-Yehiya 1984; Greilsammer 1990). This phenomenon is explained by two major factors. The first is that, being voluntary organizations, the Zionist movement and the prestate political system encouraged any basis of political activity. The second, the more crucial, is that Judaism has been a key element in the social identity of the nation (Deshen 1978; Liebman and Don-Yehiya 1983). The wide consensus to maintain national unity and to preserve the Jewish character of the organized Yishuv and latter of the state, granted the religious parties with legitimacy. Its interests have been not only respected but even identified with the national identity needs. Moreover, it resulted with an ongoing compromise arrangements known as the "status quo" (Liebman and Don-Yehiya 1984, 31–40). Therefore, in addition to many of their claims, religious political parties per se are conceived of as being legitimate. Since their establishment at the beginning of the century, the religious parties have been divided into two trends: Zionist and non-Zionist. Until the 1970s, though differing in their attitude to the state, both trends were mainly concerned with maintaining the status quo in religious matters and supplying the needs of their constituency.

The Zionist trend contested since 1956 as one party, the National Religious Party (NRP, a union of the Mizrachi and Hapoel Hamizrachi), it received between 9 percent and 10 percent of the votes and participated in most of the governments established by the Labor Party (table 3.1). The legitimacy of that partnership was never questioned; on the contrary, the NRP was considered as a political ally of the left. The non-Zionist trend (the ultraorthodox (haredi), Agudat Israel, and Poalai Agudat Israel, opposed the very idea of a Jewish state, voluntarily segregated themselves from secular and Orthodox communities, and excluded themselves from many state organizations, the salient of which are the educational system and the army. Paradoxically, in the 1950s, the ultraorthodox refused to admit the legitimacy of the state, but the state did grant them legitimization and was ready

Table 3.1. Religious Parties

	1	2	3	4	5	6	7	8	9	10	11	12	13
	1949	1951	1955	1959	1961	1965	1969	1973	1977	1981	1984	1988	1992
	National Religious Front	Mizrachi Worker	National Religious Party	National Religious Party	National Religious Party	National Religious Party	National Religious Party	National Religious Party	National Religious Party	National Religious Party	National Religious Party	National Religious Party	National Religious Party
	12.2	6.8	9.1	9.9	9.8	8.9	9.7	8.3	9.2	4.9	3.5	3.9	5
	Orthodox	Agudat Israel	Agudat Israel	Agudat Israel	Agudat Israel	Agudat Israel	Agudat Israel	Agudat Israel	Agudat Israel	Agudat Israel	Agudat Israel	Agudat Israel	Torah Judaism
	0.7	2	4.7	4.7	3.7	3.3	3.2	3.8	3.4	3.7	1.7	4.5	3.3
	Religious Women	Aguda Workers			Aguda Workers	Aguda Workers	Aguda Workers		Aguda Workers	Aguda Workers	Morasha (Aguda Workers)	Degel Hatorah	Geulat Israel
	0.6	1.6			1.9	1.8	1.8		1.3	0.9	1.6	1.5	0.5
	Religious Workers	Mizrachi Workers								Tami	Tami	Meimad	Land and Torah (Levinger)
	0.3	1.5								2.3	1.5	0.7	0.14
											Shas	Shas	Shas
											3.1	4.7	4.9

Note: Percentage of votes reported below each party.

to meet some of their special sectorial needs. This legitimation enabled negotiations between the state and the ultraorthodox parties that resulted in increasing material allocations. Thus, with the help of the state the haredi society has developed as a "society of scholars," based on the yeshivot as frameworks that prevented drift and ensured intergenerational continuity. Their success in establishing the society of scholars led to the abandonment of the principle of separatism and to more political involvement of the ultraorthodox parties, even by participation in governmental coalitions (Friedman 1991). Nevertheless, not recognizing the state left them on the margin of the political discourse.

Two major changes that occurred during the 1970s affected the two religious trends, but in completely different ways: one was the change in the political discourse of the Zionist parties, the second was the awakening of the ethnic split. Since the Likud came to power, the leading theme of the discourse was the territorial issue and the dispute over the location of the boundaries of the land. The political terminology shifted from "the State of Israel" to "the Land of Israel" and from "Israelis" to "Jewish Nation." Being committed to the Jewish nation and negating Jewish statehood, Agudat Israel found itself sharing with the dominant discourse the same legitimate terms. At the same time, this very change led to schism within the National Religious Party. The more the party entered the general discourse and identified itself with the right-wing national ideas, the more it faced internal conflict. For some, it was a reason to leave the party and to establish a new moderate one (the Matzad Party, 1984), others turned their votes to nonreligious left-wing parties. Yet, for those in the more radical circles among the Gush Emunim (Bloc of Faithful) movement, which has demanded active Jewish settlement in the territories, the party was too moderate; they left and supported the Tehiya or Moledet Parties (Goldberg 1981; Sandler 1981). In 1981 the NRP lost half of the seats it held until 1977, and it has never recovered its power (table 3.1). The awakening of the ethnic tensions led to a split within the non-Zionist and the Zionist religious parties. Tami, which was founded in 1981, was a split of the NRP, and Shas 1984 split off from Agudat Yisrael. The first tried to address religious and non-religious Sephardi constituency and failed to gain legitimacy, while Shas remained mainly within the religious circles and succeeded in gaining power and institutionalizing itself (see the following discussions on ethnic parties).

II. Jewish Ethnic Parties

Ethnic parties have been part of the Israeli political landscape since its beginning, yet ethnic identity has not succeeded in gaining social legitimacy. On the structural organizational level, the ethnic base has been approved of and utilized as a means for participation in the Israeli political system. In the early years of the State of Israel, with the entry of mass immigration from Asian and African countries into the electorate, the will of the dominant groups to stay in power resulted in the formation of satellite parties, that is, lists that appeared independently during elections but openly announced their ties to a "mother" party. Later on, the dominant parties preferred covert support of the ethnically based lists.

The broad-based parties supported the significance of ethnic origin in politics by employing co-optation tactics with the leaders of these lists and allocating political positions and jobs according to country of origin (Herzog 1984, 1986). They were the first to open their doors to new immigrants of any ethnic origin. The overall trend was a reduction in the disparity of and a continuous growth in ethnic representation, politics becoming an open, secure channel of social mobility for people of Asian or African origin (Smooha 1978; Herzog, Shamir, and Zuckerman 1989; Grinberg 1989). With the exacerbation of ethnic tensions in Israel in the 1970s and 1980s, the parties increased their efforts to include representatives of the Sephardi communities in order to neutralize the tensions as well as the potential for crystallization of a unique ethnic political identity. This politics of inclusion operated simultaneously with the politics of exclusion. On the ideological level, ethnic identity as a basis for political action was denounced and its legitimacy denied. Within the parties, although elected on an "ethnic" ticket, the deputies were expected to represent the "general interest" and not a "narrow" one, that is, not an ethnic one, defined as the "minority" interests. Therefore, Israeli politics have always been characterized by deputies who entered politics by drawing on their parochial affiliations as an expression of the democratic idea of minority representation but who almost never fought openly for their group interests.

Similarly, independent political organizations were delegitimized. Ethnicity-based parties were accused of separatism, a betrayal of the ideal, or social goal, of the "melting pot" or "integration of the exiles." Their activists were presented as peripheral by identifying them with elements that were hostile to the state, as ambitious careerists and power-hungry politicians, or simply as incapable. As a result of this stigmatization ethnic identity was never presented as an end in itself. Even when used as a focus of organization, it was presented as temporary and conditional. These were mainly "election-eve" organizations, based on personal ties and loyalties. Such weak organizational patterns reduced their electoral chances (see table 3.2). Ethnicity-based parties looked for activists of origins different from their own to gain legitimacy and deny accusations of separatism. The ethnic parties that participated in 1992 election were shaped along the same lines whether their ascriptive base was Sephardi or Russian. Thus Hatikva ("the Hope" list), initiated by Charli Bitton, veteran representative of the Israeli Black Panthers who had left the Communist Party, established the list with Leah Shakdiel. Shakdiel, of Ashkenazi origin, known as a feminist with dovish political views, explained her joining the list as follows: "I checked and found that he [Bitton] struggles for the lower class and [poor] neighborhoods [note, there is no mentioning of ethnic origin]. The change of the [party] name from The Panthers to The Hope is essentially a conceptual change. It speaks about wide and combined social struggle" (*Ma'ariv* 5 June, 1992). By such statements she tried to avoid the ethnic meaning that could be ascribed to the list. But they could not avoid the stigmatization. In a campaign tour Biton was denounced by the audience as "Frenck [means Oriental], terrorist, Arab, PLO, communist, traitor" (*Davar* 5 June, 1992), and the two were described in the media as a "strange, odd couple."

The Russian new immigrant parties of 1992 acted similarly. Their political activists did their best, before the elections, to cooperate with each other, but mainly to unite with veteran political organizations. They needed the veteran organizations for financial and administrative aid but, in particular, they needed them for legitimacy. It would appear that the failure of the absorption process should serve as a legitimate claim in Israeli political culture, yet the dominance of the melting pot and one-nation ideology seems to be stronger. Last-moment efforts to unite all the competing bodies of new immigrants were made by Natan Sharanski, a well-known Prisoner of Zion, who objected ethnic parities in general and a Russian in particular (*Ha'aretz* 24 September, 1990). He tried to compile a common list of new immigrants and veteran Israelis (*Ha'aretz* 20 May, 1992). The unification failed, and the three parties that participated in the elections were defined by the media as Russian or new immigrants parties. The Yad b'yad (Hand-in-Hand) list of pensioners and new immigrants was headed by Aba Gephen, who ran in the 1988 election at the head of the pensioners list. The new immigrants had two representatives on the list; one of the 1970 wave of immigration and the second of the new arrivals. The second list, Da (which has a double meaning: in Hebrew, it means "to know"; in Russian, "yes"), launched an independent list after a long search for veteran partners. One of the options considered was to go with Modai, finance minister in the Likud government, who headed the New Liberal Party. The party's full name, "Da, the National Movement for Democracy and Immigration," reflected the wish of the party to be identified with general problems of Israeli society and not only with the so-called narrow interests of the immigrants. This was also true of the name chosen by the third party of the Russian new immigrants: Tali (Tenua l'hitchadshut Yisrael), The Movement for Israel Renewal. As negation of ethnicity by the majority served as a mechanism to exclude ethnic identity holders from the Israeli political scene, many political activists of

Table 3.2. Ethnic Parties

1	2	3	4	5	6	7	8	9	10	11	12	13
1949	1951	1955	1959	1961	1965	1969	1973	1977	1981	1984	1988	1992
Yemenite Association	Yemenite Association	Yemenite Association	Yemenite Faction	Yemenite Immigrants List	Young Israel	Young Israel	Yemenite List	House of Israel	The Unity Party	Shas	Shas	Shas
1	1.2	0.3	0.2	0	0.2	0.1	0.2	0.5	0.07	3.1	4.7	4.9
National Union of Sephardis	Sephardis and Orientals	Sephardis and Orientals	National Sephardic Party	For Justice & Fraternity	Fraternity List		Black Panthers	Coalition of Workers & Neighborhoods	Tami	Tami		Hope
2.5	1.8	0.8	0.3	0.3	0.9		0.9	0.1	2.3	1.5		0.08
	Israeli Faithful	Sons of Yemen	Union of North-African Immigrants				Blue-White Panthers	Zionist Panthers	One Israel	Young & Immigrants		Democracy & Immigration
	0.6	0.3	0.8				0.4	0.1	0.19	0.3		0.4
		Original Religious List	Union of Independ. N. African Immigrants				Movement for Social Equality		Tent Movement	Indians		Pensioners & Immigrants
		0.3	0.1				0.7		0.03	0.3		0.3
National Union of Sephardis & Orientals							Peoples Movement		Your People	Your People		Movement for Renewal
0.2							0.5		0.02	0		0.05

Note: Percentage of votes reported below each party.

Asian or African origin were led to ignore, deny, or even be ashamed of their ethnicity. The power of these excluding practices has been expressed through the political behavior of the Sephardi Jews. They have strong aspirations for integration according to accepted rules, that is, the rules of the dominant group. These aspirations prevented crystallization of political ethnicity. Though pushed to the periphery as ethnic groups, they were offered inclusion on the basis of a wider, legitimate identity, that is, as part of the Jewish collectivity. Thus, the failure of these ethnic parties as well as their preference for broad-base parties (mainly the Likud) are the consequences of the ideological exclusion of ethnic identity in the face of the available and meaningful alternative of Jewish identity as grounds for inclusion.

The only ethnically based parties that partially overcame such stigmatization were Tami (Tradition of Israel Movement, 1981, 1984) and the ultra-orthodox party Shas (Sephardi Torah Guardians, 1984, 1988, 1992), both Sephardic religious parties. As explained earlier, religion has been a legitimate basis for organization since the early days of the political establishment of the Jewish community. Likewise, the separation between Sephardis and Ashkenazis has been institutionalized and legitimized within the religious tradition. Tami and Shas exploited the legitimacy of the religious parties and the legitimate ethnic divisions within the religious sector; they thereby bypassed the common stigmatization of ethnic parties. Both parties, by emphasizing their religious basis, deemphasized their social image as representing general ethnic protest. They thus neutralized the stigmatizing, exclusionary mechanism of ethnicity in Israeli politics and gained political power through the inclusionary mechanism of Jewish identity and traditional culture anchored in religion (Herzog 1990). Tami lost its power as it tried to expand its constituency to nonreligious circles where political ethnicity was denied. Unlike Tami, Shas campaigned in religious circles, and its claims were formulated in ethnic religious terms. Its success in 1984 and further on came from its ability to gain support of religious non-Orthodox Jews living in development towns and poor neighborhoods. The 1992 elections could have served as a good stimulus for the party to expand its constituency, but Shas did not succeed in mobilizing broader feelings of ethnic deprivation. Two events could have flared the ethnic flames: the first was the failure of David Levy's camp in the Likud's internal elections, which was followed by accusations of ethnic discrimination; the second was the declaration by the leading Ashkenazi rabbi, Shach, that the Sephardi leaders were not ready for leadership. Furthermore, the Labor claim for a policy preferring development towns to settlements in the Occupied Territories was a clear appeal to the Asian-Africans who are the major inhabitants of those towns. The election results, wherein Shas did not broaden its political constituency, show that the fear of the "ethnic demon" threatening the solidarity of Israeli society still prevailed in 1992 Israeli society. Shas has remained a legitimate phenomenon as a religious party. The ethnic split within the ultraorthodox is perceived by the secular public as entirely internal conflict. Labor and Meretz, the coalition partners, regard it as mainly religious party. The elections in 1992 indicated that within the ultraorthodox camp, the ethnic split has been sharpened and institutionalized. Shas, a party that split from the Ashkenazi ultraorthodox party, exhibited independent behavior in 1992 (see also Willis 1995). The fact that it joined the coalition with Labor, leaving behind the other ultraorthodox party and the National Religious Party, offers another proof of this trend. The coalition agreement, which gave Shas the Interior Ministry and the deputy posts in Education and Religion, goes along with the tradition of inclusion of religious parties in Israeli political system. Yet this agreement strengthened Shas and at the same time deepened the ethnic split within the ultraorthodox circles.

III. Arab Parties

The category "Arab Parties" reflects the political difficulties the parties face. "Arabs" is the term used by the dominant groups to describe their attitude toward and interaction with the non-Jewish population. At the same time, up to the past few years Palestinian identity (the term the Arabs prefer to use) has been denied and delegitimized. Consequently, in their search for legitimacy, the parties use the "Arab" identity category in the names they chose for their formal political representation. The basic contradiction between structural differentiation and symbolic delegitimation that shaped the political organization of Jewish ethnic groups holds true for Israeli Arabs. Yet, while the Jewish groups were offered a meaningful inclusionary social definition as part of the Jewish community, this was not the case with the Israeli Arabs; hence, they have developed different political behavior and political organizations. With the establishment of the State of Israel, the Arabs who remained within the borders of the state, becoming a numerical minority, were granted citizenship and were legally included in the new Israeli social collectivity. However, from the beginning, they were actually regarded as a separate entity. Invidious distinctions have marked Arab-Jewish relations in all their manifestations. Israeli Arabs have become a subordinate group, the structural separation based on their social identity serving as a particularly powerful device for control and exclusion. The Israeli regime as a whole has been designed to fragment the Arab minority, to isolate it from the Jewish majority, to make Arabs dependent on Jews, or to co-opt potential leaders of the Arab community (Smooha 1978; Lustick 1980; Zemach 1980). Between 1948 and 1966, Israeli Arabs lived under a military administration that emphasized their separation and exclusion. On the ideological level, Arab national identity was denied. Although the dominant discourse presented Israel as a nation state, it presented Israeli Arabs as part of the Arab nations, as enemies; national expression has been repressed by defining it as hostile and dangerous. While separation and exclusion characterized most spheres of interaction between the Arab minority and the Jewish majority, interaction in the political sphere differed in some respects. The right to vote and to organize politically was granted to the Arabs with the establishment of the state. As in the case of Jewish immigrants, the political parties, looking for ways to widen their constituencies, addressed themselves to the new Arab citizens. Their percentage in the population, which theoretically could grant them fourteen seats in the Knesset, made them a sought after group, especially at election time. Nonetheless, for years the government refused to refer to the Arab minority as a unique social unit. Alternative phrases have been used such as "The Minorities" (plural), Christians, Muslims, Druse, Arab population, or "the non-Jewish population." All these social categories in practice deny Israeli Arabs, or Palestinians, collective identity. This denial is opposed to the fact that in politics per se, Arabs have always been addressed and recruited on the basis of their group affiliation, their collective identity being presumed by the broad-based parties. Only the left-wing Zionist party Mapam and the Communist Party encouraged Arabs to join them as individual citizens. Similarly, as with the Jewish ethnic groups in the first two decades of the state, the Zionist parties preferred to establish satellite Arab parties (Landau 1969, Al-Haj in this volume). From the first Knesset elections (1949) up to and including the tenth Knesset elections (1981), a total of thirty-seven Arab lists (each list counted separately per election) appeared (see table 3.3). This number does not include the Communist Party and parties established as of 1984 (The Progressive List for Peace and the Arab Democratic Party), which are of a different kind and will be discussed separately. Historically, by establishing dependent and weak political configurations, the broad-based parties helped the Arabs to organize for the campaigns while keeping the dividing line between Jews and Arabs lucid. Such a policy supported both the existence of Arab lists and their structural separation. They thus controlled the Arabs parties. These parties, like many of the Jewish ethnic parties, were very often "election-eve" entities, operating sporadically for a few months at most just before the elections. They had no regular party machinery; Arabic-language publications appeared, ad hoc, just before the elections. These election-eve parties had no consistent policy regarding the Arab minority. They served as vote-catching devices and as the means of advancement for some Arab political leaders, mainly the traditional hamula chiefs. Sometimes they served as a political means for negotiations with the ruling party on some material benefits. Arab political activists, aware that the Arab vote was sought after, tried to exploit the situation to their advantage. As one of the activists quoted by

Landau said, "Would that every year were election year" (Landau 1969, 152). Another reason these lists were encouraged and supported by the broad-based parties was, if not to gain votes, at least to fragment the Arab vote and to reduce the rival parties' power (Lustick 1980; Tsimhoni 1989). Until the 1980s, several efforts by Arab activists to establish independent Arab parties ended in the co-optation of their leaders into the Arab satellite parties, mainly those of the Labor party. The meager and declining successes due to their clumsy organization and the absence of any legitimation, as well as the general decline of the Labor Party, eliminated the satellite Arab parties; instead, the Labor Party (Mapai) provided places for Arab candidates, as the "token other," on the party list. In such cases, the Arabs participated in the elections on their collective "ticket" but were expected to represent the "general interest" rather than their group's particular interests.

In addition to parties, identity-based political organizations were affirmed and even encouraged as long as they were under the control of the dominant groups. Thus, special departments for Arab affairs in the major parties and in the Histadrut (the General Labor Federation) were established. The Committee of Chairmen of Local Arab Councils was welcomed by governmental institutions as long as it limited itself to local activity and served mainly as a mediator between the authorities and the Arab population. Such a policy reflected and reproduced the perception that the Arabs, as a separate social entity, were to be kept dependent, with limited options for developing independent political collective identity. Consequently, legitimate civic demands raised by Israeli Arabs were delegitimized by the authorities and the media by labelling them "nationalistic," and by identifying the Arabs of Israel with Arabs of the neighboring Arab countries, the enemy, they were treated as potentially disloyal (Landau 1989, 75).

In extreme cases, organizations such as el-Ard (established in 1965, its expressed aim was the struggle for Palestinian Arab nationalism) were banned. Banning has been the restraining mechanism of identity-based political organizations among the Israeli Arabs for many years. For example, the leaders of the Communist Party were always conscious that their party could be banned if it went too far with proposing unambiguously anti-Israel policies (Rekhess 1988, 135). Thus, the combined structuring of all spheres of social life according to national affinity, on the one hand, and the delegitimation of Arab political collective identity, on the other, operated as an exclusionary mechanism in Israeli politics. Since 1948 this exclusive policy has channelled the Arabs' political activity either to pragmatic votes for the Zionists parties or toward the critical overtly nonnationalist, non-Zionist party—the Communists. The relative popularity of the Communist Party in the Arab communities (averaging about one-third of the Arab votes in each elections) has nothing to do with its declared ideology. Communist doctrine

Table 3.3. Arab and Communist Parties

1	2	3	4	5	6	7	8	9	10	11	12	13
1949	1951	1955	1959	1961	1965	1969	1973	1977	1981	1984	1988	1992
Communist for Democracy & Peace **3.5**	Israeli Communist Party **4**	Israeli Communist Party **3.5**	Israeli Communist Party **2.8**	Israeli Communist Party **4.2**	New Communist **2.3**	New Communist (RAKAH) **2.8**	New Communist (RAKAH) **3.4**	Communists & Black Panthers (HADASH) **4.6**	Communists & Black Panthers (HADASH) **3.4**	Communists & Black Panthers (HADASH) **3.4**	Communists & Black Panthers (HADASH) **3.7**	Communists Party (HADASH) **2.4**
Nazarath Arabs [Mapai] 1.7	Arab Democrats [Mapai] 2.4	Arab Democrats [Mapai] 1.8	Cooperation & Fraternity [Mapai] 1.1	Cooperation & Fraternity [Mapai] 1.9	Communist List 1.1	Israeli Communist Party (MAKI) 1.1	Socialist Revolution 0.1	United Arab List [Alignment] 1.4	United Arab List [Alignment] 0.6	Progressive List for Peace 1.8	Progressive List for Peace 1.5	Progressive List for Peace 0.9
Arab Workers [Mapai] 0.7	Agriculture & Development [Mapai] 1.1	Agriculture & Development [Mapai] 1.1	Agriculture & Development [Mapai] 1.1	Democracy Friends 0	Cooperation & Fraternity [Mapai] 1.4	Cooperation & Fraternity [Labor] 1.4	Cooperation & Fraternity [Alignment] 0.6	Arab Reform 0.3	Arab Fraternity 0.4	Peace & Progress 0.1	Arab Democratic Party 1.2	Arab Democratic Party 1.6
Popular Arab Block [Mapam] 0.6	Progress & Work [Mapai] 1.2	Progress & Work [Mapai] 1.5	Progress & Work 0.5	Progress & Work [Mafdal] 0.4	Peace List [Rafi] 0.5	Peace List [Rafi] 0.4	Arabs & Bedouins [Alignment] 1	Coexistence In Justice 0.1	Arab Citizens 0.1			
		Arab List – The Center [General Zionists] 0.5	Progress & Development [Mapai] 1.3	Progress & Development [Mapai] 1.6	Progress & Development [Mapai] 1.9	Progress & Development [Labor] 2.1	Progress & Development [Alignment] 1.5		Unity 0.1			
			Independent Arabs 0.4				Israeli Arabs 0.2		Initiation 0			
			Arab Labor Party [Ahdut Haavoda] 0.3									

Note: Percentage of votes reported below each party. Bold indicates links to Israeli Communist Party. Brackets indicate major party to which Arab list was connected.

has always been foreign to the Arabs' traditional culture, and the party's declared preference for class identification over national identification has not coincided with the Arabs' aspirations. Nevertheless, it has presented a reasonable solution to the impossible situation the Arabs faced in the Israeli political system. The Communist Party, although a marginal party, has been a legitimate, legal part of the Israeli political system since the prestate period. Although the Communist Party struggled to change the Zionist nature of Israel, it recognized Israel's legitimacy as an established state. Moreover, the fact that the party included both Jews and Arabs contributed to its legitimacy. It therefore enabled the Israeli Arabs to express protest without being totally excluded. The Communists perceived the Arabs in Israel as Israelis deserving equal rights, at the same time claiming self-determination for the Palestinians outside Israel.

Although the party has undergone several changes and splits, it has basically kept to the above binational pattern in order to obtain some legitimacy within the Israeli system. The Communist leaders have also done their utmost to preserve the image of a Jewish-Arab party. Until recently, the Communist Party (Hadash, its current name) has not enjoyed full Palestinian identity, despite deep involvement with and sympathies toward the emerging Arab national identity (Rekhess 1988, 128–29; Rubenstein 1985). As the 1992 elections were held against the background of the collapsing Communist regimes in East Europe and the strengthening of Palestinian identity of Israeli Arabs, the party faced ideological and financial difficulties. Yet suggestions to change Hadash to a solely Arab party failed, and the party kept its Jewish-Arab character (for more details see Al-Haj in this volume). It also kept its electoral power and three of its delegates (two Arab men and one Jewish woman) entered the thirteenth Knesset (see table 3.2). Binational affiliation as a source of legitimation also characterizes the non-Communist Progressive List for Peace, established in 1984, in collaboration with the Jewish faction the "Alternative." Although originally the party was envisaged as wholly Arab party, Muhammed Miari, the party's leader, recognized that "An exclusive Arab list would face two basic problems. First, there is no guarantee that the Israeli authorities would allow the foundation of a solely Arab movement... Secondly, one should consider the potential weight and implication of political work with regard to public opinion both in Israel and internationally" (Rouhana 1986, 130). The party won one seat in the twelfth Knesset (1988). Internal conflict between the Jewish and the Arab partners brought the party to the 1992 elections campaign as a solely Arab party. Its failure to pass the thresholds of participation should be explained on the background of power relations within the Arab community. Yet, one cannot ignore the fact that the party no longer enjoyed the quasi-legitimacy granted to co-Jewish-Arab lists, as reflected in the stridently anti-Zionist image the party had in the eyes of the

Jewish establishment (*Ha'aretz* 15 May, 1992). The exclusionary mechanism of Arab identity, then, continues to hold, even though the normative boundaries of Israeli politics have been widened. This was expressed by Miari, who was also a member of the outlawed el-Ard: "Then [in 1965] whoever spoke about the Palestinian issue was considered as coming from another planet. Now, to speak about this issue is a negotiable bill" (*Ha'aretz* 3 June, 1984). Nevertheless, subordinate groups tend to accept the ideology of the dominant group or at least do not deviate too far from it. For example, the Arab Democratic Party (ADP), founded and led by Abdel Wahab Darawsheh, indicates the growing tendency of Israeli Arabs to organize independently along affiliation lines within the limits of this sensitivity of the dominant group. The party name encapsulates this phenomenon. Although based on deep feelings of Palestinian identity, the party used the preferred terminology— "Arab"—of the dominant discourse. The party's ability to enter the Israeli political system as the first wholly independent Arab party itself exemplifies the changing of the social definition of the legitimate normative political border. Darawsheh, a former Labor MK who had resigned in protest against the then Defense Minister Yitzhak Rabin's policies of repression against the intifada, had reentered the twelfth Knesset (1988) in his own right. Such a political acts rested upon two basic factors: first, criticizing government policy toward the intifada has become part of the legitimate discourse among Zionist parties; second, the increase in self-confidence and pride of the Israeli Arabs, and the emergence of a Palestinian identity, together with the embracing of Israeli norms in Israeli-Arabs political behavior (Lustick 1990). Smooha describes this trend as a combination of Israelization and politicization (Smooha 1989; for other opinions see Rekhess 1983 and Ginat 1986). Darawshi's reputation as a moderate made him acceptable in the eyes of both Arabs and Jews, although not without reservation on the part of the latter. His independence, his personal relationships with the liberal Jewish establishment, and his declaration before 1992 elections that "we see ourselves as integral part of the political system . . . we are flexible and realistic" (*Ha'aretz* 15 May, 1992) helped him to consolidate his political power and to gain two seats in the thirteenth Knesset.

IV. Women's Parties

The experience of women in gender-based parties is not as extensive as that of the Jewish ethnic groups or the Israeli Arabs; nevertheless, they have faced similar obstacles. Four women's political parties took part in three Israeli elections, including the 1992 election, and they have not been very successful (see table 3.4). In Israel, as in many other societies, politics is considered a male domain. The Israeli case reflects many aspects of the problems of women in politics all over the world; paradoxically, it could have been different. The idea of gender equality has roots in the socialist orientation of the nation's builders. Women took an active part in the War of Independence and are conscripted into the army. Israel's multiparty system, with its proportional representation and the list system, could have paved the way for women's parties as it did for other interests represented in the Israeli parliament. Yet women are doing poorly in the political competition. Only 8 percent of current Knesset members are women, none of whom belong to the Women's Party, which was far back of the 1.5 percent threshold requested (see table 3.4). Golda Meir, the former prime minister, is an exception rather than the rule. Israeli women constitute half of the voting population, but politically they are regarded as a distinct interest group. As with the ethnic groups in the past and the Arab minority until 1992, there is a special department within the political organizations assigned to deal with their affairs. The two major parties, Labor and the right-wing Herut (now the Likud), have women's divisions. The National Religious Party does not have such a division, but this function is served by the women's organization Emuna (Azmon 1990). Organizationally, women are expected to join the women's division, to accept traditional roles, that is, to be members of committees dealing with education, welfare, senior citizens' problems, and other issues considered as belonging to women's spheres. Although they are channelled to women's activities in special frameworks on the organizational level, on the symbolic ideological level they are not "allowed" to make claims for women's interests. So-called women's interests are placed low on the public agenda, which sees the public sphere, defined mainly by issues of security and the economy, as the most significant. The private sphere, that is, domestic issues, child care and health, and their extension in education and welfare, are of little importance in the public agenda. As women in politics concentrate on these spheres of activity, they are accused of "not being able to deal with the important issues," or of "diverting public attention from the *real problems of society or* the party."

Theoretically, then, the role of women's divisions in the Israeli parties is to represent the interest of women within the parties; in practice, this is very seldom so. Women leaders are selected by the men who dominate the party apparatus, and they are usually coopted. They are expected to prefer the general interest of the party over their particularistic interests as women, and very often they do prefer to take such a stand. If they do not, they take the risk of being stigmatized as narrow-minded and selfish. Rachel Kagan, a member of the first Knesset (1949–52), elected by an independent women's list, and initiator of the Women's Equal Rights Law (1951), has described the dubious cooperation she received from other women in the Knesset, whose party or factional loyalty always took preference over their feminism. She was even told by one of them: "Stop talking about women all the time, you are becoming a joke" (Freedman 1990, 98). Women in politics, like members of other groups based on social identity, find themselves in an ongoing dilemma regarding their political identity. If they choose to be ordinary members of a party and political activists in general terms rather than as women, they find themselves categorized by the party members as "women" and are channelled into traditional women's roles. If they choose to organize within the parties on the basis of gender, they and the issues they represent are marginalized—if not completely delegitimated. Furthermore, as their divisions within the parties are not organizationally autonomous, they are dependent on party funds and controlled by the male party machine.

As the history of women's parties shows, women face the most aggressive opposition when they try to organize independent political organizations that run for election. The first women's party that participated in 1949 elections, and won one seat was Women's International Zionist Organization (WIZO), the successor of the women's party of the prestate period (Herzog 1992). Being associated with women's voluntary organization, it benefitted from the organization's experience and resources. Nevertheless, its activities were considered by the dominant culture as feminine, marginal, and irrelevant to politics. Disappointment in the lack of female representation on their party's list in the first elections after the establishment of the state (1949) led women of the religious party, Hamizrachi Workers, to run in a separate women's list, female representation being their main purpose. They failed to mobilize gender affiliation although in Judaism the separation of women and men is institutionalized in public life, and the party did not pass the 1 percent threshold in the 1949 elections (table 3.3). The unity of the religious circles was perceived as more important than women's interests. The third attempt in Israel to establish a women's party was made in 1977, when a group of feminists, members of the Civil Rights Party, left the party and established an independent list (Sharfman 1988; Freedman 1990). The "curious and friendly" (Sharfman 1988, 97) modest media coverage the party received emphasized its feminist messages. However, "the fear and hostility that feminism aroused in widening circles [was] fed by an unflagging [predominantly] negative press." Even Heda Boshes, a well-known female journalist wrote: "Feminism sometimes borders on the absurd. Feminists think that in order to demonstrate their liberation and their rights, they have to be ugly, hairy . . . perhaps they would do away with bathing" (Freedman 1990, 50). Such a statement reflects attitudes of politicians and the media and labels the feminists as an "extremist" movement. After a pro-abortion demonstration (June 1976), the press described the action the women took then as "unseemly," "scandalous," "shameless," and "hysterical" (Freedman 1990, 94–95). Under the headline "The Battle Front Has Shifted to the Home Front," Ruth Shreiber

Table 3.4. Women's Parties

1	2	3	4	5	6	7	8	9	10	11	12	13
1949	1951	1955	1959	1961	1965	1969	1973	1977	1981	1984	1988	1992
WIZO								Women's Party				Women's Party
1.2								0.3				0.1
Religious Worker Woman												
0.6												

Note: Percentage of votes reported below each party.

wrote that "Israeli men will soon have to defend a third front. It's not enough that they have to sit in the trenches and on the tanks at the borders defending our cities and towns from terrorists. In the future they will also have to defend themselves at home, against their wives" (50). These quotations not only delegitimate feminist ideas but also sustain the traditional division between gender roles, a division that is reinforced during war. War inevitably transforms the image of society into a very male-dominant image. The prolonged Arab-Israeli conflict glorifies war and heroes, emphasizes commitment to defense and to security. Women are expected to nurture, to care, and to support; family continuity is highlighted; women's concerns are played down. When women attempt to put their interests on the national agenda, they are told that the time is not yet ripe to deal with them. Moreover, women have difficulties in articulating their position on matters of general concern because these questions come to be defined as issues requiring an expertise that only men have acquired (Chazan 1984; Yuval-Davis 1980, 1987). The 1977 electoral failure of the women's party was partially a result of organizational disadvantages, including a lack of financial resources and internal conflicts; but above all it was due to the success of the politics of signification that delegitimize gender-based parties. Such politics of exclusion stifles the incentive to organize new women's parties, and it indeed took fifteen years for another party to enter into political arena. Apparently, the 1992 women's party had much more electoral potential than its predecessors. It was established in an atmosphere of emerging awareness among women of their social inequality and of increased political and social activity among women's organizations (Fogiel-Bijaoui 1992). Initially, debates in various political women's forums over the ways to enhance women's representation were pessimistic. The basic social construction of the priority of issues, and the social definition of women's issues as secondary, predominated. Two satellite parties, left and right, were considered as options. The actual decision to establish the women's party was made late in the campaign (end of April) after Ruth Reznik, the veteran feminist activist, failed in the Civil Rights Party internal elections. "Shin" (Hebrew acronym for Shivion Yizug Nashim, "Equal Representation for Women"), a small organization mainly known in feminist circles, offered her the leadership of the party. The party was delegitimated by the major parties in two ways. The first way—similar to that used with other minority groups—was to deny the relevance of identity to politics. As one of the more positive articles on the party concluded: "The only obstacle of the party on its way to its potential voters is Shulamit Aloni's arguments. 'I don't believe that this country needs a women's party . . . only those who discriminate psychologically between men and women think they need a women's party'" (*Hadashot* Supplement 23 April 1992).

The second way was to again put women in "their rightful place," the private sphere. Although the media represented the party in a sympathetic way, the political attitudes and acts of the activists were secondary to stereo-typical reports on family life and the conflict between home and politics. Especially important was the fact that most of the media coverage appeared in the local press and in the women's section of the daily press, not in the election section. Such reports transmitted latent messages about the status of party as a curiosity rather than as a serious political actor. By doing so, the media participated in marginalizing political women as well as women's interest and relevance to politics. The 1992 elections results support this analysis: while the women's party won 6,000 votes in 1977, the 1992 party won only 2,866.

V. Conclusion

The historical analysis of religious, Jewish ethnic, women's, and Israeli Arab parties indicate that their inclusion or exclusion from politics and their degree of electoral success depends to a large extent on their ability to use identity as a source of political power. This ability rests mainly on the meaning dominant groups ascribe to their social identity. While Jewish religion is perceived as bridging identity of the nation, the three ascriptive identities are defined as narrow, particularistic, and/or threatening the collectivity. The political paths the three groups (ethnic, Arabs, and women) choose vary, but they depend primarily on the options left open to them by the dominant groups. For the sake of the ideology of melting pot, Orientals largely renounce their social identity as a political claim. Their inclusion in politics is made possible on the basis of their national identity as Jews. The only niche gained for ethnic identity within the political system is through the religious parties, which are conceived as legitimate in the Israeli political culture. By basing its claim on the institutionalized separation between Ashkenazi and Sephardi religious traditions, Shas can evade both political stigmatization and denial of ethnic identity in developing its political power. As long as Shas remains an ultraorthodox phenomenon, it does not challenge the dominant ideology. The basic pattern of structural separation and symbolic delegitimation holds true for Israeli Arabs, but in more extreme ways. The major difference lies in the alternatives that each group is offered by the dominant group. The Jewish ethnic group is offered an emphasis on their identity as Jews, as a meaningful social identity in a Jewish state, as a means to integrate into the dominant parties. In the Arab case there was no meaningful alternative. In a Jewish state, where the term *Israeli* overlaps *Jewishness* to a large extent, Israeli civil religion reconciles traditional Jewish culture with contemporary political needs and values, but it excludes Arabs. Their traditions have never been deemed relevant in the formulation of

Israel's national symbols. The only alternative offered to the Arabs is to be Israelis, a social identity whose crystallization has posed a very problematic solution for them. Thus, unlike the Jewish ethnic groups, they foster a unique social identity by leaning toward the development of a national identity and the establishment of independent political parties. At the same time, they try to avoid being pushed completely out of the political game. As the 1992 elections results indicate, the fact that the national identity of Arabs is still perceived by Jews as a threat to the state affects Israeli Arab political choices. The Arab voters preferred to support the more moderate Arab party (Arab Democratic Party), or that with a binational image (Hadash), rather than the clearly nationalistic one (The Progressive List for Peace). Furthermore, half the voters voted for Zionist parties in 1992. Such votes reflect the acceptance of the hegemonic conception of Arab parties as behind bars of political legitimacy; as such, they cannot gain any political profits for their constituency. This explains their opportunist political vote, a vote for whoever gives or promises more, mainly on a personal level. The contradictory attitude of the dominant groups toward Arab parties is well illustrated in Rabin's coalition. On the structural level the coalition headed by the Labor relies on the Arab parties, which are included in the power system. At the same time, on the symbolic level, they are excluded, their absence in the coalition demoting their political weight and bargaining ability. Finally, women in political parties are not able to overcome social distinction by gender, which is taken for granted in most societies, including Israel. The fact that Israel is a society in prolonged conflict exacerbates women's situation. Thus, though gender identification structures the place of women, there is no legitimation of their interests as such in politics, and they are excluded from the "real" political game. Since gender differences cut along ethnic lines, the solution of national identification open to the Orientals does not solve the women's problem. As being part of the Jewish community does not exclude them to the extent that the Arabs are excluded, it undermines the reason for creating women's parties. In such circumstances, in comparison to other ascriptive groups, Israeli women have the least potential for entering politics and for achieving political power. The poor showing of the women's party in the 1992 elections simply continues this trend.

References

Al-Haj, Majid. 1995. "The Political Behavior of Arabs in Israel in the 1992 Elections: Integration versus Segrigation." In *The Elections in Israel— 1992*, ed. A. Arian and M. Shamir. Albany: SUNY Press.

Azmon, Yael. 1990. "Women & Politics: The Case of Israel." *Women & Politics* 10 no. 1: 43–57.

Chazan, Naomi. 1984. "Gender Equality? Not in a War Zone!" *Israeli Democracy* 3 no. 2: 4–7.

Deshen, Shlomo. 1978. "Israeli Judaism: Introduction to Major Patterns." *International Journal of Middle Eastern Studies* 9: 141–69.

Fogiel-Bijaoui, Sylvie. 1992. "Feminine Organizations in Israel—Current Situation." *International Problems—Society and Politics* 31, nos. 1–2: 65–76. In Hebrew.

Freedman, Marcia. 1990. *Exile in the Promised Land.* Ithaca: Firebrand Books.

Friedman, Menachem. 1991. *The Haredi Society: Sources, Trends and Processes.* Jerusalem: Jerusalem Institute for Israeli Studies. In Hebrew.

Ginat, Joseph. 1986. "The Arab Vote: Protest or Palestinisation?" In *The Elections in Israel—1984*, ed. A. Arian and M. Shamir, 151–67.

Goldberg, Giora. 1981. "The Israeli Religious Parties in Israel." In *Public Life in Israel and the Diaspora*, ed. S. N. Lehman-Wilzig and B. Susser, 138–57. Ramat Gan: Bar-Ilan University Press.

Greilsammer, Ilan. 1990. "The Religious Parties." In *Israel's Odd Couple: The 1984 Election and National Unity Government*, ed. D. Elazar, H. Penniman, and S. Sandler, 67–86. Detroit: Wayne State University Press.

Grinberg, L. Lev. 1989. *Public Activists in Local Government and the General Union—The Ethnic Dimension* (in Hebrew). Research no. 33. Jerusalem: Jerusalem Institute for Israel Studies.

Hall, Stuart. 1982. "The Rediscovery of 'Ideology': Return of the Repressed in Media Studies." In *Culture, Society and the Media*, M. Gurevitch, T. Bennett, J. Curran, and J. Woollacott (eds.), 56–90. London and New York: Methuen.

Herzog, Hanna. 1984. "Ethnicity as a Product of Political Negotiation." *Ethnic and Racial Studies* 7 no. 4: 520–35.

———. 1986. "Political Factionalism—The Case of Ethnic Lists in Israel." *The Western Political Quarterly* 38 no. 2: 286–303.

———. 1990. "Midway Between Political and Cultural Ethnicity." In *Israel's Odd Couple: The 1984 Election and National Unity Government*, ed. D. Elazar, H. Penniman, and S. Sandler, 87–118. Detroit: Wayne State University Press.

———. 1992. "The Fringes of the Margin: Women's Organizations in the Civic Sector of the Yishuv," in *Pioneers and Homemakers*, ed. Bernstein, D., 283–304. Albany: State University of New York Press.

Herzog, Hanna, M. Shamir, and A. Zuckerman. 1989. *The Israeli Politician: The Social and Political Bases of Israeli Labour and Herut Parties Activists* (in Hebrew). Research no. 34. Jerusalem: Jerusalem Institute for Israel Studies.

Landau, Jacob M. 1969. *The Arabs in Israel—A Political Study.* London: Oxford University Press.

Liebman, Charles S., and Eliezer Don-Yehiya. 1983. *Civil Religion in Israel.* Berkeley and Los Angeles; University of California Press.

———. 1984. *Religion and Politics in Israel.* Bloomington: Indiana University Press.

Lustick, Ian. 1980. *Arabs in the Jewish State: Israel's Control of a National Minority.* Austin: University of Texas Press.

———. 1990. "The Changing Political Role of Israeli Arabs." In *The Elections in Israel—1988,* ed. A. Arian and M. Shamir, 115–31. Boulder: Westview Press.

Rekhess, Eli. 1983. "Politicisation of Israel's Arabs." In *Every Sixth Israeli,* ed. A. Hareven, 135–42. Jerusalem: The Van Leer Foundation. In Hebrew.

———. 1988. "Jews and Arabs in the Israeli Communist Party." In *Ethnicity, Pluralism and the State in the Middle East,* ed. M. J. Esaman and I. Rabinovich, 121–39. Ithaca: Cornell University Press.

Rouhana, Nadin. 1986. "Collective Identity and Arab Voting Patterns." In *The Elections in Israel—1984,* ed. A. Arian and M. Shamir, 121–49. New Brunswick, NJ: Transaction.

Rubenstein, S. M. 1985. *The Communist Movement in Palestine 1919–1984.* Boulder: Westview Press.

Sandler, Sandler. 1981. "The National Religious Parties in Israel." In *Public Life in Israel and the Diaspora,* ed. S. N. Lehman-Wilzig and B. Susser, 158–170. Ramat Gan: Bar-Ilan University Press.

Schiff, Gary S. 1977. *Tradition and Politics: Religious Parties of Israel.* Detroit: Wayne State University Press.

Sharfman, Daphna. 1988. *Women and Politics* (in Hebrew). Haifa: Tamar Publishers.

Smooha, Sammy. 1978. *Pluralism and Conflict.* London: Routledge and Kegan Paul.

———. 1989. *Arabs and Jews in Israel: Conflicting and Shared Attitudes in a Divided Society.* Boulder: Westview Press.

Tsimhoni, Daphne. 1989. "The Political Configuration of the Christians in the State of Israel." *The New Orient* 32: 141–42. In Hebrew.

Willis, Aaron P. 1995. "The Sephardic Torah Guardians: Religious 'Movement' and Political Power." In *The Elections in Israel—1992,* ed. A. Arian and M. Shamir. Albany: SUNY Press.

Yuval-Davis, Nira. 1980. "The Bearers of the Collective: Women and Religious Legislation in Israel." *Feminist Review* 4: 15–27.

———. 1987. "Women/Nation/State: The Demographic Race and National Reproduction in Israel." *Radical America* 21, no. 6: 37–59.

Zemach, Mina. 1980. *The Attitudes of the Jewish Majority towards the Arab Minority.* Jerusalem: Van Leer Foundation. In Hebrew.

CHAPTER 4

Equal But Different?
The Gender Gap in Israel's 1992 Elections

YAEL YISHAI
University of Haifa

During the 1992 electoral campaign the Israeli public has witnessed a growing concern with the role of women in the choice of national leadership. As the proportion of women representatives in the Knesset has ranged between 6.6 percent and 10 percent, it has been widely proclaimed that women should figure more prominently on partisan lists and should be more amply represented on the decision making level. Little attention, though, has been paid to the question of their participation in the electoral process and their distinction from male participants. Does gender make a difference when it comes to political orientation, to political behavior, to casting the ballot, and eventually to choosing national leaders? Women, indeed, remain women, but does it matter? These are the main questions addressed by the paper.

In recent years the problem of gender differences in political participation has proved controversial. Within the literature three major perspectives can be identified:

1. Political inferiority, assuming that women are less active than men in political life (Lane 1961, 216; Lipset 1971, 182–84; Verba, Nie, and Kim 1980, 234; Christy 1987; Dalton 1988; Almond and Verba 1989, 325). Milbrath (1968, 116) noted that women's lower levels of participation in politics was one of the most thoroughly substantiated findings in social science.

I wish to thank Asher Arian and Michal Shamir for making the surveys on which this research is based available, and Ruth Amir, for providing me with the data.

2. Political equality, arguing that with the control of socioeconomic variables women are not different from men in regard to political participation, involvement, or interest (Bourque and Grossholtz 1984; Welsh 1980; Sapiro 1983, 59–60; Skard and Haavio-Mannila 1985; Norris 1991).

3. Political variation, suggesting that women have different patterns of behavior than men. They are more likely to participate in protest activity and to hold distinct views, either to the conservative or to the liberal poles of the political spectrum (Barnes, et al. 1979; Eduards 1981; Goot and Reid 1984; Randall 1982; Siim 1991).

The purpose of this paper is to examine these three conflicting perspectives in Israel in 1992. Whether women are inferior or equal to men in terms of their political behavior, whether they are different from them in terms of their political orientations, will be determined on the basis of survey data from the series of election studies covering national samples of Jewish respondents in 1992 and 1973.

I. Political Activity

The definition of political activity, in this context, follows the one offered by Milbrath and Goel (1977, 2) focusing not only on active roles that people pursue in order to influence political outcomes, but also on passive support activities.

Political Efficacy

Political efficacy is one of the most widely discussed concepts in political science. It constitutes the feeling that one is capable of influencing the public decision-making process (Milbrath and Goel 1977, 57). Studies of political culture have confirmed that in democratic societies, such as the United States and the United Kingdom, individual sense of civic competence is widely spread, including among women. Do Israeli women share with men the sense of political efficacy? The answer, based on the 1992 survey, tends to be positive. Respondents were asked to express their views as to the extent to which they and their friends could influence government policy.[1] The data reveal very small gender-based differences (table 4.1). The percentage of women reporting in 1992 on having a sense of political competence (38 percent) is higher than that reported by Italian and German women three decades earlier (27 percent and 19 percent, respectively) but lower than that reported by women in the United States and the United Kingdom (72 percent and 56 percent, respectively) in the same period (Almond and Verba 1989, 330).

Discussion of Political Affairs

Engaging in a political discussion is one factor in what has been termed a "communication" dimension. It is different from having subjective feelings about politics in the sense it is an active form of political participation. Living in a free society is a precondition for discussing politics. The frequency of talking politics with other people is significantly higher in the Western democracies subject to the study of political culture than it is in the other states.

Israeli respondents were asked whether, and to which extent, they discuss politics with their friends or family members. Their answers reveal similarity to the United States and the United Kingdom with 65.5 percent reporting on such discussion to some or a great extent (table 4.1). Women, however, tend to talk about politics significantly less than men. The widest difference is among those who do not discuss politics at all: only 10 percent of the men interviewed reported they never tend to talk politics with friends or relatives, whereas 15 percent of the women gave this response.

Voting

When women demanded suffrage in the institutions of self-government in prestate Israel, they were met with fierce opposition from religious groups and parties. Granting women the right to vote was considered a violation of tradition contrary to Jewish law. Despite the disapproval women won the vote as early as 1925 (Azaryahu 1980). Since then women have taken an active part in the electoral process. Elections to the Knesset have taken place thirteen times since the establishment of the state. Unfortunately, in Israel there is no public official record of voter participation by sex. As a result the only reliable evidence about the gender differences in voting comes from public opinion surveys regarding intention to vote.

Generally speaking, voter turnout in Israel is high. Although taking part in the elections is not mandatory and is not sanctioned by law, some 80 percent of the eligible population vote (Arian 1985, 133). The 1992 elections are no exception. Only 2.7 percent of the respondents stated they do not intend to cast a ballot; among these 3.3 percent were women, and only 2.1 percent men.

Partisan Affiliation

Party affiliation was evaluated on both objective and subjective bases. Formal membership in a party organization served as an objective criterion; identification with a party served as a subjective criterion. Nearly three decades of

Table 4.1. Indicators of Political Participation, by Sex, 1992

	Women (%)	Men (%)	Difference (%)	P
Sense of competence (to some and great extent)	38.0	39.5	1.5	.05
Discuss politics (to some and great extent)	61.6	70.0	8.4	.002
Party membership	6.3	11.9	5.6	.008
Voting intention	2.1	3.3	1.3	

research has confirmed the association of party identification with political participation (Milbrath and Goel 1977, 54). The impact of partisan attachment on political activity seems to be independent of the impact of socio-economic variables; at all levels of education or income strong partisans tend to participate more than weak or even moderate partisans (Verba, Nie, and Kim 1980, 308). Membership in a party is not an incentive for participation but participation itself. Only a minority among the population of Western democracies report formal membership in political parties. In Israel the situation is expected to be different owing to the high politicization of society. Yet membership is rather low—11.9 percent among men and only 6.3 percent among women. In all indicators of partisan activity women scored lower than men. The widest gap between men and women appeared in the lowest category of the scale. The proportion of women reporting they do not identify with, and are not active in, any political party was 65.7 percent, compared to 58.1 percent of men.

In conclusion, in each of the four indicators employed herein women have proved *inferior* to men in political activity, albeit not to the same extent. Women tend to be somewhat less efficacious than men; they tend to discuss politics in less frequency; they participate less in casting the vote; and finally, they tend to be less involved in partisan politics.

II. Opinions and Attitudes

Gender-based differences were traced not only in political participation but in its direction. Early feminists suggested that "a polity that included women as active participants would . . . abolish poverty, protect family life, and raise educational and cultural standards; an international society made up of nations in which women had the suffrage would not tolerate war" (Almond and Verba 1989, 325). The relevance of these suppositions to Israeli politics were tested in three aspects: (*a*) attitudes toward the Arab-Israeli conflict, (*b*) policy preferences as reflected in budgetary allocations, and (*c*) partisan identifications.

Views on Peace and Security

Israel is a nation at arms in which questions of war and peace have acquired prime importance. At the top of the political agenda is the question of territories captured in the Six Days war (1967) and these territories' inhabitants—the Arab Palestinians. The territorial issue has been a source of deep friction within the Israeli society. Political parties and public associations were pitted against each other, advocating opposite solutions to the problem of the lands and the people living on them: territorial concessions in return for peace versus annexation of the lands.

Respondents in the preelection survey were requested to state their opinions regarding four crucial aspects of the Arab-Israeli conflict. First, they were presented with a straightforward question: should Israel be required to choose between two alternatives—return most lands captured in 1967 or their annexation—what would be the respondent's individual preference? Second, should Israel accept the autonomy proposals? Third, should Israel be prepared to negotiate with the PLO? Fourth, should Israel agree to the establishment of a Palestinian state? The answers reveal that Israelis were reluctant to relinquish the territories. Less than half the respondents preferred the return of lands over annexation. Surprisingly, the proportion of doves was lower among women than among men, although the difference was marginal (38.2 percent and 40.8 percent, respectively). Furthermore, contrary to expectations, more women than men rejected the idea of granting the Palestinians in the territories an autonomy (table 4.2). When asked whether the question of the territories would affect their vote, respondents of both sexes revealed how important this issue was in their electoral considerations. An overwhelming majority (82.1 percent) of the respondents stated that the issue of lands would influence their vote to a large or to some extent. Here, too, there were no significant differences between women and men.

Policy Preferences

Whether women tend to have priorities different from those of men was examined in a series of questions relating to government expenditure. Respondents were requested to indicate whether they think the state should allocate more, less, or the same amount of money to nine different policy areas: education, the environment, religious institutions, health, security, immigration absorption, aid to the unemployed, settlement of the territories,

Table 4.2. Attitudes toward Security Policy by Sex

	Women (%)	Men (%)	Difference (%)
Willingness to return territories	38.2	40.8	−2.6
Approving autonomy (highly approve; approve)	53.5	63.5	−10.0[a]
Negotiating with the PLO	43.9	42.3	1.6
Palestinian state (certainly agree; agree)	29.1	29.0	−0.1
Influence of territorial issue on vote	82.9	81.1	1.8

[a] $p = .001$

and job production. Conventional political wisdom holds that women are expected to show greater concern for social welfare issues, supposedly due to women's maternal instincts, humanitarian compassion, extension of familial concern to public life, and narrow domestic adult role experience (Sapiro 1983). In terms of policy issues they are therefore expected to recommend increased spending on education, the ecology, health, and immigration absorption. By virtue of their alleged dovish nature they are expected to reject the possibility of increasing budgetary allocations to security; on account of their domestic roles they are expected to be less interested in "pure' economic affairs, such as creating jobs for the unemployed.

The data reveal that none of these propositions have been confirmed (table 4.3). From the range of issues presented to the respondents it appears that an overwhelming majority of the Israelis wanted to see more spending on the creation of jobs, on education, and on health. In this regard, women and men were very similar in their policy preferences. In just one policy issue was there a striking gender difference. Contrary to expectations, women wanted more money invested in security. This preference casts doubt on the widely hypothesized dovish inclination of women. The data present another interesting finding: women tended to be larger spenders than men. This is reflected in the total average of females wishing the government to spend more, compared to the men's average (57.2 percent and 54.8 percent, respectively) and in the fact that more women than men approved increased spending in almost every policy area (more men approved added spending for the environment). A possible explanation to this gap might be women's dissatisfaction with the general state of affairs, which requires more spending to amend. This hypothesis is supported by the fact that the proportion of women suggesting that the general situation in Israel is "not good" or "bad" (48 percent) was higher than that of men (42 percent).

Table 4.3. Policy Preferences (Wishing the Government to Spend More on . . .), by Sex

	Women (%)	Men (%)	Difference (%)
Education	86.1	84.2	+1.9
Environment	40.0	41.7	-1.7
Religious institutions	12.1	11.7	+0.4
Health	81.7	76.4	+5.3
Security	70.9	64.2	+6.7[a]
Immigrant absorption	51.5	48.5	+3.0
Welfare to the unemployed	57.1	52.6	+4.5
Settlement of the territories	24.0	22.2	+1.8
Job creation	91.5	91.8	+0.3
$x =$	57.2	54.8	+2.4

[a]$p = .03$

Voting Preferences

If women and men are not much different in their policy preferences, they might still be distinguished on the basis of their electoral choice. In the first phases of gender research it has been widely assumed that women lean more toward the right wing of the political spectrum and that their political orientations are more conservative than those of men (Duverger 1955; Inglehart 1977). Regardless of regime, continent or political history, women were found to penalize left-wing parties in terms of votes and membership. As Randall commented, "cumulatively the case for female political conservatism in the developed world is impressive" (1982, 51).[2]

The question of women's electoral choices in Israel was probed in a question relating to their intended voting behavior. Respondents were presented with the titles of the parties competing in the 1992 elections and were asked to indicate their choice if elections were held that day. The results do confirm a slight gender gap that is, however, not statistically significant. More men than women chose parties on the left (48.2 percent and 43.6 percent, respectively). Owing to their declared political affiliation religious parties were included in the right-wing bloc. However, European data point on clear female preferences for religious parties (Norris 1988, 222). Israeli women did not follow this pattern. When the choices for the three major religious parties (the National Religious Party, Agudat Israel, and Shas) were compared, no gender gap was evident. A minority (some 8 percent) of both sexes stated their intention to cast a ballot for a religious party.

In conclusion, the search for a gender gap in opinions and attitudes proved to be partly productive. When a gender gap is evident (and this is not often the case) women tend to be more hawkish than men. This finding is not new (Yishai 1985). Women's adherence to more militant positions has been attributed to their equivocation regarding self-identification. A more detailed examination of the possible reasons for the gender gap may cast further light on the reasons for this unusual phenomenon.

III. Some Explanations

Key differences in political participation have been analyzed according to four distinct models: development, generational, diffusion (Christy 1987, 2–6), and autonomy (Carroll 1988). The development model holds that economic development, that is, affluence, economic resources, and education (Di Palma 1970, 133–37; Rokkan 1970, 378; Milbrath and Goel 1977, 107; Baxter and Lansing 1983, 23–27), reduce sex differences. The generational model proposes that the gender differences diminish as younger, more egalitarian generations of women replace older, more traditional generations (Duverger 1955, 191). The autonomy model argues that the independence of individual women from individual men diminishes the gender gap. The diffusion model posits that sex differences narrow across time, as more egalitarian attitudes diffuse from higher status out to the rest of the population (Campbell et al. 1960).

The relevance of these explanations to the Israeli scene was examined in a series of variables pertinent to the four models offered by the literature.

The Development Model

The development model has been very popular among the proponents of political culture, suggesting a correlation between socioeconomic affluence and political participation. Studies in the United States confirmed that the gap between men and women is widest among lower-status people and narrowest among upper-status ones (Milbrath and Goel 1977, 117). It was thus assumed that economic and social development is slowly eroding the sex difference.

The relevance of the development model to Israel was examined by looking into the rates of participation and attitudes of women across the socioeconomic strata and comparing them to those of men. The variables under concern were education and ethnic origin. The educational picture among Jews in Israel is skewed: the proportion of people who have not acquired any education (up to four years of schooling) is far higher among women than among men (11 percent and 5.9 percent, respectively); the proportion is nearly equal in the higher echelons of the educational ladder (22.3 percent for women and 24.5 percent for men, respectively). Educational attainments are highly correlated with the fundamental stratifying factor in the Israeli society—ethnic origin. The forty-four years of independence have not eradicated the social differentiation between the past immigrants from Asia-Africa and their descendants (by now third-generation Israelis) and the Jews from European-American descent. The educational disparity is most conspicuous among second-generation Sephardi women (Bernstein 1991, 193), who lag far behind the attainments of their Ashkenazi female counterparts.

The findings relating to the impact of education present an equivocal picture. Education does make a difference in regard to competence, but in a direction opposite to the one expected. Women with a college education are more skeptical regarding their influence on government policy: 35.6 percent of them demonstrated a sense of competence in comparison with 41.2 of women with a secondary education. Discussing political affairs and party membership are hardly affected by years of schooling. The influence of education is highly visible, though, in regard to opinions. Women with a higher education are significantly more likely to vote Labor (59.4 percent) than their female counterparts with lower educational attainments (42.2 percent).

When the gender gap is considered, the results remain equivocal. Education has narrowed the gap regarding party membership (from 5.7 percent to 4.1 percent) but has actually increased the difference between women and men regarding political efficacy. Among the less-educated respondents the gap between men and women is only 0.2 percent, compared to 3.6 percent among those with a college degree. This stands in contrast to findings relating to other Western nations, indicating that the gender gap shrinks almost to zero among the highly educated (Inglehart 1990, 348). A marked widening of the gender gap is evident in regard to electoral choice, which is narrow among the less educated (5.5 percent), and increases with education (9.7 percent).

The data recording the influence of the ethnic factor on the gender gap are even more striking (table 4.4). Ethnic origin bears some effect on political competence and party membership. Ethnic origin does not diminish the gap between women as regards political discussions (the gap between Ashkenazi men and women is far higher than among Sephardi people). The gender gap, however, narrows dramatically when it comes to voting. The similarity between the sexes on the basis of ethnic origin is striking: electoral choice of both men and women in the Sephardi constituency is practically identical: Sephardi men, like Sephardi women, prefer right-wing parties over left-wing parties by a margin of 65.8 percent to 34.1 percent. The gender gap

Table 4.4. Political Activity and Orientations by Sex and Ethnic Identity

	Sephardim		Ashkenazim		Gender Gap	
	women (%)	men (%)	women (%)	men (%)	Sephardim (%)	Ashkenazim (%)
Sense of competence (to some and great extent)	39.3	42.2	37.4	38.9	2.9	1.5
Discuss politics (to some and great extent)	62.9	68.3	60.9	78.6	5.4	17.7
Party membership	7.3	13.4	7.0	8.8	4.6	1.8
Voting for left-wing parties (Labor, Meretz)	34.1	34.7	65.8	74.9	0.6	9.1

exists only among members of the Ashkenazi constituency, where women tend to support right-wing parties more frequently than do men. It may thus be concluded that socioeconomic variables increase the gender gap in regard to voting behavior more than other variables do.

The Generational Model

Age in itself may not be so important for crystallizing attitudes and behavioral patterns as are the life circumstances that are linked to it. Inglehart's famous thesis on postmaterialism postulates that younger age cohorts are more inclined to support postmaterialist values (including feminism) because their socialization was different from that of their parents. They grew up in peaceful and affluent societies where material considerations were set aside in favor of postindustrial orientations (Inglehart 1990). The Israeli society does not fit these circumstances. In the forty-odd years of its existence, the state has been engaged in six active wars; although it is a modern affluent society, many sectors of its population do not enjoy the standard of living prevailing in other Western countries. Notwithstanding these qualifications, the generational model is expected to explain some aspects of the gender gap. Younger women have been more exposed than their mothers to an egalitarian mood. They have grown up in a world where mass communication transcends political boundaries and have been susceptible to the feminist winds blowing from the Western world. The general change in women's role may have had an influence on their political behavior and attitudes.

The findings do provide some credence to the generational explanation. The cutting point for distinguishing between age groups was set at forty. The reason for this selection is linked to the history of the state. It has been assumed that those growing up in Israel (that is, were at the age of four when the state was established) were exposed to an egalitarian mood. The data reveal that women under the age of forty tend to discuss politics at a higher frequency than do older women (64.4 percent and 55.8 percent, respectively) and tend to have a higher sense of political efficacy than their more mature counterparts (41.6 percent and 32.0 percent, respectively). Interestingly, however, the frequency of joining parties is lower than among older women. This finding may be attributed to the fact that younger women are preoccupied with raising their children. From a different aspect this finding is compatible with Inglehart's proposition about the decline of institutionalized parties (Inglehart 1990, 363–68).

Younger women and men are thus more similar than mature age cohorts, save one aspect: voting preferences. Young men tend to prefer Labor in comparison to young women by a margin of 61.6 percent to 48.2 percent. Among the older respondents the gender gap amounts to only 2.6 percent.

The Autonomy Model

Recent studies have suggested that "independence" is a crucial variable explaining gender-based differences. The point of the autonomy argument is that women's political behavior and attitudes can best be understood if they are perceived as held by a disadvantaged or vulnerable minority, disaffected because of their status of dependency (Carroll 1988, 238). As a result of the dependency, they are expected to be less politically active and to demonstrate the characteristics identified in the early days of research on gender gap, that is, conservatism. Economic independence is associated with working outside the home. Psychological independence is associated with marital status. Those who live alone are supposedly more autonomous than are married women. Women most dependent are thus those who are married and are not employed outside their home; those least dependent are employed, single women.

During the last two decades the proportion of working women increased from 31.2 percent to 41.2 percent. Entrance into the labor force is not necessarily a sign of "independence," as women tend to concentrate in a small number of large, female-dominated occupations, especially in the service sector, where income is low. One major reason for this job segregation is the need to balance work and family obligations.

Israel is a family-oriented society in which family stability is the rule. Comparative family data reveal that marriage and divorce rates in the country are more similar to those in agrarian than in Western societies (Katz and Peres 1986). How has the combination of a growing female labor force and strong family orientations affected the political behavior of Israeli women?

Data show that independent women are indeed different from their housewife counterparts. As expected, twice as many working women as homemakers join parties (8.2 percent and 4.5 percent respectively); the former tend to the right in a far higher incidence (64.6 percent) than do nonworking women (46.0 percent). No differences were found regarding political efficacy. The fact that a woman is employed outside her home does not seem to bear impact on her ability to influence politics. Interestingly, a working woman tends to discuss politics less frequently than a homemaker does.

When marital status is controlled, the gap within the women's sample appears much less significant. In fact, the only difference on the basis of marital status is party membership. Single women tend to join parties at a higher frequency (7.7 percent) than do their married counterparts (4.6 percent). The examination of the gender gap on the basis of marital status yields familiar results: Getting married reduces the difference between men and women in regard to electoral choice, but it increases the gap in regard to other indicators of political activity. Married women do not match up to the rates of activity shown by married men. This is hardly surprising in view of the fact that, with the exception of party membership, married men are more active in politics than are their single counterparts!

In conclusion, whether or not a woman is "autonomous" and takes control of her own life does seem to influence the gender gap, although not always in the expected direction. Working outside home does partly narrow the variation between the sexes. The impact of work, however, is partly counterbalanced by the effect of marriage, which is found to widen the gender gap in all respects, except voting behavior.

The Diffusion Model

The diffusion model has two dimensions: sociological and temporal. From a sociological perspective, innovations spread from the center to the periphery, from the urban and higher status segments of society to the underprivileged, situated at the social margins (for application of this theory to women's political behavior see Hernes 1980; Poole and Zeigler 1981). There is another perspective, however, that does not rely on demographic factors to introduce change: it relies simply on time. It is not women's lesser resources and opportunities for political participation that produce a gender gap, but rather values and symbols, which are bound to change as society at large advances toward more openness and realization of injustices, as the political agenda incorporates the ideas of women's liberation (Rusciano 1992). According to the diffusion model, traditional attitudes are the primary constraint for women's equality. These attitudes, however, are not considered immutable. The test of the diffusion model lies in the comparison of women's behavior and attitudes across time. Admittedly, the diffusion model can interact with other models, since as time lapses women do gain more resources, the younger generation reaches political maturity, participation in the labor force tends to rise, and family patterns undergo change. Yet, a change across time that is not paralleled by changes explained by the other models may lend credence to the idea of diffusion.

In order to test the theory of diffusion a comparison was made between two points in time: 1973 and 1992. Data was drawn from tow preelection public opinion polls.³ During the period under discussion major changes in regard to women's status took place in terms of public awareness of women's problems and in terms of government output. How did these changes affect women's political activity?

The findings demonstrate a marked increase in the sense of political competence, which grew from 27 percent in 1973 to 38 percent in 1992 (table 4.5). The discussion of political matters is even more striking: the proportion of those reporting on being engaged in such an activity rose from 33.6 percent in 1973 to 61.6 percent in 1992. That women became more active in politics is evident also from the fact that the proportion of those stating they do not intend to vote decreased by more than half, from 7 percent in 1973 to 3.3 percent in 1992. Only in one indicator of political activity was there a decline during the period under discussion: the proportion of those women (and men) reporting party membership significantly decreased (from 14.9 percent to 6.3 percent among women and from 19.4 percent to 11.9 percent among men). These findings correspond with processes taking place in other Western democracies. In Denmark, for example, the figures of party membership are strikingly similar to those of Israel (Togeby 1992, 5).

In order to isolate the effect of time on women's political behavior, the parameters relating to men were also scrutinized. Evidently, men, too, have changed the practices of their political participation. But the effect of diffusion is far higher among women than among men. In all parameters, without single exception, the change was more noticeable among women than among men. Political efficacy, for instance, rose among men by 6.8 percent between 1973 and 1992; the equivalent figure for women is 11 percent. Discussing politics with friends has expanded for both men and women. For the former it grew by 22.4 percent; whereas for the latter, by 28 percent.

The picture looks different, however, when the gender gap is examined. Data indicate that this has narrowed only with respect to political efficacy. Women did gain more confidence in the political system as the polity has matured. A (marginal) decline is evident also in regard to their electoral participation. In other indicators, however, the gap has actually grown rather than diminished.

Findings relating to political attitudes provide stronger evidence for the impact of diffusion (table 4.5). The change of political circumstances between 1973 (before the October war) and 1992 made many questions asked in the early survey irrelevant to the later one. Comparison is thus limited only to the identical questions. These, however, cover both security and economic issues and enable the identification of temporal trends. Four conclusion may be drawn. First, the female electorate is becoming more aware of Israel's political problems. In 1973 just over half of the women stated that the territorial issue will affect their vote (to a large or some extent) against 61.2 percent of the men. In 1992 there was practically no gender gap in this regard. The proportion of women perceiving the issue of the captured lands as a major inducement for vote was slightly higher than that of men (82.9 percent and 81.1 percent respectively). These figures indicate that women are undergoing a process of politicization, that their interests are no longer confined to issues linked to domestic roles but to problems of broader political significance. Second, the data also reveal that both women and men show a lower inclination to return territories. With the passage of time, both men and women were less inclined to give up the occupied lands. In 1973 some two thirds showed moderate attitudes, compared to only one third twenty years later. Women were noticeably less inclined to return lands than men. Yet, in 1992 the gap between men and women narrowed, as women showed more compromising attitudes. Third, when respondents were asked to state their opinion regarding the extent of inequality in Israeli society, women appeared more sensitive to injustice and more aware of social inequalities. This was the case in 1973 and remained so in 1992, although to a lesser extent. In all three items the gender gap has narrowed. Fourth, when asked to report only on the influence of the economic issue on the vote, the gender gap widened. In 1973 some 40 percent of both sexes stated that economic matters would have a crucial effect on their vote. In 1992 both male and female respondents indicated increased awareness of economic issues. Men, however, felt more intensely about economic affairs, with 77.4 percent reporting on the importance of this issue in their electoral considerations as against 69.2 percent of women.

To sum up, the diffusion model, despite some limitations, does offer a partial explanation for the evolution of the gender gap.

IV. Conclusions

Is there a gender gap in contemporary Israeli politics? The answer is equivocal. Women are inferior to men when it comes to the conventional parameters of political participation (competence, discussing political affairs, partisanship, and voting turnout), but the gap is moderate, and it does not,

Table 4.5. Political Activities and Attitudes, by Sex and Year, 1973 and 1992

	Women		Men		Gender Gap	
	1973 (%)	1992 (%)	1973 (%)	1992 (%)	1973 (%)	1992 (%)
Sense of competence (to some and great extent)	27.0	38.0	47.6	39.5	20.6	1.5
Discuss politics (to some and great extent)	33.6	61.6	32.7	70.0	0.9	8.4
Party membership	14.9	6.3	19.4	11.9	4.5	5.6
Party identification	38.7	27.9	38.7	30.0	—	2.1
Nonvoters	7.0	3.3	3.8	2.1	3.2	1.2
Influence of territories on vote	54.5	82.9	61.2	81.1	6.7	1.1
Willing to return territories	64.9	38.2	69.6	40.8	4.7	2.6
Extent of social inequality	67.2	61.7	63.9	58.5	3.3	3.2
Influence of economy on vote	39.7	69.2	42.4	77.4	2.7	8.2

as a rule, apply to attitudes and opinions where women and men show a great similarity.

The attempt to look further into the gender gap by the examination of various specific, though not mutually exclusive, aspects of women's characteristics was of limited value. Education, ethnic origin, age, and social status had an unequivocal effect on the gender gap, increasing it in some cases, and shrinking it in others. One aspect was, however, clearly affected by these parameters: the higher the status of the woman (young, college educated, of European origin, working outside her home) the greater was the gender gap in regard to her electoral choice. In this regard women are *different* from men.

The analysis of the gender gap attempted to trace the influence of changes in women's status that took place during the two past decades. The women who were interviewed in 1973 came of age when the ideas regarding female quality were only incipient. Although a series of laws protecting women in the workplace were enacted the first twenty years of statehood, they had little relevance to the women's status, which remained conspicuously inferior to that of men. Between 1973 and 1992 abortion was legalized (1977), retirement age was made equal for men and women (1987), and women were promised (by law) equal opportunity in employment (1988). Women's issues such as wife battering and rape were constantly on the agenda. All these legal measures, taken to diminish the gender gap, have contributed to a rise in women's political efficacy. Furthermore, while the gender gap regarding opinions narrows across time, women do show a growing tendency to make their own electoral choices. The gender gap in voting behavior is clearly increasing. This sounds like good news for Israeli women, as a distinct electoral choice may provide a key for the future entrance of women into the political elite.

Notes

1. It is worthwhile noting that in the *Civic Culture* study respondents were asked to describe their subjective sense of civic competence in regard to an unfair and unjust law (Almond and Verba 1989, 144–45). The question in the Israeli survey did not include reference to a disturbing legislation.

2. This proposition was challenged by Norris (1988), who identified a liberal gender gap.

3. The 1973 survey was based on a national sample of 1,885 respondents (with 1,010 females and 875 males); the 1992 survey was based on a national sample of 1,180 (with 624 females and 556 males).

References

Almond, Gabriel A., and Sidney Verba. 1989. *The Civic Culture.* Beverly Hills: Sage.

Arian, Asher. 1985. *Politics in Israel: The Second Generation.* Chatham, N.H.: Chatham House.

Azaryahu, Sarah. 1980. *The Union of Hebrew Women for Equal Rights in Eretz Yisrael* (in Hebrew). Haifa: Women's Aid Fund.

Barnes, Samuel M., and Max Kaase. 1979. *Political Action: Mass Participation in Five Western Democracies.* Beverly Hills: Sage.

Baxter, S., and M. Lansing. 1983. *Women and Politics: The Visible Majority.* Ann Arbor: University of Michigan Press.

Bernstein, Debora S. 1991. "Oriental and Ashkenazi Jewish women in the Labor Market." In Swirski and Safir 1991.

Bourque, Susan C., and Jean Grossholtz. 1984. "Politics and Unnatural Practice: Political Science Looks at Female Participation." *Politics and Society* 4: 225–66.

Campbell, Angus, Philip E. Converse, Warren E. Miller, and Donald E. Stokes. 1960. *The American Voter.* New York: John Wiley and Sons.

Carroll, Susan J. 1988. "Women's Autonomy and the Gender Gap: 1980 and 1982." In Mueller 1988b.

Christy, Carol A. 1987. *Sex Differences in Political Participation: Processes of Change in Fourteen Nations.* New York: Praeger.

Dalton, Russell J. 1988. *Citizen Politics in Western Democracies.* Chatham, N.J.: Chatham House.

Di Palma, Giuseppi. 1970. *Apathy and Participation: Mass Politics in Western Society.* New York: Free Press.

Duverger, Maurice. 1955. *The Political Role of Women.* Paris: UNESCO.

Eduards, Maud L. 1981. "Sweden." In *The Politics of the Second Electorate*, ed. J. Lovenduski and J. Hills. London: Routledge and Kegan Paul.

Goot, Murray, and Elizabeth Ried. 1984. "Women: If Not Apolitical, Then Conservative." In *Women and the Public Sphere*, ed. Janet Siltanen and Michelle Stanworth. London: Hutchinson.

Hernes, Helga M. 1980. "Research Note: Predicting Support for the Women's Movement—A Diffusion Model." *Scandinavian Political Studies* 3:265–73.

Inglehart, Ronald. 1977. *The Silent Revolution.* Princeton: Princeton University Press.

———. 1990. *Culture Shift in Advanced Industrial Society.* Princeton: Princeton University Press.

Katz, Ruth, and Yohanan Peres. 1986. "The Sociology of the Family in Israel: An Outline of Its Development from the 1950s to the 1980s." *European Sociological Review* 2:148–59.

Kim, Jae O., Norman Nie, and Sidney Verba. 1974. "The Amount and Concentration of Political Participation." *Political Methodology* 1:105–32.

Lane, Robert E. 1961. *Political Life: Why People Get Involved in Politics.* Glencoe, Ill.: Free Press.

Lipset, Seymour Martin. 1971. *Political Man.* London: Heinemann.

Milbrath, Lester W. 1968. *Political Participation.* Chicago: Rand McNally.

Milbrath, Lester W., and M. L. Goel. 1977. *Political Participation: How and Why Do People Get Involved in Politics?* 2nd ed. Chicago: Rand McNally.

Mueller, Carol McClurg. 1988a. "The Empowerment of Women: Polling and the Women's Voting Bloc." In Mueller 1988b.

———. 1988b. *The Politics of the Gender Gap: The Social Construction of Political Influence.* Beverly Hills: Sage.

Norris, Pippa. 1987. *Politics and Sexual Equality: The Comparative Position of Women in Western Democracies.* Boulder: Lynn Rienner.

———. 1988. "The Gender Gap: A Cross-National Trend?" in Mueller 1988b.

———. 1991. "Gender Differences in Political Participation in Britain: Traditional, Radical and Revisionist Models." *Government and Opposition* 16:56–74.

Poole, Keith T., and Harmon L. Zeigler. 1981. "The Diffusion of Feminist Ideology." *Political Behavior* 3:229–56.

Randall, Vicky. 1982. *Women and Politics.* London: Macmillan.

Rokkan, Stein. 1970. *Citizens, Elections, Parties: Approaches to the Comparative Study of the Processes of Development.* New York: David McKay.

Rusciano, Frank L. 1992. "Rethinking the Gender Gap. The Case of West German Elections, 1949–1987." *Comparative Politics* 24:335–57.

Sapiro, Virginia. 1983. *The Political Integration of Women.* Urbana: University of Illinois Press.

Siim, Birte. 1991. "Welfare State, Gender Politics and Equality Policies: Women's Citizenship in the Scandinavian Welfare States." In *Equality Politics and Gender,* ed. Elizabeth Meehan and Selma Sevenhuijsen.

Skard, Torild, and Elina Haavio-Mannila. 1985. "Mobilization of Women at Elections." In *Unfinished Democracy: Women in Nordic Politics,* ed. Elina Haavio-Mannila et al. Oxford: Pergamon Press.

Swirski, Barbara, and Marylin P. Safir, eds. 1991. *Calling the Equality Bluff: Women in Israel.* New York: Pergamon Press.

Togeby, Lise. 1992. "The Nature of Declining Party Membership in Denmark: Cases and Consequences." *Scandinavian Political Studies* 15:1–19.

Verba, Sidney, Norman Nie, and Jae O. Kim. 1980. *Participation and Political Equality.* Cambridge: Cambridge University Press.

Welsh, Susan. 1980. "Sex Differences in Political Activity in Britain." *Women and Politics* 1:29–46.

Yishai, Yael. 1985. "Women and War: The Case of Israel." *Journal of Social, Political and Economic Studies* 10:195–214.

CHAPTER 5

Shas—The Sephardic Torah Guardians: Religious "Movement" and Political Power

AARON P. WILLIS
Princeton University

June 21, 1992. Scene: "Solemn Assembly" in Jerusalem. The various speakers, musicians, and honored rabbis are shuttled in and out. Assistants on stage maintain telephone contact with the speakers and performers, coordinating their movement between assemblies. Oriental music fills the night air with lyrics that play emotionally on the trials and tribulations of *teshuva* (repentance). Ovadia Yosef, the president of the Shas Council of Torah Sages moves off to his waiting helicopter after addressing and blessing the gathered crowd. Moments later Interior Minister Arye Deri arrives. He apologizes for being late and adds: "You have been standing here for hours . . . but this is not the only place that we have gathered. I have just arrived from Lod. Three thousand people are right now listening to the words of our master and teacher Rabbi Ovadia Yosef. We were in Pardes Katz just before. Five thousand people are there listening to words of Torah. Everyday, all over the country there are thousands of

This analysis is based on extended fieldwork in a Sephardic haredi community in Jerusalem. I thank the Mac Arthur Foundation, the Center of International Studies at Princeton University, and the Memorial Foundation for Jewish Culture for their support of this research and its writing.

people coming to these assemblies. Shas is the only one that
brings the masses of Israel to hear the sacred words of Rav
Ovadia Yosef . . ."

In the aftermath of the 1992 Knesset elections, Shas has moved to center
stage in the Israeli political arena. After its initial success in the 1984 Knesset
elections, the party has only continued to grow in terms of both voter
support and influence in key government agencies. In political terms, Shas
has played the game well, leveraging its position to gain the most from coalition agreements with the larger parties. However, in its own terms Shas is
"not a political party" but rather "a religious movement [*t'nuah*]." Largely
appealing to sentiments of "ethnic pride" and "religious tradition" among
Israel's Sephardic communities, Shas has portrayed itself as a "peoples'
movement" with a mandate for social and spiritual renewal.

The metaphor of movement was given tangible form in Shas assemblies
like the one cited above: the movement of spiritual leaders whisked from one
part of the country to another; the spiritual/moral movement of individuals
and families transforming themselves in *teshuva*; and religious/political
movement with the goals of the party elaborated and the image of nationwide community of believers offered. The sense of momentum and direction
was furthered in popular slogans like "the revolution cannot be stopped" or
"return the crown to its glorious past."

The origins of Shas in 1984 and its subsequent involvement in the
Israeli political arena has been documented elsewhere (Heilman 1990;
Friedman 1991). This essay offers a sense of the "religious imagination" that
has informed Shas's 1992 election campaign. How has the movement been
conceptualized in terms of images, stories, and symbols? I argue that in order
to understand the methods and goals of Shas as a "political party," we must
first understand what it means as a "religious movement."

I. The Campaign: "Imagining" the Movement

The Shas campaign was a multimedia affair, bringing images, symbols, and
catchy musical tunes to a diversity of communities, secular and observant
alike. At the central bus station in Jerusalem activists set up camp distributing leaflets, musical and video cassettes, and pictures of Rabbis Ovadia and
Kaduri ("the elder of Kabbalists"). Electrical generators supplied power for
video presentations. When the video was not running, tape players blasted in
several directions with the Shas election theme song:

Remember on election day
God's Torah of light
We will return the crown to the past

Our Master and Teacher, Ovadia

(chorus) Everyone is voting, only Shas
Faith we give, to Shas
To honor the Torah, with Shas
together everyone in joy

Yeshiva students with time off from their studies for this "sacred work"[1] sold the cassettes for a shekel a piece (40 cents). In trying to convince individuals to vote for Shas one student flipped the cassette open and, referring to a colorful drawing on the inside, listed off all the reasons that one should need: synagogues, ritual baths, keeping the sabbath, yeshivot, torah schools, and the Wellspring. Another activist explained that in voting for Shas one gains a share of the "merit" that accrues with all these efforts. It is "as if" one himself has physically helped to build a new ritual bath or contributed to help yeshiva students study Torah.

Shas stressed simple statements. Flipping though a newspaper with advertisements from different parties provided the greatest contrast. Whereas one party had crammed as much information and as many points as possible into their allotted space, another emphasized the photographs of its top candidates and added various points of principal. As one turned the page, Shas's message, in an equivalent space, read simply "Shas: I believe." Leaflets were handed out that captured in images one of the most profound messages of the Shas campaign. The leaflet featured two photographs and read simply, "the curse, and the blessing." On top, the walls of the Ramle prison were featured and identified; below, the "blessing" was indicated by a room full of children learning Torah—written beneath the photographs: "vote Shas, vote for life." The message was clear. While the prison represented the Sephardic past in Israel, the study of Torah stood as the future. In voting for Shas one voted for redemption and renewal of the Sephardic community in Israel.

Shas leaders were involved in highly publicized investigations into their conduct while in office. Accusations of fraud and financial mismanagement had been leaked to the press in the two years preceding the election bid. In an hour-long video production defending Interior Minister Arye Deri from police investigations, similar images of persecution and redemption were juxtaposed. Video images of thousands of Shas supporters reciting prayers, or blowing the shofar at the Western Wall were overdubbed with the sound of police sirens. The police room for the investigation was likened to a war headquarters, and the hundreds of investigators who had interviewed thousands of "witnesses," were likened to warriors. "It is not a war against Deri, it is against you. If you are Sephardic and Jewish and believe in the mitzvot and the Torah . . . if you believe in Torah schools and ritual baths, it is against you." The investigation is portrayed as a "political" ploy authorized by the highest levels of government officialdom who fear the newly found power of the Shas movement. The image of police sirens chasing Sephardic children is not new. The investigations are just another chapter in the long history of discrimination against Sephardim at the hands of secular and Ashkenazi state. "They do not even conduct investigations like this against members of the PLO," one Shas supporter complained.[2]

To Shas supporters on the street, the reaction to the investigations was indeed more varied than the single message that the video was meant to create. One man appealed to the more general metaphysical parameters of the conflict:

It is written that "what is sacred complicates itself." When Abraham, in doubt over whether to actually sacrifice Isaac or not, looked over into the bush and saw that the ram had become entangled in the brush he knew that it was a sign from God [see Genesis 22:13]. Similarly things which are sacred become entangled. Because Shas helps to sanctify the name of Heavens, people will try to bring it down.

Others appealed to a more practical sense of realpolitik: "the investigations are punishment for Shas bringing down the government. The Likud wants to clip Deri's wings, to warn him not to get too carried away with himself." Another man quietly confided in me that he believed that Deri had in fact taken money illegally for himself, "but that is part of what it means to be a minister here in Israel." As for the accusations that Deri helped to get money transferred to religious institutions associated with the Shas movement, he continued: "what party has not operated this way, the Likud funding settlements in the territories, Labor, and the kibbutzim, this is how it works." Yet another claimed that the investigations had indeed tarnished the name of Shas, but he was firm in his commitment: "as long as Rav Ovadia gives his hand to the movement, I will support it."

II. *Teshuva:* **Spiritual/Moral Movement**

The double meaning of *teshuva* (both repentance and return) was ideally suited to the Shas message. It represented the process of personal movement away from less observant and committed past to a future of spiritual fulfillment and enhanced individual destiny. At the same time, it was a symbolic "return" to the once great traditions of the Sephardic past, "to a complete Judaism, a rich Judaism, a good Judaism." These two themes were tied in to values of education, family unity, and continuity between generations, thus creating a powerful ideological thrust to the movement that Shas sought to perpetuate.

The interweaving of these various themes was skillfully done in one of Deri's preelection campaign speeches. Relating a story that was both a result of Shas activities as well as epitomizing the goals for the future of the movement, Deri created a link between past and future. He spoke on the influence which the Shas-supported Torah schools have had on Sephardic Jews who had become "distanced" from the religious customs and traditions of their forebearers:

> With a family where there are older ones already grown, what does it matter to them to send the littlest one to the talmud torah (haredi day school). It cannot be worse than what happened to the older ones in the secular schools. Friends I will tell you a child arrives at these schools at the age of four or five he knows nothing besides curses and the ways of the street. After two weeks, you can see the difference. He cleans himself up and begins to wear the clothes of *bnei torah*. He returns home from school with sacredness in his eyes, with sparks in his eyes—he answers his mother and father, yes, mother; yes, father. Later he returns home on Friday afternoon, he asks his mother to light the sabbath candles. And the mother who hasn't remembered to light the candles for who knows how long, remembers her righteous mother, and she lights the candles. Then she remembers the traditional blessings, on the education of the children, physical sustenance. What Sephardi mother can stand against this force? She begins to cry and makes the blessings that she can return in teshuva, and that the older children will return as well.
>
> The boy asks his father to take him to the synagogue. Do you know a Sephardi father in the world who could say "no" to going to synagogue with his youngest son? On the way, the father remembers when he was little and his father used to take him. During the Shir ha Shirim the father begins to feel it, and then he gets a shock, at the age of four, his son begins to chant: (*shuve shuve shulamit*) "return, return, that we may look upon thee" (Song of Songs 7:1). And the father's eyes open wide, to see his son that only two weeks ago was cursing.
>
> They arrive home—shabbat, candles, songs. In the middle of the weekly reading, he asks for his father to help him prepare

for a test the next week. The father takes the questions and answers and soon begins to get close. After another week or two the parents arrive at the school and exclaim, save us, how can we stand before this child of ours?

The educational framework that Shas provides helps to bring both individuals and entire families "back" to their religious roots. The mother and father in the story remember participating in these rituals with their parents, just as they are doing with their son. It creates stronger bonds within the family unit while creating a continuity between generations. The teshuva of individual and family is connected through Shas with a wider social movement. Deri goes on to claim that thousands of families are making teshuva every year.[3]

The newly observant (*baalei teshuva*) are an important link between Shas' haredi and masorti constituencies. This significance is reflected in the choice of a *baal teshuva* representative for the Knesset list this year. Shlomo Benezri, number six on the Shas list, tells a story that is similar to that told by many of the Shas supporters in the haredi neighborhoods of Jerusalem. He had a national-religious upbringing that made him distant from religion. He went on to a secular high school, where he was successful and popular. He had an older brother who had gone to study in a yeshiva after his army service. After he left the army Benezri went to study in a yeshiva, where he has been for the past eight years. He married and claims that since their marriage his wife's entire family has made *teshuva*. This story represents the experiences of Shas's many haredi supporters who were not raised in Lithuanian yeshivot (a majority, but no exact numbers exist). Benezri's role as Shas Knesset member serves an important legitimating function for these supporters and furthers the Shas message of teshuva as an integral component to Shas's "movement." Not long after his introduction to the Knesset, Benezri entered into the limelight in the ongoing battle of values between secular and religious Jewish culture in Israel. He publicly attacked the secular poet Haim Bialik, an iconic, if not heroic figure in secular Israeli culture, for having been an enemy to true Judaism. "He caused many, including myself, to distance themselves from religion," Benezri argued, angering many in the secular public.[4]

III. Blessings, Prayers, and a Charm

Part of what helped to characterize Shas as a religious movement, and not simply just another political party, was the invocation of "sacred" forces in the election campaign. Deri emphasizes that "Shas is the only one which brings the masses of Israel to hear the words of (our Master and Teacher) Rabbi Ovadia Yosef." The campaign is conceptualized as part and parcel of the religious movement that Shas embodies. The people they bring to speak are not just politicians but rather sages—sages who lead the congregations in prayer, teach the wisdom of past generations, and possess the merit to offer powerful blessings.

Prayers were recited that gave the assembly described above the flavor of a religious experience. This was especially true of the closing prayer (*o malchut shamayim*), which invoked the name of God in order to acknowledge God's absolute sovereignty over creation. This is the same prayer that the Sephardim use in their *slichot* (repentance) services during the High Holy days and in times of trouble throughout the year. It closed the assembly with a solemn and serious air of urgency. During the course of the assembly the audience was also blessed by Ovadia Yosef, Yitzhak Kaduri, and other important rabbis from the Jerusalem area. They recited informal blessings that were designed to ensure the health and livelihood of those assembled as well as the formal "priestly benediction" which also contained "protective" efficacy.

The invocation of sacred forces was widely misrepresented in the Israeli press. They reported that Shas was offering blessings in exchange for votes, technically a violation of Israeli electoral law.[5] The law had been passed after the 1988 elections when rabbis from the leading parties battled it out for votes by granting any who would vote for them blessings in exchange for support. This was felt by many to be an abuse of rabbinic authority and outside the pale of the modern democratic process. For the secular Israeli public these reports had the effect of exoticizing the religious parties at the same time that their voters were made to seem gullible and foolish. In fact, while blessing did play an important part in the campaign, it was never offered "in exchange" for votes. When one walked up to a Shas table they encouraged him to sign a sheet and request a special blessing from the rabbis. However, this was before one even began to discuss the pros and cons of actually voting for Shas. Similarly, at the assemblies, blessings were made for all of those assembled, but that in no way guaranteed one's vote. The blessings were not so much a quid pro quo as they were about creating a sacred atmosphere within the election process.

It was also reported that Yosef had issued a special "blessing" (*bracha*) to be said at the time of voting. It was actually more a prayer (request) than a blessing (thanksgiving). The voter asked God to recognize that he or she should participate in the merit that accrues to the Shas party for their efforts. It was more a practical act, rather than strictly a magical one. In terms of actual behavior, several "pious" individuals told me that they did not say the prayer. Others, equally pious, stressed its importance. There was no dogma on the matter.

Shas also distributed special items that had protective power. These included stickers with a "blessing over the home" and a "prayer for the road" as well as a special "charm" (*kamiya*) produced by Rav Kaduri.[6] None of these were given out "in exchange" for votes. They were available for all who were interested, and they were in fact, part of what Shas as a religious movement was all about—spreading the word of Torah. I spoke with a Sephardic taxi driver who had the "prayer for the road," complete with color pictures of Yosef and Kaduri, affixed to his steering wheel. He explained that he was voting for one of the more right-wing parties but that did not preclude his appreciation for what Shas had produced. In purely political terms Shas had failed because it would not receive a vote in exchange for the blessing. However, in the terms of a religious movement, it was successful.[7] It encouraged a bare-headed Sephardi compatriot to acknowledge the protective powers of God and the sages. The sticker reaffirmed fundamental beliefs, "returning" individuals to their own religious and ethnic roots.[8]

Rav Ovadia emphasized *gematriyot* (numerology) in his appeal to voters. In the past term Shas had a hand in the construction of 46 new ritual baths and the repair of 90, equaling a total 136 ritual baths. "In *gematriyah* 136 equals '*kol*' (voice or vote)," Ovadia declared. "Give us your voice and we will give you ritual baths." In another context he argued that the unseasonal thunderstorms in the week before the elections were a sign from God to vote for Shas. According to his argument, "thunder" (*ra'amim*) in *gematriyah* is equivalent to "Shas."

IV. Competition with Other Parties

Shas had to compete with several other parties for the Sephardic vote. Of the parties that did not gain enough votes to win a Knesset seat, the "Redemption of Israel" Party was closest to Shas in an appeal to the haredi Sephardic voter. Lead by a Sephardic rabbi associated with the Hassidic Habad movement, it stressed a connection to ethnic and religious "roots" that was similar to that of Shas. However, this "redemption" party also emphasized a connection to the principles of army service and "Greater Israel," broadcasting television ads which showed religious men in black suits doing army service or inspecting the progress of new settlements in the Occupied Territories. Rav Levinger, an Ashkenazi rabbi and settlement leader, more directly attacked Shas in an attempt to gain support from the observant Sephardic community. His Torah and the Land party emphasized settlement of the occupied territories and broadcast television images of Levinger meandering through the Arab market in Hebron with a rifle over his shoulder. Levinger attacked Deri and Shas for their efforts to gain support in Israel's Arab sector. Playing on the notion of Shas's Council of Torah Sages, Levinger offered pictures of Deri embracing Arab politicians with the caption "The Central Council of Peace Sages," thus trying to steer the traditionally more right-wing Sephardic voters away from

Shas. Both of these parties were only marginally successful in their efforts to attract Shas supporters, and neither passed the necessary percentage to gain a seat in the Knesset.

The most formidable challenge to Shas's constituency was lodged by Rav Peretz and the United Torah list. Peretz, a loyal Sephardic student of Rabbi Eliezer Menachem Shach, claimed to represent the haredi core of the Shas constituency, those students who had grown up in or studied under rabbis who had been educated in the Lithuanian yeshivot. Rav Shach had been instrumental in the development of Shas as a breakaway faction from Agudat Israel in 1984, and up until the 1992 elections he maintained a central role as spiritual and political advisor to the Shas party. However, ten days before the election, Shach made a controversial statement. Reacting to fears that Deri would try to manipulate the Sephardic vote by threatening to cut off funds to Shach's (Ashkenazi) educational network, Shach complained that "the Sephardim are not ready yet to manage affairs of religion and state . . . they are growing and developing and returning to their roots, but they still need more time to learn."[9] Shach threw his support behind Peretz, who, if elected, would be forced to work within the Ashkenazi-dominated United Torah coalition. The United Torah Party placed Peretz at the forefront of its advertising campaign, trying to convince the Sephardic public that Peretz was their representative to the Knesset. Peretz's face was ever present on United Torah's posters and in its television advertisements.[10]

Television ads showed Peretz sitting with Sephardi students, both observant and bare headed, answering questions. He claimed not just that he was a Sephardic representative in an otherwise all-Ashkenazi party but rather that he was the leader of the newly created Moriah "movement," which would tend to the spiritual needs of the Sephardic community. He offered "Judaism with a soul" and swore to protect the country from "the left." Reminding voters that Shas had brought down the government to help to form a coalition with Labor in 1990, Peretz also appealed to the more conservative Sephardi constituency. He stood on his record of dissent from the previous Shas policies and promised to enter into coalition discussions only with the Likud. He had active support on the street from an elite group of Sephardic yeshiva students studying in Lithuanian yeshivot, the *bnei torah Sephardim* (Sephardi Torah students). In more aggressive and lower profile activities, they circulated stickers that played on the Shas theme of "return the crown to the glorious past," writing instead "return the crown and glory to honesty," lodging a direct attach on Deri's integrity in the face of ongoing police investigations.

Shas did not react to the competition with United Torah Judaism (or any of the other parties mentioned above) in any direct or highly public manner. In effect they still had published an allegiance to Shach and refrained from attacking his party directly. While Peretz attempted to create the image of a break within the Sephardic community out of which his new movement could emerge, Shas continued to stress a "Sephardic unity" message, not attacking Peretz openly. However, two days before the elections an unsigned poster appeared throughout Jerusalem and Bnei Brak that went to the heart of the conflict between Peretz and Shas. "Dear Sephardic voter: support United Torah," the poster declared, "we want you to vote for us even though Sephardim only make up five percent of our yeshiva students, three percent of out torah schools, and two percent of students in our advanced study centers. God forbid that these quotas should be broken! But we want eighty percent of your vote." The poster continued in its tongue-in-check style, concluding with a direct attack on Peretz's young followers: "Today you are *bnei torah Sephardim*, but tomorrow [after the elections] you will be *"frenkim"* [a derogatory reference to Jews of North African origin]. The message was poignant in its attack on Ashkenazi institutions, which have a clear history of limiting the number of Sephardic students in their schools. It legitimated Shas's claim that years of discrimination at the hands of the secular and haredi Ashkenazi establishment could be solved only by the creation and development of an entire system of education that would cater to the specific needs of the Sephardic community.

V. The Elections to the 1992 Knesset

The election results gave the Shas movement a strong push forward. While it was anticipated that they might lose several seats, in the end Shas gained one seat, bringing their total representation to six Knesset seats.[11] Whereas in the 1988 elections Shas received 107,709 votes, they brought their total support up to 129,347 in 1992.[12] The other main haredi list, United Torah Judaism (UJT) lost support, going from seven representatives (eight, if you include Peretz) in the 1988 Knesset to only four in 1992. Apparently, many of the Sephardic students in the Lithuanian yeshivot voted for Shas despite instructions from their yeshiva leadership to support Peretz and UTJ. The UTJ also failed to bring in the *non-haredi* Sephardic voters. Shas had clearly benefited from Shach's comments the previous week that the Sephardim were not ready for leadership positions. His statement caused a backlash in which the Sephardic haredi students' connection to their ethnic roots outweighed their sense of obligation to the Lithuanian-educated yeshiva leadership.[13] Moreover, Shach's comments seems to have brought voters that had been hesitating between Shas and Likud.[14] The Likud itself had suffered from public accusations of ethnic discrimination in the placing of David Levy, then foreign minister, on their list to the Knesset prior to the elections. The words of Shach helped to move them into Shas' camp, where the message of "ethnic pride" resonated well with their sense of discrimination and frustration at the hands of the largely Ashkenazi-dominated political establishment.

Shas also drew close to 13,000 votes from the Arab sector.[15] In the year preceding the election, Deri invested in Arab Israeli communities in his capacity as interior minister. He made appearances in Arab villages and worked with clan-based and municipal leaderships to help facilitate the distribution of funds from his ministry. He appealed to the Arabs on ideological grounds claiming that (1) he was a religious man and could respect their religious values and (2) he too had known deprivation and discrimination at the hands of the political establishment. He would work to end discrimination and inequalities in the distribution of state funds. Deri found solid support among Arab community leaders, and several Shas headquarters were set up in Bedouin villages in the south. One of the leaders there said that he would support Shas because Deri was an interior minister "who could get things done and advance the plans for development in the Arab municipalities."[16]

There were also a fair number of Ashkenazi haredim who voted for Shas. Whereas in Bnei Brak, Shach's home turf, Shas had received only 5,700 votes in 1988, now they claimed more than 9,000.[17] Also, it appears that most of the 3,000 voters from the Belz Hassidic community in Jerusalem voted for Shas.[18] Their Rebbe had issued a sacred proclamation to vote for Torah Judaism, but after negotiations broke down over whether the Belz would be able to field a representative to the Knesset, their leader turned against UTJ and urged his followers to vote Shas.

Rav Ovadia turned out to be the big victor on the haredi street. Deri proudly proclaimed that while many had believed that half of Shas seats in the previous election were voters loyal to Shach, Ovadia Yosef now had the net vote with six seats.[19] Yosef had emerged as the sole leader in the Sephardic haredi community, with support for Peretz and Shach severely diminished. Shas MK Yosef Ezran enthusiastically claimed that the results of the election "prove that Shas is not just a curiosity nor a fleeting phenomenon, but rather a genuine peoples' movement."[20] Indeed, Shas has more voter support (in absolute numbers) than ever before, and it is about to embark on a massive project of institutionalization at the state's expense. Shas's ability to institutionalize is the fruit of its coalition bargaining efforts, a subject to which we now turn.

VI. Joining the Labor-led coalition

The elections to the thirteenth Knesset marked the end of fifteen years of Likud dominance and the rise of a Labor-left coalition. Labor and Meretz brought fifty-six seats to a possible coalition. With the Arab parties holding five seats, it was enough to block the Likud from forming a government.

Rabin, the Labor leader, wanted to form a wide coalition, bringing in both the more right-wing Tzomet as well as the religious parties. However, he was also in a hurry to set up his new government. At the very least, he still needed one more party to help him over the sixty seat majority necessary to form the coalition.[21] During the election campaign Shas had vowed to support a Likud government, thus appealing to voters who might have been hesitating between Likud and Shas. However, with the clear Labor victory, Shas made no excuses, and quickly came to a coalition agreement with Labor, giving Labor the majority it needed to form the new government. Shas was given the portfolio of interior minister, which it had held for the past eight years under the Likud, as well as several important deputy ministerial positions, including education and religion.[22]

Initially Deri and Shach had discussed forming a haredi block, which would include United Torah's four seats and the six from Shas. They would negotiate together, and no independent agreements would be offered to Labor. Yet, in the aftermath of their devastating loss, the United Torah Party was not as unified as the name suggested. Agudat Israel convened its own Council of Torah Sages to debate principles, leaving Shach's Degel representatives and Peretz out of their discussions. Unity was quick to return however when Shas independently announced its intention to join the Labor government. Rav Shach made it clear that he opposed Shas's decision. Shach was particularly angered by the Labor decision to offer Shulamit Aloni, head of the left-Meretz alignment, the Ministry of Education. Her "secular humanist" values were directly antithetical to those of a Torah observant Judaism, Shach argued, worrying that close to a million students in the secular-state educational system would become only more distanced from their religious roots.[23] He also feared that she might work to channel money away from the haredi Independent schools.[24]

Breaking with Shach for the first time in the battle for control of the Shas movement, Ovadia Yosef provoked a deep split between the Ashkenazi and Sephardic haredi worlds. His direct disregard for Shach's wishes were viewed as an insult to the learning and integrity of Shach, almost twenty-five years Yosef's elder. Soon other leading Ashkenazi rabbis came out with halachic (legal) decisions that participation in a coalition with Aloni as education minister was an act against the Jewish people and therefore illegitimate.[25] Yosef found himself alone in the haredi world. But he held his ground against an increasingly hostile Ashkenazi community, buoyed by Shas's resounding success in the election booth and Torah Judaism's declining stature. His move was a declaration of independence and has created a great deal of confusion in the closely intertwined Ashkenazi and Sephardic haredi worlds where Shach's overarching religious authority has held these groups together for years.[26]

United Torah supporters argued that Shas's jump into the coalition agreement was motivated by Deri's fear of prosecution on corruption charges (he is immune from prosecution as a minister; that immunity may be taken away, but it is a more complicated process and one more subject to political manipulation and bargaining). Others suggested that it had been Yosef's clear intention since 1990 to help Labor form a coalition, and that the promises to go with the Likud were empty election rhetoric. Yet, I argue that in order to understand Shas's entry into the Labor government, we need to return to its ideology as a "religious movement."

In joining the government coalition, Shas was guaranteed its pick of choice portfolios. Maintaining control over the Interior Ministry as well as taking up the deputy posts in Education and Religion will help realize Shas's commitment to channel funds to the religious needs of the Sephardic community. With Shas's "political" platform being essentially "more ritual baths and funding for Torah education in a community which has been deprived for years," other ideological considerations were clearly secondary. They were not elected with any firm commitment to either the left or the right. Their mandate was elaborated by one of the shopkeepers in the old Bucharan market in Jerusalem after the election. Echoing the movement's imagery, he explained: "Shas was created to 'spread Torah, make it great, and return the crown and glory to the past,'" adding that, "it is forbidden for Shas to sit in opposition."[27]

While the National Religious Party has chosen to sit in opposition because of the Labor position on the future of the occupied territories, for Shas this was never a question. Because of the way Shas has been imagined as a movement, it does not make sense for it to take a firm stand on this issue. Yosef has made his position clear that it is permissible to give up territories if it will save Jewish lives but "that is a decision for generals and not for rabbis." Also, Shas brings together voters, who both support and oppose issues like "greater Israel," under the unifying banner of "Sephardism" and "religious tradition." The more general rallying points of the movement thus attract a constituency that is full of contradictory political sentiments. For Shas to take a firm stand on any of the potentially divisive issues would negate its message, and effectiveness, as a religious movement. "The future of the territories is not connected to the need for Torah education within the Sephardic commu- nity," explained an official in the Wellspring organization who noted that his personal sentiments were to the right on the question of the territories.

Even before Yosef made the decision to break from Shach over the issue of coalition agreements, it was reported that Yosef intended to steer the Shas movement in a direction that was "less haredi and more ethnic," focusing on social problems unique to the Sephardic communities.[28] Initial changes may include the structure of the Council of Torah Sages. Yosef would like to increase the number of representatives on this council, bringing in younger rabbis who work more with the masorti Sephardic community and are not directly connected to Shach. This includes figures like Moshe Mazuz, the leader of the Tunisian community, or Reuven Elbaz, the Moroccan-born leader of the *teshuva* movement in Israel. Adding members to the council would serve to lessen the influence of Shach and the Ashkenazi haredim.

Yosef also intends to move Shas in a more clearly Zionist direction (Willis 1992). Whereas Shas was developed from Agudat Israel, commonly labelled a "non-Zionist" party in the academic literature, Shas has always had more of a Zionist flavor than have the other haredi parties. For one, Yosef was an employee of the state in his position as Chief Sephardic Rabbi during the 1970s, and he still wears the robe of this office in public appearances. Secondly, Shas's supporters are not easily categorized by the traditional oppositions that have been inherited from debates within the Ashkenazi community. For example, as a group, they are not committed to the dichotomy of "redemption" and "exile" which has driven many of the distinctions between "Zionist" and "non-Zionist" ideologies (see Ravitsky 1989, 1990). In Shas circles one may hear a variety of responses to the question of whether the State of Israel is part of the messianic redemption or not, or whether people should attempt to hasten this process through non-religious means. There is simply no party line on these issues. The state is problematic because it is not run in accordance with Jewish law, but it is not illegitimate.

The argument should be made that Shas as a movement actually has more in common with the Zionist-oriented National Religious Party (Mafdal) than with the haredi Agudat Israel. In its first term the Shas leadership readily took on ministerial responsibilities—something that Aguda had resisted for forty years because of reservations over the legitimacy of the state. Also, while the Aguda has provided a leadership trained in the elite of Lithuanian yeshivot, most of the Shas rank and file come from a traditional national-religious background. In fact, the issues that Shas has emphasized in this election campaign are similar to ones offered by the Mafdal in the 1965 elections, soon after many of these immigrants had come to the nascent state (Deshen 1970). At the time, Mafdal provided Torah scrolls and prayer books to promote the spiritual needs of the new Sephardic immigrants. They promised to build more ritual baths and synagogues, and they were proud of their yeshiva boarding schools. The Mafdal even provided separate assemblies for women and religious programs to "keep young women off the street." Mafdal politicians attacked the secular establishment for its abandonment of religious values—all just as Shas has done in 1992. With the present coalition agreements Shas has also taken over government responsibilities in Interior, Religion, and Education, the backbone of Mafdal's early institutional power structure.

The link between Mafdal a generation ago and Shas today is nicely captured in a story recorded by Deshen (1970, 166). He writes of a synagogue in the 1960s where levels of participation are rapidly declining among the new immigrants. During the weekdays it becomes harder and harder to get a minyan (quorum) for prayer, and, on the sabbath eve, traditional customs are not taken up by the participants. Whereas reciting the Song of Songs had been a regular practice among Tunisian Jews prior to emigration, on the day described by Deshen only one old man has taken it upon himself to recite the passage. Frustrated at the failure of others to join in, he recites the concluding benediction in the singular rather than the plural "for the merit of the Song of Songs that *I* have read and that *I* have studied . . . " In the story told by Deri, set thirty years later, the young boy shocks his father by reciting from the Song of Songs at the sabbath evening service. The dynamic has come full circle and the father who tried too hard to forget the ways of his father is brought back to them through his son. This is what Shas plays on, the sense of loss that the more secular present represents and a sentimentality for the renewal of that important connection between generations.

VII. Conclusion

The Sephardic Torah Guardians is a "revitalization movement" (Wallace 1956; Ben-Rafael and Sharot 1991). It is the attempt of individuals marginalized both economically and culturally by a dominant society to reassert certain values and forge a more coherent and meaningful lifestyle. The revitalization has been constructed through images and "image evoking or image related activities" (Fernandez 1982, 418). The prison walls are juxtaposed with Sephardic students studying Torah, creating a powerful opposition that effectively links a corrupted past with the promise of a rich future. A similar effect was created in the stories of the little boy lighting the sabbath candles with his mother, or asking his father to accompany him to synagogue on the sabbath morning. The parents who had become distanced from their parents would return again through their children. Images of "sages" blessing huge assemblies, previously distanced from religious practice, but not belief, also created a sense of religious and ethnic continuity with a golden past. These images offered meaning and direction for the project of institutionalization which stands as Shas's core goal. Its leaders have skillfully positioned themselves vis-à-vis the state in order to maximize government funding and build an institutional power base, thus concretizing revitalization goals.

Shas is also a "nativistic" movement (Linton 1943) with its stress on traditional values set in opposition to those of the dominant (Ashkenazi) society. Shas has emphasized "particular elements of culture" that have come to be symbols of nativistic authenticity and historical authority, rather than attempting to recreate the exact situation of the past. In this sense, Shas has been innovative, forging a generic Sephardic identity, which even mixes Ashkenazi styles, rather than arguing for a return to particularistic regional customs. The values and traditions that Shas has utilized to build a more general Sephardic identity play on the common experiences of these many constituent ethnicities vis-à-vis the dominant Ashkenazi "other."

The notion of religious "movement" is not so much an analytic category as it is an internal metaphor (Fernandez 1979; Kaplan 1990). Fernandez identifies three types of "movement" in the study of religious groups: analytic, moral, and architectonic. The analytic metaphor is the one that we impose as researchers trying to make sense of the phenomenon before us. Kaplan warns against use of the term as a generic category of analysis. She argues that discussions of religious movement in much of the anthropological literature has promoted an image of "unnatural," or marked, development in light of other "natural" processes of social change. As analysts we should be more concerned with representing movement in the terms of the natives' values, Kaplan suggests.

Following Fernandez and Kaplan, I underscore moral and architectonic (spatial) metaphors of movement that are internal to the values of the people themselves. Realized in symbols, stories, and prayers, the "movement" was imagined and given concrete form in physical, moral, and political realms of experience. It helped to link individuals who themselves were embarking on a personal journey of self-transformation in *teshuva* (moral movement) with a wider group of individuals and families, all "moving" together. Moreover, an architectonic (spatial) sense of movement, was given form in images of the religious leaders being shuttled from one part of the country to another, spreading their word of truth and blessing. Movement imagery provided the symbolic link among individuals around the country— helping to make local experience national in scope. Finally, in the context of Israeli political culture, Shas's self-appellation of "movement" is part of an effort to adopt "the terms and categories" of the dominant culture "so as to resist them" (Kaplan 1990, 14). Goldberg explains: "there is hardly an image more embedded in labor Zionist rhetoric than 'movement' (t'nuah)."[29] To appropriate the notion of "movement" and to use it to build an institutional force on par with the early influence of these other two pioneering groups is to symbolically transform Shas into a pioneering movement with its roots fundamentally placed in the legitimacy of the contemporary Israeli state.

Finally, as an internal metaphor, Shas's self-conceptualization as a "religious movement" largely prescribed the "political" goals of the organization and its positioning vis-à-vis possible government coalitions. The movement, as imagined, was given direction in terms of its own particular "logic" (Comaroff 1985; Lan 1985). Shas's direction necessitated a successful capture of state power and influence in the interest of furthering their educational goals. To have shied away from the possible coalition with Labor, as both Mafdal and Aguda had done because of ideological reasons, would have flown in the face of Shas's mandate for government participation. In the case of Shas, the ideological distinctions that had proved so divisive to the Ashkenazi parties over the years—questions over the importance of the land of Israel, or the legitimacy of the secular state—were secondary to a party built upon the logic of "religious movement" and "Sephardic unity." For Shas, the only political course that made sense was the one that would bring it the greatest amount of responsibility, and thus influence, in the new government. That is what they achieved in their coalition with Labor.

The movement has received a great push forward with the recent election results and coalition agreement. Ovadia Yosef has skillfully maneuvered his party into the core institutions responsible for funding religious life in the state. Shas has the opportunity to become a weighty institutional force in the coming years. However, at the time of press, Arye Deri has resigned his post at the Interior Ministry and has been indicted on charges of receiving bribes, fraud, falsification of corporate documents, and violating the public trust. Deri welcomes the coming court proceedings as a chance to vindicate himself after "having been tried and convicted in the press over the past three years." Whether Deri will ultimately be exonerated, or whether the movement can function in his absence, are just two of the contingencies that are sure to effect Shas's future as a religious movement.

Notes

1. Ovadia Yosef argues that time off from Torah study was acceptable to help Shas's "sacred" effort. He even went so far as to allow individuals to sell their teffillin (phylacteries), a highly symbolic move, if it meant that it could provide the bus fare to the polling station. (However, this was permissible only if you had access to a neighbor's teffillin for the next days).

2. Haredi Shas supporters often made reference to their treatment as somehow less than the Arabs. They liked to point out that even the Arabs got funding for their own school system or for gas masks during the Gulf War (they charge that the state was unwilling to provide special masks for the beards of religious men.)

3. Deri quotes a number that would equal eighty-four hundred families per year—probably an exaggeration, and no "official" numbers exist to substantiate him. However, anyone who rides a public intercity bus in Israel can clearly "see" the numbers of Middle Eastern Jews, clad in dark suites, beards, and fedora hoats, growing noticeably over the past ten years.

4. *Ma'ariv*, 8 January 1993.

5. Election Law 122.6, noted in *Ha'aretz*, 1 June 1992.

6. Kaduri is known for his power of "practical kabbalah," the manipulation of worldly forces through esoteric knowledge and ritual.

7. While I admit distinguishing the "religious" from the "political" is a dubious business, the point here is made for emphasis. Shas is not just about "politics."

8. Aviad (1983) notes the connection between religious return and enhanced ethnic identification. The identities are conjoined in a "homecoming metaphor."

9. *Ha'aretz*, 14 June 1992.

10. It is ironic that Peretz played such a public role in the United Torah campaign. After the dismal election results Peretz was forced to resign his position to an Ashkenazi loyal to Shach. He went out complaining of "another instance of discrimination against the Sephardic community."

11. Shas began the 1988 government with six representatives. When Peretz left in 1990 he took his seat with him. Going into the 1992 elections Shas had control of only five Knesset seats.

12. Quoted in Friedman 1991; 1992 figures are quoted in *Ha'aretz*, 29 June 1992.

13. *Ha'aretz*, 23 June 1992.

14. *Ha'aretz*, 25 June 1992.

15. *Yediot Aharonot*, 26 June 1992. The first Knesset seat was approximately forty thousand votes, but those thereafter went for twenty thousand each. The Arabs' thirteen thousand votes were thus a helpful boost to Shas's Knesset presence.

16. *Ma'ariv*, 19 June 1992.

17. *Yediot Aharonot*, 26 June 1992.

18. *Ha'aretz*, 25 June 1992.

19. *Ha'aretz*, 25 June 1992. Deri's observation is based on the argument that Ezran, Pinchasi, and Peretz were loyal to Shach, but now Yosef controls all six seats with Shach's influence heavily diminished.

20. *Ha'aretz*, 24 June 1992.

21. The Arab parties are not usually asked to be part of the government.

22. Pinchasi later also received a deputy portfolio in the Finance Ministry.

23. Aloni, in an interview shortly after she took over the Education Ministry, set as her aim "to teach children to question their parents," a thought that is anathema to the haredi sensibilities.

24. *Ma'ariv*, 17 July 1992.

25. *Yediot Aharonot*, 17 July 1992.

26. Ovadia Yosef's grandchildren were threatened in their elite Lithuanian day school, and parents complained that they didn't want their children sitting next to the descendants of "he who went against Rav Shach."

27. *Ma'ariv*, 25 June 1992. It is interesting to not that the enthusiast repeated the exact words of the Shas campaign slogan.
28. *Ha'aretz*, 26 June 1992.
29. Personal Bitnet communication, 11 November 1992.

References

Aviad, J. 1983. *Return To Judaism: Religious Renewal in Israel*. Chicago: University of Chicago Press.

Ben-Rafael, E. and Sharot, S. 1991. *Ethnicity, Religion and Class in Israeli Society*. Cambridge: Cambridge University Press.

Comaroff, J. 1985. *Body of Power, Spirit of Resistance: The Culture and History of a South African People*. Chicago: University of Chicago Press.

Deshen, S. 1970. *Immigrant Voters Israel*. Manchester: Manchester University Press.

Fernandez, J. 1979. "On the Notion of Religious Movement." *Social Research*, 36–62.

———. 1982. *Bwiti: An Ethnography of the Religious Imagination in Africa*. Princeton: Princeton University Press.

Friedman, M. 1991. *The Haredi Society: Sources, Trends, and Processes* (in Hebrew). Jerusalem: The Jerusalem Institute for Israel Studies.

Heilman, S. 1990. "The Orthodox, the Ultra-Orthodox, and the Elections for the Twelfth Knesset." In *The Elections in Israel—1988*, ed. A. Arian and M. Shamir. Boulder: Westview Press.

Kaplan, M. 1990. "Meaning, Agency and Colonial History: Navosavkadua and the Tuka Movement in Fiji." *American Ethnologist* 17, no. 1 (February) 3–22.

Lan, D. 1985. *Guns and Rain: Guerrillas and Spirit Mediums in Zimbabwe*. Berkeley and Los Angeles: University of California Press.

Linton, R. 1943. "Nativistic Movements." *American Anthropologist* 45: 230–40.

Ravitsky, A. 1989. "Exile in the Holy Land: The Dilemma of Haredi Jewry." In *Israel: State and Society, 1948–1988*, ed. P. Medding. Oxford: Oxford University Press.

———. 1990. "Religious Radicalism and Political Messianism in Israel." In *Religious Radicalism and Politics in the Middle East.*, ed. E. Sivan and M. Friedman. Albany: SUNY Press.

Wallace, A. 1956. "Revitalization Movements." *American Anthropologist* 58 (April): 264–81.

Willis, A. 1992. "Redefining Religious Zionism: Shas' Ethno-Politics." *Israel Studies Bulletin*, 8, no. 2 (fall) 1–2.

CHAPTER 6

The Political Behavior of the Arabs in Israel in the 1992 Elections: Integration versus Segregation

MAJID AL-HAJ
University of Haifa

I. Parliamentary Elections and Political Marginalization

Prior to the first Knesset elections in 1949, Israeli policy makers had a dispute regarding the granting of Arab citizens the right to vote (Benziman and Mansour 1992, 201). Palmon, the prime minister's advisor for Arab affairs at that time, argued that granting Arabs the right to vote would serve as a catalyst driving them to question the Jewish character of Israel. Palmon's stand was not accepted. Eventually those who supported the voting rights of Arabs gained the upper hand. The participation of Arabs in these elections was massive, and some 79 percent of them cast their ballots. Yet, the participation of Arabs in the political system was passive, and their share in the national power center was marginal. The circumstances that prevailed at the beginning of Israeli statehood facilitated political control of the Arab population. As a result of the 1948 war the Palestinian Arabs who remained in Israel became a small, vulnerable minority constituting only 13.5 percent of the total population (Al-Haj and Rosenfeld 1989, 206). Nearly all of the Palestinian Arab middle and upper classes—the urban landowning, mercantile, professional, and religious elite—were no longer present in Israel. The vast majority of Arabs in Israel were then placed under military government, which restricted their movement. The military apparatus was used to control the Arab population. For this purpose the traditional clan—*hamula*—leadership was revived. The goal behind it was to gain control over the entire population via a few key people, while simultaneously preserving internal divisions

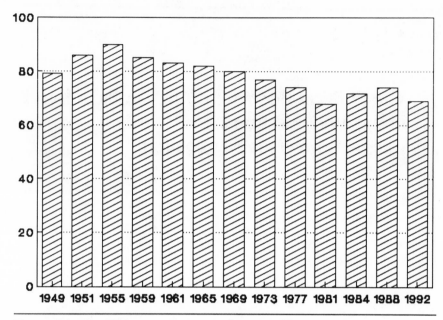

Figure 6.1. The Turnout among the Arab Population in Israel over Time, 1949–1992, in percentages

among Arabs so as to counteract the formation of a collective national identity (Al-Haj and Rosenfeld 1989, 207; Lustick 1980).

At the national level the partisan participation among Arabs was very minor. It is true that Arab citizens were not eager to join existing parties and to enter nationwide politics (Landau 1969). Nevertheless, the main reason for this trend was the lack of a political organization that could have appealed to Arab citizens. Arabs were not accepted members in the Zionist parties except Mapam, nor could they identify with the basic ideology of these parties (Nakhleh 1975; Landau 1969).

Arab affiliated lists were one of the most efficient instruments of channelling Arab votes, in particular until the late 1960s (Landau 1969; Abu-Gosh 1972). These affiliated lists were initiated and backed by Zionist parties, mainly the Labor Party, which was the principal force in the Israeli establishment until 1977 (Shokeid 1982, 122). The object of these lists was not the political mobilization of the Arab populations but rather the "catching" of Arab votes through traditional means of persuasion (Landau 1969). The structure of the Arab affiliated lists was tailored to fit the deep social territorialization of the Arab population and the traditional character (Nakhleh 1975).

These lists claimed the representation of several factions of the Arab population. Their candidates were carefully selected in order to encompass the main divisions among the Arab citizens: geographic region, religious group, prominent hamulas, and large Arab localities (Landau 1969; Lustick 1980). Until the seventh Knesset elections (1969) the Arab affiliated lists were the major political framework among the Arab minority. During that period their power ranged between 30 and 50 percent of the Arab votes. Since the early 1970s the Arab affiliated lists have decreased in power. In the tenth Knesset elections (1981) they did very poorly, and none of them were elected to the Knesset (Al-Haj and Yaniv 1983). Since then the Arab affiliated lists have disappeared from the national political arena.

II. From Passive to Active Participation

The vanishing of the Arab lists is both an outcome and reflection of the political transition that has occurred among the Arabs in Israel: from passive to active participation. The abolishment of the military government and the growing accessibility of the Jewish population have facilitated the contact between Arabs and the Jewish center. The increasing level of education and the growing number of young Arabs have increased the awareness of Arabs about the rules of the "political game" and decreased the power of the traditional methods of persuasion (Rosenfeld 1978; Smooha 1989).

The politicization process among Arabs has been accompanied by a strong national awakening. Several factors have brought about this trend, among them: the renewed contact between the Arabs in Israel and their brethren in the West Bank and Gaza after the 1967 Israeli occupation; the rise of the Palestinian National Movement and the increasing international recognition of the PLO; and the results of the 1973 war, which boosted the feelings of dignity among the Arab minority (Rekhess 1989).

The increasing politicization of the Arab population has fostered internal political competition within the Arab population, not only between traditional and nationalist segments, but also among the latter as well. This has, in turn, increased the voting percentage among the Arab population (figure 6.1).

Through active participation Arabs sought to penetrate the national power system and take part in the decision making apparatus. For this purpose the predominantly Arab parties have adopted a fairly pragmatic approach. Since the Likud came to power in 1977 the DFPE and later (1984) the Progressive List for Peace (PLP) had cooperated with the Alignment in several ways, such as the election of Hillel (Labor) as the speaker of the Knesset in 1984, against the Likud and the right-wing parties candidate (*Al-Hamishmar* 25 February 1990).

Table 6.1. Arab Vote, 1949–1992

	Arab Voters			Breakdown of Arab Vote				
Knesset	Year Elected	Arab Voters as % of eligible voters	Voting turnout (%)	Communist Party, Since 1977, DFPE (%)	PLP (%)	Arab List Aligned with Mapai (%)	Labor Party (%)	Total Zionist Parties[a] (%)
First	1949	6.6	79	22	—	28	10	—
Second	1951	7.5	86	16	—	55	11	26
Third	1955	8.2	90	15	—	48	14	23
Fourth	1959	7.9	85	11	—	42	10	26
Fifth	1961	8.3	83	22	—	40	20	29
Sixth	1965	8.6	82	23	—	38	13	27
Seventh	1969	8.4	80	28	—	40	17	27
Eighth	1973	8.5	77	37	—	27	13	29
Ninth	1977	8.9	74	50	—	16	11	21
Tenth	1981	9.8	68	37	—	12	29	45
Eleventh	1984	10.4	72	32	18	(Arab democratic party)	26	50.4
Twelfth	1988	12.0	74	34	14	11	17	42
Thirteenth	1992	11.8	69.7	23.2	9.2	15.2	20.3	52.3

[a] Labor Party and votes for other Zionist parties.

In the 1988 elections, the predominantly Arab parties made an unprecedented step in their effort to share the national power center. They declared their willingness to support a coalition led by the Alignment and the other leftist Zionist parties under certain conditions (Al-Haj 1990). The required conditions, such as the promotion of the peace process with the Palestinians and the equality for the Arab citizens in Israel, were not specific. Virtually most of these principles were declared by the leftist Zionist parties during their electoral campaign among the Arab population. Darawsheh, the head of the Arab Democratic Party (ADP), had even gone further in his pragmatic approach. Throughout his electoral campaign he emphasized his intention to be included in the political consensus in Israel as a legitimate partner with Zionist parties (*Ha'aretz* 10 November 1989).

The same situation was evident in the 1992 elections. However, an important difference came to expression between the PLP and the DFPE, on the one hand, and the ADP, on the other. The first emphasized that they would support the Labor party and Meretz in order to prevent the Likud from forming a coalition government. But they clearly declared that even in a coalition was formed they would not be an integral part of it since they could commit themselves to agree to the government's policies (interview with MK Hashim Mahamid).

Despite this pragmatic approach Arabs have remained politically marginalized, in the sense that their effect has not come to expression in the nationwide parliamentary politics. One factor responsible for the political marginalization of the Arab minority in Israel is the exclusion of Arabs from Israel's nation-state building. It has been repeatedly emphasized that the formal policy toward the Arabs in Israel is directed by three main contradicting principles: the democratic feature, the Jewish-Zionist feature, and security concerns, (Smooha 1980; Lustick 1980; Rouhana 1989). While the first principle drives toward equality and integration of Arabs, the other two pull in the opposite direction. When these features are juxtaposed it is clear that the national feature and security considerations gain the upper hand (Carmi and Rosenfeld 1988). As a result, Arabs have only "partial membership" in the Israeli society. They are excluded from the main national organizations in Israel and from its legitimate core political culture (Ben-Rafael 1982; Lustick 1980). While non-Zionist ultraorthodox parties are considered legitimate partners in the government coalition, the Arab parties are not (Galnoor 1989, 40).

The trend of political marginalization of the Arab minority is also affected by the nature of the Arab-Jewish relations in Israel. Most of the interpersonal relations between Arabs and Jews are formal, technical, and characterized by asymmetric minority-majority relations (Mari 1988). This asymmetry is also reflected in the political sphere. While large scale, well organized Jewish parties and associations have continuously penetrated the Arab minority, there has been no corresponding effective penetration of the Jewish majority by the predominantly Arab parties (Cohen 1965).

Despite the fact that the leadership of the DFPE and the PLP was almost equally divided between Jews and Arabs until the 1992 elections, the support they received from the Jewish population was negligible. Upon the formation of the Joint List in the recent Histadrut elections (1989) the DFPE insisted that a Jewish member of the Communist Party chair the list (al-Ittihad 26 November 1989). That might have negatively affected the popularity of this list among the Arab population without bearing any fruits from the Jewish population (Ha'aretz 20 November 1989).

In the recent Knesset elections (1992) a vocal dispute was evident among the Arabs in Israel regarding the returns Arabs in Israel have had in taking part in the parliamentary politics. Those who expressed their doubts indicated pragmatic reasons, not just ideological ones (interview with Ibrahim Nemir Hussein, May 1992).

The immediate result of the disappointment of Arabs with their peripheral political status was a drop in the turnout among Arabs from 74 percent in the 1988 elections to nearly 69 percent in the 1992 elections. As a matter of fact, this marks a new trend among the Arabs in Israel, after a trend of increasing participation in the Knesset elections during the past decade (figure 6.1).

III. The 1992 Elections

Political and Social Divisions

One of the central issues presented by the Arab public in the 1992 elections was the formation of a unified Arab list. However, this was not the first time that efforts had been made in this direction. In 1977 the DFPE, which was initiated by the Communist Party, was established with the aim of becoming the sole representative of the Arab population. Although it received more than 50 percent of the Arab votes in the 1977 elections, the DFPE failed to become the recognized voice of the Arab population. Furthermore, the goal of universal Arab representation highlighted a contradiction embodied in the very structure of the DFPE itself: its effort to respond to the national orientation of the Arab population and at the same time to preserve its international communist character by maintaining a Jewish-Arab partnership within the party (Al-Haj and Yaniv 1983).

The political unification of the Arab population has remained an unrealized goal. In the 1984 elections the split within the Arab population had just increased when the PLP, headed by Muhammad Miari, was formed. The political split among Arabs was further widened with the declaration of Darawsheh to leave the Labor Party and form a new party—the ADP. Although having similar political platforms, the three predominantly Arab parties failed to unify. In the 1988 elections they even failed to reach a surplus vote agreement, a legal arrangement that regulates the counting of votes not utilized in distributing Knesset seats. As a result they wasted nearly two seats (Ginat 1989).

After the aforementioned elections, strong pressure was exerted by the Arab public on its leadership to set aside personal disputes and unify the ranks. This trend has brought the formation of a unified predominantly Arab list in the 1989 Histadrut elections (*Al-Ittihad* 29 November 1989). This list, however, was not that successful. It gained only 33 percent of the Arab votes, much to the disappointment of the Arab population (Kupty 1992). The reasons behind the relative failure of this list are beyond the scope of this chapter. Nevertheless, one of the reasons that has been repeatedly mentioned is the fact that this list was headed by a Jewish member of the Communist Party. This occurred despite the fact that the list was meant to be purely Arab, with the main support coming from the Arab voters (Kupty 1992).

The attempts to form a unified Arab list received an impetus in the 1992 elections. The raising of the required quota from 1 to 1.5 percent of the nationwide votes (nearly forty thousand votes) was a central catalyst for the efforts in forming a joint Arab list. It was feared that the split of the Arab vote might bring about a situation in which none of the predominantly Arab parties would pass the threshold (Regev 1991). The endeavors of forging a unified Arab list were accelerated by the indirect intervention of Arab leaders outside of Israel. A group of Arab representatives from Israel were invited to Cairo. Ibrahim Hussein, the chairman of the National Committee of Arab Local Authorities, together with Miari and Darawshi, responded to the invitation. It is believed that they met with senior figures of the PLO and the Egyptian government. The discussions focused on the possibility of forming a joint Arab list that would include the predominantly Arab parties (*Al-Hamishmar* 25 April 1992). For this purpose a special committee was formed, and it was headed by the chairman of the National Committee of Arab Local Authorities. The committee held a series of meetings with representatives of the different political groups among the Arab population including DFPE, ADP, PLP, the Islamic Movement, Abna' el-Balad, and the newly formed group called the "independents."[1] However, all the aforementioned efforts proved futile. The main dispute was on the order of the candidates of the ADP and the PLP on the list. Each wanted to head this list and to gain maximum representation for his party. Eventually, the PLP ran on its own, and a representative of the independents (Muhammad Zeidan) joined the

ADP in the third place. The failure of the predominantly Arab parties to form a unified list has just deepened the leadership crisis and increased the gap between the leadership and the public among the Arab population. This has opened the way for the revival of traditional forms of political behavior based on religious and kinship-*hamula* affiliations.

Religious Divisions

Religious origin of candidates played a major role in the composition of most political parties. Labor decided to allocate the twentieth slot for a Muslim candidate and the thirtieth slot for a Druze one. This decision has outraged Christian members of the Labor Party, since the Christian candidate was pushed into a marginal slot (*Kul-Hazafon* 20 March 1992). Leaders of the Labor party sought to prevent a crisis with the Christian community. Subsequently a Christian candidate was allotted the forty-sixth place (*Kul-Hazafon* 20 March 1992). Christians were also disappointed because the Christian candidate was placed only in the fourth place on the DFPE list, which is considered unlikely to win election. The same happened with the Christian candidate in the ADP.

Zionist and non-Zionist parties alike tried to take advantage of this disappointment of the Christians. A group of Christian political activists called for the formation of a Christian party (*el-Sinnarah* 17 April 1992). This attempt was not successful, however, and the group turned to Yitzhak Modai, a former financial minister, in order to join his newly formed list. Modai turned down the request of this group to place a Christian candidate (Wadi Asi, mayor of Fasuota) in the second place. However, Modai promised to consider a financial assistance to the Catholic Church in the Galilee (*Kul-Bo* 27 March 1992).

The PLP also tried to utilize the aforementioned situation in order to attract Christian votes. After the PLP council elected its candidate, the PLP decided to change the order and place a Christian candidate, Saad Khouri, in the second place (*el-Sinnarah* 8 May 1992). This unexpected step was directed to gain the support of the Christian community and was severely criticized by some PLP members (Ghanim, 1992, 21).

Religious solidarity was especially evident among members of the Druze community, even those affiliated with the DFPE, which had denied for a long time the significance of religious and other traditional considerations. In the 1992 elections, however, the situation was radically altered. Druze members of the DFPE strongly protested that the Druze candidate was not placed in a realistic slot (*Jerusalem Post* 18 May 1992). The Likud continued its traditional connection with the Druze community. A Druze candidate, Asad Asad, was elected for a secured place in the Likud slot (29th). This act turned the Labor and the Likud Parties into the main competitors for nearly thirty-three thousand Druze votes.

From Arab-Jewish to Arab Structure

In addition to the religious element, the national element has played a prominent role in the composition of the predominantly Arab parties. In this sense there has been shift in the structure of the predominantly Arab parties from Arab-Jewish to mainly Arab. The ADP, which was formed as an Arab party, has increasingly emphasized its "Arab Character." Throughout the election campaign, Abd el-Wahab Darawshi, the head of the ADP, repeatedly mentioned that the main achievement of his party is the very fact of it being an *Arab* party.

However, the main change toward Arab orientation was manifested by the DFPE and PLP. After forty-four years of being the only genuine Jewish-Arab party, at least at the leadership level, the DFPE made a major step in the 1992 elections toward Arabization. While the list of the Communist Party (and later that of the DFPE) had always been headed by a Jewish member, in the 1992 election an Arab member, Tawfiq Ziad, was placed at the top of the list. A severe dispute came to the forefront regarding the candidacy of Tamar Gozansky. Accusing her of being too Zionist, Arab members opposed her placement in an advanced slot (*Hadashot* 12 April 1992). On the background of this dispute, some veteran Jewish communist members even threatened to quit the party. Eventually Gozanky was elected for the third slot.

The same trend of Arabization also holds true for the PLP. As mentioned earlier, the PLP was established in 1984 as an Arab-Jewish party. But in the 1992 elections this party took on a strong Arab character. In an interview Muhammad Miari, the head of the PLP, justified the decision of Arabization of his list by the changing political circumstances and the electoral voting pool, as the vast majority of his supporters are to be found in the Arab sector (*Zafon I* 10 April 1992).

This trend has outraged some of the Jewish leading members of the PLP. Mati Peled, who was one of the main Jewish partners and a former MK for the PLP, severely criticized the idea of forming a unified Arab party. He defined the idea as an "Arab racism, which is harmful even to the interest of Arabs themselves" (*el-Sinnarah* 17 January 1992).

Citizenship Issues

In the 1992 elections, citizenship issues were placed at the center of the election campaign of each party. While in the 1988 elections national issues, mainly the intifada and the peace process, occupied a central place in the propaganda of the predominantly Arab parties, in the recent elections these parties focused in particular on citizenship equality of the Arab population in Israel.

Citizenship equality was the core issue presented by newly formed Arab political groups. A number of Arab intellectuals from the Galilee (among them Dr. Muhammad Sakran and Dr. Rashid Awisat) announced the establishment of a new movement called "the Avenguard." The members of this movement emphasized that the main issues they will address are equal rights and day-to-day matters (*Ha'aretz* 28 February 1992).

Shortly before the elections a new Arab-Jewish movement was formed under the name of Mitaq el-Musawa, "Constitution for Equality." The founders of this party are mainly ex-members of the Maki, the Israeli Communist Party (*Kul-Haifa* 10 April 1992). The focal point of this movement is citizenship equality, which, according to the movement, could be achieved only by changing the character of the State of Israel from Jewish-Zionist to a state for all its citizens. In addition, this movement requests autonomy for the Arabs in Israel, including autonomous administration for their educational and cultural institutions. Eventually this list decided not to run in the Knesset elections (*el-Sinnarah* 17 April 1992).

Voting Behavior

The massive support given by Arabs to the Jewish-Zionist parties was one of the main features of the 1992 elections. These parties received, for the first time, more than 50 percent of the Arab vote (table 6.2). Except for Meretz, all the Zionist parties gained more support among Arabs than they did in former elections (1988).

Undoubtedly, Meretz had hoped to increase its power among Arabs, mainly among educated youth. These hopes were not baseless, since in the 1988 election both Ratz and Mapam (two of the three components of Meretz) received 8 percent of the vote. But the failure of Ratz to place any of its Arab members in an advanced place on the list outraged the Arab supporters. The only secured place for an Arab (ninth place) was designated by Mapam for Walid Sadiq. However, Meretz had already lost some of its sympathy it had among Arabs before the elections. This occurred in the wake of the attack of Yossi Sarid, one of the prominent members of Ratz, on the PLO because of its support to Iraq during the Gulf War.

All Zionist parties have sought to share the Arab vote since 1949 (Shokeid 1982; Nakhleh 1975). Their approach toward the Arab population was based on paternalism and individual interest (Ben-Rafael 1982, 215). Hence, they had maneuvered through local Arab *hamula* heads and notables in order to minimize their costs and maximize their gains. They received between 25 and 50 percent of the Arab votes (table 6.1).

The Zionist parties' traditional tactics were to argue that only through establishment parties can Arabs promote their case. This approach was especially adopted by the Labor Party (Shokeid 1982). The National Religious Party (Mafdal) adopted a particularistic approach. The party's long-standing

Table 6.2. The Arab Vote in the Twelfth and the Thirteenth Knesset Elections

Parties	DFPE	Labor	PLP	ADP	Meretz	Likud	Mafdal	Shas	Other	Total
Years										
1988 12th Knesset	33.4	16.4	14.3	11.3	10.6	6.7	3.1	0.5	3.7	100.0
1992 13th Knesset	23.2	20.3	9.2	15.2	9.7	8.4	4.8	4.9	4.3	100.0

Note: The results are based on the findings provided by the elections central committee. These findings do not include the voting of mixed Jewish-Arab cities, where about 10 percent of the Arabs live.

control of the Ministry of the Interior and the Ministry of Religions allowed it to penetrate the Arab communities, through its connections with traditional leadership (Al-Haj and Rosenfeld 1990). The Likud, unlike other Zionist parties, sought from its inception to concentrate on two main particularistic groups: the Druze and the Bedouins.

The aforementioned tactics were also evident in the 1992 Knesset elections, with Shas joining the search for Arab votes. The latter (a Sephardic Orthodox party) has partially replaced the Mafdal (National Religious Party) not only among Jews but among Arabs as well. By controlling the Ministry of the Interior, Shas has gained a very important tool for political recruitment, since the Arab minority in Israel is highly dependent on this ministry. The limited access of Arabs to the national opportunity structure has increased the importance of Arab local authorities as a channel for the allocation of resources and benefits. The failure of the government ministries to hire Arab university graduates turns local authorities into major employers. These graduates are forced to compete for jobs in their localities, whether within the municipal administrative system or in secondary schools, where teachers are hired by the municipality. The projects carried out by the municipalities also become an important economic source for contractors and entrepreneurs. In addition, even Arab localities lacking municipal status are dependent on the Ministry of the Interior in order to gain formal recognition (Al-Haj and Rosenfeld 1990).

This background may explain the fact that a number of Arab mayors justified their support for Shas in the 1992 elections by the need to develop their communities. For example Abu-Romi, who is the mayor of Tamra and is affiliated with the DFPE, insisted that he supported Shas in order to "respond to the needs of the local population and to secure more budgets and services" (*Ha'aretz* 20 July 1992). Whether or not Abu-Romi was accurately projecting Shas's impact on his community, his support increased the votes Shas received in Tamra from 3 in the 1988 elections to 570 in the 1992 elections. The same holds true for Baqa el-Gharbiyyeh, where Shas gained 1,050 votes in the 1992 elections as compared to only 3 votes in the 1988 elections, due to the support of a local politician (*Ha'aretz* 20 July 1992).

Traditionally, the Arabs in Israel have been close allies for left-wing parties (from the Labor Party left). However, since the Likud came to power in 1977, this situation has somewhat changed, albeit gradually. The Likud has based itself as an establishment party through the allocation of personal benefits and the cooptation of some local leaders. But it was clear for the Likud that its effect among Arabs is mainly limited to traditional groups, in particular Druze and Bedouins. In the 1992 elections the Likud secured a place for a Druze candidate with the aim of attracting support from the Druze community. Indeed the Likud was the second largest party voted for among the Druze. It received about 27 percent of the Druze votes while the Labor Party received 31 percent (Institute for Israel Arab Studies 1992, 17). Altogether the right-wing parties received 18.1 percent of the Arab votes in 1992, as compared to 14 percent in 1988. That is to say, despite the slight increase in support of Jewish right-wing parties, the vast majority of Arabs (about 78 percent) voted for what are considered to be left-wing parties.

Except for the Arab Democratic Party (led by Darawshi), the other predominantly Arab parties lost a considerable part of their power among the Arab population. The PLP was the main loser. The votes it received were not enough to meet the minimum vote quota. Therefore after eight years of activity it failed to gain representation in the Knesset.

It has been repeatedly argued that the PLP failed because the Arab voters were disappointed by the refusal of its leader, Muhammad Miari, to join with the ADP in a united Arab list (see Institute for Israeli-Arab Studies 1992, 2). This argument might be partially true. However, it would be simplistic to think that one reason is responsible for this result. To this explanation we should add the poor organizational base of the PLP, the internal competition and disputes within the party, the shift of the Arab public interest from national issues to citizenship matters, and the clear stand of PLO representatives in favor of the ADP.

As indicated earlier, the PLP was the only predominantly Arab party to continue focusing first and foremost on national issues, including Palestinian symbols, the intifada, and Palestinian identity. It seems that Arab voters chose rather to support those parties inclined to improving their day-to-day life and enhancing integration of Arabs into Israeli society. In addition, even before the elections Palestinian representatives were quoted as saying that the PLP should quit in favor of the ADP because the former held less of a chance winning, and if both of them ran there was the risk that neither would pass the required quota.

Muhammed Miari argued that these declarations were "just a joke" created by Darawshi to promote his own interests. Miari even published a letter, signed by Arafat, indicating that the PLO had no intentions of intervening in the dispute between Arab parties (*el-Sinnarah* 22 May 1992).

The DFPE also decreased in power from 33.4 percent of the Arab vote in the 1988 elections to 23.2 percent in the 1992 elections. The loss of the DFPE was fairly well expected in the light of the decline of the communist ideology all over the world and the internal divisions with the DFPE itself. Some of the DFPE leaders even expressed their satisfaction at losing only one seat in the Parliament since the expected result was much worse (table 6.2).

The DFPE suffered a loss in almost all Arab settlements except for some localities in the Galilee. In Umm el-Fahm, the largest Arab town in the Triangle, the DFPE received about two-thirds of the vote in 1992 as compared to 45 percent in the 1988 elections (see report of the Institute for Israeli Arab Studies 1992, 7). The same trend holds true for Muawiya, a nearby small village, where the DFPE received 50 percent of the votes in the 1992 elections. This can be attributed to the fact that the MK Hashim Mahamid originated from one of the largest *hamulas* in Umm el-Fahm, one that also extends to nearby villages. Therefore, support for the DFPE mainly reflects solidarity with MK Mahamid on an individual and *hamula* basis. Aside from these localities, the DFPE lost considerable support among all other segments of the Arab population: in urban localities it has decreased from 43.1 percent in 1988 to 32.7 in 1992; in large villages from 35.7 to 22.2; in small villages from 19.8 to 11.5; in Bedouin settlements from 4.3 to 2.8; and in Druze villages from 15.7 to 7 percent (Osetzky-Lazar 1992, 15–17).

The decrease in support of the DFPE among the Druze by almost 50 percent may be explained against the background of their disappointment that the Druze candidate was pushed to a marginal place. Druze voters shifted to the Labor party to support the Druze candidate. This result formed a considerable loss for the DFPE among a traditional segment of the Arab population in which the DFPE invested a lot of energy and resources over a long time in order to gain a stronghold. As mentioned earlier, the ADP was the only Arab party to increase its power among Arab voters (from 11.3 percent in 1988 to 15.2 percent in 1992). The fact that the ADP presented itself as a unified Arab list after forming a coalition with the independent group led by Muhammad Zeidan reinforced its stand among the Arab population. Moreover, the fact that Abdallah Nimr Darwish (one of the leaders of the Islamic Movement) and Ibrahim Hussein (the chairman of the National Committee for Arab Local Authorities) strongly supported Darawshi contributed to his success among Arabs. It should be indicated, however, that Darawshi appealed especially to traditional segments and leadership among the Arab population. The ADP was the only party to give an advanced place to a Bedouin candidate (Talab el-Sani). This party came in first among Bedouins in the Negev, receiving 38 percent of the votes. In some of the Bedouin tribes the ADP had a sweeping victory. It received 75 percent in Abu-Ruqayq, 60 percent in al-Asam, and 56.8 percent in Aroar (Report of the Institute for Israeli Arab Studies 1992, 13).

In the Aftermath of the Elections

As indicated earlier, the support of the Arab voters for the Labor Party and Meretz, has contributed to the restoration of the Labor Party dominance after nearly fifteen years in which the Likud was in power. For this reason, the Likud and other right-wing parties accused the new government of being dependent on Arab support. This sentiment was strongly expressed by

Sharon, the former housing minister. In an article published in *Yediot Aharonot* (3 July 1992) he indicated:

> the genuine political upheaval in the state of Israel did not occur in 1977 but in 1992, since the rise of the Likud just replaced one Jewish political block by another. In the 1992 elections a completely different thing took place and it is worrisome and scary: For the first time in the history of the state [Israel], the Arab minority—in particular the anti-Zionist part amongst it— has determined who will be in power in the State of Israel and who will shape its future.

Representatives of the Labor Party also praised the contribution of the Arab vote for assuring a majority block against right-wing parties (*Jerusalem Post* 26 June 1992). Sheikh Abdallah Nimr Darwish, one of the leaders of the Islamic Movement, indicated in an interview that he was pleased with the results of the Knesset elections. He added that these results form a victory for Israelis and Palestinians who advocate the principle of peace in exchange for territory. But Sheikh Darwish added that the real test now is to see whether Rabin will activate that principle (Institute for Israeli-Arab Studies 1992, 8).

The questions might be asked, Has the aforementioned fact brought about a turning point in the political status of the Arabs in Israel? What are the returns of the massive political support given by the Arab voters to the Zionist parties? It is too soon to fully answer these questions. Nevertheless, some initial conclusions may already be drawn.

The structure of the new coalition does not bear any change whatsoever, as far as the partnership of the Arab parties is concerned. For the time being this coalition, which is composed of sixty-two MKs, includes three parties: Labor (forty-four MKs), Meretz (twelve MKs), and Shas (six MKs). The role of the predominantly Arab parities is confined to supplying tacit support without taking any part in the coalition. This is so despite the fact that the ADP, led by Darawshi, expressed its wish to join the government coalition and asked for the appointment of an Arab minister (*Ma'ariv* 24 June 1992). This wish, however, has not been met and among the sixteen ministers in the Labor government there are no Arabs. It is true that two Arabs were appointed as deputy ministers (Walid Sadiq, deputy minister of agriculture, and Nawaf Massalhah, deputy minister of health). However, this does not form a turning point since in the 1970s two Arabs served in the post of deputy minister (Abd el-Aziz Zuabi, deputy minister of health, and Gabir Moadi, deputy minister of transportation). In addition, even these deputy ministers complained of their marginal status and limited authority (interview with Walik Sadiq, 14 December 1992).

The developments after the 1992 elections have increased the disappointment of Arabs because of the wide gap between expectations and reality. Salim Jubran, a prominent Arab intellectual, expressed this disappointment:

> in the recent Knesset elections all Zionist parties sought to gain the support of Arab voters. Without the Arab vote the Labor Party could not come to power. It received direct support of Arab voters and the support of the Arab Knesset members. But nothing has occurred as far as the participation of Arab MKs is concerned. They have remained marginal as before, having no position in the new government. The Labor Party wants the Arabs as voters, not partners. In this sense, the Arab votes are kosher but the Arab MKs are not." (Interview 9 October 1992; see also his article in *Al-Hamishmar* 11 November 1992)

The minor returns for the Arabs despite their contribution to the political change is also reflected in the agreements signed between the Labor Party on the one hand and the DFPE and ADP, on the other. As a matter of fact, these agreements are more a statement of intentions that goes hand in hand with the declared policy of the Labor Party regarding peace, social issues, equality for the Arab population in Israel, and legislation as unpublished letters from the Labor Party to the DFPE and the ADP on 9 July 1992 indicate.

The part of the agreements concerning citizenship rights of the Arab minority in Israel includes twenty-seven points that cover different fields where the Arabs are discriminated against. Throughout several points the Labor Party declares that the new government will pursue the full integration of Arabs in all areas and bridge the gaps between Arab and Jewish settlements in the fields of education, industry, agriculture, social services, health services, and employment of Arab university graduates. It was promised that a series of committees would be formed in order to investigate the Muslim endowments (Waqf), the irrigation of the lands of el-batouf, the forty unrecognized villages, and other related issues. In this agreement it was promised that within six months a committee would be created, headed by the prime minister, to deal with the issues of Arab education, budgets for Arab local authorities, the issue of "illegal houses," the inclusion of Arab settlements in the project of "neighborhood renovation," and regulations of property tax.

Undoubtedly this agreement includes many important points, which, if fulfilled, would tremendously improve the status and conditions of the Arab populations. However, the way the agreement is presented and phrased makes it a mere statement of intentions that does not necessarily commit the Labor Party to implement its promises. Therefore, the agreement has been severely criticized by the Arab public. The changes mentioned in this agreement have been described as cosmetic, as leading to no tangible improvement in the situation of the Arab population (interview with MK Hashim Mahamid 12 November 1992).

It should be indicated that the document presented by the Labor Party to the DFPE and the ADP does not include any breakthrough in terms of the official collective status of the Arabs in Israel. It relates to Arabs as a cultural and religious minority, rather than as a national minority (Institute for Israeli-Arab Studies 1992, 4). In addition, it ignores many of the requests of the predominantly Arab parties in terms of the Palestinian issue and equal rights for the Arab citizens.

IV. Concluding Remarks

This chapter deals with the political behavior among the Arabs in Israel in the 1992 Knesset elections. Our analysis shows two contradictory trends. At the organizational-leadership level there was a clear transition from Arab-Jewish organizations to mainly Arab organizations. This was reflected in the new reorganization of the predominantly Arab parties. In the DFPE the role of the Jewish members imminently decreased, and an Arab member was placed, for the first time, at the top of the list. The same held true with the PLP, where the Jewish-Arab partnership has almost come to an end. The trend toward political segregation among Arabs was also manifested by the unsuccessful endeavors to form a unified Arab list.

At the individual-public level there was an opposite trend toward increasing support of Zionist-Jewish parties. This was reflected in the fact that for the first time these parties received more than 50 percent of the Arab votes. In this sense, except for Meretz, all the Jewish parties increased their power among Arabs.

These contradictory trends highlight the gap that exists among Arabs between leadership and public. The failure to form a unified Arab list has just intensified the leadership vacuum among Arabs and enabled Jewish parties to attract more Arab votes. It has also opened the way for the resurgence of traditional forms of political behavior, including the manifestation of kinship-*hamula* and religious solidarity.

However, these two contradictory trends do not reflect different political orientations, since they are only tactical and not strategic. In this sense both the Arab leadership and public have adopted an adjustment strategy in which citizenship issues are placed at the center. Unlike the 1988 elections, where national-Palestinian issues were placed at the first priority in the propaganda of the predominantly Arab parties, in the 1992 elections the status and rights of the Arab citizens came to the forefront. In addition, along with the Arabization of the predominantly Arab parties, the leaders of these parties declared their will to participate in the national power center by supporting a Labor-Meretz coalition.

Our analysis has indicated that while the Arabs in Israel have contributed to the restoration of the Labor regime, the benefits of Arabs from this political upheaval have been so far negligible. Predominantly Arab parties are still considered an illegitimate partner in a government coalition. In addition, these elections have not brought, as yet, any breakthrough in the integration of the Arabs in the decision making apparatus. The declaration of intentions of the new government toward Arabs is elusive and not binding. This declaration merely aimed at securing the support of predominantly Arab parties in order to block the possibility of forming a Likud government while concurrently increasing the maneuvering power of the Labor party.

We may conclude that despite adopting an adjustment strategy, Arabs are still placed in the margins of the parliamentary politics. This fact, along with the transition to Arab political organization, may just reinforce political segregation among the Arab minority in Israel. As a result, two directions may evolve simultaneously. At the parliamentary level, we may hypothesize that there will be further Arabization of the DFPE and increasing pressure to form a unified Arab list. At the local level, we may expect to see an increasing importance of local government and autonomous institutions among Arabs, including the reorganization of extra-parliamentary organizations. The latter direction may be strongly supported by the Islamic Movement, Abna'el-balad, and other groups that find it difficult to take part in parliamentary politics because of the Jewish-Zionist character of the State of Israel.

Note

1. The "independents" are composed of several local council members, intellectuals, and prominent figures among the Arabs (*Jerusalem Post*, 1 January 1992).

References

Ben-Rafael, Eliezer. 1982. *The Emergence of Ethnicity: Cultural Groups and Social Conflict in Israel.* Westport: Greenwood Press.

Benziman, Uzi, and Atallah Mansour. 1992. *Subtenants* (in Hebrew). Jerusalem: Keter Publishing House.

Carmi, Shulamit, and Henry Rosenfeld. 1988. *Changes in Class-National Relations in Palestine-Israel: A Political Economy Perspective.* Tel Aviv: International Center for Peace in the Middle East.

Central Bureau of Statistics. 1989. *Statistical Abstract of Israel, 1989.* No. 40. Jerusalem: Central Bureau of Statistics.

Cohen, Abner. 1965. *Arab Border Villages in Israel.* Manchester: Manchester University Press.

Galnoor, Itzhak. 1989. "The Israeli Elections: The Flight from Freedom and Responsibility." *Tikun* 4 no. 1:38–40.

Ghanim, Asad. 1992. *The Arabs in Israel towards the Elections for the 13th Knesset* (in Hebrew). Givaat Haviva: Institute for Arab Studies.

Ginat, Joseph. 1989. "Voting Patterns and Political Behavior in the Arab Sector" (in Hebrew). In *The Arab Vote in Israel's Parliamentary Elections, 1988,* ed. Jacob Landau, 3–21. Jerusalem: Jerusalem Institute for Israel Studies.

Abu-Gosh, Subhi. 1972. "The Election Campaign in the Arab Sector." In *The Elections in Israel—1969,* ed. A. Arian, 239–52. Jerusalem: Jerusalem Academic Press.

Hadashot, 12 April 1992 (in Hebrew).

Al-Haj, Majid. 1990. "Elections under the Shadow of the Intifada in the Arab Sector in Israel: Advertisement and Results." In *The Elections for the 12th Knesset among the Arab Population in Israel,* ed., J. Landau. Jerusalem: Jerusalem Center for Israeli Studies.

Al-Haj, Majid, and Henry Rosenfeld. 1989. "The Emergence of an Indigenous Political Framework in Israel: The National Committee of Chairmen of Arab Local Authorities. *Asian and African Studies* 23:205–44.

———. 1990. *Arab Local Government in Israel.* Boulder: Westview Press.

Al-Haj, Majid, and Avner Yaniv. 1983. "Uniformity or Diversity: A Reappraisal of the Voting Behavior of the Arab Minority in Israel." In *The Elections in Israel—1981,* ed. A. Arian, 139–64. New Brunswick, NJ: Transaction.

Institute for Israel Arab Studies. 1992. "The Arab Sector and the Knesset Elections, 1992" Beit Berl: Institute for Arab Studies. *Kul-Bo* 27 March 1992.

Kupty, Makram. 1992. "The Experience of the Joint List for the Histadrut Elections: Its Repercussions on the Political Behavior of the Arabs in Israel" (in Arabic). In *The Arab Citizen and the 1992 Elections,* ed. Makram Kupty, 79–99. Nazareth: The Galilee Research Center.

Landau, Jacob M. 1969. *The Arabs in Israel: A Political Study.* London: Oxford University Press.

Lustick, Ian. 1980. *Arabs in the Jewish State: Israel's Control of a National Minority.* Austin: University of Texas Press.

Mari, Sami. 1988. "Sources of Conflict in Arab-Jewish Relations in Israel." In *Jewish Arab Relations in Israel: A Quest in Human Understanding,* ed. John Hofman, 21–44. Bristol: Wyndam Hall Press.

Nakhleh, Khalil. 1975. "The Direction of Local Level Conflict in Two Arab Villages in Israel." *American Ethnologist* 23 (August):497–516.

Osetzky-Lazar, Sara. 1992. *The Elections for the 13th Knesset among the Arabs in Israel* (in Hebrew). Givat Haviva: Center for Arab Studies.

Regev, Avner. 1991. "Everything Depends on the Required Quota" (in Hebrew). *Al-Hamishmar* 13 October.

Rekhess, Eli. 1989. "The Arabs in Israel and the Territories: A Political Linkage and National Solidarity (1967–1988)" (in Hebrew). *Hamezrah Hehadash* 1989:165–91.

Rosenfeld, Henry. 1978. "The Class Situation of the Arab National Minority in Israel." *Comparative Studies in Society and History* 20 no. 3 July: 374–407.

Rouhana, Nadim. 1989. "The Political Transformation of the Palestinians in Israel: From Acquiescence to Challenge." *Journal of Palestine Studies* 18 no. 3 Spring:38–59.

Shokeid, Moshe. 1982. "The Arab Vote and the Israeli Party System." In *Distant Relations, Ethnicity and Politics among Arabs and North African Jews in Israel.* New York: Praeger.

Smooha, Sammy. 1980. "The Control of Minorities in Israel and Northern Ireland." *Comparative Studies in Society and History* 22 no. 2 April:256–80.

———. 1989. *Arabs and Jews in Israel: Conflicting and Shared Attitudes in a Divided Society.* Vol. 1. Boulder: Westview Press.

CHAPTER 7

Voting Trends of Recent Immigrants from the Former Soviet Union

AHARON FEIN

Tazpit Research Institute, Jerusalem

I. Introduction

Interest in the political positions of immigrants to Israel from the republics of the former Soviet Union began during 1990 when it became clear that the number of such immigrants was growing from month to month and that their percentage of the voting public in Israel was becoming most significant. This attention reached a high level after what was an average yearly immigration of some fifteen thousand in the early 1980s rose to the same number arriving per month beginning with the end of that decade (Florsheim 1991).

The particular interest in the political positions of these immigrants was influenced to a certain extent by the political situation that was created in Israel as a result of the 1984 and 1988 elections. In those elections a clear victory was achieved, by neither the right-wing bloc, led by the Likud, nor the left-wing bloc, led by Labor. The general feeling that developed as a result of the new immigration was that these immigrants constituted a new factor in Israeli society that would likely bring about an end to the political deadlock that had developed among the veteran citizenry over a period of years. This deadlock necessitated numerous compromises in the creation of coalition governments and in the decision-making process involving the peace initiative with the Arab states, as well as in the economic and social spheres.

In this article we shall attempt to examine the voting trends of the immigrants from the former Soviet Union and to evaluate their influence on the results of the Israeli elections of June 1992. With the aid of information gathered in a series of surveys conducted among these immigrants prior to the elections, we shall try to identify the processes that contributed to the formation of their political stance. These surveys were carried out by the Tazpit Research Institute once every few months during the period between April 1990 and May 1992. In each survey the sample consisted of eight hundred immigrants who arrived in Israel between September 1989 and up to two months before the date on which the survey was taken. We also sought to identify the experience of these immigrants as voters undergoing the process of socialization under a democratic regime.

II. The Electoral Power of the Immigrants

During the period between September 1989 and June 1992, 375 thousand immigrants arrived in Israel from the former USSR republics. Since under the Israeli Law of Return, Jews are entitled to receive Israeli citizenship upon request, these immigrants received Israeli citizenship immediately upon their entry into Israel. This citizenship conferred upon each immigrant eighteen years of age and older the right to vote. For technical reasons, this voting right was in fact granted to all of those who had arrived by mid-March 1992, by which time the official voting list was established. As a result, 240 thousand new immigrants from the former Soviet Union received notification of their inclusion in the voting register and of their right to participate in the elections.

The wave of immigrants that arrived in Israel from the former Soviet Union up to mid-March 1992 increased the country's total population by 7 percent. Since the percentage of older people among these immigrants was relatively higher than in the veteran Israeli population, the actual percentage of the new immigrants in terms of eligible voters reached 8 percent. This meant that the immigrants had the potential voting power to elect between 9 and 10 representatives to the 120-member Knesset. This number is based on the assumption that the total of immigrants exercising their right to vote would be 10 percent lower than in the veteran population.

Information on elections held in Israel in the past would indicate that about 80 percent of the eligible voters actually exercised their right to vote. Taking into consideration that hundreds of thousands of eligible voters are not in the country on any given election day (Israeli law does not provide for absentee voting by mail), it can be estimated safely that approximately 90 percent of those eligible voters who were in the country on election days did actually vote, with only 10 percent failing to do so.

Among new immigrants, nearly all of those who were eligible to vote in the June 1992 elections were in the country on election day. Assuming that 20 percent of them would not exercise their voting right, their potential to influence the election outcome would still be proportionally equal to that of the veteran population (i.e., 80 percent). From surveys taken just before the elections, it became clear that 75 percent of the immigrants were certain that they would go to the polls on election day. Among the remaining 25 percent, the level of that certainty was lower. It is noteworthy that on election day in Israel, the various political parties operate extensive operations intended to bring reluctant voters to the polls. If needed, these operations help in providing easier access to polling stations and in arranging transportation to the polls.

The high level of awareness regarding the electoral power of the immigrants created great interest in those processes influencing the determination of their political positions and their voting trends. This also found expression in the survey activities that attempted to follow this process.

III. Determination of Political Positions

The process of absorption and adaptation to a new society and environment is a complex one of desocialization, in which the immigrant separates himself from certain norms to which he had become accustomed in the country of his origin, and resocialization, in which the immigrant learns new norms that are acceptable to the new society in which he hopes to become absorbed. These processes of desocialization and resocialization in the political sphere were most radical in particular for the immigrants from the former Soviet Union. These immigrants had to undergo an experience of passage from a communist society, which had limited their freedom of expression and political organization, to a democratic society which permitted substantial rights of expression and political organization. In contrast to their former situation, the immigrants found in Israel a wide range of parties and party organizations that they were asked to join. They were made aware as well of the possibility of creating new political alternatives (Yishai 1981).

Additionally, their experiences had been as residents of a large nation, in which the political influence of each voter is rather small, but the immigrants discovered that in Israel the individual voter has substantial influence: a relatively small group of twenty-three thousand voters was sufficient in 1992 to elect one member to the Knesset. The immigrants also learned that one such Knesset member, whose vote may be crucial to the establishment of a government coalition, can influence the allocation of resources and the furthering of interests that are important to the voter, and that his or her lone vote can influence decisions made by the government and the Knesset.

Aiding the immigrants in learning to recognize the political dynamics in Israel and to understand their own electoral power were the many articles that were published on the subject in the Russian language press, in the Russian language electronic media, and also in information provided to them by politicians.

The immigrants were made aware of the possibility of creating a separate political framework as well as the possibility of their becoming integrated into the existing political establishments. This process of political socialization operated among the immigrants at a different pace than the parallel socialization processes in other areas related to their absorption (Horowitz 1978). In those other areas, which required the learning of prevailing societal norms, each immigrant had to proceed at a pace that was compatible with individual characteristics, personal needs, and the environment in which the immigrant found herself or himself.

In the political area, the fixed election date dictated to a great extent the pace and the time in which the immigrant had to make a decision. The formation of political positions of the immigrants did not take place in a vacuum. Various elements relating to the areas of contention among the Israeli political parties, especially involving the peace issue, were a part of this process. In the background, there were critical murmurings as to the success of the government in coping with immigrant absorption problems. The immigrants could not remain apathetic to matters relating to the absorption process. In many instances one could see the constant connection that was made, sometimes not at the immigrants' initiative themselves, between the immigration absorption process and the effort to direct the immigrants toward forming certain political stands. For example, the minister of absorption, who at the time was a member of the Shas religious party, directed resources toward bringing the immigrants closer to the Orthodox religious outlook. This activity, which provided certain benefits to the immigrants, was intended to encourage a more favorable outlook not only toward religion but also toward religious parties. This matter was subject to a great deal of criticism from the secular parties as well as from the immigrants themselves, who dissociated themselves from it since in most cases their own Jewish identification was not in harmony with the Orthodox Jewish approach. In this way, the immigration absorption process became a political issue in which the immigrants found themselves in the midst of the debate and sometimes were even asked to state their own positions on the matter, and they did.

In one area one could see the activities of the leftist parties, especially Meretz, which sought at every opportunity to examine whether immigration absorption was not being utilized to increase the settlement in the territories captured in the Six Days war. This was accompanied by exposure of the immigrants to the issue of the territories taken in 1967 and attempts to expose them to the vehement public debate over the possibility of relinquishing territories for peace. The United States, which granted $400 million in loan guarantees for immigrant absorption, also demanded commitments that this money would not be used to direct immigrants to homes in those disputed territories, and even asked later to inspect those territories to ascertain that indeed immigrants had not settled in those areas (General Accounting Office 1992). In this connection, one can see how the immigrants found themselves at the center of a political struggle, while they themselves were engaged in trying to solve their housing problems.

Additionally, the opposition parties of the time, led by Labor, accused the Likud government of not doing enough for immigrant absorption and not providing reasonable services in terms of employment opportunities or construction of housing for the immigrants. These claims received a certain reinforcement from the government comptroller's reports, which pointed to a lack of proper allocation of resources intended for furthering immigrant absorption. The immigrants found themselves, in the midst of this political muddle, at the center of a bitter confrontation between the political parties in the run-up to the elections.

In principle, the immigrants understood that there were two main possibilities: (1) organize a political framework of their own and concentrate their electoral power in an immigrant political party or (2) spread their strength and join existing parties. In any case, they understood that they had to solidify their political stands and to act accordingly on election day.

Regarding those issues that were current, the immigrants came to understand that the veteran voters were especially absorbed with the debate over the peace process and the possibility of exchange of territories for peace. On the domestic side, the question of the honesty of public officials occupied a central position. In contrast, the immigrants were mainly interested in problems involving housing, employment, and overall absorption into the country (Wolffsohn 1987).

The heightened consciousness of the immigrants from the former Soviet Union of their political strength and the identification of thousands of immigrants who came to Israel from the Soviet Union during the 1970s and 1980s as an element that could lend a hand to political organizations presented to the new immigrants the possibility of establishing their own immigrants' party. This possibility aroused great interest among the immigrants even before they actually got into the practicalities of establishing a party and choosing political leaders.

Figure 7.1 presents the position the immigrants regarding an immigrant party. One can see that in the first stages of the election campaign there was a relatively high interest in establishing an immigrants' party. This interest decreased steadily as the election drew closer. In the end, despite the fact that there were two parties in the running that identified themselves as immigrant parties, neither one succeeded in winning enough votes to gain the minimum 1.5 percent of the total vote required in order to elect a representative to the Knesset. In April 1991, a bit over a year before the elections, 53 percent of the immigrants tended toward support of an immigrants'

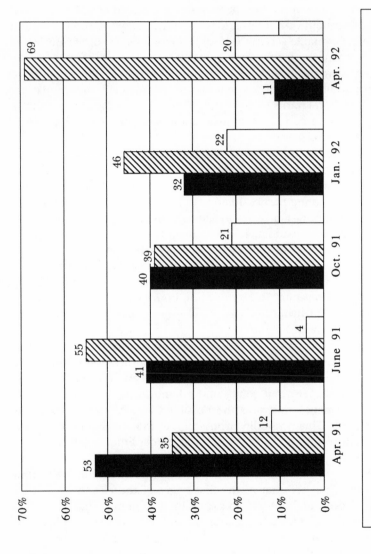

Figure 7.1. Support for Immigrants' Party and Veteran Parties

party. In a survey taken in April 1992, just two months before the elections, only 11 percent still said that they would support an immigrants' party.

A partial explanation of the reduced support for an immigrants' party can be seen in the correlation between the amount of time the immigrant had been in the country and endorsement of a party of immigrants. Analysis of the relationship between amount of time in the country and support for an immigrants' party, in each of the surveys, clearly exhibits this direct inverse relationship. Since the height of the immigration occurred in 1990, when some 189 thousand immigrants came to Israel from the Soviet Union, the first survey of April 1991 covered, for the most part, those who had been in the country a relatively short period of time; they tended more toward support of an immigrants' party.

Thereafter, in 1991 and early 1992, immigration fell, which meant that the percentage of immigrants who had been in the country for a longer period and underwent a process of acculturation rose in the later poll surveys. This contributed to the reduction of support for an immigrants' party in those surveys and their total failure in the elections.

The connection between amount of time in the country and the reduction in support for an immigrants' party can be viewed to some extent as an indication of successful absorption, since the immigrants were able to find for themselves political frameworks that suited their political views. Looked at in this way, an immigrants' party can actually be said to be an antithesis to absorption and interaction with the existing society. The experience of absorbing the immigration from the former Soviet Union does not, therefore, point toward signs of discrimination by the larger society, nor does it indicate resistance to accept those immigrants and to integrate them into the social and economic system. The immigrants felt keenly the openness of the veteran society to accept them. Additionally, the successful absorption of those immigrants who came to Israel from the Soviet Union in the 1970s proved to the newer immigrants that they were indeed welcome to become integrated into Israeli society (Voronel 1976).

Further, these new immigrants began to find themselves being accepted for positions in universities, hospitals, industry, research, services, and other areas. The more veteran an immigrant was, the less likely that he would be attracted to support an immigrants' party. The immigrants had the feeling that the various elements of society were working to assist in their absorption and that this absorption did have a high national priority. The criticism that existed concerned the absorption activities and focused mainly on the efficiency of the services offered and the way in which resources were being used to further the process.

IV. Issues and Party Preferences

The extent of support by the Israeli public for relinquishing territory captured in 1967 in exchange for peace has been seen in recent years—and particularly prior to the elections of June 1992—as one of the major factors in Israeli politics. Thus, supporters of rightist parties tend to oppose concession of territory in exchange for peace, while supporters of left-wing parties tend to demonstratively support this possibility. The immigrants were exposed to this issue within the framework of their socialization process involving Israeli politics. Along with exercising their right to vote, the immigrants had to form their own positions on this issue, which, for the veteran citizens, at least, constituted a broad indication of political leanings.

From the data shown in figure 7.2, one can see a general tendency of opposition by the immigrants to concession of territory for peace. This tendency was rather steady until the Gulf War at the beginning of 1991 and became even slightly more firm immediately after the war. According to the numbers obtained in April 1991, 75 percent of the immigrants opposed such concessions within the framework of a peace agreement with Arab states.

Thereafter, one can see a trend of weakening in the support of that position, and in January 1992 only 54 percent opposed relinquishing territory for peace. This trend was mirrored by an increase in the percentage of immigrants who supported conceding territory for peace as well as an increase in the number of those who were still undecided on this issue. Under the assumption that the attitude of the immigrants toward concession of territory for peace could be seen as a sign of their support for parties of the right or the left, then the reduction in opposition to concession could be seen as a reduction in their support for the right-wing parties as well.

But it is important to see these trends in light of another issue that troubled the immigrants: their absorption problems. On the face of it these two issues are different, yet the parties of the left succeeded in linking the two by arguing that their problems could be alleviated if the money invested by the government in the territories would be allocated to immigrant absorption. The U.S. government's policy in early 1992 gave credence to this linkage. It demanded that the Likud government stop its building projects in Judea, Samaria, and Gaza so as to be eligible for the $10 billion in loan guarantees designated to help in the immigrant absorption process. This left no doubt as to the relationship between the two issues. Thus the immigrants were faced with a dilemma, whether to support the Likud policy that rejected these demands, thus jeopardizing the loans needed for adequate immigrant absorption, or to compromise along the positions of the left parties.

The change in the position of the immigrants regarding concession of territories can be explained as a result of this link, which was underscored by

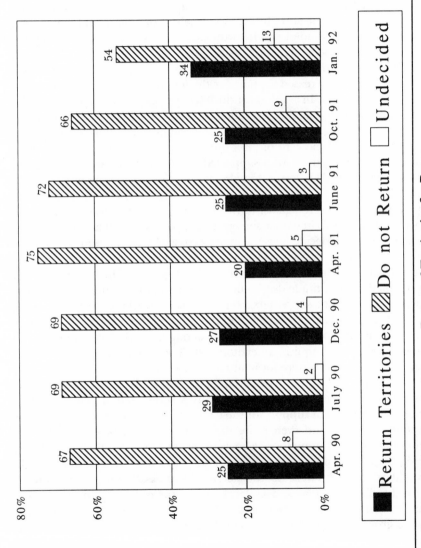

Figure 7.2. Immigrants' Tendency to Agree on Return of Territories for Peace

the opposition parties of the time (in particular the Labor and Meretz), between investment in the territories and the government's inability to allocate adequate resources for immigrant absorption. This resulted in creating a rising trend among the immigrants to see the advantage in conceding territory. One can also say, in a general way, that the extended and intensive efforts made by Labor and Meretz to put before the immigrant voters their political positions yielded results, with many of the immigrants accepting their arguments on the territorial issue.

Whether for the first or the second reason, the trend corresponded to a degree with their increased support for the left-wing bloc and their reduced support for the right. In a survey conducted in January 1992, 56 percent of the immigrants thought that the government should agree to the U.S. demands to freeze new building projects in Judea Samaria and Gaza so as to receive the loan guarantees; 33 percent did not think so, even if it jeopardized the loan guarantees. Among those who supported territorial concessions, 84 percent were for accepting U.S. terms, but also among those who opposed giving up territories, 42 percent were willing to accept the American dictate. In that survey, 54 percent were against territorial concessions for peace, down from more than two-thirds in earlier surveys. It is apparent then that when the new immigrants had to decide between their needs and their position on the territories, the level of opposition to territorial concession was reduced, and they came closer to the political positions of the left parties. The dilemma is well represented in the attitude distribution of the immigrants within each political bloc. Among left-bloc supporters, 80 percent supported accepting U.S. terms for obtaining the loan guarantees, but the split between support and opposition to territorial concessions was 52:40. Among the right-bloc adherents, 75 percent opposed relinquishing territory, yet we see a similar split on the loan guarantees: 42 percent were for it and 53 percent against.

The immigrants' party preferences were strongly related to their level of satisfaction in their absorption. In a survey conducted in March 1992 we found that the level of support for the left bloc increased the less satisfied the respondents were, and even more strikingly—the level of support for the right diminished. Among those who were very satisfied with their situation in Israel, 44 percent declared support for the right bloc. In contrast, only 16 percent of those who were not satisfied at all expressed support for parties of the right. The personal and collective concerns of immigrant absorption thus combined to produce the move away from hawkish positions and toward growing support for parties of the left.

V. Trends in Party Preferences

From surveys conducted between April 1991 and May 1992, one can see a clear drop in the support of the immigrants for the right-wing parties as opposed to an increase in support of the left-wing bloc. As we can see in figure 6.3, 46 percent said in April 1991 that they supported political parties on the right, while only 21 percent said they supported those of the left. By the time we examined the results of the survey of May 1992, however, 48 percent said they supported the left-wing parties, and only 20 percent said they supported the right-wing group (Carnegy 1992).

As to the possibility of support for one of the religious parties, we can see from the numbers that while at the beginning stages of the immigrants' absorption some 4 percent felt that they would support a religious party, over a period of time this support dwindled, and in the end only 1 percent said that they would support a religious party. This low level of support can be traced to the immigrants' outlooks being quite distant from the Orthodox approach of the religious parties. The immigrants, too, felt hurt by the demands made by religious leaders concerning their Jewish status. Also, the fervent activities of the religious circles and the allocation of resources by the Ministry of Immigrant Absorption for spiritual-religious absorption ran against the grain of the immigrants' world-view.

VI. Influence of the Immigrants on the Election Results

From the results of the surveys taken before the elections and on the basis of the survey taken among them after the elections, one can see a clear trend of increased support by the immigrants for the left-wing bloc led by the Labor Party. Since free and democratic elections are based on the principle of the secret ballot, it is difficult to determine with absolute certainty how the immigrants from the former Soviet Union voted. But at the same time, the consistency of the data obtained in the various surveys strengthens the feeling that the immigrants massively supported the left-wing bloc headed by the Labor. Strengthening of the supposition that this support was indeed translated into votes can be seen by analysis of the vote for the Labor Party in specific communities. The analysis shows that while Labor increased its strength by a national average of 12 percent, its gain in those communities that absorbed a large number of immigrants was substantially above that average. If we look at Ashdod, for example, a city that has absorbed a great many immigrants, the vote for the Labor Party increased by 40 percent, from 23.4 percent of the total vote in the previous election of 1988 to 32.8 percent in the June 1992 elections. In Upper Nazareth, another city with a substantial new immigrant population, the Labor Party vote increased by 26 percent, from 39.6 percent of the total vote in 1988 to 49.9 percent in June 1992. A similar trend can be seen also in Kiryat Yam, another community that has absorbed a substantial number of immigrants. There, Labor Party support went up by 28 percent, from 33.4 percent in 1988 to 42.5 percent in 1992. A

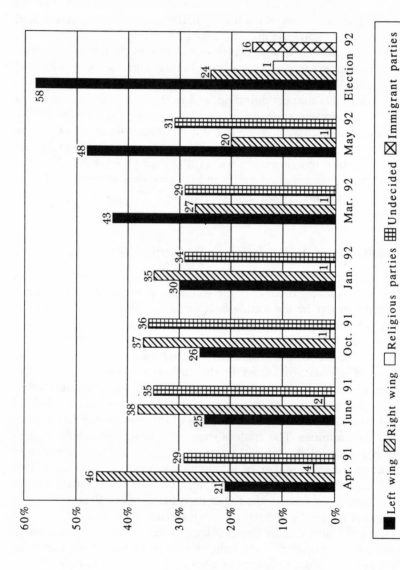

Figure 7.3. Support for Major Political Blocks in Israel

similar trend can be seen in most of the communities in which sizeable numbers of immigrants can be found. In each of them, the support for the Labor Party increased by a far higher percentage than the national average (*Yediot Aharonot* 1992).

On the basis of these statistics, one can state that the election outcome, in which the left bloc led by Labor won sixty-one mandates as opposed to the fifty-nine mandates won by the right-wing and religious parties led by the Likud, resulted from the support given by immigrants to the left bloc. Their vote, despite their short period of residence in the country, can be said to have brought about the change in the government and the termination of the stalemate between the two large blocs that had existed for so long (Beyer 1992).

Even later surveys taken among the immigrants on matters concerning foreign affairs and security showed that the immigrants still had a stronger tendency to back right-wing concepts than was true among the general population. Therefore, one can assume that their support for the left-wing parties headed by the Labor party in the 1992 elections was influenced mainly by their criticism of Likud government policies regarding absorption services. Seen in this way, their vote for the Labor Party and other left-wing parties should be viewed as a protest vote.

References

Alon, Gidon. 1992. "Elections Results." *Ha'aretz*, 25 June.

Beyer, Lisa. 1992. "From Russia with Votes." *Time Magazine*, 22 June.

Carnegy, Hugh. 1992. "Immigrants Cast Their Spell over Israeli Elections." *Financial Times*, 8 April.

"Election Results." 1992. *Yediot Aharonot*, 24 June.

Etzioni-Halevy, Eva, with Shapiro Rina. 1977. *Political Culture in Israel: Cleavage and Integration among Israeli Jews.* New York: Praeger.

Fein, Leonard. 1967. *Politics in Israel.* Boston: Little, Brown & Co.

Florsheim, Yoel. 1991. "Soviet Jewish Immigration to Israel in 1990—A Demographic Profile." *Soviet Jewish Affairs* 21, no. 2: 3–10.

General Accounting Office. 1992. *Israel—U.S. Loan Guarantees for Immigrant Absorption.* Report to the Chairman, Committee on Appropriations, U.S. Senate.

Horowitz, T. 1978. "Fear of Choice: The Soviet Jew in an Open Society." *Jerusalem Quarterly* 8 (Summer): 110–22.

Knesset. 1950. *The Law of Return.*

Lissak, Moshe, and Emanuel Gutmann. 1971. *Political Institutions and Process in Israel.* Jerusalem: Hebrew University of Jerusalem.

———. 1979. *The Israeli Political System.* Tel Aviv: Am-Oved.

Voronel, A. 1976. "Aliah of the Russian Intelligentsia." Committee of the Israel Public Council for Soviet Jewry, Tel Aviv.

Weiss, Shevah. 1973. *Politicians in Israel.* Tel Aviv: Achiasaf Publishing.

Wolffsohn, Michael. 1987. *Israel, Polity, Society and Economy, 1882–1986.* Atlantic Highlands, N.J.: Humanities Press International.

Yishai, Yael. 1981. "Soviet Immigrants in Israeli Politics." *Soviet Jewish Affairs* 11, no. 1: 19–28.

PART III

Nonvoting Constituencies

CHAPTER 8

The PLO and the 1992 Elections—
A Skillful Participant?

HILLEL FRISCH
The Hebrew University of Jerusalem

For the PLO, beset by internecine strife in the territories and the Likud's second mass settlement drive, the 1992 election campaign represented one ray of hope. Large-scale settlement confirmed the view prevalent in the PLO since 1984 that a government monopolized by the Likud presented the worst scenario for Palestinians. Fortunately for the PLO, factionalism within the Likud revolving around a Sepharadi leader pitted against the Likud's Ashkenazim, a theme in Israeli politics that the PLO always researched with a microscope and then magnified considerably, suggested that the Likud was really weakening, improving by default the prospects of a Labor government (*Filastin al-Thawra* 7 June 1992). How then could the PLO participate from afar to ensure the change of government that would dramatically curtail the settlement drive and possibly improve Palestinian prospects in the peace process?

The PLO, the following article will attempt to argue, responded by making a qualitative change in its policy from past elections, preferring active participation in order to directly influence the vote for parties that could form the government rather than focusing exclusively on the Arab vote and the consolidation of an Arab electoral bloc. The change stemmed from radically different circumstances. Until the intifada at least, the Palestinians could only think defensively, defending the territories from Israeli state-building encroachment. From 1988, but particularly with the initiation of the Madrid peace talks, what government came to power could have an important impact on the fortunes of the peace process. Whether this involvement is one more indication of the PLO's willingness to recognize the State of Israel and its formal institutions, however, remains ambiguous.

I. Government Formation and PLO Electoral Strategy

Though PLO involvement in the Israeli electoral process dates back to the 1977 general elections when, for the first time, it urged Arab voters to vote for the Democratic Front for Peace and Equality (DFPE), it was only in the 1984 elections that the PLO perceived that the Arab electorate could be utilized as a means to influence the formation of a government more suitable to Palestinian interests (*Al-Ittihad* 10 May 1977; *Ha'aretz* 13 July 1984).

The results of the 1984 elections (which seemed to confirm the institutionalization of a two-party system in Israel), and the formation of the national unity government in their wake, alerted the PLO to three seemingly uncontestable facts. First, in the stalemate that prevailed between the Likud and Labor and its respective allies, in which both shared fifty-four seats apiece, the institutionalization of the Arab voting bloc focused around predominantly Arab parties, such as the DFPE and the newly formed Progressive List for Peace (PLP), could in the future ensure a Labor government beholden to the Arab vote. Technically, the Arab voting bloc was short of the twenty thousand votes necessary to place a seventh member in the Knesset (Yanai 1990, 157). That would have given Labor the edge in coalition formation had Labor been able to overcome ideological reservations concerning coalition with Arab parties to form a government of the Jewish state.

At the very least, the PLO felt that the institutionalization of an Arab voting bloc forced the Likud into a unity government. The formation of that type of government, and that was the third lesson the PLO learned, indeed mattered: The unity government reduced expenditures on settlement in the West Bank by nearly 80 per cent (Amnon Rubinstein, *Ha'aretz* 16 April 1992).

II. The 1988 Campaign: Endorsing the Zionist Center and Left-of-center Parties

In his article on the 1988 elections, Lustick pointed to the growing number of Israeli Arabs in the past fifteen years who have voted for parties of integration as opposed to either establishment parties with selective spoils to distribute, or to nationalist non-Zionist parties (Lustick 1990, 120–21). Voters for those parties, including the newly formed Arab Democratic Party (ADP), wanted to effectively influence policy by voting for parties that indicated clear positions on Palestinian national rights and equality in allocations between Jews and Arabs as well as a firm commitment to joining a Labor-led coalition.

Augmenting the strength of these parties was exactly the reasoning behind the PLO's call to Arab voters to vote for "parties of peace" in the 1988 elections:

The campaign to end the black Israeli occupation of the West Bank, the Gaza Strip, and Jerusalem and enable the Palestinian people to exercise its right to national determination and the establishment of its independent state on its national territory, involves the internal Israeli arena and the Jewish front as well.

The position which the Arab voter and the Arab vote occupies in Israeli society and the influence which it might wield on the internal balance of power requires it [the vote] transcend the stage of expressing protest and its maturity to a level of effectiveness and solid influence.

Owing to the uniqueness of the position which the Arab masses occupy in the internal Israeli arena and its corollary in terms of joint action with the peaceful and democratic Israeli forces, they will become more than capable in influencing the Israeli decision provided that they use this electoral weapon in the campaign for peace. (*Filastin al-Thawra* 30 October 1988)

A separate call addressed to Jewish voters similarly advised them to vote for parties of peace without specifying the exact names of these parties (*New York Times*, 24 October 1988).

By placing coalitionable Zionist and non-Zionist parties on equal footing with the non-Zionist protest parties, nationalist Palestinians who might have felt constrained ideologically to vote for protest parties, the Democratic Front for Peace and Equality and Muhammad Mi'ari's Progressive List for Peace (PLP), could now choose parties freely. The PLO essentially favored parties of integration over parties of protest by undermining their ideological attractiveness.

Thus, the PLO's pronouncement of 1988, in relation to previous directives to Arab voters since 1977, seemed to indicate a culminating point in a long process of increasing recognition of the state and its institutions. That process emerged out total denial of the state and its institutions in the course of the 1960s, developed into an awareness of the importance of the Israeli Arab electoral bloc, and culminated in veering the Arab vote from the extreme and non-Zionist left side of the party spectrum toward voting directly for center and left-of-center Zionist parties (Shilo 1982, 72–73).

The irony of PLO policy hardly escaped its detractors. What one can view as being linear progression, from the point of view of normalization of relations between the PLO and Israel and the PLO and Israeli Arabs, can be seen as viciously circular from another more radical perspective of Palestinian institution and nation building within Israel. From this perspective, Palestinians within Israel expended considerable energy ridding themselves of institutional Zionist penetration into the Arab sector only to find that ten years later, the PLO, the institutional manifestation of Palestinian nationalism, was inviting Zionist parties back in (Salim 1992).

One may argue whether the parties of integration and the Zionist parties of old are essentially the same, but certainly by endorsing all parties, the PLO gave priority to the electoral process and its influence on the peace process over specific mobilization of Israeli Arabs.

III. The 1992 Elections—The Politics of Disengagement

Yet the PLO did not repeat its endorsement to vote for all parties advocating peace in the 1992 elections. In fact, it made no official pronouncement whatsoever to either Arab or Jewish voters (Kahlil 1992, 78). The omission stemmed not from lack of involvement but rather from deep concern over the elections. The PLO wagered that since a Labor victory was very likely and that it would be secured this time through the Jewish vote, it would be unwise as an adversary national movement to openly side with it. For unlike national movements that often arouse the sympathy of key political groups in the metropole, the PLO is perceived by the overwhelming percentage of the Jewish electorate as an organization that has persistently used indiscriminate violence in seeking to destroy the State of Israel. The Israeli Communist Party and the PLP, both parties that leaned over backward to attract Jewish votes, have never been successful in drawing more than three thousand Jewish votes; their histories indicate that, in part, this is because they identified with the PLO as a positive political force in the region (Osetzki-Lazar 1992, 14).

The PLO and Labor Party adherents that advised them might have exaggerated the extent of such resentment (Abu Zayyad 1992, 4–5). The historical weakness of single-issue parties with the Jewish electorate (with the exception of parties on the right, which are outside the pale of PLO influence altogether) seems to indicate that PLO endorsement, which focuses on one issue alone, however crucial, is not effective either way.

External considerations also prevailed in the decision to avoid open involvement in the elections. Too much endorsement of Labor might harm Palestinian prospects in the peace process in the aftermath of a Labor victory by giving the impression that Labor positions per se were acceptable to Palestinians.

Little wonder then that the voices emanating from the PLO and the Palestinian delegation varied. 'Nabil Sha'th, one of 'Arafat's advisors, emphasized the PLO's neutrality: "We are not concerned with the rule of any alliance or prime-minister in Israel. Rabin is not our model. He advocates a steel fist and breaking the bones of the intifada youth. There is not much difference during a transitional period but we do not want to rely on this or trust any Israeli politicians until we see results at the negotiating table" (Sha'th 1992b).

Hanan 'Ashrawi's statement on the eve of the election reflected Palestinian elite desires more truthfully, especially those emanating from the West Bank:

> We are a people under occupation who have to, in a way, deal with the policies that the government takes. This is particularly important due to the peace process, because we are involved in a process and we want to make sure that there is an Israeli Government that is a peace government that will deal with the peace process seriously and take the necessary mature steps and brave positions pertaining to the peace process and the negotiations. We are following them closely, yes. That is why we think that Israel does need, in essence, a strong government with a vision, with genuine commitment to peace that is capable of taking such historical decisions and that will reflect a constituency of peace, which we are sure exists in the Israeli public. ('Ashrawi 1992)

'Ashrawi emphasizes the basic elements of what the Labor government should be. It should be strong, hence PLO support for parties of integration. It should be ready to change positions in a manner deemed necessary by a constituency of peace without quibbling over whether that constituency forms the majority. The Israeli public significantly is not broken down into its Jewish and Arab components. The particular West Bank perspective comes through in her opening statement. She is not only a spokeswoman of Palestinians regarding a peace process but also one concerned with government policies relating to the affairs of a people under occupation. Yet, in a previous statement she repeated the theme that a Rabin government would deflect pressure on Israel to the Palestinians.

IV. Using the Peace Process to Embarrass the Likud

Although not the case in previous elections, in 1992 the PLO felt it could utilize its influence in the peace process to facilitate Labor's electoral success in a number of ways. The PLO was anxious to demonstrate that a link existed between the peace process and economic welfare, an issue of perhaps greater concern to the swing voters than the Palestinian issue per se. It hoped to create an atmosphere in which Israelis would recognize that a vote for the Likud would jeopardize the peace process and ultimately U.S. loan guarantees (Sha'th 1992a). To continue the peace talks on an optimistic note, then, entailed the risk that Israeli voters might feel that they could have their cake and eat it too, thus helping the Likud retain the undecided in its camp. The PLO called upon the other Arab members to postpone the sixth round of peace talks in Washington in order to emphasize to Israelis that as long as the Likud was in government the freezing of loan guarantees would continue (*Ha'aretz* 6 June 1992).

On a more positive and subtle note, Palestinian analysts, particularly in the territories, pressed the PLO to raise the issue of confederation with Jordan within the framework of the peace talks and time that dialogue so that it would take place just before Israeli elections. These analysts hoped to demonstrate Palestinian flexibility within the contours of a "Jordanian option" based on land for peace so often evoked in the past by Labor and rejected by the Likud, once again emphasizing that a Labor victory would create a dynamism in the peace talks to which the PLO could respond.

Tactically, the PLO orchestrated a well-publicized meeting between 'Arafat and 'Ashrawi and Faisal al-Husayni on 18 June in Amman. Though the substance of the meeting, winning recognition that the Palestinian delegation and the PLO are one and the same, was clearly related to the peace process, the timing was designed to create a dilemma that would strike at the credibility of the Likud. To arrest the Palestinian delegates and al-Husayni, the PLO reasoned, would have been condemned by the U.S., stressing the troubled relations purportedly existing between the U.S. administration and Israel. Failure to enforce the law would demonstrate that the Likud government was in fact negotiating with the PLO, suggesting that just as it was forced to make the concession on this issue it would be forced to eventually concede on matters relating to statehood; however, the process would be longer and more costly to both sides than under a Rabin led government (*Al-Quds* editorial 21 June 1992).

How much of an effect these moves had in persuading former Likud supporters, the waverers, or the new Russian immigrants to vote for center and left-of-center parties, is hard to assess. One thing is, however, certain: the peace process presented the PLO for the first time with the opportunity to wield some kind of positive, albeit indirect, influence on the Jewish public.

V. The PLP Episode

At least on one occasion the PLO did intimate its preference that Israeli Arabs, the only potential voters who were likely to be directly influenced by the PLO, vote for the ADP, a coalitionable party, rather than for the PLP, even though this party was most closely formed in the PLO's own image. The PLP is more dedicated to a particularistic Palestinian ideology and identity than either the DFPE, dominated by the Israel CommunistParty, or the ADP, which has over the years identified strongly with Arabism and Islamism

(Sulayman 1992, 86–87). The PLP was launched in 1984 with extensive PLO support that included the use of *Al-Fajr*, the East Jerusalem daily and organ of the PLO mainstream, as its mouthpiece in order to counterbalance the DFPE's *al-Ittihad* published in Haifa (*Ha'aretz* 13 July 1984). The latter was the only radical Arabic newspaper published within Israel at the time. The party had also ruled out the possibility of joining a government coalition, resulting in a secession from the party of one prominent founder, the (Anglican) Reverend Riah Abu al-'Asal, along with a considerable number of followers (*Arabs in Israel* 1992).

Specifically, the PLO might have been displeased with Muhammad Mi'ari's behavior during negotiations aimed at merging the ADP and the PLP in one party. Mi'ari had insisted on heading the prospective list despite the party's many splits and failure in organizing effective party branches (Rabinowitz 1992).

The PLO expressed its displeasure when *al-Diar*, the ADP weekly newspaper, publicized a letter purportedly written by Mahmud 'Abbas (Abu Mazen), a close advisor to 'Arafat and member of the PLO executive committee, calling on the PLP to withdraw from the elections. The same newspaper quoted a number of members of the Palestinian delegation and other prominent Palestinians such as Faisal al-Husayni, allegedly supporting that view. While the delegation members vehemently denied these statements, the PLO made do with a statement reiterating its neutrality in its stance on Arab parties, rather than denying the authenticity of 'Abbas's letter (*Al-Watan* 5 June 1992).

VI. The PLO and the Unified Arab Party

Was the PLO displeased by the failure of unity or, more specifically, the prospect that unity would improve the chances of a party headed by Darawshi and thus, indirectly, the prospects of a coaltionable party? Given the PLO's past promotion of political pluralism in the Arab sector, it was probably interested more in bolstering the center in the 1992 elections than in either unifying parties or creating a plural Arab electoral bloc as in the past.

Of the three alternatives, the PLO least sought the unification of parties. Its record of involvement clearly demonstrates this. In the 1981 elections it reversed its decision to support the DFPE despite its success in achieving a majority of Arab votes (51 percent) in the elections four years previously (Yaniv and Al-Haj 1983, 154). In 1984, the PLO continued to endorse the DFPE along with the PLP, a more Palestinian nationalist alternative that appeared on the electoral scene in 1984, but only after employing a divide-and-rule strategy. Throughout the campaign it promoted the nationalist

PLP. (As one major PLP slogan succinctly put it: "Our letter on the ballot is "Fe for Filastin"; Theirs [the DFPE] is vav. There is no waw (vav) in Filastin.") But after building up the PLP, the PLO endorsed both parties (*Kol Ha'ir* 22 July 1984). In 1988, it warmly endorsed 'Abd al-Wahab Darawsha's ADP rather than employ the threat to refrain from doing so as a means of pressuring him to join forces with the PLP or the DFPE (*Filastin al-Thawra* 21 August 1988, 18 September 1988).

The PLO's strategy of promoting a plural electoral block seemed to bear fruit. The same 1981 elections that reflected PLO animosity toward the unified Arab party, also demonstrated the limited electoral attractiveness in the Arab Sector of a party dominated by Communists. The DFPE's share of the vote declined from 51 to 37 percent, suggesting that in 1977 the party reached its vote-getting peak and that another specifically Palestinian party was needed to attract votes away from the Zionist parties. In 1984, the combined share of votes for the DFPE and the PLP in the Arab sector slightly exceeded the DFPE's share in 1977 (52 to 51) percent). Similarly, the endorsement of the ADP in addition to the other two predominantly Arab parties in 1988 increased the non-Zionist parties' share of the vote to 58 percent. The institutionalization of pluralism, it would then seem, only served to expand the Arab electoral bloc. Of course, one never knows what could have been the electoral effect of a unified Arab party, particularly in attracting those who abstained from voting in elections.

While PLO preference for an electoral bloc rather than a united Arab party can be rationalized on electoral grounds, that preference preceded the quest for such a bloc, suggesting that the roots of such a preference lie elsewhere. The PLO as a diaspora center to territorial Palestinian communities must always be weary of the possibility of being superseded by institutions in territorial Palestine, much as, in the Zionist movement, the territorial center superseded the movement and leadership in the diaspora (Sandler and Frisch 1984, 7). In both the territories and among Israeli Arabs, the PLO cultivates mobilization through organizational diffusion and fragmentation, even though the purpose and the means of that mobilization are different (Frisch 1991). A unified Arab party among Israeli Arabs, who are acknowledgedly latecomers in Palestinian institution-building, could, under certain circumstances, seek to repartition Palestine and abandon—or at least marginalize—the role of the diaspora PLO. It was only natural then, that the PLO opposed the creation of one Arab party among Israeli Arabs, preferring that several parties with common platforms regarding the issue of Palestinian statehood scurry for its endorsement at each election. Only if an ascendant Islamic Movement decides to contest the elections directly might the PLO reconsider the unified Arab party option. In that case the creation of a unified nationalist party will only institutionalize disunity among Israeli Palestinians rather than forge it.

VII. Electoral Politics and the Politics of Identity

Does growing involvement imply that the PLO recognizes the Arab voters as loyal citizens of the state? Many changes have taken place in the role the PLO has allocated to Israel's Arab citizens. In the first decade of the PLO's existence, Israeli Arabs essentially had no role in creating or recreating the Palestinian polity. Palestinian institution-building, most notably the establishment of the PLO and other organizations that promoted Palestinian identity, was a diaspora event, the handiwork of leaders residing in the farthermost reaches of Palestinian diaspora.[1] Essentially the history of the renewed Palestinian national movement chronicles the spread of Palestinian political identity from core groups in the diaspora back to geographic Palestine. For the PLO, then, the Palestinians within Israel were important only in so far as they reflected Israeli iniquity and immoral behavior. In this capacity they were not only passive sufferers but also marginal ones compared to their fellow Palestinians in the occupied territories (Shilo 1980, 64–65).

In the mid-seventies, the PLO altered their role radically. Israeli Arabs, after the violent land day event of 31 March 1976 in which five Arabs lost their lives, were now perceived by the PLO as fellow Palestinians with considerable potential to mobilize against the state. One is struck by the extent to which the Palestinian radicalization perspective introduced by Ben-Dor in his article on Israeli Arabs in the 1977 general elections became the reigning ideological perspective within the PLO (Ben-Dor 1980, 178).[2]

Such a perspective, however, could hardly be squared with the results of the 1981 general elections, where the majority of Israeli Arabs not only failed to respond to the PLO call to boycott the elections but also voted overwhelmingly for Zionist parties (Yaniv and Al-Haj 1983, 154.) The DFPE's share of the Israeli Arab vote dropped from 51 to 37 per cent, while the vote for Labor among Israeli Arabs substantially increased. To a certain extent, it was Israeli Arabs, through the Israeli electoral process, who defined their role in the PLO scheme of things in a manner presumably comparable to that used by American Jews in U.S. elections, where they attempt to achieve more pro-Israeli policy by affecting American presidential and congressional elections (Herzberger, *Ha'aretz* 20 July 1984).[3] The power of the Palestinian Arab at the polling booth as an ideological motif (together with the demographic theme of the fecund Palestinian mother whose offspring would undo Israel from within) replaced the image of the Israeli Arab as a Palestinian demonstrator and Land Day combatant(*Filastin al-Thawra* 23 October 1988).[4]

Can one assume from changing role allocations, then, that the PLO imputed different meaning to Palestinian identity among Israeli Palestinians than Palestinians elsewhere? Despite the changes in roles, the terms identifying Israeli Palestinians changed far less. The PLO in 1988 was still calling the whole of Palestine "the occupied homeland" and bringing out a journal bearing that name, identifying Israeli Arabs "our people inside (1948)" or "inside the occupied Arab Palestinian territories (1948)," to draw on two examples from the very same article that championed the Arab electoral role in promoting the peace process (*Filastin al-Thawra* 23 October 1988). None of these terms can be squared easily with an ethnic lobby role model.

Even in the 1992 campaign, 'Arafat publicized a statement addressed to Arab voters that suggested that PLO stances regarding Israeli elections were momentary and tactical: "Land Day occurs this year in proximity to the Parliamentary elections in Israel. The Knesset is an Israeli institution, enforcing Israeli laws and furthering the Israelis' own interests. Nevertheless, it is our duty to wield political warfare in this arena. By means of a united Arab front, you will succeed in minimizing the arrogance and racism of the Israeli government which has recently been turned against Jews from Oriental descent as well" (*Al-Ittihad* 31 March 1991).

Finally, there seems to be little correlation between PLO encouragement of particularistic institution-building in the Arab sector for the purpose of promoting the national minority idea and the move electorally towards promoting the Zionist center (al-Batal 1992).[5] Evidently, the PLO promotes different agendas to promote short-term and long-term goals. The mutual promotion does however constrain and limit the effectiveness of PLO electoral support for the Zionist center.

VIII. Assessing PLO Influence on the Arab Vote

Influencing Arab Voter Participation

No matter how far the PLO has moved to promote the Israeli center, it still has a clear, vested interest in reducing the numbers of Israeli Arabs abstaining from voting altogether. The 7 to 8 percent voting gap characterizing Jewish and Arab participation rates since 1984 could easily have cost the Arab sector one Arab member of Knesset, assuming that the differential participation rate is composed of nationalists or Islamisists who would vote for Arab parties (Reiter and Aharoni 1992, 43). It is no wonder that the PLO has emphasized the importance of voting in its calls to Arab voters since 1984 (*Filastin al-Thawra* 23 July 1984; *New York Times* 15 October 1988). The PLO's influence on participation rates is probably the only aspect of its relationship to the election process that can in some measure be tested quantitatively. One can analyze the relationship between the official PLO position and the participation rate in recent general elections. It would be worthwhile to take into consideration the effect of another possibly important variable, new

Table 8.1. Relationship between Participation Rate, New Voters, and PLO Stance, Israeli Elections 1973–1988

Year	Participation Rate (%)	New Eligible Voters as % of total eligible voters	PLO Position
1973	77.0	13.9	Boycott
1977	73.4	15.0	Endorses DFPE
1981	69.2	17.6	Boycott
1984	73.6	11.6	Endorses PLP, DFPE
1988	69.6	31.1	Endorses Arab parties
1992	70.2	7.1	Endorses all parties for peace

Source: Data for 1977–88 were derived from Reiter and Ahroni, p. 43. Data for 1992 were provided by the Labor Party's Election Committee.

eligible voters as a percentage of total voters in the Arab sector on the same phenomenon. Presumably more youths than adults tend to abstain from participation in elections on ideological grounds.

Analyzing the relationship between these two variables on Arab voter participation yields little evidence that the PLO influences a citizen's decision to vote in the elections. For example, one notes a decline in participation rates between 1973 and 1977 (77.0 to 73.4 percent), despite the fact that the PLO opposed participation in the 1973 elections and endorsed voting for the DFPE in 1977 (table 8.1). The decline might have more to do with the increase in young prospective voters between 1973 and 1977, (15.0 percent compared to 13.9 percent) than to PLO intervention. The participation rate continued to decline in the 1981 elections, yet it is hard to discern whether this was a result of the PLO boycott or of the youthfulness of the eligible electorate. The percentage of new voters reached a new high of 17.6 percent. Data for the next two elections hardly clarify matters, for if the increase in the 1984 participation rate might be associated with the PLO call to vote (from an estimated 69.2 to 73.6 percent), why did the same position not prevent a decline in participation rates in 1988? Again, a marked surge of young potential voters in 1988 compared to their growth in 1984, (33.1 [*sic*] to 11.6 percent), might better explain the decline. In the 1992 elections, the participation rate dropped slightly despite Arafat's early call to vote and despite the precipitous drop in the percentage of new eligible voters. It is possible that some of the decline can be attributed to those within the Islamic movement who favored boycotting the 1992 elections, thus offsetting the PLO's positive stance towards participation (*Arabs in Israel* August 1992, 3).[6] While the PLO's basic position has not prevented lower participation rates, it might have influenced its stabilization around the 70 percent level.

Voting for Zionist/Non-Zionist Parties

PLO endorsement seems to have even less influence on whether Arabs vote for Zionist or non-Zionist parties. In 1981, the PLO's call to abstain from voting coincided with an increase in votes for Zionist parties (from 49 to 61 percent). And while the 1984 and 1988 elections seemed to confirm PLO influence on Arab voting patterns—in the 1984 elections the call to vote for non-Zionist predominantly Arab parties met with a positive response (their share of the vote increasing from 37 to 52 percent) and in the 1988 elections the call to vote for parties of peace might have influenced the heavy vote for both these parties and the CRM—the results of the 1992 seriously question that assumption. Even though 'Arafat urged Arabs to vote for non-Zionist parties, they attracted only 47 percent of the vote in 1992 (*Arabs in Israel* August 1992, 3).

Voting for Parties of Integration/Protest Parties

Only among the "nationalists," those who vote ideologically for Arab parties (excluding in this regard the DFPE), does the PLO seem to influence voting. In the 1984 and 1988 elections the PLO in effect helped fragment the Arab vote, as we have seen, by endorsing on each occasion the party most recently formed. In 1992, by contrast, the PLO might have influenced the shift in votes that took place from the PLP to the ADP. The ADP's share of the Arab vote increased from 11.3 to 15.2 percent, while the PLP's share declined from 14.3 to 9.3 percent. It would be difficult, however, to quantify that influence among the many, probably more important, factors that led voters to make the switch (*Al-Sinara* 26 June 1988).

IX. The 1992 Election Results, the PLO, and the Israeli Arabs

For the PLO, the outcome of the 1992 elections was the best imaginable. In addition to completely excluding the Likud from government, the mathematics of government coalition-building vindicated both the older PLO policy of cultivating an Arab electoral bloc with its newer emphasis on shifting their voting to coaltionable parties. At long last there was a chance of forming a government where the support of the Arab Knesset members would be crucial. With Labor's forty-four seats and Meretz's additional twelve, the five members of Knesset from the DFPE and ADP could have given the government the necessary, though slim, majority. Though that prospect never materialized, their role in Rabin's successful negotiations in forming the government was far from negligible. The Arab bloc prodded Shas to enter the government at substantially lower costs to Labor than would have prevailed had it not made up the balance. Shas, once having joined, sought Arab support for the coalition in order to ensure the government's longevity (*Arabs in Israel* 1992, 4).

At the same time the election results demonstrated the PLO's limited influence on deciding the immediate outcome. If many Palestinian Israelis decided to vote for Israeli parties as part of its policy to use the Arab vote to influence electoral outcomes directly, too many voted for the wrong kind. The increase in Arab votes for small, Jewish-based parties, many of which took no clear stance on the Palestinian issue, increased from 4 to 7.2 percent (excluding Shas). Worse still was the fine performance of Likud that increased its vote in the Arab sector from 6 to 7.6 percent. Nor does Shas's success, a tenfold increase in Arab votes from the previous elections, conform to the gist of the PLO's endorsement. Shas, exposed to pressure both from right-wing centers of religious legitimacy and a right-wing electorate base, has never explicitly endorsed a land-for-peace platform.

In sum, an analysis of the PLO role seems to suggest that the PLO does not influence Arab voting behavior in a direct way. One cannot, however, totally discount the PLO's role in the crystallization of an Arab voter bloc in the past decade that influences the formation of government coalitions. Nor can one conclusively learn of the PLO's basic positions regrading the state and its institutions from such involvement. A gap continues to persist between the PLO's strategy of electoral involvement in the Israeli election process, implying recognition of the state and its institutions, and its frames of reference to the state's Palestinian Arab citizens and their role within it.

Notes

1. Of the twelve core leaders of Fath who came to dominate the PLO as we know it today, at least nine resided outside areas of former Palestine in the late 1950s and early 1960s when Fath was formed (Abu 'Amru 1987, 193–98).

2. The Central Council of the PLO in August 1977 held that Israeli Arabs and Palestinians in the occupied territories played the same role: "While warning certain lax and suspect elecments against being led astray by the schemes of the Zionist enemy, the council has the highest appreciation of the heroic role played in the struggle of the masses of our people and the national leadership in Galilee, the Triangle, the West Bank and Gaza Strip and their loyalty to the PLO" (*Journal of Palestine Studies* 1978, 174).

The PLO adopted the same stance in 1981 as well: "In its discussions and resolutions the Council expressed its great pride in the level of struggle...in the occupied homeland, in the extend of unity and cohesion they have achieved, and in their full allegiance to the PLO. The Council commended the heroic struggle of the masses of our people in Galilee, the

Triangle, the Negev, Jerusalem, the West Bank and Gaza Strip (*Journal of Palestine Studies* 1981, 193).

3. Arthur Herzberger expresses a dissenting view of the Jewish vote. He argues that Jews vote consistently for Democrats and support liberal policies out of fear of "muzhik" violence disadvantage can unleash. They are haunted more out of memories of the past in the old country rather than out of specific concern for Israel.

4. In the issue preceding the election, *Filastin al-Thawra* (23 October 1988) reflected this new conceptualization of the Israeli Arab on its cover with the title "The Arab Vote in the Israeli Elections: The Weapon of Democracy and the Weapon of Demography." Obviously, the PLO in the mid and late 1980s accorded a different role to Israeli Palestinians than to Palestinians elsewhere, and, paradoxically, Israeli citizenship was the key factor behind such differentiation.

6. The movement's influence was surprisingly limited, due to its inability to speak in one voice. While 'Abd Allah Nimr Darwish, the founder of the movement, purportedly supported the ADP, Sheikh Raid Salah, the young mayor of Um al-Fahum, issued a call to ban the elections, and Sheikh Kamal Khatib of Karf Kana, and Islamic Movement stronghold in the Galilee, supported the PLP. Nevertheless, where they were regionally strong, participation rates were low, meaning that they had a stronger effect on reducing participation than on voting patterns.

References

Abu 'Amru, Ziad. 1987. *Usul al-Haraka al-Siyasiyya Fi Quta' Ghazza* (The Basis of the Political Movement in the Gaza Strip). Acre: Dar al-Aswar.

Abu Zayyad, Ziad. 1992. "Al-Intikhabat al-Israiliyya al-Muqbila: Hudud al-Murahana al-Filastiniyya." (The Coming Israeli Elections: The Limits of the Palestinian Wager). *Shu'un Filastiniyya* 231–32:3–12.

Arabs in Israel. 1992. 2 no. 6:14.

'Ashrawi, Hannan. 1992. Interview (in Arabic). Amman Jordan Television Network, 19 June (FBIS-NES—22 June).

Al-Batal, Hassan. 1992. "Al-Jalil: Al-'Awda al-Sughri" (The Galilee: The Lesser Return). *Filastin al-Thawra*, 10 May.

Ben-Dor, Gabriel. 1980. "Electoral Politics and Ethnic Polarization: Israeli Arabs in the 1977 Election." In *The Elections in Israel—1977*, ed. Asher Arian. Jerusalem: Jerusalem Academic Press.

Frisch, Hillel. 1991. "Between Diffusion and Territorial Consolidation in Rebellion." *Terrorism and Political Violence* 3 no. 4:39–62.

"Al-Jinni al-Sepharadi La Ya'ud lil-Qumqum" (The Sepharadi Jinni Does not Return to the Bottle). 1988. *Filastin al-Thawra*, 30 October.

Khalil, 'Awad. 1992. "MTF wal-Intikhabat al-Israiliyya: Min al-Inkar ila'l-Rihan 'ala'l-Taghyyir" (The PLO and the Israeli Elections: From Denial to Betting on Change). *Shu'un Filastiniyya*, 233–34:65–84.

Lustick, Ian. 1990. "The Changing Political Role of Israeli Arabs." In *The Elections in Israel—1988*, ed. Asher Arian and Michal Shamir. Boulder: Westview Press.

Osetzki-Lazar, Sara. 1992. *The Elections to the 13th Knesset, among the Arabs in Israel* (in Hebrew). Givat Haviva: The Center for Arab Studies.

Rabinowitz, Dani. "The Price of Personal Honor." *Haaretz* May 15, 1992.

Reiter, Yitzchak, and Reuven Aharoni. 1992. *Olamam Hapoliti Shel Araviei Israel* (The Political World of Israeli Arabs). Beit Berl: Hamerkaz le-Heker Hevrati be-Israel.

Salim, 'Afif. 1992. "Al-Muktashifun al-Judud" (The New Discoverers). *Al-Nahar*, 1 May.

Sandler, Shmuel, and Hillel Frisch. 1984. *Israel, the West Bank and the Palestinians: An Intercommunal Conflict.* Lexington, Mass.: Lexington.

Sha'th, Nabil. 1992a. Interview. PLO Radio, San'a, 5 May (FBIS, 8 May 1992).

———. 1992b. Interview. BBC Television, London, 17 June 1992 (FBIS-NES, 18 June 1992).

Shilo, Gideon. 1982. *Aravei Israel be-Einei Medinot Arab ve-Ashaf* (Israeli Arabs as the Arab States and the PLO See Them). Jerusalem: Magnes.

Sulayman, Ibrahim. 1992. "Ha-Fragmentizatzia ha-Politit ba-Migzar ha-Aravi" (Political Fragmentation in the Israeli Arab Sector). Master's thesis, Hebrew University of Jerusalem.

Yanai, Nathan. 1990. "The Resumption of a Communal Coalition Tradition." In *Israel's Odd Couple*, ed. Daniel J. Elazar. Detroit: Wayne State University Press, 169–92.

Yaniv, Avner, and Majid Al-Haj. 1983. "Uniformity or Diversity: A Reappraisal of the Voting Behavior of the Arab Minority in Israel." In *The Elections in Israel—1981*, ed. Asher Arian. Tel Aviv: Ramot, 154.

CHAPTER 9

U.S.-Israel Relations and Israel's 1992 Elections

BARRY RUBIN
The Hebrew University of Jerusalem

U.S. policy has an important effect on Israel's internal and electoral politics. At the time of Israel 1992 elections, the open hostility of President George Bush's administration toward Prime Minister Yitzhak Shamir's government surely influenced the behavior of Israeli politicians and voters.

At first glance, this factor would seem to have benefitted Labor and contributed to its victory. But it is difficult to evaluate the extent or even the net consequence of that influence, because it is inherently so contradictory and highly subjective.

I. The Course of Events

Preelection Friction

After the 1991 Gulf War and the USSR's collapse, U.S. policy makers perceived that many of the circumstances previously hindering progress on Arab-Israeli peace had been altered. Arab states were weaker, more inclined to put a priority on good relations with Washington, and less eager to pursue the conflict with Israel. The PLO had been internationally isolated and discredited. U.S. leaders also felt they needed to make an effort on the issue to hold together the Gulf War coalition and to take advantage of these circumstances.

As soon as the war ended, Bush and Secretary of State James Baker began working on the peace process. In March 1991 Baker said on *Meet the Press* and *This Week with David Brinkley*, that "We have got to find a way for the

Arab states and Israel to make peace," and "a way for Israel and the Palestinians to begin a dialogue. We cannot let this historic opportunity pass" (*Jerusalem Post* 12 March 1991).

The administration would not reestablish the U.S.-PLO dialogue because, Baker said, the PLO leaders had "damaged themselves significantly" by siding with Saddam Hussein in the Kuwait crisis. In his victory speech to Congress on 6 March, Bush said that any diplomatic settlement must be based on trading "territory for peace" and respecting "legitimate Palestinian rights" (*Jerusalem Post* 18 February 1991; *International Herald Tribune* 8 March 1991).

He had "no illusions" about the difficulty of the task, said Baker in testimony to the House of Representatives Foreign Operations Subcommittee on 22 May 1991. "But I also had a strong sense that the Gulf War might have created some new possibilities for peacemaking in the region and that the U.S. has a unique obligation to help explore the possibilities. It would be very sad, of course, if it turns out that the old obstacles are more formidable than new opportunities. But I think it would be sadder still if the U.S. failed to energetically pursue a chance for peace, because such chances don't come along very often in the Middle East."

The Gulf War, Baker said, acted as a "grim reminder" of the danger of conflict and the state-to-state dimension of the Arab-Israeli issue while also showing that Israel and the Arab states "sometimes find common ground between them." Baker based his initiative on six points: the need for a comprehensive settlement based on UN resolutions 242 and 338; a two-track process of simultaneous Israel/Arab states and Israeli/Palestinian talks; the Camp David formula of an interim arrangement to be followed by an agreement on the territories' permanent status; Palestinian representation by residents of the territories; U.S.-USSR cosponsorship of a conference as a "launching pad" for direct talks; and no imposed settlement by the United States (*New York Times* 14 June 1991, 19 June 1991).

In his endeavor to promote negotiations, Baker made eight trips to the Middle East between March and October 1991; each one included meetings with the leaders of Egypt, Israel, Jordan, Saudi Arabia, and Syria, along with talks with a Palestinian delegation in Jerusalem. In his trips in March, two in April, mid-May, June, and July, he tried to resolve barriers to initiating talks. Baker also met with Israeli Foreign Minister David Levy in Washington on 13 June.

Baker and the Bush administration realized that Israel and the Arab governments had to agree to any actions. "It goes without saying," said Baker on one of his trips, "that you're not going to have a conference until the countries that are the participants . . . make a firm decision that this is what they want" (*Los Angeles Times* 17 May 1991).

To encourage Israel to participate in talks, the United States also took some steps to improve bilateral relations. In March 1991, Congress agreed to give Israel $650 million to offset costs incurred during war. In his speech to the UN in September, Bush successfully urged the repeal of a UN resolution equating Zionism and racism. "This body cannot claim to seek peace and at the same time challenge Israel's right to exist," he said (*New York Times* 6 March 1991; *International Herald Tribune* 24 September 1991).

During this period, though, Baker particularly criticized the construction of new Jewish settlements on the West Bank, commenting that they obstructed peace. He personally resented how settlers tried to establish new communities to "greet" his trips to Israel (*International Herald Tribune* 25 and 29 April 1991). The administration made clear its strong opposition to the creation of new settlements in the West Bank. When Israeli Housing Minister Ariel Sharon visited Washington in May, the White House ordered Secretary of Housing and Urban Development Jack Kemp not to receive his counterpart officially, in order to punish Sharon for his active role in building settlements. Instead, the two men met at Israel's embassy (*New York Times* 2 May 1991).

The key breakthrough on the Arab-Israeli peace process came in June, and it was confirmed during Baker's sixth trip in July, with Syria's agreement to attend direct talks with Israel. He then pressed Israel, Jordan, and the Palestinians for their agreement to attend. Baker said to Israel, "This is a moment of historic opportunity [since] Israel now has Arab partners willing to engage in direct negotiations" (*International Herald Tribune* 19 July 1991, 3–4 August 1991; *The Economist* 20 July 1991 for text of Baker's remarks in Jerusalem on 22 July 1991).

The problems in structuring negotiations were gradually resolved, and on 30 October the Madrid conference began. The Bush administration's thinking, summarized the *New York Times*, was that "only on the basis of 'real peace' and Arab respect for Israel's 'reasonable' security needs does Mr. Bush expect Israel to make concessions. But, he made clear, he does expect concessions, specifically including territorial concessions as well as 'fairness' to Palestinians" (*New York Times* 31 October 1991; *Washington Post* 18, 19, and 27 October 1991).

Bush, in his speech at the Madrid meeting, stressed that the U.S. would only be a "catalyst" to help the parties themselves end the state of war and achieve "real peace. . . . Treaties, security, diplomatic relations, trade, investment, cultural exchange, even tourism." Any agreement must be acceptable to all sides, give the "Palestinian people meaningful control over their own lives and fate," and provide for the acceptance of Israel and meet that country's "reasonable security needs" (*The Economist* 2 November 1991; text in *Washington Post* 31 October 1991).

The administration was aware that it could not impose a settlement but might use pressure to break specific roadblocks. Of these, it identified Israeli settlement in the territories as a key problem. Bush and Baker personally considered such activity to be, as Baker told Congress on 22 May, the biggest obstacle to peace. He had been particularly angered by settlers' establishing small new settlements timed to coincide with his visits to Israel (*New York Times* 23 May 1991; *Jerusalem Post* 24 May 1991.

The question became the most contentious issue in U.S.-Israel relations when Israel requested that the United States guarantee $10 billion in loans Israel sought to build housing for Soviet Jewish immigrants. Aside from the opposition to new settlements, the White House's hostility to the proposal was heightened by a post–Cold War domestic mood for reducing foreign aid, an economic recession, and some criticisms of Israel's economic policy.

In July, Bush said that there "ought to be a *quid pro quo*" between freezing settlements and receiving the guarantees. Baker asked Shamir to delay the request, though seventy-one senators signed a joint letter urging going ahead with the guarantees (*International Herald Tribune* 6 September 1991).

In September, Bush met with Senate supporters of Israel and asked them to accept a four-month delay in considering the issue, claiming that immediate action would threaten the peace process. "If Congress chooses to press forward now, we stand a very real chance of losing the participation of either our Arab or Israel's negotiating partners." He promised not to seek any further delay after January 1992 (*New York Times* 10 September 1991).

As part of its campaign on the question, the administration leaked critical reports on the Israeli economy. When pro-Israel citizens came to Washington to urge congressional support for the proposal, Bush spoke at a press conference of "a thousand lobbyists descending on Capitol Hill." Bush, wrote *New York Times* columnist Leslie Gelb, "stepped in front of the cameras . . . and declared political war on Israel." He threatened to veto the loan guarantees' measure if Congress passed it. Congress accepted the requested delay, as it wanted neither a confrontation nor alleged responsibility for damaging the peace process. In addition, there were insufficient votes to override Bush's veto, and public opinion was not enthusiastic about new foreign commitments (*International Herald Tribune* 19 June, 1991, 13 September 1991).

Thus, as 1992 began and an Israeli election loomed on the horizon, U.S.-Israel relations were also troubled by policy differences and personal friction between the two countries' leaders as well as the loan guarantee issue (*Washington Post* 18 March 1992, 23 March 1992; *New York Times* 22 March 1992).

On 24 January 1992, Baker suggested to Israel's ambassador that, as a compromise, homes already begun could be finished but no new ones started. "The choice is Israel's," Bush said, on "whether she wants to take action which would permit the strong support of both the legislative and executive branches for these loan guarantees or not" (*Washington Post* 5 February 1992, 18 March 1992).

In principle, then, the Bush administration was willing to give loan guarantees to the Shamir government, but only on condition that it stopped expanding settlements. Such a step, however, was totally antithetical to the Shamir cabinet's policy, and on 17 March, Bush officially rejected Israel's request (*New York Times* 7 February 1992).

Friction also occurred on some other issues. In January, the U.S. voted for a UN resolution that "strongly condemns" Israel's deportation of Palestinians, the harshest it ever supported (*Washington Post* 7 January 1992).

In March, U.S. officials leaked a State Department report speaking of a "systematic and growing pattern" that Israel was illegally selling U.S. military technology—including cluster bombs and aircraft radars—to China, South Africa, Ethiopia, and Chile. Another leak claimed Israel had sent Patriot missiles to China. Assistant Secretary of State for Politico-Military Affairs Richard Clarke, who oversaw such matters, rejected the claims as "specious on their face" and lacking hard evidence. A U.S. investigating team cleared Israel of some accusations while the others remained unproven (*New York Times* 15 March 1992; *Washington Post* 16 March 1992, 2 April 1992, 3 April 1992).

That same month, U.S. Assistant Secretary of State for Human Rights and Humanitarian Affairs Richard Schifter resigned the post he had held for six years. Some sources said his motive was a dispute with Baker, who supported issuing State Department human rights reports more critical of Israel than Schifter wanted (*Washington Times* 3 March 1992).

Another controversy broke out in March after former New York city mayor Edward Koch wrote in his *New York Post* column, "When Baker was criticized recently at a meeting of high-level White House advisers for his belligerent attitude toward Israel, he responded, '[Fuck the Jews]. They didn't vote for us.'" The White House and State Department denied this incident happened. But Democratic presidential candidate Arkansas Governor Bill Clinton, referring to this and other events, said the administration's "strident rhetoric, public and private, against Israel [and] the Jewish community . . . has broken down the taboo against overt anti-Semitism" (*New York Times* 28 March 1992, 2 April 1992).

Bush responded with an open letter, ostensibly to a Jewish supporter's sympathetic questioning, which spoke of his "anguish" over U.S.-Israel tensions, while reiterating his opposition to more settlements. Baker denied Clinton's charge, saying that "nothing is more abhorrent to me" than anti-Semitism (*Washington Post* 2 April 1992).

At this point, the administration made some attempt to ease the friction. After all, Israel was still participating in the U.S.-sponsored peace negotiations, whose fourth round ended in early March. Vice President Dan Quayle addressed an April meeting of the pro-Israel lobby—the American Israel Political Action Committee meeting—as "fellow Zionists." "I am here as George Bush's vice president," he continued, "to underscore his commitment to Israel. The bumps in the road trouble him and all of us deeply, but they do not change or threaten the basic principles behind our relationship" (*Washington Post* 8 April 1992).

Still, the friction continued, sometimes fostered by unintended acts. In May, State Department spokesperson Margaret Tutwiler routinely affirmed U.S. support for UN Resolution 194 of 1948 in a daily briefing, setting off a controversy, since, in the atmosphere of U.S.-Israel strain, some Arab and Israeli observers saw this as support for a "right to return" for Palestinian refugees. The U.S. government denied any such implication (*New York Times* 15 May 1992).

But during all these minor crises, the administration's actual conduct of the peace talks was relatively friendly to Israel's position. After all, the U.S. government insisted the talks be direct, coincide with the Camp David framework, and rule out PLO participation. The administration let the parties negotiate among themselves, putting forward no plan of its own (*New York Times* 16 May 1992).

Baker also criticized Palestinian negotiators for "posturing" and urged them to focus on negotiating specific proposals, "pocket the gains" where possible, "and begin real negotiations." The U.S. government insisted on an interim period of autonomy and made no stipulations about the final outcome (*Washington Post* 6 March 1992). The administration was also angry with Jordan for continuing covert trade with Iraq despite the UN embargo. Congress held up $30 million in economic aid and $27 million in military assistance to that country (*Washington Post* 13 March 13 1992, 6 September 1992).

Thus, while there was a fair amount of U.S.-Israel friction, there was also a great deal of cooperation on the main diplomatic issues. The policy differences paralleled previous periods of divergences, including those of 1982–83 and 1988–90.

Celebrating Rabin's Victory

Relations took a sharp turn for the better after the Labor party victory in Israel's June election and the installation of Yitzhak Rabin as prime minister. This event was warmly welcomed in the United States. The *New York Times* editorialized, "The change to the pragmatic Mr. Rabin offers new possibilities for a land-for-peace compromise vainly sought by successive American Presidents. . . .For President Bush, who has suffered harsh criticism from some American Jews, the results vindicate a long, tenacious peace initiative." The *Washington Post* argued that from an American viewpoint the election result "is a good one" (Anti-Defamation League 1992).

Baker traveled to the Middle East right after the Israeli election to survey the prospects for peace talks, commenting, "It's a real pleasure to be going to Israel under circumstances in which I anticipate that we will not be met with the opening of a new settlement" (*Wall Street Journal* 20 June 1992).

A few hours after Rabin was sworn in, Bush invited him for a visit. On 10–11 August, Bush hosted Rabin at his Kennebunkport, Maine, home in an extremely friendly atmosphere. The president promised to seek quick congressional approval on loan guarantees now that the two countries agreed on "basic principles." Bush spoke warmly of Israel as the U.S.'s "strategic partner." Despite some quibbling on service charges for the guarantees, the measure quickly progressed through Congress (*New York Times* 12 August 1992).

The administration also moved to improve U.S.-Israel military cooperation. It announced plans to sell Apache and Black Hawk helicopters to Israel from U.S. stockpiles in Europe and to preposition up to $300 million in equipment there, in addition to $100 million already in place. These steps had been previously approved by Congress but had been held up by the White House during the previous era of bilateral friction. These acts were intended to balance U.S. sales of F-15s to Saudi Arabia and to signal a warmer relationship with the new Rabin government. According to some sources, the sale to Saudi Arabia was delayed because the White House thought it would be easier to obtain Rabin's than Shamir's acquiescence (*Washington Post* 27 September 1992).

II. Politics, Ideology, and Patron-Client Relations

These events, and the sharp difference between Bush's behavior toward the Shamir and Rabin governments, raise questions about the effect of U.S. policies on Israel's elections. On this matter, the perceptions of the parties are as important as their intentions.

Israeli Perspectives

On the Israeli side, efforts by U.S. policy makers to have some impact on domestic politics could backfire, especially since what is involved concerned punishments rather than rewards. Israelis often reject such interventions on patriotic, nationalist grounds, seeing them as treating Israel like—in the words of Prime Minister Menachem Begin in the early 1980s—a "banana republic." By acceding to U.S. pressures, Israel would be seen to lose both dignity and sovereignty, becoming subject to ever-increasing coercion from Washington. This reaction could apply across the political spectrum.

Moreover, especially on the right and center, American proposals were perceived as threatening. During the campaign, for example, Shamir accused the U.S. of trying to force Israel's return to its 1967 borders, complaining it had ceased to be an "honest broker."

Moves to force Israel to cease settlement in the occupied territories immediately and—potentially—to give up territory or even negotiate with the PLO were perceived as posing a threat to Israel's interests or even survival. Thus, U.S. pressures mobilized support for Shamir's government in certain sectors.

At the same time, however, the perception of U.S. strategy is more subjective than American observers might realize. While playing on Israeli patriotism against American bullying, the Likud made two arguments. First, it suggested that bilateral relations were not in a state of crisis and that U.S. loan guarantees would be granted to a Shamir government after the Israeli elections. Second, voters were urged to make Shamir's continued incumbency a *fait accompli*, a fact to which the U.S. government would have to accede. At that point, relations would allegedly improve.

On the left, in the Meretz bloc and Labor's dovish faction, there was the hope that U.S. influence would press the Shamir government harder and thus help them gain victory. But it was hard to speak openly of such a recourse to a foreign factor or make explicit a tactic of worsening one's own country's position in order to benefit politically. Thus, the left's approach was to blame the Shamir government for the deterioration of relations with the United States.

Another important issue—perhaps the most important—was the material factor. By denying loan guarantees to Israel as long as the Shamir government continued its settlement policy in the territories, U.S. policy refused to help improve Israel's housing or job situation at a time of massive immigration and high unemployment. Indirectly, this bad situation influenced immigrants from the USSR—first-time voters—to react critically against the incumbents and vote in relatively high numbers for Labor and Meretz.

In short, the left portrayed the position of the right as wrong, stubborn, isolating Israel from its U.S. ally and, hence, undermining Israel's security. The United States, it argued, was reacting against Shamir's mistaken policies. The right urged mistrust for the United States and for supporting Israeli patriotism against U.S. pressure. Steadfastness, it argued, would produce a future reconciliation.

The U.S Position

But to what extent was the United States acting in regard to affecting Israel's electoral outcome? This aspect was, in fact, a very secondary factor for U.S. policy makers, who were motivated by broader conceptions of interests and strategy.

The Bush administration considered that advancing Arab-Israeli negotiations was important for maintaining the U.S. regional position. In that regard, it sought Israeli concessions on various points in order to advance the talks. It was especially persuaded by Arab arguments that the continued Jewish settlement in the West Bank and Gaza was a barrier to successful diplomacy.

Within the context of U.S. policy, Bush and Secretary of State James Baker accepted the notion that the American position in the region rested on preserving the good will of the Arab states. The events surrounding the Kuwait crisis of 1991 seemed to provide an opportunity to make progress on Arab-Israeli negotiations as well as making the U.S. government feel a need to show its own efforts in that direction.

At the same time, there was a good deal of personal friction between the patrician U.S. leaders and Shamir. As a superpower, America underestimated Israel's security concerns and its far more fragile situation. Lacking knowledge of the Arab world, U.S. policy makers often overestimated both its moderation and options. Consequently, the Bush administration put a relatively heavier burden on Israel to make compromises, directing U.S. leverage at Israel rather than using U.S. power to push for Arab concessions (Rubin 1992).

But the administration's goal was diplomatic success. Thus, while this prompted some pressure being put on Israel, it also limited such measures, since the administration needed Israeli cooperating in starting, continuing, and progressing in the peace process.

Aside from U.S. national interests, the administration sought success in the Middle East negotiations to enhance its domestic image as highly competent statesmen. This was an especially important factor as the 1992 U.S. presidential elections approached.

Concern about the Jewish vote might enhance the administration's desire to improve relations with Israel but—as we shall see below—the Republican White House did not expect to win many of these ballots. In addition, the two elections' timing allowed Bush to continue his hard line toward Shamir until well after Israel's June balloting, yet shift his stance well before the U.S. election in November. This fact formed a basis for the claim by some Shamir supporters that the Israeli prime minister's reelection in June would not prevent Bush from moving to improve bilateral relations in September or October.

Officially, of course, the Bush administration maintained a posture of noninterference in domestic Israeli politics. This position was largely true, and it was reinforced by Washington's knowledge that such activity could well be counterproductive. Moreover, while U.S. presidents had generally preferred having a Labor Party counterpart ever since the Likud first took office in 1977, diplomacy required dealing with the incumbent government. And the greatest American diplomatic success, the Camp David agreements, had been reached with Prime Minister Begin.

Attempting to act as if Labor was in power had not benefitted previous U.S. diplomatic initiatives. For example, the 1982 Reagan peace plan, drawn up in Washington along the lines of the Labor Party opposition's positions, was rejected by Prime Minister Begin. During the Labor-Likud national unity government of 1984–86, Secretary of State George Schultz pressed peace plans trying to achieve a breakthrough when Prime Minister Shimon Peres headed the coalition for two years before turning over his office to Shamir.

In another period of high activity beginning in 1989, the U.S. government found it difficult to deal with another national unity government in which Foreign Minister Peres and Prime Minister Shamir often took contradictory positions. When U.S. initiatives forced the coalition to break down in early 1990, however, it was Shamir—not Peres—who emerged at the head of a center-right cabinet.

The frustrations of dealing with the Arab side along with these other experiences taught U.S. policy makers that there could be no peace settlement without an Israeli government's agreement. And if that regime was led by a Likud prime minister, U.S. strategy had to be to find proposals acceptable to him.

In this context, during 1991 and the first half of 1992, the Bush administration was trying to change the Shamir government's policy, not displace it. Shamir's encouragement for increasing the rate of Jewish settlement in the territories—coupled with apparent opportunities available in the post-Gulf war period, Israel's request for U.S. loan guarantees, and pressures for austerity within the United States—set the stage for friction in bilateral relations.

The effect of U.S. policy on Israeli 1992 elections, then, was coincidental rather than a matter of design. At the same time, of course, the U.S. government had no incentive to reward the Shamir coalition and thus to strengthen its popularity at home.

If Shamir had met the U.S. conditions on loan guarantees—or even offered a compromise—Bush would have granted the loan guarantees even before Israel's elections. But such a concession would have compromised Shamir's own platform and ideology. His apparent belief that once he won the elections—and Bush faced his own voters—U.S. policy would change made him more unyielding. The four-month gap between Israeli and U.S.

elections and the failure to reach an agreement before the former did not help Shamir at the polls.

Any objective damage from U.S.-Israel relations to Shamir's electoral fortunes arose from policy conflicts, not from a coherent U.S. design to remove him from office. The 1992 Israeli elections showed the importance of relations with the United States but did not prove great U.S. influence over Israeli domestic politics.

Indeed, the ensuring events further illustrated Israel's independent decision making. The United States acted more as facilitator and observer than as mediator during eleven rounds of talks in Washington held in 1992 and 1993 between Israel and Jordanian/Palestinian, Syrian, and Lebanese delegations. Moreover, the real progress was made elsewhere, in direct secret meetings between Israel and the PLO held mostly in Norway. These exchanges led to the Israel-PLO agreement signed in Washington on 13 September 1993.

The fact that the signing ceremony was held on the White House lawn and hosted by President Bill Clinton—who defeated Bush in the November 1992 election and entered office in January 1993—symbolized the important role played by the United States in the long peace process. Without Rabin's election victory in Israel, bilateral, direct exchanges between the local parties had determined the outcome. Indeed, the PLO's comprehension of the limits of U.S. influence on Israel—showing that it must satisfy Israel's government and not merely the White House—was a necessary precondition for success. As Said Kamal, PLO Ambassador to Cairo and one of those preparing the agreement, later commented, "The PLO felt that in its alliance with the United States, Israel makes its own decision, and the American role is to provide support and guarantees, no more" (*Al-Ahram* article cited in *Mideast Mirror* 8 September 1998, 18–9; see also Rubin 1994).

References

Anti-Defamation League. 1992. "Big 50 Press Survey: The Election Victory of Israel's Labor Party and Yitzhak Rabin." Anti-Defamation League, New York, July.

Rubin, Barry. 1992. *Cauldron of Turmoil: America in the Middle East.* New York: Harcourt, Brace, Jovanovich.

———. 1994. *Revolution until Victory? The History and Politics of the PLO.* Cambridge: Harvard University Press.

PART IV

Political Communication

CHAPTER 10

The 1992 Campaign: Valence and Position Dimensions

JONATHAN MENDILOW
Rider University

Critics have pointed to a disparity between the issues on which the 1992 electoral campaign turned and the consequences of the election itself. The Hebrew term *Mahapach* (upheaval) is popularly used to denote the far-reaching shifts in style, ideology, and policies of the new government, especially as regards the Israeli-Palestinian and Israeli-Arab conflicts. The campaign, by contrast, had focused chiefly on leadership and domestic system-management. It was long on personal attacks and negative criticisms of performance and short on positive substantive messages. While this general assessment is a reasonable one as far as it goes, it tends to deflect attention from subtle but important changes in direction and style during the campaign itself, and it obscures the logical sequence of the tactics employed. A closer consideration of the appeals launched by the main contenders as the campaign proceeded may help to clarify the nature and significance of what took place and thereby allow us to speculate on the degree to which the electoral competition and its results indicate more than a temporary phenomenon.

I. The Argument

The exercise of the basic democratic right to vote demands of the citizen that he coordinate complex decisions on two distinct planes. He must pass judgment on the performance of those currently in office, their leadership, and achievements. He must also take a stand on divisive issues of principle. Voter preference usually involves both a positive evaluation of a party's performance and the acceptance of its basic outlook. But individuals, and societies as aggregates of individuals, do not move in fixed grooves. Apart from constant generational and migrational changes in the electoral pool, there are the noncommitted, who may switch their votes from election to election. These are not to be confused with defectors, who alter their choice due to changes in their basic positions or switch sides temporarily due to what they consider to be failures in performance of a party with whose ideology they nevertheless continue to identify.

Because of the uncertainty caused by all these noncommitted voters, a central problem confronting electoral strategists is the necessity to choose the type of appeal best suited to their needs. A party can concentrate on what Donald Stokes called "valence issues," that is, noncontroversial matters and issues of leadership and system management geared to link it with conditions and attributes favored by the general electorate and to link its rivals with those generally valued negatively. Thereby it seeks to gain short-term support without necessitating decisions on questions of principle. Alternatively, a party can concentrate on "position issues," that is, divisive questions "that involve advocacy of government actions from a set of alternatives over which a distribution of voter preferences is defined" (Stokes 1966, 171). Thereby it seeks to gain long-term support by converting the defectors and noncommitted to its principles. In practice, the two strategies are usually combined, and the outstanding question is, in what proportions?

Parties, of course, are not totally rational actors. They are complex organisms, each with its own bounded rationality reflecting its history, program, electoral base, and internal dynamics. They must also take into account the counterbuffeting of rival parties in the election boxing-ring. However, except in the case of "missionary parties," strategists in search of electorally profitable issues need to assess the potential effect of their mix on the targeted public. Consciously or unconsciously, they must base their decisions on a set of hypotheses about the factors that influence the choice of various categories of voters and the relative payoff to be gained from different weightings accorded to these factors. Such considerations are obviously conditioned by place, time, and the agents involved. Nevertheless, there may be broad similarities in the gamesmanship of parties operating in broadly similar contexts.

A case in point is the general resemblance between the strategies adopted in 1992 by Labor and the Likud. Both based their calculations on the fact that an unusually large proportion of the electorate consisted of voters without clear party loyalty: an exceptional number of young first-time voters, the huge wave of new immigrants, and increasing numbers of potential defectors, especially from the incumbent Likud. Polls indicated that a large proportion of all these were primarily concerned with problems of unemployment and housing and that they were troubled by failures of leadership and government performance against the background of a deepening social and economic malaise. Labor's plan of action was predicated on the assumption that while this common denominator on the domestic performance and leadership plane worked in its favor, it did not imply the automatic acceptance of its ideological positions. The decision therefore was to base the appeal to such voters mainly on valence issues, to ignore divisive position issues as far as possible, and not to allow the Likud to deflect attention from leadership and system-management. A similar evaluation led the Likud at the beginning of the campaign to focus on position issues and thereafter to try to corner Labor on problems related to the fate of the Occupied Territories. After polls had shown that the effort to sidetrack the undecided was countereffective, the decision was made to pay labor back in its own coin and to shift the emphasis from an "incumbency style" to a "challenger-style" (Trent and Friedenberg 1991, 63–87): to devote greater attention to arousing suspicions on the character and performance of the Labor leaders and to hark back to failures in system-management of labor-led governments. The consequence was a "unidimensional" campaign conducted almost throughout on valence issues, where each of the main rivals was to a large extent the mirror image of the other.

Some variation of the theses on party adaptation and change that first saw light in reference to the European multiparty systems of the mid-'60s may help to clarify further what took place. Until recently, critics have argued that parties addressing themselves to electorates that increasingly direct their attention away from matters of principle to questions of system-management gradually abandon their ideologies (see, e.g., Wolinetz 1979; Golden 1986). Instead of targeting restricted sections of the population, they aim their appeal at all those whose interests "do not adamantly conflict" (Kirchheimer 1966) by concentrating on uncontroversial issues, performance, leadership, and personalities. The Likud's reassessment of its tactics early in the campaign would confirm the contention that the pressures of competition force main rivals to emulate one another; the adoption of "catch-all" tactics by one compels others to follow suit, thereby altering the style and very nature of party competition.

Such a thesis cannot however account for the behavior of the Israeli electorate. In Europe, the rise of catch-all parties was attributed to ideological indifference bred of the growing dependence on mass consumer goods, the standardization of norms and patterns of living, and the blurring of the traditional lines of cleavage. Such processes were evident in Israel too. But preoccupation with questions of leadership and system management in 1992 owed not a little to conditions that were largely the reverse: widespread social and economic anxiety as well as the emergence of the young, the immigrants, and other groups with specialized interests. This may account for the widespread dissatisfaction with what we have called the "unidimensional" nature of the campaign. It might also explain why polls indicated a growing demand, especially among the undecided, for a two-dimensional campaign in which valence issues of leadership and performance would be firmly based in positions on controversial issues of principle, thereby offering a more complex yet coherent choice.

Significant modifications of strategy in midcampaign would pose a problem for any party, but in the case of Labor and the Likud the difficulty was compounded. The gravamen of the discontent was grounded in the social and economic spheres, and it was precisely here that the difference between the two parties was at its narrowest. Labor had largely moved away from a socialist to the market orientation long favored by the Likud, while such matters as the need for immigration absorption and subsidized housing for young couples were never in question. The main bone of contention was over issues of national security, which Labor, as mentioned above, was not eager to bring up. However, the predicament of the Likud was even greater. Incumbents must run in the final analysis on their record. They may lay blame for failures on the opposition or minimize the extent of difficulties, but they cannot credibly shift their principles at a moment's notice. Challengers, on the other hand, can more easily advocate new principles to guide policy. This may explain why the Likud responded by making changes in emphasis and tone rather than in content, while Labor was able to come up with a more substantive feedback. What had been a wedge issue intended to win over from the Likud the development towns and poorer urban neighborhoods was now expanded to constitute a central national issue: the change of priorities from the development of the settlements in the Territories to the satisfying of urgent needs within Israel proper. Nevertheless, since the problem was not the destiny of the Territories nor of the settlements, other parties, including Tzomet on the Likud's right and Meretz on Labor's left, were free to join in the call for a change of priorities, to come out with more fundamental agendas of change, and even to vie for the same voters.

What follows falls into three parts. The first offers a bird's-eye view of the patterns of appeal launched by the two main parties in the campaign as a whole, and it seeks to explain how and why they deviated from those of 1988. The second tries to show how a campaign largely run on valence issues created pitfalls for the main parties and forced them to readjust their strategies. The conclusion raises questions concerning the use of valence and position issues in electoral campaigns run at a time of social and economic malaise as against times characterized by widespread feelings of relative prosperity.

II. The Shift in Style, 1988–1992

Electoral campaigns in Israel usually extend over about two months. In the first half, propaganda is disseminated chiefly through the press and through parlor meetings and mass rallies. The second, formal phase, centers on daily television and radio electoral programs, each party being allotted time in proportion to its strength in the outgoing Knesset. As in all elections, public interest intensifies as the fateful day approaches, reaching a climax in the final weeks. 1992 constitutes an interesting deviation. Until the last few days, the closer the campaign approached its zenith, the more public interest seemed to dwindle to its nadir. Whereas on the first day of the television blitzkrieg some 60 percent of the electorate watched the programs, by the end of the first week that number was roughly halved (Gallup poll, *Jerusalem Post* 12 June 1992; see also Geocartography and Teleseker polls, *Yediot Aharonot* 12 June 1992). When asked to evaluate the performance of the various parties, viewers gave, on the average, the barely passing grade of six on the scale of one to ten, with the large parties falling well below the median (Smith polls, *Ma'ariv* 12 June 1992). Though the leaders of Labor and the Likud denied that the public was apathetic (see, e.g., *Ma'ariv* 19 June 1992), both parties felt compelled to cancel the massive rallies that had traditionally served as the grand finale of the campaign and had attracted hundreds of thousands in previous elections.

On the face of it, the reason for the lackluster reaction was obvious. The head of the Labor information headquarters summed up the party's campaign as successful because it refused to stray from its purpose of presenting the government as corrupt and incompetent and of presenting Rabin as possessing the qualities required of a prime minister. "The Likud," he claimed, "repeatedly tried to drag us into such issues as Peace, the Territories, or the Histadrut [trade union movement], but we refused to yield to such provocations" (MK Ben-Eliezer, quoted in *Ma'ariv* 23 June 1992). However, commentators from across the board were at one in viewing this "success" as precisely the source of the problem. A prominent figure on the left defined the campaign as an exercise in autism (Benvenisti 1992a), while the communication expert of a party on the right complained that "all sides are slinging mud, none address the issues, and the whole affair is a terrible bore" (Yariv Ben-Eliezer, quoted in Gershon 1992). A distinguished political scientist asserted that "we have been fed junk by 'gimmickmeisters'" (Shlomo Avineri, quoted in *Jerusalem Post* 10 June 1992), and a leading advertizing specialist concurred that "the large parties are concerned only with addressing envelopes without any messages inside. There is no difference between them" (David Tamir, quoted in Gershon 1992).

The content analysis presented in table 10.1 of the Labor party and the Likud electoral appeals appearing on the Israeli television may serve to test such impressionistic observations.[1] The choice of the audiovisual medium reflects the fact that its use intensifies the messages and achieves a greater degree of saturation, especially where parties are allotted time on a daily basis. The effects are strengthened by the level of technical sophistication, an element that was prominent in 1992. Critics have decried the use of the television with its manipulative effects as stifling meaningful discourse and replacing content by showmanship, technical tricks, and emotive images. But campaign techniques in themselves are neutral. They can be put to the service of campaigns waged in position or valence-issue terms with equal effectiveness.

The point can be illustrated by comparing the 1992 Israeli television campaign with that of 1988 (table 10.1). The figures in the columns referring to the contents of the appeals in 1988 reflect a highly ideological campaign, largely focused on controversial foreign policy and security issues. These appeared in 37 percent and 29 percent of the net broadcast time of Labor and the Likud, respectively. By contrast, in 1992, such issues were taken up in only 5 percent of Labor's messages and 3 percent of the Likud's. In the case of Labor, the difference in ratios between position and valence issues in the two campaigns was somewhat lessened by the increased time devoted to controversial domestic issues. The almost doubling of the latter from 8 percent to 15 percent raised the total percentage of position issues to 20 percent (as against 45 percent in 1988). With the Likud however no such compensatory trend took place, and, in fact, stands on controversial domestic issues that in 1988 had appeared in 7 percent of the net time virtually disappeared altogether in 1992. Consequently, position issues appeared only in 3 percent of its 1992 television campaign as compared with 36 percent in 1988.

The figures relating to the other content categories confirm that most of the interparty sparring was indeed over valence issues. What is noticeable is not only the increased time devoted by each party to such issues in the 1992 campaign but also the degree of parallelism between them. As expected, the Likud hammered for more than a third of its time on its achievements in office (34 percent as against 8 percent in 1988) while seeking in a further 15 percent (as against 12 percent in 1988) to warn against the consequences of a Labor victory. Labor dealt with general, noncontroversial issues in some 13 percent of its net time, up from a mere 3 percent in 1988. Nevertheless, both parties spent most of their time on the same issues and in almost the same proportions: leadership (Labor 49 percent and Likud 45 percent, up from 36 percent and 30 percent, respectively) and criticism of rivals (37 percent and 41 percent, up from 20 percent and 21 percent). The similarity between the two parties was even greater than the numbers alone suggest. Both listed rival activists and party branches that they had won over to their side, and

Table 10.1. Content Analysis of Labor and Likud Electoral Appeals
Appearing on Israeli Television, 1–22 June 1992 and 4–29 October 1988

	Labor		Likud	
Content of Appeal	1988 (%)	1992 (%)	1988 (%)	1992 (%)
Exploiting the reputation of leaders	36	49	30	45
Past achievements and positive party traits	9	5	8	34
Criticism of rivals on grounds of poor leadership or failures in system management	20	37	21	41
Fears (war, unemployment, etc.)	7	1	12	15
Unity	—	—	—	2
General noncontroversial issues (democracy, peace, etc.)	3	13	5	4
Continuity	—	—	—	6
Confident assurance of electoral victory	5	6	—	1
Stands on controversial domestic issues (state religion, priorities in allocation of resources, etc.)	8	15	7	0
Stands on controversial foreign policy and defense policy and defense issues (settlement in occupied territories, relations with U.S., etc.)	37	5	29	3
Others	9	9	14	3
N (seconds)	8,573	4,403	9,220	4,676

Note: Content percentages relate to the time alloted to each item. Since each broad-casting second may contain more than one of the content items, the total percent of content item to broadcasting time does not equal 100. Each broadcast was divided into seconds and each content idea was rounded to the nearest whole minute. Percentages were rounded to the nearest whole number.

both claimed that such listing on the part of the other side was a sign of panic. Labor accused the minister of health of personal corruption and pointed to his failure in office. The Likud accused former Labor Ministers of corruption and pointed to the failure of the Histadrut health network. Both pointed an accusing finger at the internal backbiting and rivalries within the opposite camp. Labor portrayed Prime Minister Shamir as out of touch with the people and incapable of governing. The Likud pointed to Rabin's collapse shortly before the 1967 war and his poor record as prime minister as evidence of his incapacity for governing. Finally, shortly before election day Shamir even accused Labor of appropriating the Likud's slogans (*Ma'ariv* 22 June 1992).

Such comparisons, both between the campaigns and between the parties, give rise to two questions. One is more general: What lay behind the dramatic difference between the styles of the electoral competition in 1988 and 1992? The other is particular to 1992: How can one explain the increase in the weight given to controversial domestic issues in the otherwise valence-style campaign of the Labor party, and why was this not paralleled by the Likud?

The treatment of the second question hinges on that of the first and will therefore be deferred to the following section. However, both gain added meaning when one keeps in mind that during the decade preceding the elections the main dispute between the two major parties had been over the fate of the West Bank and Gaza Strip. Indeed, the right-left continuum had become virtually conterminous with the hawk-dove continuum (Shamir 1986). It was precisely over dissensions as to how to proceed with the government's peace initiative of May 1989 and how to react to the U.S. involvement in it that the Labor Party left the National Unity government to become the mainstay of the opposition. Labor and the Likud were themselves far from monolithic, and each had its own hawks and doves. Even during the period of their cohabitation, the centripetal tendencies had been countered by the increasing power of the more extreme wings of each. Whether or not this centrifugal tendency reflected a need in both parties to accentuate the differences that distinguished them from each other (Inbar 1992: 26–28, 149–56), it accelerated after the partnership dissolved. The shift further to the right of Prime Minister Shamir's coalition following its inclusion of the parties of the far right meant the strengthening of the right wing of the Likud that had now become the center of the government spectrum. After the temporary lull caused by the Gulf War, this manifested itself in an unprecedented spurt of building activity over the Green Line.[2] This provided the Labor party as a whole with ammunition to attack government and justify its walkout, and it allowed the left wing within it to express more stridently positions that had earlier been somewhat muted.

Nor did the fact of Israel's participation in the American-brokered peace negotiations reduce the tensions between the Likud-led coalition and Labor or those within each. That Shamir's government agreed to take part in negotiations within the framework, however circumscribed, of what amounted to an international conference, indicated a sidestepping of earlier rejections. It reflected a new post–Gulf War reality in which a refusal to accept the U.S. invitation would have invited serious consequences (see Atherton 1992). But the Likud partners of the far right jibbed at any negotiations, let alone the suggested interim solution of Palestinian autonomy. And in this they found support among not a few members of the Likud itself, most vociferously expressed by Housing Minister Ariel Sharon. Despite the effort to placate internal opposition by intensifying settlement building, the government lost its Knesset majority when Tehiya and Moledet finally left the coalition in January 1992 in protest against what they perceived as excessive concessions to the Palestinians.

These strains acted in turn to aggravate the debate between the Labor hawks and doves, and it came to a climax in the party convention in late November 1991. The need to adopt a new party platform prior to the Knesset elections would in any case have stirred up controversy. But the assessment that the date would have to be advanced and that the elections would determine Israel's stand in the peace talks added fuel to the fire. Following on stormy confrontations, failures to resolve differences in behind-the-scene negotiations, and threats by several MKs to bolt the party and form a more radical coalition with the small parties to the left of Labor, both sides had to make do with less than they sought. The doves withdrew their amendments to the proposals of the Platform Committee, and the hawks were resoundingly defeated. However, if the former failed in their efforts to obtain clear commitments to their positions, the latter had to accept a clear shift to the left in the provisions, including a call for territorial compromise in the Golan Heights, as a way to achieve peace, and a recognition of "the legitimate and national rights of the Palestinians."

Another flash point within and between the two parties was produced over choice and ranking on the slates of Knesset candidates. At issue were the individual positions in the party hierarchies, but the contest had obvious programmatic ramifications. Labor had instituted primary elections, so that candidates had to present their individual positions and campaign for the votes of the party membership. The Likud adhered to the practice of selection by ballot in the Central Committee, resulting in acrimonious competition among camps within the party. In Labor, embattled hawks warned against those who "are tainting Labor as increasingly leftist, making [it] indistinguishable from the Citizen Rights Movement and Mapam, . . . linking it in the voter's mind with the lunatic fringe" (MK Michael Bar-Zohar, quoted in

Honig 1992). In the Likud, Foreign Minister David Levy, leader of the relatively moderate camp, confided on the eve of the crucial vote in the Central Committee that he contemplated resigning from his post if the outcome would be the triumph of the hawkish camps led by Shamir and Sharon. This, he warned, would blur distinctions with the parties of the extreme right and lead to "a negation of the peace process, prolonged confrontation with the U.S., loss of the loan guarantees, the dwindling of immigration from the USSR, and the deterioration of our relations with Europe" (quoted in Ben-Porat 1992). As it turned out, both these premonitions of the outcome proved correct. Yizhak Rabin was elected to head the Labor slate as the party nominee for the premiership. However, most of the other hawks, including front-benchers like Motta Gur and Shoshana Almoslino, did poorly and found themself occupying lower slots. Dovishly inclined competitors tended by contrast to do surprisingly well. As for the Likud, Levy himself retained his place in the top party leadership, but his supporters fared poorly, and an alliance between the Shamir and Sharon camps ensured the decisive triumph of the hawks.

Paradoxically, the very polarization goes some way to explaining what rendered the shift from emphasis on position to emphasis on valence issues possible. Campaign strategies commonly reflect a desire to appeal to two kinds of constituents: the party faithful and the uncommitted. The protection of a party's electoral base involves the assertion of basic principles and the highlighting of ideological differences so as to reinforce group-antagonism with other parties. Though such an appeal is not necessarily incompatible with one directed to the uncommitted, the stronger the confidence of the committed in their party's policies, the freer the choice of appeal presentable to the uncommitted. The tilt of Labor to the left and of the Likud to the right placed the two on the eve of the campaign in a similar situation. Both could take their ideologically minded supporters for granted and could therefore concentrate on targeting those without clear party loyalty. However, the possibility of conducting a campaign in valence-issue terms does not automatically imply the desirability of so doing. And it is there that the symmetry broke down. As the elections loomed closer it became progressively evident that Labor's preference would be to change its 1988 approach by stressing valence issues, whereas the Likud's would be to keep to its focus on position issues.

The rationale of the change can already be seen in Rabin's suggestions at the Labor Party convention for a campaign strategy that would justify his bid to lead the party slate. The convention took place against the background of a rise in the popularity of the Likud, now buoyed up by the hopes raised in the general public by the opening of the peace talks in Madrid in 1991, and the plummeting of the popularity of Labor, whose ammunition seemed to have been stolen. Polls conducted by Hanoch Smith in the first part of November (*Jerusalem Post* 24 January 1992) indicated, for example, that if the elections had been held at that time, Labor would have received only 22 percent of the vote (down from 31.5 percent in 1988), whereas the Likud would have garnered 37 percent (up from 36 percent in 1988). Worse still, the combined strength of the right would have reached 54 percent, and it would do so even without counting the ultrareligious parties, which were expected to join a Likud-led coalition. Such results, confirmed independently by other polls (notably Mina Zemach's, see Honig 1991), gave credence to Rabin's arguments that the party should concentrate its attention on the new voters and on disappointed Likud voters and that the appeal should center on government's failures in the economic sphere and in the absorption of the new immigrants rather than on its record in the sphere of national security.

The import of this suggestion becomes obvious once we take into account the fact that some 260 thousand of the 400 thousand immigrants who had arrived since 1988 were eligible to vote and that some 400 thousand young voters had been added to the voting list. They alone could account between them for twenty-five Knesset seats, and it was they who tended to be especially concerned over authoritative allocations of resources and over government performance, seeing that they were the most exposed to unemployment, housing shortages, and the skyrocketing cost of rental accommodations resulting from the large immigration. The spillover effects also hit other voters, such as young couples or families worried by the impact of the budgetary difficulties on the educational system, thereby creating a ripple effect of disgruntled potential defectors among those of them who had hitherto supported the Likud. Labor's problem however was that in previous elections, on balance, more of the young tended to vote for the right than did the general electorate, while among those who voted for the left showed a greater preference for the parties to the left of Labor than did the general electorate (e.g., Katz and Levinsohn 1989). As for the new immigrants, polls consistently showed their clear predilection for the right. In December 1990, no fewer than 69 percent of new immigrants polled answered the question, What is preferable: giving up territory in exchange for peace, or not giving up territory? in favor of the second alternative. And in the following April, 46 percent declared they would support the right, as against 15 percent who favored the left, with 29 percent undecided (Tatzpit polls, *Jerusalem Post* 31 January 1992). Over and above the fact that Shimon Peres had led Labor in four consecutive electoral failures and that his image had been tarnished by repeated personal attacks by the Likud, he was associated with the dovish ideological side of the party. As such, the argument went, he would be distrusted by a more hawkishly inclined electorate. Rabin, by contrast, was not directly linked to any electoral defeat, and in view of his military record and service as minister of defence under Shamir himself no one could suspect him of being weak-kneed on security issues. He could therefore establish a good rapport with such voters and lead a campaign focusing on government's lack of leadership and failed stewardship of the economy. This interpretation was backed by polls that consistently indicated that Rabin would be more electable than Peres; and the trend became increasingly pronounced as the Labor primaries drew near. To take but one typical example, a Smith poll found that in January 1992, 63 percent of the sample thought Rabin would draw more votes for Labor, as against 14 percent who thought that Peres would be the more popular. The same poll also indicated that Labor led by Peres would gain 28 percent of the vote as against the Likud's 33 percent, but under Rabin the figures would be 36.5 percent as against 28 percent (*Jerusalem Post* 24 January 1992).

Such figures reflect additional factors in the period between the Labor convention and the primaries that militated against the Likud and that worked in Labor's favor, and in favor of Rabin's candidacy for first place on his party's list. Most evident of these was the escalation of the strains with the U.S. administration over the provision of $10 billion in loan guarantees requested by Israel for the absorption of immigrants. At stake was the condition set by Washington that Israel agree to a settlement-freeze in the Occupied Territories. Jerusalem argued that such a demand should be part of the peace negotiations, that accepting it would constitute a unilateral concession to the Palestinians, and that in any case there was no connection between the humanitarian issue of absorption and the fate of Gaza and the West Bank. On top of these problems however was the fact that what was demanded touched the raw nerve of the Likud's ideology, and this on the eve of an electoral campaign with the parties of the extreme right waiting to point an accusing finger at any sign of weakness. After fruitless attempts at compromise, the government opted for the lesser of two evils, gambling on the dividend of a tough stance to offset the electoral costs of popular economic anxiety and on the belief that the elections would precede any further aggravation of economic difficulties.

Nevertheless, the decision exacted a heavy toll. Widespread public ambivalence on the issue had already been revealed by Smith polls in late August 1991, that is, even before President Bush called for the postponement of any decision for 120 days. In response to the question whether the U.S. policy was good for Israel, 48 percent answered in the negative with only 21 percent responding positively and 27 percent unsure. But in response to the question, Should Israel freeze settlement activities in Judea, Samaria, and Gaza in the event of the U.S. setting it as a condition for the granting of the loan guarantees? 57 percent were in favor of the freeze and only 32 percent rejected it (*Jerusalem Post*, international edition, week ending 28 September 1991). As the tensions between Washington and Jerusalem escalated in December and in the first quarter of 1992, polls showed a shift of opinion, especially among the immigrants. As noted earlier, 69 percent of the immigrants rejected in December 1990 the "land for peace" formula. The number dropped to 54 percent in January 1992 and to 46 percent by early May 1992. At the same time, polls revealed a swing away from the right. In April 1991, 46 percent of the immigrants supported the right; in October the number dropped to 37 percent; in January, 35 percent and in early May, a mere 19 percent (Tatzpit polls, *Jerusalem Post* 31 January 1992; *Ma'ariv* 8 May 1992).

The emphasis on social and economic woes depended however on preventing the Likud from turning the tables by accusing the U.S. of interfering in the elections and insinuating that Labor was conniving with it at the expense of national security. Thus, for example, Planning and Economics Minister David Magen was already voicing the charge that "the opposition is harming the national interest under the artificial camouflage of feigning concern for the unemployed and the poor . . . [it is] trying to sow demoralization and despair" (Wallfish, 1992). In these circumstances, Rabin's reputation and record gained in value, since Rabin, unlike Peres, could hardly be the target of such accusations. A further impetus to this emphasis on personality was given by the ongoing debate on electoral reform that climaxed early in January with the crucial second Knesset reading of a bill, to become operative in 1996, for the direct election of the premier. This aroused great public interest, not only because of the anticipated influence on the interparty processes and interparty competition, but because supporters of the bill from both sides of the left-right divide argued that it would serve to break the gridlock that hampered coalition formation and often turned minor parties into kingmakers. The fact that most of the Likud members opposed the bill, with Shamir even prophesying electoral disaster if it were passed (see Goell 1992a), added credence to Labor's pooh-poohing of Shamir's leadership and encouraged Labor to underscore the leader rather that the party as a whole. Finally, what may have worked in favor of Rabin's candidacy was the proximity of the primaries to the opening of the campaign due to the advancement of the elections. This made the electoral consequences of the process more concrete, and it brought home to the rank and file the need to balance ideological and pragmatic considerations. An example of this climate of opinion was the statement by MK Uzi Baram, himself a dove, that Rabin's election to head the list did not signify any change of ideology: "All Labor wanted was to win. That was all. And it knew that only Rabin can deliver victory over the Likud" (interview in *Yediot Aharonot* weekend supplement, 21 February 1992).

In light of all the above, it is understandable that the Likud saw no reason to shift the terms of the debate away from the security concerns that usually upstage other issues in Israeli campaigns. If anything, the discontent of Levy's Sephardi followers, the growing tensions with the U.S., and the constant harping of the media on the likelihood of further economic deterioration strengthened the resolve to base the party's appeal on what Shamir described as a "two-track approach: keeping Eretz Yisrael along with an unrelenting effort towards peace" (*Jerusalem Post*, international edition, week ending 15 February 1992). Indeed, as he put it at the end of April, "tacticians without ideology will not achieve anything . . . the top priority is ideology" (*Jerusalem Post* international edition, week ending 25 April 1992). A few days later, the state comptroller published her annual report together with a special report on government corporations. These accused government of serious mismanagement, waste, and nepotism, and they even recommended criminal investigations in several instances. This sharpened even further the need to shy away from the issues of the economy, immigrant absorption, and system management.

The concentration on the same segments of the electorate turned the first skirmish of the campaign into what can be called a "battle of agendas." Both the Likud and Labor presented to the public the agenda on which they wished to run and awaited reactions that would establish the grounds on which the campaign as a whole would be fought. Though there had already been brushes between the parties after February when it became clear that new elections were imminent, the rallies officially opening the party campaigns clearly indicated their proposed lines of attack. That of the Likud began with filmed excerpts of speeches by the revered late leader Menachem Begin on the subject of the territorial integrity of the historical Land of Israel, followed by impressions expressed by new immigrants who had toured the Occupied Territories. The themes of continuity and the realization of the vision were reinforced by the fact that the keynote speech was delivered by Begin's son, MK Benny Begin, who dismissed contemptuously any territorial compromise with the Arabs and stressed the strategic and redemptive significance of the Territories: "It will probably take Labor a full decade to appreciate the success and salvation contributed to the State by the Settlements in Samaria, Judea and Gaza. They reject building in densely occupied Arab areas . . . they do not yet understand that these, by the grace of God, will be densely occupied Jewish areas" (*Hadashot* 4 May 1991). The rally was immediately followed by a tour of the Occupied Territories conducted for reporters and accompanied by a cavalcade of busses filled with new and veteran immigrants.

The opening rally of the Labor Party a week later was in stark contrast to this emotional and ideological display. It was a meeting of party activists with the chairmen of the various campaign headquarters and with Rabin as the main speaker. In his well-known laconic style he outlined the main themes: Labor as the party representing national consensus and the replacing of corrupt and ineffectual government by one capable of exploiting the potential offered by mass immigration and a modern economy. "Our slogan is no longer 'let my people go' but 'let my people be absorbed,' and it is here that [government has] failed" (*Hadashot* 11 May 1992). The party, he proclaimed, must create an atmosphere of confidence in victory, leadership and national *esprit de corps.* In the field the efforts took two forms. Before the electronic campaign began, party activists established contact with some half-million voters through parlor meetings and home visits to discuss specific interests and concerns. Many of these local meetings were deliberately held in Likud bastions and were organized by regional headquarters headed by prominent Labor leaders of the same ethnic background as the local inhabitants (Louvlavski 1992; Sand 1992). Concurrently, rallies in which the main speaker was usually Rabin himself were conducted in major Likud strongholds. They were designed to draw the attention of the media by challenging the Likud in its home bases, forcing it to react. The cogency of this tactic may be better appreciated once we adopt the media agenda-setting perspective according to which though the mass media "may have little direct effect on political opinions . . . they have a significant cumulative effect on cognitions—the agenda of issues that voters have opinions about" (McCombs, Einsiedel, and Weaver 1991, 14).[3] The heated opposition at the Labor rallies directed attention to Rabin's leadership, to his attacks on government performance, and to the extent of the impact of both on dissatisfied Likud voters.

In mid-May, the Likud campaign headquarters decided that organized tours of the Occupied Territories were counterproductive and that the emphasis of the campaign should be shifted away from the settlement issue.[4] Polls showed that not only the young and the new immigrants[5] but even traditional Likud supporters regarded unemployment, social and economic problems, and system management as their main concern. Typical examples are the Geocartography Institute polls that found that the number of waverers had significantly grown at the expense of the Likud. They found that 21.6 percent of the potential Likud defectors pointed to unemployment as the main reason for their vote, 18.9 percent to socioeconomic conditions, 16.2 percent to government corruption and inefficiency, and 13.5 percent to the appeal of Rabin as a leader. Only 1.7 percent mentioned the settlement issue at all (*Hadashot* 1 June 1992). The conclusion was that henceforth stress would be laid on doubts as to the ability to govern of Labor in general and of Rabin in particular. A campaign of persuasion would be opened, one in which all Likud MKs and Ministers would personally contact Likud defectors and waverers (*Ha'aretz* 1 June 1992). Though faint ideological echoes persisted, mainly in the attack on Rabin as a Trojan horse of the extreme left, the debate thereafter was largely conducted on Labor's turf, namely leadership, system management, and corruption.[6] There was a hint of resignation in the statement of Minister Nissim, head of the Likud campaign headquarters, when he defined the television campaign as "our greatest chance . . . Labor will have no answer to our messages" (*Ma'ariv* 2 June 1992).

III. The Television Campaign

Now that we have noted the general shift of the center of gravity in both the Labor and the Likud campaigns, we can turn to the second question posed earlier, namely, how is one to explain the weight given by Labor in its television appeals to controversial issues, and why was this not paralleled by the Likud?

Table 10.2 reveals that actually an appreciable change did take place in the propaganda of Likud as well. If one compares the content of the appeals during the first four days with that of the rest of the campaign, the change undertaken by both parties becomes even more prominent. In the Likud's appeals what is especially noticeable is the diminution of its criticism of Labor from 50.4 percent between June 1 and 4 to 37.4 percent between June 5 and 22. Similarly, the attempt to arouse fears of what a Labor government might do fell from 17.6 percent to 14.2 percent. This in turn involved less time being devoted to controversial foreign policy and security issues (from 5 percent to 2.1 percent), since much of the attempt to sow fear had been on grounds that Labor would play into the hands of the extreme left and the supporters of the PLO. Conversely, more time was spent on positive presentations of Likud leaders (from 30.4 percent to 50.6 percent) and on practical achievements of the Likud-led government (from 27.9 percent to 35.9 percent). What stands out, however, is that the low percentage of time in which controversial principles were raised was further reduced (from 5 percent to 2.4 percent) and domestic position issues were mentioned in no more than 0.2 percent of the total time.

Labor too reduced its criticism of the Likud and its leaders (from 44.1 percent to 35.3 percent). But the outstanding change was in the rise of controversial issues from 1.4 percent to 25.6 percent, most noticeably in the domestic sphere (from 0 percent to 19.3 percent). The reason for the shift in the appeals launched by both parties[7] may be found in the negative feedback received in the first four days. Summing up the campaign, the head of the Labor Party information headquarters acknowledged that it was brought into consideration that the concentration on valence issues might involve "a

Table 10.2. Content Analysis of Labor and Likud Electoral Appeals Appearing on Israeli Television, 1–22 June 1992

Content of Appeal	Labor			Likud		
	June 1–4 (%)	June 5–22 (%)	Total TV Campaign (%)	June 1–4 (%)	June 5–22 (%)	Total TV Campaign (%)
Exploiting the reputation of leaders	55.3	47.3	49.2	30.5	50.6	45.5
Past achievements and positive party traits	6.8	4.5	5.1	27.9	35.9	33.9
Criticism of rivals on grounds of poor leadership or failures in system management	44.1	35.3	37.4	50.4	37.4	40.7
Fears (war, unemployment, etc.)	—	0.7	0.5	17.6	14.2	15.1
Unity	—	—	—	—	2.7	2.0
General noncontroversial issues (democracy, peace, etc.)	5.3	14.9	12.7	3.8	3.7	3.7
Continuity	—	—	—	4.9	6.6	6.1
Confident assurance of electoral victory	10.1	4.1	5.5	2.7	—	0.7
Stands on controversial domestic issues (state religion, priorities in allocation of resources, etc.)	—	19.3	14.7	—	0.3	0.2
Stands on controversial foreign policy and defense issues (settlement in occupied territories, relations with U.S., etc.)	1.4	6.3	5.1	5.0	2.1	2.9
Others	1.2	12.0	9.2	2.6	2.9	2.8
N (seconds)	1,045	3,358	4,403	1,188	3,486	4,674

Note: Content percentages relate to the time alloted to each item. Since each broadcasting second may contain more than one of the content items, the total percent of content item to broadcasting time does not equal 100. Jingles and time devoted to broadcasting the party's initials were not counted. Each broadcast was divided into seconds, and each content idea was rounded to the first tenth of a percent. "Others" refers to instances in which three checkers failed to include broadcast time under any of the content readings.

price in terms of those hesitating between Labor and Meretz" (Haim Ramon, quoted in *Ma'ariv* 23 June 1992). The price however was badly underestimated. Polls taken after the first four days showed that 1 percent of the voters already indicated their decision to change from Labor to Meretz (Smith polls, *Ma'ariv* 5 June 1992, 12 June 1992). Meretz itself contacted by phone as many as eighty thousand households chosen from those voting centers where in 1988 a high proportion of votes had been cast for labor and the parties on its left. Its findings showed the number of hesitants between Labor and the left had jumped from 3.5 percent in 1988 to 19 percent (Temkin 1991). More ominous still were the reactions of those to whom Labor primarily directed its appeal. The party's secretary general explained, as the reason for the revision of the style and content of the broadcasts, that the target audience demanded "more concrete positions" and had little patience for what had been offered it (MK Micha Harish, quoted in *Ha'aretz* 8 June 1992). The same phenomenon was described more bluntly after the elections by Arie Rotenberg, the Labor television campaign manager. On the very first day, he stated, "we were inundated with criticism on our lack of relevance. Reactions by the general public as well as by our own members were a call to stop with the jingles, technical trickery and vicious attacks on the Likud. People wanted to hear solutions instead." It was, he concluded, "virtually a public rebellion in a demand [that we] come to the point" (Rotenberg 1992).

What facilitated the switch was the availability of an earlier propaganda item that could readily be overhauled and applied to the immediate situation. In previous elections as well as in the early phases of the 1992 campaign, Labor had accused the Likud of reneging on its promises to the poorer urban neighborhoods and the development towns, where a high proportion of its followers were concentrated. In its enthusiasm for the settlements, it had been channeling the resources so badly needed to the Occupied Territories. Yet in 1988 Labor had not pressed the argument, partly because interparty debate focused directly on the questions of peace and the destiny of the Territories. The issue again played a minor role at the beginning of the 1992 campaign because of Labor's decision to turn the elections into a plebiscite on the Likud's leadership and economic stewardship. Now the theme of a change of priorities and diversion of resources from the Territories to Israel proper was given pride of place. However, it was no longer limited to just one segment of the population but deepened and broadened to cover the priorities of the nation as a whole, thus allowing all domestic areas of policy to be brought within its scope. Such comprehensiveness in turn added to the attacks on government and enabled Labor to promise social and economic reform without entering the minefield of the future of the Territories.

A week after election day, the head of Labor's campaign information headquarters drew the various stands into a coherent argument to make clear "what we repeatedly said and Rabin emphasized in his campaign regarding the [need for] a fundamental change of national priorities." A brief listing of his main points may help to illustrate the use to which the call for "new priorities" was put. The government's settlement activities, he argued, were counterbalanced by its failure to intervene in social and economic matters. As a result, society was becoming increasingly polarized, and the standards of health, education, welfare, and other services were steadily deteriorating. The outer front of prosperity and ever-expanding settlements hid a backyard of neglect, illiteracy, unemployment, and drug use. If Israel was not to become a Third World country, investment in the facade must cease forthwith and the money diverted to clearing out the backyard junk. "It was this commitment to national and social change which lay behind the electoral *volte face*" (Ben-Eliezer 1992).

Reading between the lines of Labor's pronouncements reveals, beyond the shift of focus from Greater Israel to Israel proper, two further dimensions. Evident in the insistence on fostering the well-being of the individual citizen was a conception of the nation as an aggregate whose success is measured by that of all its members, thus reversing the Likud's subordination of the individual to the abstraction of the nation as a mystical entity. Such a view squared with its vision of Israel's future as wedded to its historical past, which contrasted with Labor's pragmatic concern with the present. The difference, to take one example, is clearly discernible in Shamir's plea to the new immigrants to consider themselves as an inseparable part of the Israeli people: "Your concerns with the problems of absorption should give way to the overriding destiny of the nation . . . of which you are now members. I call upon you to rise above your immediate interests as individuals and to think today of the supreme interests of the state" (*Israel TV* 5 June 1992).

The extent of the modification of Labor's line of propaganda must be estimated in the context of the rest of its campaign, in which valence issues remained predominant. However, the effect was by no means insignificant, as attested by the Likud's reaction. Toward the end of the campaign it hesitantly returned to the settlement theme, but this time defensively, in an effort to play down the cost of its policy. The total investment in the Occupied Territories, it was now claimed, was no more than 1 percent of the national budget. All the rest was invested in immigration absorption, in the poor neighborhoods, and in stimulating the economy (*Israel TV* 20 June, 1992). No less than 93.7 percent of government investment in housing was within Israel proper (*Israel TV* 21 June 1992), as was most of the road building and infrastructure development (*Israel Radio* 18 June 1992, 21 June 1992). Such claims, which stretched general credibility to its limits were, as critics quickly pointed out, signs of the Likud's awareness that its central credo was working against it among the undecided (e.g., Abramovitch 1992). This had become clear even earlier, as shown by the quickly abandoned attempt to appropriate the Labor slogan and to claim that it was popular young Likud leaders like MK. Moshe Katsav who had "changed the national priorities and brought about an upheaval" (*Israel TV* 8 June 1992). Toward the end of the campaign, in a similar forlorn hope, the popular mayor of Yavne pleaded for a change of national priorities that would elevate education to the top of the list (*Israel TV* 20 June 1992).

Other parties also tried to base their propaganda on a call for a far reaching change of national priorities and for a shift of accent onto the social and economic concerns of the citizen within Israel proper. That this line had been taken early in the television campaign by Meretz was to be expected, for it had always crusaded against poverty, religious bigotry, and gender and national discrimination, and it had tirelessly campaigned on issues such as improvement of welfare and social services. Indeed, the largest faction in Meretz was the previously independent Movement for Citizens' Rights. Even before the campaign got underway, polls conducted by the party revealed that the main attraction it held for its supporters as well as for those of Labor and for the undecided was its stand on social issues, including anticorruption. Forty percent of its members and supporters pointed to the party's positions on social and economic issues as the first or second determinant of their preference, and an additional 22 percent attributed their choice or preference to the anticorruption stand. Only 20 percent gave defense and security issues as a main (first or second) factor. The more general polls revealed a similar picture: 40 percent regarded social and economic factors as the first or second reason for considering a vote for Meretz, 35 percent pointed to the stand on corruption, and again only 20 percent pointed to defense and security issues.[8]

What came, however, as one of the greatest surprises of the campaign was Tzomet's successful call for a similar change of national priorities. Despite its strong endorsement of the policy of settlement in the Occupied Territories and its participation in the Likud-led government after Labor had left the National Unity coalition, its situation differed significantly from the other right-wing parties. This was because of its independent line on a number of issues, including its support of electoral reform, which led it to temporarily withdraw from the government. In a press conference opening the party's campaign, the founder-leader, MK Rafael Eitan, exploited his nonalignment with the Likud to redefine Tzomet's position in the party spectrum as "a central party" intent with presenting an alternative to those Likud defectors who distrusted Labor (*Hadashot* 11 May 1992). In the following days he came out with a series of programmatic declarations designed to shift emphasis in the party's message toward social and economic issues and suggest a well-thought-out and moderate alternative on the territorial question (see Sand 1992). By the beginning of the television campaign, parallel with Labor's call for changes in the national priorities, Tzomet was able to present its own more detailed and radical version. In a markedly unequivocal and trenchant style, it put forth a set of positions amounting to a complete reordering of the social and economic system, alongside major legal, electoral, and governmental reforms. Perhaps the most outspoken demands were those to stop all monetary favoritism of the religious institutions, to put an end to the release of religious seminarists from military conscription, and to raise education to the top of the national priority list. Such positions, along with the call for new ethical standards in government, brought the party close to the principles advocated by Meretz. "Tzomet," one critic complained, "has become more and more a carbon copy of Shinui [the former independent centrist faction of Meretz] . . . and like it may well enter into unexpected coalitions" (Shnitzer 1992). "The right-wing has disappeared all of a sudden," asserted another critic, "now that Tsomet has become a party of the center, chiefly concerned with good government and education, . . . its social and economic program is in fact that of the Left" (Shohat 1992).

Nor was such an appraisal confined to professional critics. The Meretz telephone campaign mentioned earlier found that after the first week of television some 3.5 percent of those polled (corresponding to 1 1/2 to 2 Knesset mandates) wavered between Meretz and Tzomet (*Ha'aretz* 8 June 1992; Temkin 1992). Subsequently, party and external polls confirmed the trend in all parts of the country, especially among the young first-time voters and the Likud defectors (*Ha'aretz* 20 June 1992). Of special interest are the Smith polls, which indicated that fully half of Tzomet's gains were made during the first days of the television campaign (Silver 1992a), and the Gallup finding that several days before the voting most of the first-time voters who still wavered hesitated between Meretz and Tzomet (*Hadashot* 20 June 1992).

Several explanations were offered for this wavering between parties at the opposite ends of the political spectrum. For Rabin, it was a sign of the weakening of the party system, exposed by the tendency of voters to pin their faith in the charisma of individual leaders rather than on the parties that they had come to despise (*Hadashot* 29 June 1992). For others, hesitancy between the two parties was due to the rejection of ideology by a relatively affluent electorate that deferred consideration of divisive issues to some distant future and was concerned with only marginal improvement of the status quo (Benvenisti 1992b). Yet others saw it as resulting from the ideological coming together of the two parties on the religious issue. This suited the tunnel vision of young voters troubled by unemployment and freedom from conscription of religious seminarists, two issues that were linked by the fact that the minister of labor was a rabbi and leader of an ultra-Orthodox party (Goell 1992b). This diversity of explanations exemplifies the general bewilderment shared by Meretz itself. "We were at first dumbfounded, and by the time we figured out what had happened it was too late to do anything about it," one of its MKs admitted. "What apparently lay behind it was that young voters were fed up with the large parties and looked for such as would address them straightforwardly. Meretz and Tzomet represented in their eyes an authentic, non-evasive ideological approach. . . . Had we realized this in time we would have pressed home that they [Tzomet] are hawkish and promoters of settlements" (Temkin 1992).[9]

The argument offered in this chapter is that these explanations are all partly, and none wholly, right. The vacillation between parties that had hitherto been seen as holding extreme positions in the political spectrum and the disconcertment this evoked were symptomatic of what occurred in the entire campaign, and they help to explain the election results. It was not that young voters forgot or were oblivious of Tzomet's positions on the Occupied Territories. Rather, it was that the entire issue was overshadowed by more immediate concerns on which the two parties overlapped. Moreover, both were small ideological parties noted for their uncompromising stands. In the campaign they strengthened their image by a common style of direct, unadorned, and unambiguous presentation of position issues. The fact that the large parties campaigned mainly in valence-issue terms highlighted this common denominator. In the final analysis, what had earlier separated them was subordinated to their common stands and to their credibility, now that many of the voters had changed their conception of the ideological spectrum.

IV. Conclusion

Schumpeter (1942), Downs (1957), and others formulated a conception of political parties as entrepreneurs angling for maximum sales in a competitive market. In the context of the post–World War II Western multiparty systems, this implied the rise of "catch-all" parties, de-emphasizing ideology to respond to the demands of the widest range of voters. The prognosis assumed however a continued prosperity that did not occur. Today one may enquire what happens to parties attempting to campaign in catch-all style in conditions the reverse of those postulated. The problem is sharpened, since widespread economic anxieties and a sense of failure in system-management tempt parties, chiefly but not only those in opposition, to campaign in valence-issue terms, whether to concentrate the voters' minds on the failures of government or to deflect their minds from them and to claim successes.

The Israeli case points to the danger that the adoption of such strategies by the major contenders may lead to extensive voter frustration.

The 1992 campaign was launched at a time when large groups within the electorate were exceptionally concerned with questions of system-management and the social and economic performance of government. Labor correctly identified the need to base its appeal to such voters on the issues that perturbed them, and the Likud was forced to follow suit. Neither, however, discerned the full nature of the perturbation. At this point it may be more fitting to shift from the market to a medical analogy. Patients suspecting a serious illness will not be reassured by doctors who merely enumerate the symptoms, put the blame on previous practitioners, and vaguely promise a cure. What they look for is an identification of the nature and causes of the sickness, a proposal of treatment, and an explanation of how it will work. What has been dismissed as public indifference was in reality the baffling of such expectations. There was a widespread feeling that both large parties were tarred with the same brush and that the party system had failed in that the main parties had neglected to structure an adequate choice between them. From this perspective the "virtual rebellion" after the first days of the television campaign could be interpreted as a groundswell of support for the return of meaning to electoral participation.

Large parties basing their strategy on valence issues in conditions such as in Israel provide opportunities for minor parties to profit electorally. Less fearful of alienating specific segments of the electorate, they can rush in with clearer position issues for which they are not likely to be held to account. But in defining the choices confronting the electorate, campaign tactics also create conditions that affect the existing lines of cleavage. When Labor made national priorities its leading position issue, it sought to meet the call to provide grounds for meaningful choice while bettering its position within the existing lines of cleavage. However, before the change could achieve the intended effect, Tzomet stole Labor's thunder and won over significant numbers of the undecided voters, thereby undermining party cleavages. National security remained a major line of cleavage and continued to exert a strong impact on the vote. But now this issue forked off in two directions: on the question of the destiny of the Territories, Labor and Meretz strongly differed with Tzomet. On the position of their place in national priorities, all three found themselves in the same boat. Election results showed that the parties most closely associated with the outgoing government's settlements policy, Likud and Tehiya, lost heavily: the former eight of its forty Knesset seats and the latter all its three seats. The biggest winner was Tzomet, which profited from both directions and quadrupled its representation from two to eight MKs. Next came Labor, which garnered five additional seats (thirty-nine to forty-four) and Meretz (ten to twelve MKs).[10]

Will the right-left cleavage be reestablished, or will the crisscrossing issue of the ordering of national priorities eventuate in lasting fault-lines? The question assumes different meanings in relation to each of the main parties. Will Labor's last-moment ploy become the organizing principle of its ideology, bringing together its security, foreign, and domestic policies? Or will it be put aside and only taken out again to be used as a wedge issue in future elections? As the core of the new government, it must be judged by its record. Here the test will be not only whether but how successfully it will carry out the pledge to change national priorities. As for the Likud, the question hinges on the degree to which its Greater Israel ideology will be incorporated as an integral part of the wider schemata which will include an emphasis on socioeconomic problems of Israel proper. The choice was astutely put by a party leader: "Is it possible to address ourselves to some of these issues [which dominated the campaign] even if it requires a certain moderation of some of our traditional positions? If we will not be able to find appropriate answers . . . we will become irrelevant" (Ehud Olmert, quoted in Silver 1992b).

Notes

1. The data appearing in tables 10.1 and 10.2 were generated according to the following procedures: (*a*) the Labor and the Likud television campaign appeals were videotaped; (*b*) jingles and time devoted to broadcasting the party's acronyms were deducted; and (*c*) each party presentation was reviewed independently by two viewers and divided as far as possible into content segments. Where simultaneous oral and visual messages were not consistent, each was segmented separately; (*d*) each segment was timed and categorized by the two panelists according to the list of content appeals prepared by the author; (*e*) in cases of disagreement, the author served as judge; and (*f*) where all three failed to include the broadcast time under any of the content items, the segment was listed under the category of "others." For content analyses of electoral appeals in the Israeli context see, among others, Torgovnik 1972; Elizur and Katz 1980; Caspi and Eyal 1983; Herzog 1990.

2. Though no official figures have been published, on-site counts made by the antisettlement "Peace Now" movement revealed that during the 1991 calendar year more than 15 percent of the nonmilitary budget was devoted to infrastructure and more than 13,000 housing units were added to the settlements (*Jerusalem Post* International Edition, week ending 1 February 1992). These figures were later challenged by the Council of Jewish Settlements in Judea, Samaria, and Gaza, which disclosed the number of 16,500 units plus hundreds more in the site-preparation stage (*Ma'ariv* 23

July 1992). Whatever the true number may be, the significance becomes clearer when we consider that during the preceding twenty-three years the total numbers of homes built in the settlements was about 20,000.

3. For a further analysis of the agenda-setting function of the media, see Protess and McCombs 1991. However, there are critics who regard agenda-setting as "a plausible but unproven idea" (McQuail 1987, 276).

4. It is worth noting that the minister who was the foremost proponent of abandoning the settlement issue was no other than Ariel Sharon, pugnacious defender of the settlers and the one who contributed perhaps more than anyone else in government to the settlement efforts in the Occupied Territories.

5. To illustrate the point one may refer to polls relating to each of the categories. In mid-May Geo-cartography polls found that the proportion of undecided voters who had previously voted Likud was twice (34.8 percent) that of those who had previously voted Labor (18 percent) and that their main concern was the economy (Degani and Degani 1992a). Another Geocartography poll found that 34 percent of the Russian immigrants placed absorption as their leading concern, 20 percent the economy, and 11 percent social issues. Only 16 percent pointed to defence and security (Degani and Degani 1992b). Telseker polls found that a far greater number of young voters than in previous elections were either wavering (25 percent) or decided for the left (42 percent). The main topics at issue were government efficiency, the place of religion in national life, and which party could best deal with the economy (*Yediot Aharonot* 22 June 1992).

6. An interesting indication of this situation was given by private advertisements, published in the national press by nonparty groups such as the Peace Now movement or even by concerned individuals like industrialist Steff Wertheimer, calling on the electorate to examine the party positions on crucial issues before casting their vote. Wertheimer's advertisement, for instance, ran: "all [the parties] have forgotten the essentials . . . Don't waste your vote on irrelevancies. I am not running for the Knesset, but I am suggesting you base your choice on . . . [a list of issues that should be examined by the voter]" (*Ha'aretz* 17 June 1992). For the Peace Now ad, see, e.g., *Ha'aretz* 8 June 1992).

7. In the Likud's case, this may have also reflected the fact that several days before the television campaign began Rabin cut the ground from under the feet of the Likud by granting a press interview in which he frankly discussed the past problems on which the Likud based its attacks, including his brief collapse under the strain preceding the Six Days war. Subsequent polls indicated no significant drop in his popularity (see *The Jerusalem Report* 18 June 1992, 6). Most interesting were the Modi'in Ezrahi polls (*Hadashot* 3 June 1992) which revealed that 37 percent of those undecided felt that the

attacks on Rabin were harming the Likud and an additional 37 percent felt uninfluenced by them. No less significantly, Likud voters themselves were evenly divided, with 39 percent feeling the attacks harmed their own party, 35 percent the Labor, and the remainder believing they had no effect.

8. Unpublished polls conducted by Peres, Yochanan, and Dafna 11 April 1992, The Stands Taken by Young Voters in the Election, for the Meretz Party. I wish to thank the Ratz faction secretary-general, MK Benny Temkin, for permission to use this material.

9. This belated explanation conforms with the stronger demands made by the party youth headquarters several days before the elections day to "launch an immediate attack on Tzomet with a view to exposing its hypocrisy and the hawkishness of Raful [its founder-leader]" (MK Ron Cohen, quoted in *Ha'aretz* 14 June 1992).

10. Another party that may have profited from the blurring of the left-right cleavage is the National Religious Party (NRP), which gained an additional Knesset seat (from five to six MKs). One of the reasons was the return of Meimad voters to the fold. In 1992, Meimad had split off in an effort to attract those Zionist religious voters who defined themselves as centrists on the issue of the Territories, as against the right wing tendencies of the mainstream NRP. Failing to pass the electoral threshhold, most of its members returned in 1992. The argument offered by one of its prominent leaders is illuminating. The NRP, he maintained, represents an entire way of life. The decrease in importance of the territorial and settlements issues means the increase in importance of such elements that make the party "a camp." "Admittedly, we in the center may feel like orphans. But I am sure that the party as a whole will adopt a wiser line" (Shalom Rosenberg, quoted in *Ha'aretz* 8 June 1992).

References

Abramovitch, Amnon. 1992. "The Floating Votes are Drifting Ashore." *Ma'ariv Weekend Supplement,* 19 June.

Atherton, Alfred L., Jr. 1992. "The Shifting Sands of Middle-East Peace." *Foreign Affairs* 86:114–33.

Ben-Eliezer, Benjamin. 1992. "The Backyard." *Ma'ariv* 20 June.

Ben-Porat, Yeshayahu. 1992. "Despicableness." *Yediot Ahronot* weekend supplement, 10 April.

Benvenisti, Meron. 1992a. "An Autistic System." *Ha'aretz,* 14 June.

———. 1992b. "The Prosaic Sobriety of the Voter." *Ha'aretz,* 19 June.

Caspi, Dan, and Chaim H. Eyal, "Professionalization Trends in Israeli Election Propaganda, 1973–1981." In *The Elections in Israel—1981,* ed. Asher Arian. 235–58. Tel Aviv: Ramot.

Degani, Avi, and Degani, Rina. 1992a. "44% Have Still Not Decided for Whom They Will Vote." *Yediot Aharonot*, 15 May.

———. 1992b. "Where Will the Russian Vote Go?" *Yediot Aharonot*, 22 May.

Downs, Anthony. 1957. *An Economic Theory of Democracy*. New York: Harper.

Elizur, Judith, and Elihu Katz. 1980. "The Media in the Israeli Election of 1977." In *The Elections in Israel 1977*, ed. Asher Arian. Jerusalem: Jerusalem Academic Press.

Gershon, Michal. 1992. "Everybody is Shooting Everywhere." *Ma'ariv Election Supplement*, 22 June.

Goell, Yosef. 1992a. "How Labor Could Win Next Time." *Jerusalem Post*, international edition, week ending 18 January.

———. 1992b. "Voters Have Punished the Likud." *Jerusalem Post*, 26 June.

Golden, Mariam. 1986. "Interest Representation, Party Systems, and the State: Italy in Comparative Perspective." *Comparative Politics* 18:279–301.

Herzog, Hanna. 1990. "Was it on the Agenda? The Hidden Agenda of the 1988 Campaign." In *The Elections in Israel—1988*, ed. Asher Arian and Michal Shamir. Boulder: Westview Press.

Honig, Sarah. 1991. "Grim, Party-Pooping Polls Rain on Labor Parade." *Jerusalem Post*, international edition, week ending 30 November.

———. 1992. "Right Gets Righter, Left Gets Lefter." *Jerusalem Post*, international edition, week ending 5 January.

Inbar, Efraim. 1992. *War and Peace in Israeli Politics: Labor Party Positions on National Security*. Boulder: Lynn Rienner.

Katz, Elihu, and Levinsohn, Hanan. 1989. "Too Good to be True: Notes on the Israeli Elections of 1988." *International Journal of Public Opinion Research* 1:111–23.

Kirchheimer, Otto. 1966. "The Transformation of the Western European Party System." In *Political Parties and Political Development*, ed. Josef LaPalombara and Myron Weiner. Princeton: Princeton University Press.

Levitzki, Naomi. 1992. "The Debts of the Likud: Everyone Blames Everybody." *Yediot Aharonot*, 21 August.

Louvlavski, Naomi. 1992. Interview. 1 June.

McCombs, Maxwell, Edna Einsiedel, and David Weaver. 1991. *Contemporary Public Opinion, Issues and the News*. Hillsdale, N.J.: Lawrence Erlbaum.

McQuail, David. 1987. *Mass Communication Theory: An Introduction*. Beverly Hills: Sage.

Protess, David L., and McCombs, Maxwell, eds. 1991. *Agenda Setting, Readings on Media, Public Opinion, and Policymaking*. Hillsdale, N.J.: Lawrence Erlbaum.

Rotenberg, Ariel. 1992. Interview by Ronit Hurowitz. *Hadashot*, 26 June.

Sand, Etti. 1992. "Electoral Strategy, 92." *Davar*, 26 June.

Schumpeter, Josef. 1942. *Capitalism, Socialism and Democracy.* New York: Harper.

Shamir, Michal. 1986. "Realignment in the Israeli Party System." In *The Elections in Israel—1984*, ed. Asher Arian and Michal Shamir. New Brunswick, N.J.: Transaction.

Shnitzer, Samuel. 1992. "The Floating Votes are Drifting Ashore." *Ma'ariv*, 19 June.

Shohat, Orit. 1992. "The Right-Wing has Disappeared all of a Sudden." *Ha'aretz*, 26 June.

Silver, Eric. 1992a. "The Rise of Raful." *Jerusalem Report*, 16 July.

————. 1992b. "A Farewell to Ideology?" *Jerusalem Report*, 26 July.

Stokes, Donald E. 1966. "Spatial Models of Party Competition." In *Elections and the Political Order*, ed. Angus Campbell, Philip E. Converse, Warren E. Miller, and Donald E. Stokes. New York: John Wiley and Sons.

Temkin, Benni. 1992. Interview, 17 August.

Torgovnik, Efraim. 1972. "Party Factions and Election Issues." In *The Elections in Israel—1969*, ed. Asher Arian. 21–40. Jerusalem: Jerusalem Academic Press.

Trent, Judith S., and Robert V. Friedenberg. 1991. *Political Campaign Communications.* 2nd ed. New York: Praeger.

Wallfish, Asher. 1992. "Poisonous Politics are Becoming Passe." Jerusalem Post, international edition, 11 January.

Wolinez, Steven B. 1979. "The Transformation of Western European Party Systems Revisited." *West European Politics* 2:4–28.

CHAPTER 11

Voters as Consumers: Audience Perspectives on the Election Broadcasts

GADI WOLFSFELD

The Hebrew University of Jerusalem

Televised advertisements have become a central component of the Israeli election campaign in recent years. Millions of shekels are poured into the production of these commercials, and their content and tone have an important impact on the pace and agenda of the election campaign. The newspapers carry daily reviews of the previous evening's broadcasts as various pundits attempt to rate the effectiveness of the ads in the perennial attempt to determine who is "winning" the campaign. The underlying question appears to be, Who is doing the best job at manipulating the public?

The controversy over whether or not these ads should be broadcast takes place during every election campaign. In addition to making the usual complaints about the dominance of "style" over "substance," many commentators are alienated by the often vicious attacks of the two major parties on one another. Questions are also raised about whether or not the ads really have any effect on anyone. This controversy continued during the 1992 election campaign, and concerns over the waste of public monies were fueled by press reports that the number of people who were viewing the election broadcasts had declined.

In order to evaluate the utility of the election broadcasts, or whether or not there is a need to change the existing format, we need to be more specific about their purpose. The approach that will be adopted in this article is best described by Joslyn (1990) in which he calls on researchers to look at elections campaigns as "occasions for civic education." While the intended goal of the election broadcasts is persuasion, they also provide an important channel for the dissemination of political information about the candidates and positions of the various political parties. This type of information can be valuable for many citizens, including those who have already decided on how they will vote. The broadcasts can also serve other positive functions such as stimulating a greater level of political interest, discussion, and participation in the election campaign.

We see voters as intelligent *consumers* of political information (Himmelweit, Humphreys, and Jaeger 1985; Popkin 1991) who are perfectly capable of evaluating whether or not the election broadcasts are meeting their needs. This perspective differs from a good deal of the previous research in political communication, which looks almost exclusively at the "effects" of such commercials on candidate images and voting behavior (see, e.g., Biocca 1991; Kaid, Nimmo, and Sanders 1986; Kaid and Boydston 1987). The ideas which are presented in this article do, however, dovetail rather well with the "uses and gratifications" school of thought, which also looks at these issues by looking at the needs of the audience (Blumer 1985; Blumer, Gurevitch, and Katz 1985; Caspi 1984; Caspi and Levinsohn 1993; Donohew, Palmgreen, and Rayburn 1987).

The starting point for any evaluation of these broadcasts should begin by comparing what the public expects from these broadcasts with what they are getting. Accordingly, we shall examine the 1992 election broadcasts by asking voters about the utility of the election broadcasts. The discussion will be divided into two sections. The discussion in the first section will look at the attitudes and behavior of the general public. It is important to look at such issues as the size of the audience for such ads, reasons for watching and not watching the ads, and the general level of satisfaction with what is being broadcast.

The second part of the study will focus on a more specific group of consumers: the undecided voters. Many voters in this group should be actively searching for political information in order to make their decision about their final "purchase." It will be useful to find out about the size and nature of this group and who among them find the broadcasts helpful as a voting guide. We shall also present some results that indicate the amount of help voters say they received from the one political debate that was televised as compared to the other political ads that were broadcast. All of these factors will allow us to better evaluate the overall utility of the broadcasts for the electorate.

In this paper we shall attempt to answer these questions based on a national survey that was carried out a few days after the election in 1992. The survey was carried out by the Guttmann Institute of Applied Social Science Research in Jerusalem.[1] The survey was conducted by telephone among five hundred and four Jewish adults above the age of 19.[2]

Table 11.1. Television Viewing for Three Elections

Amount of Viewing	1981ª (N = 1,111) (%)	1988 (N = 508) (%)	1992 (N = 504) (%)
All or almost all	61	33	25
3–4 times each week	⎤	23	12
1–2 times each week	15 ⎟	12	23
Infrequent	⎦	7	21
None	23	26	19

Note: The survey in 1981 was carried out using personal interviews while the surveys in 1988 and 1992 were carried out by telephone. No survey data were available for the 1984 election.

ª In 1981 the response categories were all, some, and none. The 15 percent figure refers to all of those who answered some.

I. The General Public: A Shrinking and Sceptical Audience

The first question that should concern consumer advocates is whether or not people are using the product. There's not much point in investing so much money in public education if a good deal of the population is cutting class. Survey data published during the election campaign suggested that the television ads were attracting a smaller audience than in previous elections. It is possible to examine this question directly by utilizing data collected during two previous election campaigns: 1981 and 1988.[3]

As can be seen in table 11.1, people were indeed watching fewer ads in the election campaign of 1992. While 61 percent of the population reported watching all (or almost all) of the ads in 1981, that figure decreased to 33 percent in 1988 and to 25 percent in 1992. There was also a dramatic drop since the previous election in the percentage who were watching the ads several times a week.

It is important to emphasize however, that these findings suggest not that *fewer people were watching the ads* but rather that *people were watching the ads less.* The percentage of citizens who watched at least one set of broadcasts remained fairly stable over the years and may have even increased slightly in 1992. Most voters apparently decided that there was no need to watch the broadcasts every night and preferred to tune in from time to time. Although presumably one could argue for the convenience of being able to choose which night to watch, the fact that 63 percent of the population watched two or fewer ads a week should cast certain doubts about the wisdom of broadcasting the commercials six nights a week, at least under the present format.

Table 11.2. Campaign Interest for Three Elections

Frequency of interest	1981 (N = 1,111) (%)	1988 (N = 508) (%)	1992 (N = 504) (%)
All the time	31	23	21
Most of the time	29	26	24
Occasionally	27	26	34
Never	13	25	21

Why did the voters watch fewer ads in 1992? The primary reason offered by pundits was that the decline in viewing was indicative of a more general indifference to the 1992 campaign. Dozens of news articles, radio broadcasts, and several television features were devoted to a discussions about the lack of popular interest in the campaign. The political parties were reported to be having much more trouble mobilizing volunteers to work in the campaigns, and the numbers who were attending rallies appeared to be much smaller than in previous elections.

The notion of political indifference, in a sense, places the "blame" for a lack of viewing on the voters. If the Israeli public is simply not interested in the political campaign, then there is really not much the political leadership can do to better inform them. Yet, it has been documented that Israelis have one of the highest levels of political interest in the Western world (Wolfsfeld 1988), and thus the potential for viewing should be very high.

The evidence collected for the present survey does not support the notion that the decrease in viewing in 1992 was related to a drop in interest in the campaign. In addition to the previously discussed questions about viewing habits, respondents in the 1981, 1988, and 1992 elections were also asked: "How much do you take an interest in and follow the election campaign: in newspapers, the radio, and television?" The results of this comparison are presented in table 11.2. While there does seem to have been a decrease in voter interest when one compares the extremely heated campaign of 1981 to that of 1988, there was no further drop in interest between 1988 and 1992. Although one would hesitate to reject the many claims of party activists on the basis of one survey question, these findings do cast some serious doubts as to whether or not the extent of voter indifference was as widespread as was claimed.

Another explanation that was offered for the decline in viewing had to do with changes in the mass media system in Israel. The introduction of cable television to Israel, while not yet complete, offered many Israelis the option of watching something possibly more attractive than election propaganda. The

Table 11.3. Reasons for Not Watching Election Broadcasts

Reason	Percentage of Respondents
Preferred to do other things	36
Already decided on vote	12
They had nothing new to say	12
Don't like when people try to "trick" me	9
Didn't want to watch political propaganda	8
Don't believe the claims and promises of political parties	8
Not interested in politics	8
The politicians didn't relate to me seriously	5
Watched cable television	1
Watched something on another channel	1
I didn't understand what they were talking about	1

Notes: Total $N = 508$; total exceeds 100 percent due to rounding.

survey sample was divided into two groups according to whether or not the respondents had access to cable television in their homes. Although in some geographic areas this might be related to other demographic variables, the fact that many major cities still had not yet installed cable offered a reasonable test of the "cable hypothesis." When we compared those with cable to those without, *no significant differences* were found in the extent to which either group watched the political commercials. It would seem then that peoples' decisions about how many broadcast ads to watch are unrelated to the number of program alternatives they face.

An additional way to approach this problem is to simply ask those voters who watched the smaller number of broadcasts about their reasons for not viewing. We asked those who watched less than once a week why they didn't watch. As can be seen in table 11.3, the most popular reasons were that they preferred to do other things, that they had already decided how to vote, and that the ads had nothing new to say. A further refutation of the cable hypothesis comes from the fact that only 2 percent of those who didn't watch said that it was because they were watching something else on television.

It is also noteworthy that so few Israelis suggested that they weren't watching due to a lack of interest in politics. Most Israelis are interested in politics and, as shown, do follow the campaign in the news media. The most reasonable conclusion is that the election broadcasts are simply not providing the type of information and format that would attract a wider audience.[4] This point becomes even clearer when we look at the public's attitudes towards the ads.

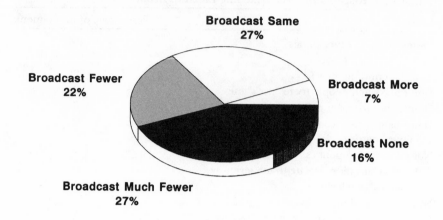

Broadcast Same
27%

Broadcast Fewer
22%

Broadcast More
7%

Broadcast None
16%

Broadcast Much Fewer
27%

Figure 11.1. Public Attitudes toward Frequency of Ads

Total does not equal 100 percent due to rounding.

Attitudes Towards the Ads

In general it can be said that most Israelis have a negative attitude toward the election broadcasts. This is perhaps best illustrated by their responses to questions about whether they would like to see more or fewer ads broadcast during election time. As can be see in figure 11.1, the majority of Israelis would prefer to see fewer political ads on television, and a meager 7 percent would like to see more.[5] It is perhaps meaningful to point out that the 16 percent of those sample who suggested that the ads be completely discontinued did so without that possibility having even been mentioned by the interviewers.

People are also very unlikely to find the ads very helpful in deciding for whom to vote. Although we shall deal with this issue more directly in the second section of this piece, it is important to note that only 2 percent of the sample reported that the ads offered them a good deal of help in this direction, and another 7 percent reported that it offered them some help.[6] If this is considered one of the primary functions of these broadcasts, they are clearly missing the mark.

Another way to gauge how seriously voters are taking the ads is to look at some of the reasons they give for watching them. Previous work on this topic (Caspi 1984; Caspi and Levinsohn 1993) has concluded that voters are much more likely to watch for reasons of entertainment than for voting guidance.

The gap is especially dramatic when one asks respondents to list the "most important reasons" for watching. When this question format is used, the proportion listing voting guidance as their principal reason for voting ranges between 2 percent and 11 percent of the public (Caspi 1984).

In the present study we used a more conservative measure that attempts to gauge whether or not voting guidance was *one* of the reasons for viewing the election ads. The respondents were presented with five different motivations that had been found important in previous studies and asked whether each of them was one of the reasons they watched the programs. The results are presented in figure 11.2, and it is useful to bear in mind that the proportions refer only to those who actually watched a number of broadcasts, rather than to the whole electorate.

It is important to recall that this survey was conducted after the conclusion of the election campaign. Therefore these replies tell us something about how people came to think of these broadcasts as well as why they initially chose to watch. As in the past we find that the most frequently cited reason for watching the election broadcasts in 1992 was entertainment. This was the only motivation cited by a majority of the audience, and this suggests that most viewers do not take these broadcasts very seriously.

The other motivations, on the other hand, fall much closer to the notion of civic education. The fact that a significant minority of viewers did turn to the ads in order to get information for the purposes of political discussion and debate, to keep up with the electoral race, and to obtain help in their voting decisions is one of the few findings that suggests something positive about these ads. It could be argued that the use of entertainment is a perfectly legitimate means of achieving some more significant educational goals.

In general, however, the evidence presented here suggests that the Israeli election broadcasts are not meeting the needs of the general public. People are watching fewer broadcasts than in the past, and a large majority would like to see fewer political ads put on the air. The major reason for watching is entertainment, and considering the public cost of these ads, the broadcasts are not realizing their potential.

We turn then to the second part of the discussion, which focuses more specifically on the utility of the ads for undecided voters.

II. Undecided Voters

Undecided voters should provide the most motivated audience for the election broadcasts. Certainly they are the primary target for the political ads, and at least some of these citizens should be expected to use these broadcasts as a source of information in making their final decision. In this essay "undecided

Percent Saying Yes

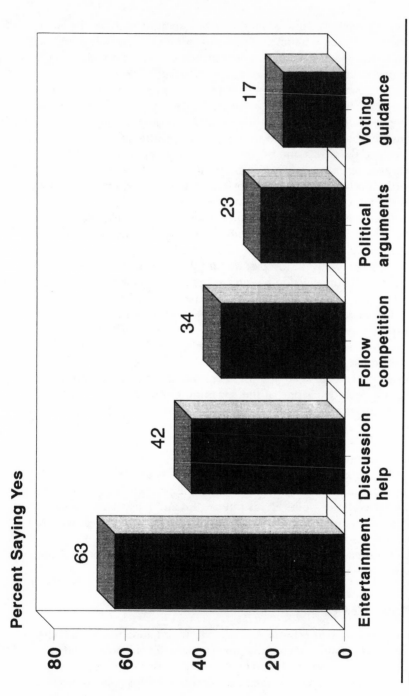

Figure 11.2. Viewing Motivations

Note: Figures indicate the percentage of respondents who said yes to each category. Respondents were allowed to say yes to more than one category.

voters" refers to those respondents who reported (after the election) that they had debated between two parties before making their final choice.[7] A surprisingly high 49 percent of the voters fall into this category. We also made a further distinction between "internal floaters" (34 percent of the sample), who debated between two parties within the same political camp, and "external floaters" (15 percent) who weighed the options of voting for parties from two different camps.[8]

It is helpful to begin by telling something about the social background and interests of these three groups before turning to an account of their attitudes and behavior with regard to the election broadcasts. We shall, throughout these analyses, attempt to better understand the undecided voters by comparing them in background, attitudes, and behavior to committed voters. In terms of age, undecided voters tended to be younger than committed voters. Thus, while only 23 percent of those who were over the age fifty-six reported being undecided, 64 percent of those between the ages of twenty and twenty-five fell into this category. As we might expect, then, political commitment is something that grows with time.

In detailing the differences in education, it is important to distinguish between internal floaters and the external floaters. Those voters with higher levels of education were the least likely to be external floaters. Thus, only 9 percent of those who finished a university degree were external floaters, while 17 percent of those with less education fell into this category. There were no significant educational differences on the other hand between committed voters and internal floaters; those with a university education were just as likely to fall into one of these categories as the other.

These results have a certain internal logic about them. Studies have shown that greater education leads to more political interest and a greater tendency to think about politics in an ideological manner (Barnes and Kaase 1979; Converse 1964; Neuman 1986; Wolfsfeld 1988). As the platforms of the small parties tend to be more ideologically focused, they are more likely to appeal to the better-educated voters. In the present sample, for example, 50 percent of the college-educated respondents said they voted for small parties in the 1992 election, while only 34 percent of the least-educated group did so. While many educated voters considered the option of voting for small parties, very few contemplated the much more drastic step of voting for the other political camp.

The variations among the three groups in terms of political interest also provide meaningful insights into the ways in which they relate to the political broadcasts. Two separate questions were asked about political interest. The first asked about the extent to which the respondent had a *general interest in politics*. This was the first question on the questionnaire, and it was designed to tap a long-term preoccupation with the world of politics. The second question, which was discussed earlier, was designed to measure *campaign interest* by asking more specifically about the extent to which the respondent expressed an interest in the campaign by following it in the mass media. Although the two variables are correlated with one another (r = .31) the distinction between the two types of political interest proved to be a useful one.

The results shown in figure 11.3 show that while there are significant differences among the groups in terms of general political interest (X^2 = 19.24, p < .001), there are no such differences when it comes to following the campaign.[9] The fact that undecided voters have less long-term political interest than committed voters do makes perfect sense. The fact that such differences disappear at election time, however, is a far more intriguing finding. It suggests that many citizens normally uninvolved in politics suddenly develop an interest during the election campaign. Lacking previous interest, they remain unencumbered by many political commitments, a seductive prize for all of the political parties.

This state of affairs offers an important opportunity for those who hope to use the election broadcasts as an opportunity for civic education. Television has become a truly mass medium whose visual format can attract an extremely large audience. The fact that so many Israelis tend to watch television news on a regular basis (Cohen, Adoni, and Bantz 1990) demonstrates the potential for these broadcasts. Only television can provide political information in a format that can appeal to almost everyone, even those who do not normally read about politics in the newspapers.

This line of argument is given support by the fact that we found no significant differences in the amount of broadcast viewing by the three groups. This is consistent with the earlier finding about a lack of difference in campaign interest, which, it turns out is the best predictor of broadcast viewing (r = .53). This reinforces the notion that election campaigns can serve an important equalizing function by closing the gap between those who are more or less involved in politics.

Despite the similarity in viewing patterns, however, there are critical differences in the ways in which each voting type relates to the political ads that reflect each group's needs. There is a good deal of evidence pointing to the fact that *the weaker the level of political commitment the more seriously the viewers relate to the broadcasts*. The first piece of evidence is presented in figure 11.4 which, shows that it is the external floaters who are most like to watch the ads either to gain voting guidance or to follow the competition and that they are the least likely to view the ads as a form of entertainment. The differences with regard to voting guidance are especially significant and offer an important clue to what follows.[10]

The most important question from a consumer's viewpoint is whether voters are in fact getting help from the election broadcasts in making their

Percent in "High" Category

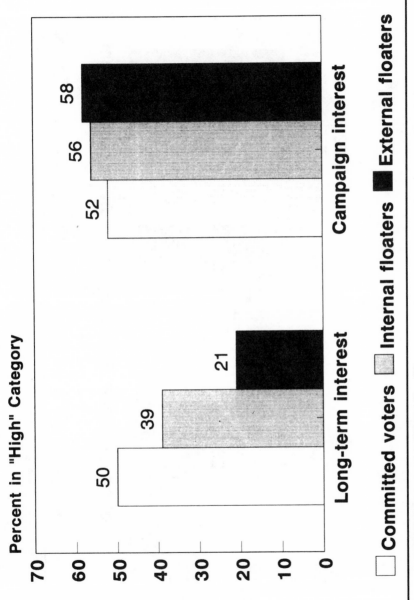

Figure 11.3. Political Interest and Voter Profiles

Percent Saying Yes

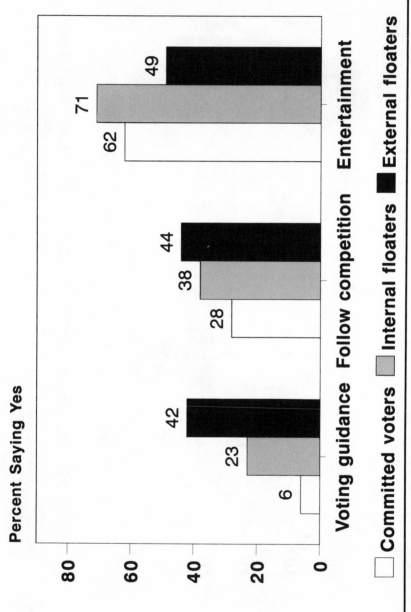

Figure 11.4. Voter Profiles and Viewing Motivations

voting decision. There were two questions in the survey that related to how much help the viewers felt they were getting from the broadcasts. The first was a general questions about how much the broadcasts helped them make their voting decision.[11] The second question focused more specifically on one particular broadcast: the debate between the two candidates for prime minister than has become a standard part of the election campaign.

The standard method in the past few elections is for the two major parties to devote some of their broadcast time to debates in which an assumedly neutral journalist asks questions of the two candidates for prime minister. Seventy-one percent of the respondents in our survey reported watching the debate in the 1992 election, a understandably far higher number of people than would view the election broadcasts on a more typical night. Those respondents who reported watching were asked whether the debate had helped them in their voting decision. We calculated the percentage in each voting type who reported either "no help" from the ads, "reinforcement" of their previous intention, or help in a "decision change" about how they were going to vote.[12] The results presented in figure 11.5 show the percentage of each type that received some kind of help from the debate and the percentage that received help from the much more numerous political ads.

Once again we find important differences among the different voting types. The external floaters form the group that gets the most help in their voting decision from both the political ads and the debate. The differences between the committed voters and the internal floaters are less consistent, but it is the external floaters who feel the most positive about the information they are getting from these broadcasts during the election campaign.

Yet another confirmation of this pattern of results can be found by examining the differences in attitudes about how many ads should be broadcast. Although, as was shown, most Israelis would like to see fewer ads broadcast, there are once again significant differences among the three groups. While 71 percent of the committed voters wanted fewer broadcasts, 65 percent of the internal floaters felt that way, and only 51 percent of the external floaters wanted fewer ($X^2 = 12.12$, $p < .01$). The external voters clearly got more out of these ads than did the other two groups.

Let us try to put all of this into some type of perspective. Those citizens who find themselves debating between the two major political camps during the election campaign turn out to be the least educated members of the population, the youngest, and the ones who have the least long term interest in politics. Many of these voters do become interested at the time of the election and then depend on the television broadcasts for information that apparently helps them in their voting decision.

It is important however not to exaggerate the size of this group. Only fifteen percent of all those who were surveyed fell into the category of exter-

Percent Saying Yes

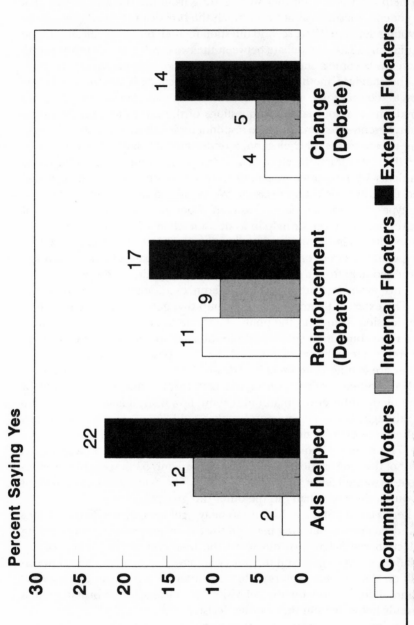

Figure 11.5. Help from Ads and Debate

nal floaters, and while 40 percent of these voters hoped to receive voting guidance from the broadcasts, only 22 percent actually did. To put it differently, if we remove all of the people who did not watch the broadcasts as well as those who denied getting any help from the ads, we are left with about 3 percent of the public who claim to have used the ads to make an internal camp decision and about 2.5 percent who used the ads to decide between the two camps.

It is true that the last few elections in Israel have been very close and that even a small percentage in either direction could have determined the shape of the government. However, when one looks at those few external voters who had the potential of changing the election outcome, one finds that they split fairly evenly between the two camps.[13] Even the most media-centric of observers would have a hard time using these data to make a case that the election broadcasts had a major impact on the final election results.

III. Conclusion

The overall conclusion of this article is that the election broadcasts in Israel are not meeting the needs of the voters. The election campaign offers an important opportunity to get citizens involved in the political process. The vast majority of Israelis are watching fewer ads than they did in the past, and it is clear that they are not satisfied with what they are seeing. Most voters do not take these ads very seriously, and most would prefer to have fewer ads broadcast.

At the same time, one can not ignore the half-full side of the glass. This was one of the first studies in Israel to show that the televised ads and the debate do have an impact on an important segment of the voting public. While further research is needed to better specify this process, it is clear that many less committed voters do exploit these broadcasts as a source of information for voting guidance.

The fact that many of these voters appear to be less-educated and less-interested in politics in between the elections can be thought of in either a positive or a negative light. On the one hand, it could be argued that television serves as a great equalizer in that it not only creates a general excitement about the election campaign but also offers useful information for those who might otherwise be left out of the democratic process. The fact that no correlation was found between education and either campaign interest or viewing can be cited in support of this position. A more cynical perspective however would point to the generally low level of the ads and raise questions about the manipulation of the uninformed through style rather than substance. This becomes an especially important issue, because it is those who float between the two camps who ultimately determine the election.

In any case, it is clear that some type of reform is warranted. There are many alternatives that can be considered, but one possibility that seems especially appealing is to decrease the number of ads while increasing the number and scope of the political debates. Some might argue that this type of format would attract even a smaller, more elite audience than those who now watch the broadcasts. Yet, the admittedly small amount of evidence that was presented in this paper showed that it was the less-sophisticated external floaters who reported receiving the most amount of help from the one debate that was held. We also found no differences in the educational level or long term political interest between those who watched and did not watch the debate.[14]

The key to planning and evaluating such changes, we would argue, is to look at these broadcasts as an incomparable opportunity for inform the public. Policy makers would be well advised to consult the voters about what they would like to get out of such broadcasts rather than depend exclusively on the advice of professional politicians. This would be surely offer one way to narrow the rather large gap that now exists between public expectations and government performance in this field.

Notes

1. I want to thank Chana Levinsohn, of the institute, who provided a great deal of help in both designing the questionnaire and carrying out the survey.

2. It should be noted that over the years the institute has found very few differences when comparing this sample size to the more conventional sample size of more than one thousand.

3. Data for 1981 and 1988 were graciously supplied by Dan Caspi and Chana Levinsohn (see Caspi 1984 and Caspi and Levinsohn 1993). All three surveys were carried out by the Guttmann Institute for Social Science Research. In 1988 there were two surveys that dealt with this topic. We chose to present the one that took place between October 19 and 23 because it was the closest in size, method, and timing of interviews to the one carried out in 1992. A comparison with the other survey results leads to exactly the same conclusions about the decrease in viewing in 1992.

4. There are of course other possible explanations for the decrease. An important factor that was not mentioned in the public discourse was the change in the broadcast time of the election ads. In all previous elections the ads had been given the slot immediately after the evening news, which is by far the most popular program in Israel. In 1992 the ads were shown *before* the news, and this may very well have had a detrimental effect on the size of the viewing audience.

5. Four percent would like to see many more, and three percent would just like to see more.

6. Respondents were also asked whether they thought the ads were helpful to "others." In keeping with what is known as the "third person effect" (Davidson, 1983) in communication, 23 percent, that is, a somewhat larger group, believed that the ads probably helped other voters to decide. This suggests that many are overestimating the utility of the ads in this regard, and this may offer one reason why so many ads are being broadcast.

7. The question asked was "Between which parties did you deliberate (*Mitlabet*) in you decision who to vote for?" A total of eighteen response categories were included, one of which was "I did not debate, it was clear to me who I was going to vote for in the elections."

8. Religious parties were considered to be part of the right-wing camp, as all of them had expressed a preference to continue their coalition with the Likud.

9. Note that the results are summarized by looking at the percentage who fall into the "high" category among each group; this is an arbitrary dividing point. The "high" category in long-term political interest was composed of those respondents who answered that they followed politics "a very great deal" or "a great deal" on a six-point scale. The "high" category in the campaign-interest scale was composed of those saying they followed the campaign "all the time" or "most of the time." We also looked at the alternative definition for high campaign interest that excluded the "most of the time" respondents. The results were essentially the same: although the external floaters exhibited somewhat *less* campaign interest than the other two types, the differences were still not statistically significant.

10. The statistical differences for these groups are as follows: Voting guidance ($X^2 = 52.39$, $p < .001$), follow competition ($X^2 = 5.98$, $p < .05$), and entertainment ($X^2 = 7.06$, $p < .05$). No significant differences were found with regard to two of the motivational variables: for use in political arguments and for use in political discussions."

11. The question was: To what extend did the election broadcasts help or hinder you in your decision about who to vote for? The response categories were: (1) the broadcasts helped me very much, (2) helped, (3) didn't help and didn't hinder, (4) hindered, and (5) hindered very much.

12. The initial response categories were: (1) reinforced my previous decision who to vote for, (2) changed my previous decision who to vote for, (3) helped me decide because before that I didn't have any decision, (4) the debate did not help me to decide, and (5) the debate didn't change anything for me. Those who gave responses four and five were placed in the no-help category, those who gave response one were put in the reinforcement category, and those who gave responses two and three were placed in the decision-change category.

13. When one looks at all of the external voters one finds that 51 percent reported voting for a right-wing or religious party, and 48 percent for a left-wing party. Looking at the even smaller number who say that the ads helped them in their decision, it turns out that 58 percent voted for the left, and 41.7 percent voted for the right.

14. The format of the debates could also be varied as was graphically illustrated in the presidential debates held during the American election in 1992.

References

Barnes, Samuel M., and Max Kaase, eds. 1979. *Political Action: Mass Participation in Five Western Democracies.* Beverly Hills: Sage.

Biocca, Frank (ed.). 1991. *Television and Political Advertising, Volume 1: Psychological Processes.* Hillsdale, N.J.: Lawrence Erlbaum Associates.

Blumer, Jay G. 1985. "The Social Character of Media Gratifications." In *Media Gratifications Research: Current perspectives,* ed. Karl E. Rosengren, Lawrence A. Wenner, and Philip Palmgreen. Beverly Hills: Sage.

Blumer, Jay G., Michael Gurevitch, and Elihu Katz. 1985. "Reaching out: A Future for Gratifications Research: Current Perspectives." In *Media Gratifications Research: Current perspectives,* ed. Karl E. Rosengren, Lawrence A. Wenner, and Philip Palmgreen. Beverly Hills: Sage.

Caspi, Dan. 1984. "Following the race: Propaganda and Electoral Decision." In *The Roots of Begin's success,* ed. Dan Caspi, Avram Diskin, and Emanuel Gutmann. Kent, England: Croom Helm.

Caspi, Dan, and Chana Levinsohn. 1993. "To influence and to be Influenced: The Election Campaign to the 12th Knesset." In *Who's the Boss in Israel,* ed. Daniel J. Elazar and Shmuel Sandler. Detroit: Wayne State University Press.

Cohen, Akiba A., Hanna Adoni, and Charles R. Bantz. 1990. *Social Conflict and Television News.* Sage Library of Social Research 183. Newbury Park, Calif.: Sage.

Converse, Phillip. 1964. "The Nature of Belief Systems in Mass Publics." In *Ideology and Discontent,* ed. David E. Apter. New York: Free Press.

Davidson, W. Phillips. 1983. "The Third Person Effect in Communication." *Public Opinion Quarterly* 47:1–15.

Donohew, Lewis, Phillip Palmgreen, and J. D. Rayburn II. 1987. "Social and "Psychological Origins of Media Use: A Lifestyle Analysis." *Journal of Broadcasting & Electronic Media* 31:255–78.

Himmelweit, Hilde, Patrick Humphreys, Marrianne Jaeger, and Michael Katz. 1981. *How Voters Decide.* London: Academic Press.

Josylyn, Richard A. 1990. "Election Campaigns as Occasions for Civic Education." In *New Directions in Political Communication,* ed. David L. Swanson and Dan Nimmo. Newbury Park, Calif.: Sage.

Kaid, Lynda Lee, and John Boydston. 1987. "An Experimental Study of the Effectiveness of Negative Political Advertisements." *Communication Quarterly* 35:193–201.

Kaid, Lynda Lee, Dan Nimmo, and Keith Sanders, eds. 1986. New *Perspectives on Political Advertising*. Carbondale: Southern Illinois University Press.

Neuman, W. Russell. 1986. *The Paradox of Mass Politics*. Cambridge: Harvard University Press.

Popkin, Samuel L. 1991. *The Reasoning Voter: Communication and Persuasion in Presidential Campaigns*. Chicago: University of Chicago Press.

Wolfsfeld, Gadi. 1988. *The Politics of Provocation: Participation and Protest in Israel*. Albany: SUNY Press.

CHAPTER 12

Caveat Populi Quaestor: The 1992 Preelections Polls in the Israeli Press

GABRIEL WEIMANN

University of Haifa

Three heated and close campaigns were conducted during 1992: British, American, and Israeli elections were all held within a period of six months (April to November 1992). All three campaigns attracted worldwide attention and massive media coverage. All of them were accompanied by public opinion polls and surveys, monitoring the standing of parties and candidates. The prevalence of the polls was inspired by the extremely close contests between Labor and the Conservatives in Britain, the Likud and Labor in Israel, and between Bill Clinton and George Bush in the presidential race in U.S. However, despite the popularity of the polls and their prominence in the mass media, the results were rather disappointing: the British polls failed to predict the winners, experiencing the most disastrous result in the history of polling in the United Kingdom.[1] The Israeli polls, though accurately predicting a change of government, failed to predict the gap between the leading parties and the resulting coalition.

Two decades ago Philip Meyer suggested that "journalists would be wrong less often if they adapted to their own use some of the research tools of the social scientists" (Meyer 1973, 3). Sixteen years later, in spite of growing criticism of his notion of the emergence of "precision journalism," Meyer kept his optimism: "the media have made considerable progress in understanding and interpreting election polls . . . The proliferation of polls will, of course, force journalists to become more proficient at interpreting them" (Meyer 1989, 1). However, the emergence of "precision journalism" was not as fast growing as the popularity of mass-mediated polls. This tendency was noted by Bogart, who claimed that "public misunderstanding of opinion surveys can be expected to continue as long as the mass media ignore or belittle their technical intricacies" (Bogart 1972, 23), and by Wheeler, who argued that "the reader of opinion polls is given no hint that they may not be trustworthy" (Wheeler 1976, 16). A study of poll reports in the U.S. press led researchers to conclude: "The way methodological information about polling is reported in the media tends more to reassure than alert the audience about the possible defects of poll data" (Paletz et al. 1980, 506).

The present chapter examines the way preelection polls were reported by the Israeli press during six election campaigns. The analysis focuses on the methodological and statistical problems revealed in press reports on polls. While most studies of this kind measure the accuracy of the reported polls by comparing their predictions with the actual results, the present study highlights the errors made in presenting, analyzing, and interpreting polls results throughout the campaign.

I. Data

Data for this study come from a systematic content analysis of fifteen daily newspapers published in Israel[2] during the election campaigns of 1969, 1973, 1977, 1981, 1984, 1988, and 1992. The coders were trained to analyze any report on polls published during the three months preceding each election, and they used a preset manual of coding categories (see Charlebois 1979; Stone and Morrison 1976; Weimann 1983a, 1983b, 1990). The following components were recorded for each report ($N = 1531$):

1. Form of coverage: space allocation, placement in the paper, and source of sponsorship. Space was measured by column inches devoted to reporting a poll and its results and to analysis or interpretation of polls.
2. Content of coverage: inclusion of information on sampling method and sample size, wording of questions, rate of "don't know" and "undecided" answers, method of interviewing, timing, measures of intensity of opinion, identification of pollster, and the prediction made by the poll.
3. Style of coverage: "horse-race" polls (focusing on predictions, personal popularity) or issue-related polls (focusing on issues and attitudes).

The coders were trained prior to the investigation and were subjected to an inter-coder reliability test. This test involved the comparison of the evaluations of different coders when analyzing the same text (Holsti 1969, 135–42).

The coefficients of reliability (i.e., the average proportion of agreement between pairs of coders) were, for the 1992 data, .92 in form, .89 in content, and .92 in style. Data for previous elections came from our database on press reports of preelection polls, updated every campaign (Weimann 1990).

II. Reporting the Polls

The Proliferation of Polls

When looking for the origins of election polls, many turn to 1936 when Gallup, Roper, and Crossley conducted polls on the Roosevelt-Landon Race. However, others cite the presidential straw polls conducted by a news magazine, the *Literary Digest*, in 1916 or similar newspaper straw polls going back to the mid-nineteenth century (Robinson 1932; Jensen 1969, 1980). It appears that 1824 has been cited as the starting date of polls by most reviewers of the election polls' history (Smith 1990). The Israeli press began reporting preelection polls only during the election campaign for the seventh Knesset (1969). None of these polls were initiated or commissioned by the press; most came from political bodies that leaked partial results to the press. However, the following campaigns witnessed a dramatic change in press coverage of polls. Table 12.1 presents several measures that demonstrate this trend, which reached its peak in 1992.

The data in table 12.1 reveal the gradual and consistent increase in the number of dailies covering polls (from 3 in 1969 to 15 in 1988 and 1992), in the number of reports on polls during the three months preceding the elections (from 16 in 1969 to 421 in 1992, when on average 4.6 reports on polls were published every day), in space allocation (from 172 column inches in 1969 to 9,411 in 1992), and in prominent placement (from 7 percent on the front page in 1969 to 27 percent in 1992). The growing popularity of polls in the Israeli press is also revealed in the frequency of reporting: the average number of reports per newspaper increased from 5.3 reports per paper in 1969 to 19.6 in 1981, 27.2 in 1988, and 28 in 1992. In 1992 the Israelis were flooded with polls: some of the dailies published several polls in the same issue and devoted more space to analysis and discussion of these polls.[3]

The growing attractivity of polls has caused changes in the relationships between the press and polling agencies. *Ha'aretz* was the first paper to sponsor private polls (in 1973). Soon, the three major dailies commissioned their own polls, each paper contracting a different pollster. Consequently, while in 1973 only 9 percent of the reports covered polls sponsored by the reporting paper, the rate increased to 37 percent in 1977, 48 percent in 1984 and 1988, and 56 percent in 1992, when several dailies signed contracts with more than one pollster.

Table 12.1. Measures of Polls Coverage, 1969–1992

	1969	1973	1977	1981	1984	1988	1992	Rates of Change from 1969–73 to 1988–92
Number of dailies reporting polls	3	6	8	11	13	15	15	3.11
Number of reports on polls	16	52	109	216	308	409	421	12.20
Average number of reports per newspaper	5.3	8.7	13.6	19.6	23.7	27.2	28.0	3.94
Average number of reports per day	0.1	0.6	1.2	2.4	3.4	4.5	4.6	13.00
Space allocated for polls (column inches)	172	513	1297	6927	8122	9365	9411	28.41
Placement:								
front page (%)	7	12	15	21	24	25	27	2.73
inside page (%)	93	88	85	79	76	75	73	–1.22
Sponsorship by:								
reporting paper (%)	0	9	37	47	48	48	56	11.55
other papers (%)	5	22	28	33	32	30	27	2.11
political bodies (%)	71	49	22	11	12	16	14	–4.00
unspecified (%)	24	20	13	9	8	6	3	–4.88
Total sponsorship (%)	100	100	100	100	100	100	100	100

Table 12.2. Changes in Contents of Polls Reports

	Percent of reports including item					
	1973	1977	1981	1984	1988	1992
Sample Size	54	86	92	90	90	91
Definition of population	56	68	84	80	76	82
Sampling error	0	6	9	8	8	7
Method of interviewing	29	32	51	50	52	53
Wording of question	14	21	28	35	36	28
Refusal rate	63	71	88	80	67	64
Timing of poll	38	51	64	66	65	67
Intensity of opinion	0	8	11	10	10	9
Identification of pollster	75	87	96	95	94	96
Identification of sponsor	30	49	66	76	88	73
N	(52)	(109)	(216)	(308)	(409)	(421)

Reporting (or not) Methodological Deficiencies

The emergence and prevalence of polls in the Israeli press is manifest not only in the changing form and prominence of poll reports but also in the contents of the reports. The comparisons presented in table 12.2 indicate that content elements have changed significantly.

In the 1970s press reports of preelection polls in Israel read merely as a short summary of results and predictions. But in the subsequent campaigns the reports have become more richly textured and detailed. Nevertheless, as table 12.2 reveals, such enrichment has been rather selective. Comparison over the years shows that the reports have become more informative as to sample size, definition of population, and identification of pollster and sponsor. To a lesser extent, an increase has also been noted in reports containing information regarding method of interviewing, wording of questions, and timing. However, the reports still do not adequately define or interpret methodological intricacies such as sampling error, rates of "don't know," or "undecided" answers. It appears that these problems are more evident in the Israeli case. Comparison of the Israeli data with the findings of studies on reporting polls in the American press (Paletz et al. 1980; Miller and Hurd 1982; Cantril 1991) reveals that the Israeli press provides less adequate information about methodological deficiencies than does the American press. While 71 percent of the American reports include the polling questions, the rate in the Israeli press in 1992 was 28 percent. Moreover, while 31 percent of the former include information on sampling errors, only 7 percent of the latter contain such information. Similar differences are found regarding the definition of the population (91 percent and

Table 12.3. Interpollster Variance, 1969–1988

Party	Average Deviations, by Year						
	1969	1973	1977	1981	1984	1988	1992
Labor	5.6	6.2	7.4	5.8	6.1	5.6	5.4
Likud	4.3	5.7	7.1	6.0	5.4	5.3	5.1

Note: Average deviations were calculated for the number of seats predicted by polls published within the same week.

82 percent respectively) and method of interviewing (62 percent and 53 percent respectively). The absence in the Israeli polling industry of agreed standards of reporting polls (such as the American Association for Public Opinion Research standards; see Gollin 1988 and Cantril 1991) may contribute to these differences.

The Interpollster Variance

Even more troubling was the variance across reports, or the interpollster variance. One of the measures of polls' accuracy is the comparison of the predictions made by polls conducted at the same time. This measure, known as the interpollster variance, was applied to the polls published during the seven campaigns. The comparison was made in terms of average deviations in the number of seats predicted for each of the two leading parties (Labor and Likud) by polls published during the same week. Table 12.3 presents these deviations for each campaign separately.

The predictions made by Israeli polls reveal interpollster variance that exceeds the sampling error (actually it is about double the variance expected by the standard sampling error stated by these polls). On average, the polls' predictions vary by 6.01 seats for the Labor and 5.55 for the Likud (the differences in deviations between the two parties are statistically insignificant). Higher variance was recorded for the smaller parties. The deviations do not vary significantly over the campaigns except for the 1977 election, in which the highest interpollster variance was observed. It was more surprising to find such variance between reports on the same poll. This is explained by differing interpretations of the same results by different reporters or political analysts.

"Horse-Race" Journalism

One of the popular criticisms of poll reports in the media is related to their focusing on superficial aspects of public opinion and politics. Several studies

Table 12.4. Poll Reports according to Type

Type of poll	1973 (%)	1977 (%)	1981 (%)	1984 (%)	1988 (%)	1992 (%)
Prediction polls	46	41	42	52	60	61
Personal popularity	8	22	24	28	28	32
Issues and attitudes	46	37	34	20	12	7
Total	100	100	100	100	100	100
N	(52)	(109)	(216)	(308)	(409)	(421)

(Broh 1980; Paletz et al. 1980; Rokeach 1968; Stovall and Solomon 1983) reveal this tendency of poll coverage to deal exclusively with the "horse-race" aspects of the political campaign. Table 12.4 presents a comparison of types of polls reported in six campaigns. The reports were classified according to their main theme: predicting the elections' results (prediction polls), personal popularity polls, and polls that focus on issues and political attitudes.[4]

The Israeli press clearly displays a consistent trend toward horse-race imagery. In every campaign the "prediction polls" were the most popular reported, and this preference has been increasing over the years (from 46 percent of the reports in 1973 to 61 percent in 1992). Moreover, there has been a consistent increase in the popularity or "candidate-centered" reports, a trend more noteworthy in Israel, where voters choose among parties, not candidates. The comparison in table 12.4 reveals the decline of reports on issues and political attitudes (from 46 percent of the reports in 1973 to only 12 percent in 1988 and 7 percent in 1992). Thus, we find that more and more polls reported in the press deal with predictions or personalities rather than with political issues. Polls appear to be used more often to rate parties and candidates than to study the voters, the decision making process, and the political issues involved.[5]

The findings of the content analysis of press reports on polls highlight the dramatic changes in the quantity, prominence, and contents of press reports on polls and in the relationships between the media and the polling industry in the Israeli society. These trends reached a peak in the 1992 elections. One should examine the to the specific circumstances of the Israeli political system, campaigns, and media structure during the 1992 campaign to understand the factors causing the failure of the polling industry. In fact, by looking at the 1992 campaign and the way the polls were reported we may learn about the factors shaping the interaction among four Israeli systems: the political system, the mass media system, the polling industry, and the Israeli electorate. The following discussion deals with the complexity of the circumstances in the 1992 campaign that explain the obsession to forecast, the transition to the "horse race" format, and the lingering failure to provide accurate predictions.

III. The 1992 Campaign: Why Did the Polls Fail?

Several factors, some unique to the Israeli setting and others challenging every pollster, affected the accuracy of the reported poll. Let us highlight some of the most important factors, based on the analysis of the 1992 post-election data.

Is the "Representative Sample" Really Representative?

The majority of poll reports (86 percent) included a statement claiming that the poll is based on a "representative sample." While the size of the sample was almost always adequate ($N > 1,200$) a problem stemmed from the method of sampling. Most of the published polls (82 percent) were based on a standard sample drawn from the urban Jewish population, thus misrepresenting several subpopulations: (*a*) Israeli Arabs, (*b*) new immigrants, (*c*) soldiers, (*d*) settlers in the occupied territories, (*e*) Ultrareligious groups (e.g., haredic Jews), and (*f*) residents of nonurban areas (e.g., kibbutzim, moshavim). These voters are rarely represented in the polls, though they compose 36 percent of the voters. Moreover, their political views differ significantly from those of the standard samples. Table 12.5 is based on a comparison of the voting preferences of certain misrepresented groups and the standard samples, based on a retrospective analysis of polls (Katz and Levinson 1992).

Although the polling industry in Israel is well aware of the problems related to the standard method of sampling, the press reports rarely include any qualifications or warnings regarding the misrepresentation of certain subpopulations. As table 12.5 reveals, the standard samples in 1992 did not represent a third of the eligible voters and especially groups whose voting patterns differed significantly from those of the sampled population. Moreover, the misrepresented groups were participating in the elections, determining a fate of one-third of the Knesset's seats.

The pollsters attempted to overcome the misrepresentations by using "estimates" of the voting patterns of the groups they did not sample. These estimates were based (Katz and Levinson 1992, 1) on their voting in the previous elections. However, the validity of such estimation is questionable due to shifts in public opinion and political circumstances. Moreover, the estimates related to the Russian immigrants, recently arrived, could not rely on past voting and consequently were very biased (contrary to popular

Table 12.5. The Represented and the Misrepresented and Their Voting Behavior (1992 Elections)

Group	Number of Eligible Voters	% of Electorate	% Actually Voting	% Voting Left[a]
Israeli Arabs	375,000	11	73	86
Russian immigrants	300,000	9	65	75
Jewish Settlers	40,000	1	90	10
Age 18–20	280,000	8	75	45
Kibbuzim	86,000	2	90	90
Haredic Jews	175,000	5	80	5
Total	1,256,000	36		
Surveyed[b]				
April 1992	2,144,000	64	89	48
June 1992	2,278,000	67	89	51

[a] All the left and center-left parties combined.
[b] Based on the population sampled by four pollsters: Modiin Ezrahi, Gallup Israel, the Guttman Institute, and Geocartography.

predictions, this group preferred voting for the Labor party). Again, this reliance on estimation is hardly ever reported when the polls' results are presented in the press.

Deciding for the "Undecided"

The undecided, "don't know," and "no answer" in the Israeli preelection polls compose 25 percent to 30 percent of the surveyed samples,[6] and thus further weaken the validity of the predictions. This high rate may be explained by the Israeli multiparty system, in which many parties compete (twenty-six parties in 1988, twenty-five parties in 1992). Most of the undecided are in fact "floating" between the big parties and their satellite parties, though in 1992 a certain shift from Likud to the Labor was recorded. Unlike voters in other countries, most of the Israeli undecided do vote in the elections (voting turnout in Israel is between 80 percent and 90 percent). However, popular reports on polls are presenting a predicted distribution of Knesset seats, thus relying only on the decided respondents. As seen from table 12.2, the rate of undecided and "don't know" are not included in a third of the published polls. Moreover, the majority of the 1992 published polls (78 percent) based their predictions on the sample without the undecided category, but the reports mentioned this fact very rarely. Only 14 percent of the reports presented distributions that included the undecided as a separate category.

More sophisticated attempts to identify the voting intentions of the undecided by studying their political attitudes are rare (accounting for only 8 percent of the 1992 published polls). Predictions based only on the decided actually assume that the distribution of the undecided will be similar to those who decided earlier. This assumption, found to be false, led to the failure of the polls to predict the success of the Likud party in the 1977 and 1981 campaigns.

Manipulations and Double Loyalties

Wheeler (1976) points to the manipulation of polls and their results by politicians, parties, and campaign experts. However, our data revealed declining publication of polls commissioned by political bodies (see table 12.1). While in 1969 71 percent of the published polls were sponsored by political bodies, the rate declined to 49 percent in 1973 and to 16 percent and 14 percent in 1988 and 1992, respectively. This may be explained by the growing skepticism of the media toward such polls, despite the constant flow of "results" and predictions leaked by politicians and campaign organizations.

Pressures on the pollsters may come not only from political bodies but also from the mass media. In his study on the accuracy of preelection polls in the 1982/1984 Israeli campaigns, Shamir found that "mass media pressure for highly processed predictions is liable to result in less accurate reports" (Shamir 1986, 62). The media's thirst for predictions and ratings, the need for exciting and newsworthy projections, provide a structural constraint on the accuracy and validity of the polls and a threat to the professional standards of the polling industry.

Recently, another troubling trend was noted in the polling industry: double loyalties of pollsters. In 1992, most of the leading pollsters signed contracts with both a political party and a newspaper (sometimes by several papers). For example, Dahaf, a polling organization and an advertising agency, ran the Likud campaign, conducted polls for the Likud, signed a contract with a newspaper (*Yediot*) to publish polls' results and analysis, presented polls on the Israeli television news, and conducted the exit polls on election day. Almost all the other pollsters combined party contracts with press contracts. Such double loyalties raised the question of bias to favor the party's interests. Dahaf, for example, was accused of publishing pro-Likud findings and, in fact, was predicting a right-wing victory of 61 seats (out of 120). Throughout the campaign, Dahaf's predictions were more favorable to the Likud than were those of all the other pollsters.[7]

The Changing "Climate of Opinion"

One of the main factors affecting the accuracy of polls' predictions is the changes of voters' preferences. The Israeli climate of opinion during the 1992 campaign was very unstable. Several trends were recorded during this campaign, all of them weakening the predictability of the results.

1. One-way shifts: unlike previous campaigns, in 1992 there was a significant shift of voters, moving not within a political bloc (left or right) but among the blocs. According to the surveys, most of the shifting votes were from Likud to Labor: about 16 percent of those who voted Likud in 1988 preferred Labor in 1992. The shift was mostly one way as only 1 to 2 percent of the 1988 Labor voters preferred the Likud in 1992 (Katz and Levinsohn 1992, 4). Most of the shifting occurred during the short campaigning period.

2. Political realignment: the Israeli left has been redefining its political positions, moving toward the ideological center on both territorial and economic issues. In its 1992 campaign the Labor party presented a more central image than ever before, trying to appeal to a wider range of voters, including Likud supporters. The classic Labor-Likud distinctions became more obscure, thus weakening the traditional association between political attitudes and party affiliation.

3. Personal campaigns: though Israeli voters choose among parties, the 1992 campaign was more than ever a personal contest. This was the strategy of the Labor party, basing most of its appeal on its candidate for the post of prime minister, Yitzhak Rabin. By highlighting his military experience, his tough stance with regards to the Palestinian issue, and his good relationships with the leaders of Western nations, the Labor campaign became almost a presidential campaign. This strategy was effective, leading numerous voters to support Rabin while not favoring the Labor party. However, it created an additional problem for pollsters whose standard questions on voting for parties did not match the personal contest format. As table 12.4 reveals, many polls applied the personal comparison questions (with 1992 being the peak in these polls' popularity), but their predictions were based on the routine party-preference question.

4. The perceived "climate of opinion": the pollsters themselves often argue that the publication of the polls affect voters, thus changing the distribution of opinion they try to reflect. The frequent publication of polls in the mass media is suggested to serve as a constant flow of reflections on the climate of opinion. If not directly affecting attitudes, it shapes the perception of the state of public opinion—a sense of who is leading, who is losing—and may, consequently, lead to a spiraling process of silencing those who perceive themselves as supporting the minority (on the notion of the "spiral of silence" see Noelle-Neumann 1974, 1976, 1984). The fact that the polls often distort the actual "climate of opinion" (Shamir 1986; Weimann 1990) may shape a distorted perception among the voters. However, there is no massive empirical support for such effect in Israel. All that we can relate to this is that in 1992 the public sensed the coming victory of Labor and that this realization interacted with or supported the shift toward Labor. Table 12.6 presents the perceived "climate of opinion," studied by three surveys of the Guttman Institute.

The public perceptions of the climate of opinion changed according to the shifts reported by the polls. From a losing position in 1988, Labor moved to a perceived lead in April 1992, one that became even stronger a week before election day in June 1992. There is clear correlation between the growing support for the Labor as recorded and reported by the polls and the perceived dominance of Labor as a likely winner. We cannot establish any causality between the two, but there is clear evidence that most of the public has an established estimate of the climate of opinion and that such estimates vary in accordance with the polls' reports.

Table 12.6. The Perceived "Climate of Opinion"

	October 1988 (%)	April 1992 (%)	June 1992 (%)
The Likud will win	24	18	16
The Labor will win	15	41	50
The same	40	25	22
Unable to estimate	13	9	8
No opinion	9	6	5
Totals	101	99	101
N	508	506	507

Source: Data indicate the distribution of answers to the question: "According to your impression now, what will be the results for the Likud and the Labor in the coming elections?" (Katz and Levinsohn 1992, 6)

IV. Conclusion

How precise is precision journalism? Meyer (1989, 5), offering a somewhat self-fulfilling prophecy, argues that polls have become increasingly accurate and that the journalists have become more proficient, adding, "if precision journalism, in the form of pre-election and exit polls, helps the electorate to communicate with itself and bring about consensus, then there is hope for the brave new world of direct democracy." However, the recent British pollsters' fiasco and the Israeli faulty reports of preelection polls can hardly support Meyer's exuberant impression. It appears that the emergence of precision journalism has led to a growing acceptance of polls as both important and newsworthy. However, when this growing reliance on surveys and polls is not accompanied by increasing familiarity and understanding of the statistical and methodological problems involved in polling, and when standards for reporting polls are nonexistent or poorly observed, the results of such "precision journalism" may be hazardous to the democratic process (Donsbach 1987).

A previous analysis (Weimann 1990) examined the correlation between measures of press coverage and the accuracy of the reported polls (the overall error calculated by the mean deviation of polls' predictions from the actual results). The accuracy of reported polls, tested by the actual results of the elections, was found to be strongly related to two variables. It appears that the more methodological deficiencies were reported, the smaller is the prediction error ($R = -.51$) was. The reports that carefully detailed the methodological problems, thus limiting the value of predictions based on the poll, were more accurate in their predictions. The study's conclusion was: "when the campaign is nearing its peak the 'obsession to forecast' is more evident, making polls more newsworthy and prominent, but less cautious about polls deficiencies and more focused on ratings and predictions than on political issues and attitudes" (Weimann 1990, 405).

The Israeli case of the 1992 elections may serve as an extreme example of what Cantril labelled "the uneasy alliance between the media and polling" (1991, 72). Let us conclude with his alarming observation:

> polls are no different from other types of information that come into the newsroom. News judgement must be made about their reliability and their pertinence to an emerging story line. But, as with other kinds of scientific or technical information, journalistic criteria alone are not sufficient to assess the adequacy of a poll. In this sense, polling represents an uneasy alliance between journalism and the social sciences. Each field has its own criteria of professional competence. More often than not, it is when these criteria come into conflict that controversies about the polls flare up.

Notes

1. The five major pollsters, Gallup, Harris, ICM, MORI, and NOP reported an average 1.3 percent Labor lead, while the final result was a 7.6 percent lead for the Conservatives. In the previous thirteen British elections between 1945 and 1987, the average error of the final polls published on the eve of the election was only 1.4 percent.

2. This includes all eight Israeli dailies published in Hebrew, one in English (the *Jerusalem Post*), two in Arabic, and five in European languages such as Hungarian, Russian, Rumanian, French, and Yiddish. While the first papers to report polls were the Hebrew dailies, the rest joined in later, mainly during the 1977/1981 campaigns.

3. For example, the leading daily (*Yediot Aharonot*) published repeatedly the predictions of three different pollsters, side by side.

4. In the Israeli campaigns the issues of security, the occupied territories, negotiation with the Palestinians, the absorption of new immigrants, inflation, and economic stability were the leading themes and the major factors shaping the voters' preferences. Studies of the issues dominating the Israeli campaigns and their influence on voters (see, e.g., Elizur and Katz 1979; Katz and Levinsohn 1989) reveal the centrality of these issues in determining voting in Israel. Moreover, they indicate that the campaigns themselves focused on these issues with changing emphases from one campaign to another.

5. Broh argues that these type of predictions combined with personal ratings are the characteristics of the horse-race coverage of polls: "For journalists, the horse-race metaphor provides a framework for analysis. A horse is

judged not by its absolute speed or skill but in comparison to the speed of other horses and especially by its wins and losses. Similarly, candidates are pushed to discuss other candidates; events are understood in a context of competition; and picking the winner becomes an important topic. The race—not the winner—is important" (Broh 1980, 528).

6. Even in the poll conducted on 14–15 June 1992, a week before the elections, by the Guttman Institute, 14 percent were undecided and 10 percent refused to answer.

7. This became a public issue following the elections, forcing Mina Zemach, Dahaf's pollster, to defend her professional ethics (see *Yediot Aharonot* 30 June 1992 22; *Hadashot* 3 July 1992, 9–11).

References

Atkin, C.A. 1969. "The Impact of Political Poll Reports on Candidates and Issue Preferences." *Journalism Quarterly* 46:515–21.

Bogart, L. 1972. *Silent Politics: Polls and the Awareness of Public Opinion.* New York: John Wiley and Sons.

Broh, C. A. 1980. "Horse-race journalism: reporting the polls in the 1976 elections." *Public Opinion Quarterly* 44:514–29.

Cantril, A.H. 1991. *The Opinion Connection: Polling, Politics, and the Press.* New York: CQ Press.

Charlebois, C. 1979. Multiple Measures in the Study of Press Response. *Journalism Quarterly* 56:851–56.

Crespi, I. 1980. Polls as Journalism. *Public Opinion Quarterly* 44:462–76.

Donsbach, W. 1987. "Are Poll Data Hazardous to the Health of Democratic Elections?" Paper presented at the Annual Conference of the International Communication Association (ICA), Montreal.

Elizur, J., and E. Katz. 1979. "The Media in the Elections of 1977." In *Israel at the Polls*, ed. M. R. Penniman, 227–54. Washington, D.C.: American Enterprise Institute.

Gollin, A. E. 1988. "Polling and the News Media." *Public Opinion Quarterly* 51:86–94.

Holsti, O. R. 1969. *Content Analysis for the Social Sciences and Humanities.* New York: Addison-Wesley.

Jensen, R. 1969. American election analysis: A case history of methodological innovation and diffusion. Pp. 226–243 in Seymour Martin Lipset (ed.), *Politics and the Social Sciences.* New York: Oxford University Press.

———. 1980. Democracy by the numbers. *Public Opinion* 3(1).

Katz, E. and H. Levinsohn, 1989. Too good to be true: Notes on the Israeli elections of 1988. *International Journal of Public Opinion Research* 1(2):111–22.

————. 1992. "Predicting the 1992 Israeli Elections: A Retrospective Analysis." Guttman Institute of Applied Social Research, Jerusalem, June.

Mendelsohn, H., and I. Crespi. 1970. *Polls, Television and the New Politics.* Scranton: Chandler.

Meyer, P. 1973. *Precision Journalism.* Bloomington: Indiana University Press.

————. 1989. "Precision Journalism and the 1988 elections." Paper presented at the Esomar Conference on Opinion Polls, Seville, Spain, February.

Miller, M. M., and R. Hurd. 1982. "Conformity to AAPOR Standards in Newspaper Reporting of Public Opinion Polls." *Public Opinion Quarterly* 46:243–49.

Noelle-Neumann, E. 1974. "The Spiral of Silence: a Theory of Public Opinion." *Journal of Communication* 24:43–51.

————. 1976. "The Dual Climate of Opinion: The Influence of Television in the 1976 West German Federal Elections." In *Elections and Parties,* ed. M. Kaase and K. von Beyme 137–69. Beverly Hills: Sage.

————. 1984. *The Spiral of Silence.* Chicago: University of Chicago Press.

Paletz, D. L., et al. 1980. "Polls in the Media: Content, Credibility and Consequences." *Public Opinion Quarterly* 44:495–513.

Robinson, C. E. 1932. *Straw Votes: A Study of Political Prediction.* New York: Columbia University Press.

Rokeach, M. 1968. "The Role of Values in Public Opinion Research." *Public Opinion Quarterly* 32:547–59.

Roper, B. W. 1986. "Evaluating Polls with Poll Data." *Public Opinion Quarterly* 50:10–16.

Shamir, J. 1986. "Preelection Polls in Israel: Structural Constraints on Accuracy." *Public Opinion Quarterly* 50:62–75.

Smith, T. W. 1990. The first straw: A study of the origins of election polls. *Public Opinion Quarterly* 54:21–36.

Stone, G. C., and J. Morrison. 1976. "Content Analysis as a Key to Purpose of Community Newspapers." *Journalism Quarterly* 53:488–94.

Stovall, J. G., and J. H. Solomon. 1983. "The Poll as a News Event in the 1980 Presidential Campaign." *Public Opinion Quarterly* 48:615–23.

Turner, C. F., and E. Krauss. 1978. "Fallible Indicators of the Subjective State of the Nation." *American Psychologist* 33:456–70.

Weimann, G. 1983a. "Pre-election Polls in the Israeli Press." *Journalism Quarterly* 50:315–26.

————. 1983b. "Every Day is Election Day: Press Coverage of Pre-election Polls in Israel." In *The Roots of Begin's Success: The 1981 Israeli Elections,* ed. E. Gutman, A. Diskin, and D. Caspi. London: Croom Helm.

————. 1990. "The Obsession to Forecast: Pre-election Polls in the Israeli Press." *Public Opinion Quarterly,* 54:396–408.

Wheeler, M. 1976. *Lies, Damn Lies and Statistics: The Manipulation of Public Opinion.* New York: Liveright.
Wilhoit, G., and T. Sup Auh. 1974. "Newspaper Endorsement and Coverage of Public Opinion Polls in 1971." *Journalism Quarterly* 51:654–58.

PART V

Reforming the System

CHAPTER 13

The Rise of Instrumental Voting: The Campaign for Political Reform

TAMAR HERMANN
The Open University of Israel

I. Introduction

The unprecedented electoral victory of the Likud in 1977 seemed at the time to have marked a crucial turning point in Israeli politics, first and foremost as it put an end to the Labor party's prolonged domination in the national political arena. Its significance seemed even greater in the light of the prevalent interpretation of this electoral shift as an outcome of the Israeli voters' growing awareness of their ability and right to use their votes to penalize the ruling party for malfunction and corruption. This perception led to high hopes for the development of a genuine competitive political system in which the party in power would periodically be unseated and replaced, thereby bringing new ideas, people, and practices into the political establishment. It was believed that the attentiveness of the nation's representatives to the voters' demands and needs—and their accountability—would increase in view of the voters' electoral clout. For about fourteen years, however, these expectations came to naught. Long-standing partisan affiliations and loyalties, on the one hand, and traditional enmities, on the other, apparently continued to be central in determining the citizens' electoral preferences; military fiascos, economic stagnation, and governmental turpitude failed to produce a political reversal.

In 1992, following an intense campaign focusing on the ruling Likud Party's incompetence and its leaders' corruption and inattentiveness to the public's grievances, the Labor Party won a decisive victory. This shift seemed to indicate that the notion of reward/punishment voting had finally worked its way into the Israeli political culture. Such an interpretation was propounded by Professor Uriel Reichman, who is perhaps the single individual most identified with the pro-reform campaign of the late 1980s and early 1990s in Israel. In an article published in the daily *Ha'aretz* less than a week after the ballot boxes had been closed and the votes counted, Professor Reichman wrote: "The slogan 'We are fed up with your corruption' was addressed to the political system at large. However, only some of the politicians got the message. The public has rewarded the Labor and Tzomet parties, which it associated with the hope for democracy of another kind, and has punished the Likud party, which it perceived as entrenched in the maladies of befouled reality" (Reichman 1992).

This argument regarding the immediate cause-and-effect relation between the parties' conduct and their respective electoral attainments—or losses—may be attributed to wishful thinking, or even to biased analyses by those personally involved in the campaign in their desire to claim its success. However, similar views of the electoral outcome were expressed by people clearly unfettered by any vested interests. For example, in several television programs broadcast right after the elections, people interviewed on the streets and in workplaces stated candidly that they had not voted according to their traditional electoral preferences because they wanted to punish the ruling party for its malfunctioning and flagrant corruption rather than because they had changed their basic political views. Such an awareness of the electoral mandate as conditional upon performance was evidence of a change in Israeli voters' political mentality. It supports a growing tendency to reconsider the long-standing characterization of the Israeli public as keenly interested but "authority-directed" politically or, at least, as very slow in reacting to their government's deficiencies and failures (e.g., Lehman-Wilzig 1992).

This chapter suggests that the 1992 electoral shift marked a decisive stage in the progressive change in Israeli citizens' perception of their standing vis-à-vis the political establishment. The formerly dominant "ideological voting," which is quite stable by its nature and less contingent on performance, has given way to "instrumental voting," which is highly dependent on the politicians' achievements and hence basically alterable. This change thus neither fell out of the blue nor was a trivial consequence of objectively changing conditions. It was prompted and accelerated by vigorous pro-reform activity that fostered the notions of politicians' accountability and of attentive citizenship. The link between the extraparliamentary reform campaign and the Israeli voters' new perception of civil potency was not, however, a direct one.

It is suggested here that this change was brought about gradually by the effective work of the reform campaign's hard-core activists', sometimes carried out at the grassroots level, at other times at the political establishment level, and occasionally at both levels simultaneously, which is not unusual insofar as extraparliamentary movements are concerned. A combination of three basic orientations of such movements—the value orientation, the participation orientation, and the power orientation—is discerned. In other words, these movements make a simultaneous effort to instill their values into the surrounding political culture, to create a solid basis of public support, and to influence policy making through the building up of close ties with the political establishment (Turner and Killian 1972). In most cases the success of extraparliamentary movements in realizing their aspirations in all three orientations is uneven. This is so in the specific case dealt with here, where the greatest success appears to have been in bringing about a conceptual change, while mobilization of public participation and exertion of influence on the decision-making process were less successful.

II. Enhancement of the Notions of Politicians' Accountability and Instrumental Voting

In order to grasp the full meaning and significance of the political reform campaign of the late 1980s and early 1990s, one should employ two historical perspectives. The first perspective refers to the campaign's concrete aim—electoral reform: it therefore focuses on earlier endeavors to change the national electoral system. The second perspective has to do with modes of operation: it thus concentrates on previous extraparliamentary campaigns and political protest. Since an unprecedented combination of content and methods was the most significant feature of this campaign, both components must be dealt with concomitantly. To emphasize one at the expense of the other would unavoidably lead to an incomplete understanding of this new development in Israeli politics.

The pure proportional representation (PR) electoral system, inherited from the Zionist institutions of the prestate era and used through and including the 1992 elections, has been a huge political bone of contention since the early days of the State of Israel (Brichta 1992).[1] Long and extensively debated within the political establishment, this issue was a kind of microcosm of national and partisan politics, with a representative blend of rational and emotional elements. Those in favor of the replacing the PR system, a group headed for a long time by Israel's first Prime Minister David Ben-Gurion, argued with much zeal that it unavoidably leads to broad coalitions, which in turn obstruct the party in power from governing effectively. They therefore advocated adopting a majoritarian system, such as the British one, which would produce a definitive victor. They also claimed that the PR system turned the notion of political accountability into a meaningless ideal, as it actually severed the connection between the voters and their representatives.

The advocates of the PR system argued, with much the same passion, that PR provided for an accurate reflection of the entire broad spectrum of political opinion and enabled the smaller parties to have at least some representation and political impact. Moreover, they maintained, since regional interests are of only minor importance in the Israeli context there is no need for regional electoral representation.

Major parliamentary efforts to reform the system were made several times: in 1948, before the first general elections; during the term of the third Knesset (1955–59); in 1965 after Ben-Gurion left Mapai and founded the Worker's Party (Rafi), which inscribed the reform issue on its banner; and during the 1970s and 1980s, when several private bills proposing mixed constituency-proportional systems were submitted to the Knesset. Although these efforts were fruitful in raising the politicians' awareness of the need for some reform of the system, they failed either to overcome parliamentary barriers to the implementation of any reform or to attract the interest and attention of the general public. As the following parts of the paper show, both of these aspects changed radically as the extraparliamentary reform campaign gained momentum in the late 1980s.

The extraparliamentary modus operandi of the reform campaign was, like its purpose, not a new phenomenon in the Israeli political milieu and had emerged intermittently in Israeli political life throughout the years (Lehman-Wilzig 1992). However, in the case of the reform campaign it was exceptional in terms of scope, continuity, vigor, resources, and visibility. The extraparliamentary character of the campaign was fostered first and foremost by the fruitless parliamentary efforts made earlier to alter the political system. It was also invigorated by the sharp increase in the disillusion and even contempt felt by the grass roots for the political establishment and its methods. In addition, mass mobilization was facilitated by the fact that the focal issue was nonpartisan and both sufficiently important and general to bring together people of the political left and right, disparate party affiliations, varying socioeconomic strata, and diverse ethnic backgrounds. This contrasts sharply with other extraparliamentary struggles, like those of the peace movements, ultranationalist organizations, ultrareligious groups, or protestors demanding greater social or economic assistance from the state, each of which by definition had a limited mobilization potential.

The reform campaign differed from other Israeli extraparliamentary initiatives in that beyond striving for the realization of a concrete goal, it aimed to transform the basic rules of the political game. The fact that it was also openly supported by major parties and focal individuals of the political establishment, as well as by some wealthy private entrepreneurs, invested it with both the legitimization and the material resources that are so crucial—albeit usually difficult to get—for citizens' initiatives.

Reinforcement of the notions of politicians' accountability and instrumental voting were not incidental by-products of the reform campaign. In fact, the implementation of these two notions constituted the original raison d'etre of this endeavor from its inception and one of its manifest goals. The major catalysts for action, as delineated in various publications of the Movement for a Constitution for the State of Israel, the organizational and ideological cornerstone of the reform campaign, were the parliamentary deadlock that followed the 1984 elections and the shameless interparty deals that were made in order to break through it. The widespread loathing for the political establishment that this incurred, accompanied by frustration with blatant civil inefficacy, stirred up the citizens' sense of urgency and of the need to seek out a legal way to enforce the politicians' accountability to their constituencies and, at the same time, reduce their dependency on their coalition allies. However, no actual steps in this direction were taken during the next two years.[2] (For a chronology of major dates and events of the campaign, see the Appendix.)

The first sign of activity in this direction occurred in 1986 with the organization of the Constitution Drafting Committee, which consisted of a group of professors, mainly from the Tel Aviv University law faculty. As reflected by its name, the focal point of this group's activity was the drafting of a constitution, and such a proposal was presented to the public in the summer of 1987. The two main issues of this proposal were the revision of the electoral system and the adoption of the Basic Law: Human Rights. Both issues dealt with the relationship between citizens and the authorities and with restrictions limiting government powers. The first was meant to increase the politicians' accountability by the adoption of a constituency-based electoral system, and the second to protect the citizens from arbitrary decisions of the authorities in matters of civil rights. The public's rapid and positive response to the committee's initiative was an unequivocal indication of its ripeness for the message of political reform. In a survey carried out in November 1987 by Teleseker, 65.8 percent of the respondents supported the adoption of a constitution. The notion of the public's right and ability to present demands to the politicians became even more popular in the late 1980s and early 1990s. For example, in the massive rally against the politicians' malfeasance during the parliamentary deadlock following the 1988 elections, placards expressing this notion were flaunted. One particularly explosive placard punned that "if you politicians don't depend [*teluim*, in Hebrew] on each other then you'll hang [also *teluim*] by each other" (*Ma'ariv* 13 November 1988).

The idea of large-scale public protests was also promoted by the Movement for Governance Reform, the second and more "plebian" and radical spearhead of the reform campaign. Its activists sometimes used rather dramatic means to transmit the message of their very pithy motto: "[We are] fed up with [your] corruption." For example, in April 1991, while picketing against the Knesset's intention to postpone the vote on the electoral reform bill, the protestors smeared mud on their clothes and Avi Kadish, the chairman of the movement, announced, "This is the last time that we, the citizens, will wallow in this disgusting mud. If the electoral system is not changed, we will see that those who sit in the Knesset building will be covered with this stuff." As expected, the politicians in the establishment did not exactly appreciate this very graphic style of pressure, and the activists using it were blamed even by some of their fellow activists of damaging their mutual cause by it (Landau 1991). However, the taboo on this kind of rhetoric and normative argumentation was clearly shattered.

The view that the genie was out of the bottle was expressed by Avi Kadish in an article, published in December 1991, in which he presented an optimistic assessment of the campaign's impact: "Until two years ago the general public's involvement in the debate on the character of Israeli democracy was minimal and non-committal. The result was paralysis and bankruptcy of the system of government. But the 'dirty tricks' have driven the citizens out to the streets, and the uncompromising will of the public has become the catalyst of the transformation process . . . The grassroots pressure will force the politicians to take into account the public's opinion and feelings . . . It should be noticed that beyond the fundamental change of the system of government, what we see here is a normative and psychological transformation of supreme significance" (Kadish 1991). The facts seemed to sustain this view. In March 1992, a few days before the second and third readings of the bill on the direct election of the prime minister, a Gallup survey was made in which 68 percent of the respondents considered reform to be a solution, direct or indirect, to the state's most pressing political problems; 74 percent wished to see the changing of the political system as a primary or at least a secondary issue in their party's platform; and 15 percent said that they would not vote for a party that did not include the express commitment to a governance reform in its platform.

In an interview, held a few days before the elections on 23 June 1992 but published only after them, Arie Rotenberg, one of the reform campaign's hard-core activists and, as a professional public relations specialist, the manager of the Labor Party's election propaganda, expressed the feeling, widespread in this party, that the public had become deeply aware of its power:

> The public surprised everybody, including us. This is a turning point. It is the end of the era in which the politicians can fool the people. In the last three elections, when the campaign started

and the tom-toms began to thunder, everyone went back to his old camp. Thousands of voters returned to the Likud . . . To my mind, this time, for the first time, the winners of the elections will be those who listened to the people . . . What we see is a stunning process of maturation which this nation underwent . . . The politicians will realize that there is an electoral price for their inattentiveness at crucial times. The transformation, this time, belongs first and foremost to the people! (Horwitz 1992)

Rotenberg's lucid comments express the virtual essence of the main arguments presented in this chapter on the campaign. The following parts of the analysis will deal with the intricate process by which this transformation in Israel's political culture was fostered by the reform campaign.

III. Public Mobilization and Participation

Classical liberal theory argues that political participation at the grassroots level is an invaluable instrument for the development of the general public's political maturity and, hence, of a truly accountable government. There is no doubt that the modifications in Israeli voters' motivations during the late 1980s and early 1990s were accompanied by a noticeable increase in their political activism. However, it is also necessary to examine the extent to which this period was characterized by such grassroots political vigilance and whether this increase could have presaged the electoral shift of June 1992.

At the beginning of his abovementioned article, Reichman made the assertion that "in April 1990 a powerful wave in Israeli society crested. For years the citizens had gazed with growing contempt at the parliamentary power struggles . . . On this wave of contempt, the Movement for a Constitution for Israel was raised high" (Reichman 1992). At the end of 1991, Avi Kadish also described the proreform activity as a powerful grassroots struggle "[in which] were invested the hopes, frustrations and disappointments of hundreds of thousands of citizens" (Kadish 1991). Such a favorable presentation of the reform campaign, used by its leaders in order to buttress the democratic legitimacy of their struggle, raised considerable doubts in other circles. Critics of their perception have argued that the grassroots involvement in the reform campaign was sporadic and ad hoc and that, in fact, no mass movement had actually ever been established.[3] As the following overview of the participatory aspect of the reform campaign will attempt to demonstrate, both views, that of Reichman and Kadish and that of their critics, are—paradoxical as it may appear—empirically correct.

The first phase of the reform campaign, the Drafting Committee's preparation of its proposal for a constitution 1986–87 was, without a doubt, basically nonparticipatory insofar as the general public was concerned. The costly preparation and wide circulation of the proposal (according to certain estimates, at a cost of more than five hundred thousand dollars. See Barnea 1988) was made possible financially by the generous support of several Israeli entrepreneurs, such as Steph Wertheimer and Al Schwimmer, and a number of Israeli and American foundations, such as The Bronfman Foundation and The Friends of Tel Aviv University Law School. This short list of benefactors is indicative of the sort of people and institutions interested and involved in the proreform activity at this stage. The social composition of this group, in addition to its formal-legal orientation and the professional jargon it used, clearly precluded its ability to constitute a basis for grassroots mobilization.[4] Reichman and his group, aware of the need for broadly based legitimization while addressing the decision makers, and in order to attract the general public's attention and win its support, used the services, both voluntary and hired, of first-class public relations professionals.

Due to the committee members' high professional status, upper-class social connections, and considerable resources, no less than because of the importance of the issue itself, the constitution proposal received vast media coverage and considerable public attention. The Movement for a Constitution was established, however, only in January 1988, in a mass rally organized by the committee. This operative shift, which marked the beginning of the second phase of activity, was meant to put greater visible pressure on the political leaders, who seemed reluctant, or at least sluggish, about responding to the committee's initiative. The impending elections, scheduled for later in the year, apparently also prompted the change of gears into a broader range of action. However, as the agenda of the new movement was clearly laid down from above, and the general public was asked only to attend the rallies and support the platform as given, it appears that the mass mobilization effort was more instrumental than ideological.

The next switch sustains this assessment. In June 1988 the new elections bill successfully passed its first reading in the Knesset, and it appeared as if the campaign, with its limited but devoted avant-garde and inclusive ad hoc body of supporters, was beginning to bear the desired fruits. No further pressures from below seemed necessary, at least not for the time being. Therefore, the exclusive character of the campaign was in fact reconstituted for a while.[5] But as the stormy interparty preelection struggle gained momentum, the practical involvement of the politicians engaged in efforts to transform the system faded away. The leaders of the Movement for a Constitution were shunted aside, greatly disappointed and very angry. They again sought and encouraged the active support of the public, which at this stage remained fairly inactive, apparently awaiting the results of the coming elections. The 1988 elections, however, brought in their wake yet another parliamentary deadlock as neither the Likud, with forty mandates, nor the Labor, with thirty-nine, succeeded in constituting a viable coalition. This impasse, and far more the excessive benefits offered by the major parties to the small ultrareligious parties in return for joining the coalition, infuriated many Israelis and provoked them out of their usual political lethargy. It became widely acknowledged that such political paralysis could be averted only by fundamental political reform. Under the movement's auspices, thousands of people again rallied in Tel Aviv on 12 November. They demanded a broad coalition that would invest the energy and devotion necessary to changing the electoral system to one ensuring a single clear-cut victor able to govern the nation effectively.

The deadlock was resolved by the formation of the second unity government. Nevertheless, it was quickly realized, and acknowledged, that this was a poor solution, as it resulted in an oversized and cumbersome government and a small and ineffective opposition. Consequently, the leaders of both the Likud and Labor parties, first and foremost out of their partisan considerations but apparently also due to their realization that the spreading civil discontent could no longer be ignored, cooperated in nominating, in March 1989, a bipartisan committee for reform of the electoral system. The committee was chaired by MK Gad Yaacobi of Labor, who had been involved for many years in various efforts to reform the Israeli electoral system. The attention of the committee again shifted to those MKs partial to electoral reform. Activity at the public level did not cease at this stage, but the actions taken, rather than being massive and demonstrative, were local and nonconflictive and more symbolic. For example, the Movement for a Constitution together with the mayor of the wealthy town of Ramat Ha'Sharon declared a local "Constitution Week." This cooperation was an indication that the campaign had become completely "respectable" under the overarching principles of the Israeli polity and that electoral reform was now considered legitimate.[6]

In March 1990 the second unity government broke down, following the tireless attempts of Labor Party, when still a prominent partner in this government, to free itself from this undesirable partnership and constitute its own government by offering some flagrant benefits to certain MKs in return for their parliamentary support. This unscrupulous conduct, labeled the "dirty trick" by Yitzhak Rabin himself, invigorated the public rage against the political leadership. The reform campaign—until then virtually identical to the Movement for a Constitution—entered the third phase of activity, which was characterized by unprecedented participatory features. This phase, which was also the campaign's most vigorous and radical, was launched by two individuals, Avi Kadish and Shachar Ben Meir. In late March, in the Rose Garden facing the Knesset, they began a hunger strike, which was extensively covered by the media (Melamed and Chalfon 1992). Unlike the Constitution Committee at its inception, Kadish and his colleagues in the new Movement for Governance Reform had neither a clear platform nor a concrete program for reforms. In their numerous interviews and statements during the strike, in the last days of March and early April, they called upon the public only to fight for a radical change in the political system that would prevent such disgraceful wheeling and dealing in the future and would enhance greater accountability on the part of the nation's elected representatives. That this message was rather vague was apparently not perceived as a problem by the thousands of Israelis of wide-ranging political affiliations, ages, and social backgrounds who came, unorganized and on their own initiative, to sit with the hunger strikers in order to express support in their struggle. The only notion clearly shared by all of the people, there and throughout the country, was loathing for the professional politicians and their shameless behavior.

Public interest and involvement in the campaign mounted quite rapidly as hundreds of students demonstrated on their campuses, various small groups calling for reform were established all over the country, pro-reform petitions were circulated and signed by hundreds of thousands citizens, and so on. A massive public demonstration was organized in Tel Aviv on 7 April and attended by all of the movements and groups involved in the campaign. More than 100 thousand people (almost 250 thousand, according to the organizers' estimates) came to hear the various speakers calling for reform. Optimistic, and applauding and cheering, they were hardly aware that under the facade of camaraderie the organizers were already struggling bitterly among themselves over the leadership of what showed every sign of being one of the strongest and most profound protest movements the country had ever seen.[7]

The activists' claims of the public's solid and active support of the endeavor's underlying ideas and solutions, and hence of the campaign itself as a resounding success in terms of mobilization, appeared to be well grounded in April 1990. However, by mid-May it became clear that the efforts to establish and sustain a mass movement had actually failed. Not only were most of the thousands of people who had signed the petitions or participated in the rallies unwilling to go beyond such noncommittal actions, but those who were interested in becoming or staying active were put off by the clashes between the different factions involved in the campaign. The struggles over matters of prestige and the offensive language used by the rival parties within the campaign seemed to many virtually the same as the ugly infighting of the professional politicians, which the campaign leaders denounced with increasing fierceness in order to catch the attention of the media and the public.

When its leaders realized that the masses would not stay active for long, the Movement for a Constitution reinvigorated its efforts to mobilize support in the upper political echelons. The activists of the Movement for Governance Reform, on the other hand, well aware of their ultimate dependency on the active backing of their grassroots supporters, preferred to take a somewhat different course of action to forestall the loss of support. They transferred their emphasis from massive protest on a national scale to more local and low-key activities, feasible without large-scale public participation. Regional chapters were established and put in charge of organizing local initiatives and sustaining networks of activists to be called upon when needed. Another important fact to note is that from about that time on this movement's affairs were organized and controlled from a central office located in a luxurious hotel in Tel Aviv, a service provided free of charge by the owners of the hotel, who supported the cause of reform. Once again, connections with the upper classes were established, a development known to have a moderating effect on the agenda of extraparliamentary movements. Thus, both components of the campaign, regardless of their actual contacts with the masses at any specific time, continued to present themselves as the tip of the iceberg, attributing the visible decline in mass participation to the advanced phase of activity, one characterized by routinization.[8] Nevertheless, it was clear to all observers, supporters and opponents alike, that the campaign's mobilization potential was more limited then had been estimated.

As 19 June 1991 drew near—the day that the Law, Constitution and Justice Committee of the Knesset was to finish its deliberations on the bill for direct election of the prime minister and present it to the Knesset for its second and third plenary readings—public pro-reform activity was revitalized by the Movement for Governance Reform, although not to its mid-1990 level. Huge placards proclaiming the crucial date were displayed along the main roads and at the entrances to the larger cities, picket lines demonstrated in front of the Knesset building, and large (and costly) advertisements were placed in the newspapers, all to remind the public of the significance of the date and thus to urge the Knesset committee to meet the deadline. However, the deadline turned out to be deceptive, and the vociferous pressure engendered by these activities backfired, urging into action those MKs who opposed the bill. These MKs succeeded in obstructing Labor's initiative to compel the Knesset to vote on the bill before the beginning of the summer recess. Their triumph made the Movement for Governance Reform the target of fierce criticism from all sides, including its former ally, the Movement for a Constitution. Kadish and his fellow activists were accused of cheap populism, impatience, over-militancy and political shortsightedness. Such accusations apparently heightened the public's uncertainty and doubts regarding the advantages of massive political participation. And, indeed, fewer than one thousand people attended what was supposed to be a mass rally organized by the movement in order to express the citizens' anger at the indefinite postponement of the readings.

After the summer of 1991, the fourth (and up to this writing the last) phase of activity, active public participation in the reform campaign, has been low. Early in 1992, when the readings of the bill for direct election of the prime minister seemed to be at stake again, the idea of transforming the campaign into a political party was seriously deliberated. It was promoted especially by the leaders of the Movement for a Constitution, against the position of the Movement for Governance Reform, which advocated adherence to the extraparliamentary modus operandi. While there were apparently other reasons for the final decision not to change strategy, it may well be that the plan was dropped mainly because it was realized that the mobilization problems from which the reform campaign had suffered all along would probably become even more severe if it turned into a single-purpose political party aiming at a typical "public good." However, the flow of information on the ongoing proreform endeavors, both within and outside of the Knesset, remained extensive, keeping the issues of proper representation and politicians' accountability on the national agenda.

IV. Targeting the Political Establishment

On the level of the campaign's interaction with the political establishment, three main factors were most significant: the differential relations between the reform campaign and the two major parties, the disparity between the goal and the methods of the campaign, and the prolonged and quite dismal history of parliamentary efforts to reform the electoral system. As a result of these three factors the relationship between the campaign's leadership and the politicians was multifaceted, much like its interactions with the general public, and it swung—even more sharply than in the public's case—from cooperation to discord and back again.

It is quite clear that despite its facade of political impartiality, the reform campaign's relationship with each of the two major parties was basically different. Being the party in power, the Likud was the natural target for criticism of the government's malfunction and reluctance to change the electoral system. And, indeed, in the survey of Teleseker mentioned above, 17 percent of the respondents said that the Likud was responsible for the recent failures to change the system. This was not an erroneous impression, however, as Prime Minister Shamir openly and strongly opposed the proposed electoral reform. In June 1990, delegates of the reform campaign met with Mr. Shamir and tried to draw his attention to the growing public dissatisfaction and its possible repercussions. The newspaper reports of the meeting described the extreme tension and unconcealed antagonism of both sides. The first speaker for the group, David Meital of the Movement for Governance Reform, confronted Mr. Shamir outright by affirming his and his colleagues' resolution to take steps against the government's unresponsiveness: "Does Your Excellency understand? The People are angry. And we are angry at you and the politicians who sit idly and exploit every good thing in this land. Your Excellency does not understand, and he surely does not feel. The earth is quaking under your feet. We came here to warn you, a wave of protest is going to wash you all away" (Bar 1990).

The link between the Likud's official opposition to the reform and the voting in the elections was laid bare a year later, with the approach of the 19 June deadline for the second and third readings of the bill for direct election of the prime minister. Large advertisements in the daily newspapers showed an ostrich with its head in the sand and the caption "Mr. Shamir, you can't run away from the consequences." The advertisement went on to say: "We're not talking ideology now, we're talking mandates. Seats. The Likud is going to loose three mandates if it again obstructs the bill for the direct election of the prime minister . . . Our next encounter will be in the voting booths" (Ha'aretz 1992).

Relations with the Labor Party were clearly more positive, and this party expressed its support of the campaign's causes more and more openly as the elections neared. However, this rapprochement apparently had another aspect, for on personal, social, and ideological grounds the hard-core activists, especially those of the Movement for a Constitution, were always closer to the Labor Party than to the Likud. Certain observers claimed that this proximity was based on practical interests, such as the long-standing vested financial interests of the old Ashkenazi elite in the formerly dominant party and this elite's difficulties in adapting to the unfavorable status it encountered following Labor's 1977 electoral defeat. Had Labor remained in power, these observers argue, the reform campaign would have been far more moderate, if it had emerged at all (Nitzan 1990).

The disparity between the campaign's goals and its methods was the second factor that influenced its relationship with the political establishment. The relationship between an extraparliamentary movement and the authorities contains by definition a certain element of conflict, because in most cases the main raison d'etre of such a movement is the modification of some aspects of the existing sociopolitical order. The nature and depth of the desired changes determine the movement's position vis-à-vis the political establishment: the more radical the changes, the more confrontational the movement's relations with the authorities usually become. Various studies have shown that in a pluralistic democratic context the ability of a radical movement to bring the decision makers to willingly take steps in the direction it advocates is usually very limited because of the threat to the existing order it embodies. A moderate movement, on the other hand, has a better chance of introducing its demands into the national agenda, but by definition its prospects of bringing about a comprehensive or a fundamental political change are low. The application of this theorem to the case of the Israeli reform campaign presents a problem, as there was a clear disparity between the campaign's goals and its methods of operation. On the ideological level the changes it demanded, particularly in the more advanced phases of its activity, were quite fundamental and thus, as expected, provoked resistance within the establishment. On the operative level, however, during all the years it was active, the campaign remained fairly moderate and nonviolent, in practice if not in rhetoric, a feature that, in turn, had a positive impact on its relations with the political establishment. These relations were therefore characterized by a mixture of mutual heed and reciprocal give and take, the respective salience of each changing in almost perfect negative correlation with the campaign's ups and downs in public mobilization.

This complex situation was further complicated by the third factor mentioned above, the prolonged history of parliamentary efforts to change the electoral system and the ongoing commitment and activity for electoral reform of certain politicians within the establishment, including several Likud MKs. Thus the campaign for reform could neither step into a vacancy nor claim the prerogative of having conceived the reform idea. Ideas for reform usually emerge and are formulated at the elite level, not at the grassroots one. Professional politicians, probably because of their close acquaintance with the system, seem to be more prone than laymen to advocate electoral reform as the remedy for national political maladies. Gradually the general public starts to share the elite's sense of crisis, but time and some professional guidance are needed before the point is reached where the citizens realize that electoral reform is the best solution possible. Nevertheless, the elites' leading position is gradually eroded, for when the masses join the reform campaign they often introduce their own concerns and perspectives into the agenda (Weir 1992).

Generally speaking this theoretical description fits the Israeli case, as the extraparliamentary reform campaign was indeed preceded and influenced by various partisan initiatives for a change of the electoral system. Moreover, most of the time it was closely intertwined with the ongoing parliamentary struggle over the proposed new electoral bills. At the same time, it should be noted that the extraparliamentary campaign's leadership, despite its close cooperation with those MKs who tried to promote the electoral reform by parliamentary means, was intellectually self-reliant from its inception, mainly because its most prominent activists were widely acknowledged experts in electoral issues. Therefore they did not need the politicians' guidance, at least not in the planning stages. Furthermore, the reform campaign had started immediately with a profound demand, the adoption of a full, written constitution, but after 1990 demanded much more: a fundamental revision of the national political modus operandi.

No wonder, then, that the political establishment as a whole, including the parties of the opposition that exploited the public's readiness for reform in their election campaigns, was not especially eager to adopt the reform as it was outlined in the constitution proposal. The two main reasons were the practical difficulties likely to be incurred, such as the anticipated objections of the religious parties to a Bill of Rights, and, perhaps an even weightier consideration, because it meant narrowing the parties' latitude for political maneuvering. And, indeed, the minister of justice in the first unity government, Avraham Sharir of the Likud, supported by his ministry staff and by Yosef Harish, the legal adviser to the government, rejected the professors' initiative on the controversial ground that it would nullify the legislative work done earlier in having eight of the eleven planned basic laws passed in the Knesset.

Vast publicity, general attention, and extensive media coverage made it impossible for the politicians to ignore the proposal. This was particularly true for the opposition, which could not but notice the advantages of utilizing the prevailing public discontent and readiness for change. In light of past experience, the authorities first tried the strategy of cooptation in order to deal with the new challenge presented by the Constitution Drafting Committee. The committee members were invited several times to the Knesset, officially to give professional advice but probably also as a means to soften their criticism. In December 1987, for example, only a few months after the publication of the constitution proposal, the Reichman group was invited to take part in the discussion of the Human Rights Bill in the Knesset's Law, Constitution and Justice Committee (Margalit 1987).[9] While some of the politicians who worked with Reichman's group were apparently motivated by a real interest in receiving legal advice from first-class experts, others were clearly prompted by the idea of forestalling the radicalization of the group by absorbing it into the establishment. Either way, the doors of the establishment were opened to the group members, thereby intentionally or unintentionally giving their initiative and skills official recognition and legitimization—as well as considerable media exposure.

Cooperation with the political elite was obviously also facilitated by the committee's basic belief in the political establishment's potential capacity to correct itself. This belief apparently did not vanish even after its members became bitterly disappointed by the politicians' inattentiveness and lack of action, although it eroded considerably later on. It is not surprising, then, that the brochure published by the Movement for a Constitution (1991) just before the decisive vote in the Knesset on 19 June 1991, was prefaced by acknowledgements of the committee's deep appreciation for MKs Linn, Libai, Zidon, and Rubinstein "for their devotion and creative and energetic activity for the cause of governance reform" and to Vice-Ministers Magen and Netanyahu and MKs Rabin and Yaacobi "for their tireless support for the realization of the idea of direct election of the prime minister". The general public's support and pressure were mentioned only briefly in the short historical overview of the campaign.

The Committee members' enthusiastic cooperation with professional politicians, as well as the quick shift of focus from the crowded city squares to the carpeted halls of the Knesset, was public knowledge. They were often criticized for seeking honor and causing the campaign to lose its raison d'etre: "The Dean of the Law Faculty, Professor Uriel Reichman, and his fellow professors are frequently found in the Knesset cafeteria. The group mingles comfortably with those MKs who act as their lobbyists for speeding up the adoption of the constitution . . . Reichman, more than anyone else, should know that a constitutional framework does not guarantee a democratic government" (Tzimuki 1989).

The second half of 1988 was a low point in the movement's relations with the political establishment, which then, just a few months after the optimistic fanfare with which the new elections bill passed the first reading in the Knesset, turned a deaf ear to the demands for reform. One explanation for the government's reluctance to continue working on the bill between June and November 1988 was the religious parties' open threat not to join the coalition after the coming elections if the entire issue were not dropped (Arian and Shamir 1990). The highly disappointed pro-reform activists denounced the politicians' "desertion" as a typical example of political opportunism that the provisions in the reform proposal were meant to forestall, at least in part. In a press interview on this matter, Reichman, in high dudgeon, criticized the parties of both the left and the right: "We are used to saying that the right is brutish and the left moral. This is untrue. The same instruments, the same methods, the same cheap rhetoric, the same hypocrisy [are used by both]. This is a gang that you simply cannot trust" (Barnea 1988).

The March 1990 crisis aggravated the relations of the reform activists with both major parties. The members of the Movement for a Constitution picketed outside Labor Party headquarters against what they defined as the party's surrender to the excessive and insolent demands of the ultrareligious parties. They held up placards condemning the "horse trading" and even more biting ones such as "Shamir and Peres—both of you deserve a kick in the rear." The threat of electoral reprisal in the upcoming election was also brandished. As described above, the antiestablishment rhetoric became even more radicalized with the emergence of the Movement for Governance Reform. The activists of this movement were from the start openly skeptical about the ability of the political system to correct itself. This was expressed in so many words in the brochure (1990) explaining its objectives and courses of action: "It is not to be expected that the political system will effect changes on its own initiative . . . The protest movement, therefore, has to coerce the political system into making these changes, rather than wait for development from within."

In the spring of 1990 the two movements seemed to find common ground for cooperation: their shared loathing and distrust of the politicians and the parties. But their disparity in tone and attitude toward the political establishment was soon to have its effect, and indeed after a while their roads actually diverged: the Movement for a Constitution forged anew its connections with Labor and cooperated with Likud politicians, such as Linn, Magen, and Netanyahu, who openly supported electoral reform, whereas the Movement for a Governance Reform stuck to its basic antiestablishment position of disassociating itself from all political parties. The difference between the two strategies became highly visible in the spring of 1991 when the two movements' disagreements over the 19 June deadline deteriorated into a rupture. At the time it looked like a self-defeating domestic controversy between the two spearheads of the reform campaign, but in retrospect it appears to have had some salutary effects on the voters, who reconsidered their electoral options. The cooperative strategy favored by the Movement for a Constitution did not disqualify any politician or party per se but referred only to their manifested positions on the specific issue of reform. This promoted the notion that the national political arena should be perceived as a "free market" in which the politicians offer their "goods" and the public decides what to "buy" on the basis of cost-benefit calculations rather than on long-standing ideological loyalties. No less important in sustaining the public skepticism of the decision makers' integrity and skills, however, was the outcry of the Movement for Governance Reform against the politicians' Machiavellianism and their narrow partisan attitudes toward fundamental national problems.

The change in attitude, fostered by the reform campaign, can also be traced to the party level. Labor's adoption of the primaries system is one indication of the new weight attributed by the party's leaders to the preferences of its rank and file. Another indication of the inculcation of the reform message is found in the electoral platforms of various parties. Three of them, Labor, Tzomet and the New Liberal Party, put the issue of reform at the center of their platforms; they advocated structural and procedural changes almost identical with those promoted by the reform campaign. These three parties also supported direct election of the prime minister and committed themselves to the implementation of the new elections' law in the elections for the next Knesset. The Labor Party's platform, in addition, expressed its commitment to the replacement of the existing proportional representation electoral system by a mixed one similar to that suggested by Reichman and his colleagues, and it took it upon itself to promote the formulation of a Bill of Rights.

Tzomet openly advocated changing the Israeli system of government in order to put an end to the minor parties' disgraceful extortion of the major parties during coalition negotiations and to establish an efficient executive branch. The platform of the New Liberal Party (which, unlike Labor and Tzomet, proved to be an electoral fiasco, probably due to the unpopularity of its leader, Yitzhak Modai), called for the establishment of a referendum as the main democratic instrument for resolving decisive national issues, supported the adoption of a constitution, and called for separation of the three branches of government. The Moledet Party's platform also included some suggestions for political reform, but its proposals, in particular one regarding the strengthening the Knesset vis-a-vis the government, were the antitheses of those of the reform campaign. Meretz did not refer specifically to the electoral reform in its platform but, much in the spirit of the reform campaign, advocated a more participatory political system. All three electoral losers in 1992, Likud and the religious Mafdal in their highly detailed platforms and the communist Hadash in its compact one, had made no mention of the need for political reform.

While it is impossible to prove that there was any substantial cause-and-effect relationship between a party's stand on the reform issue and its electoral achievements, the fact that the major winners in the 1992 election had advocated reform, whereas the losers had ignored or brushed it aside, seems to strongly suggest that electoral reform was a central factor in determining the election results.

V. Conclusions

Just as one swallow does not make the spring, so too one electoral campaign with even the most unique features is not in and of itself a significant symptom of a real change in the national political culture. However, when it follows and is linked to a chain of extraordinary and accumulative political activities, is was the case here, there is a strong reason to believe that it can be taken as an indication of some meaningful change.

Looking at it from such a wider perspective, the voting in the 1992 elections—which weakened certain political parties enough to put them out of the Knesset (Tehiya), strengthened others as much as fourfold (Tzomet), and opened a wide gap between the two major parties—seems to have been more than a "ballot incident" or an episode. The electoral shifts apparently reflected the deep dissatisfaction of many Israelis with the functioning of the existing political system in general and of the party in power in particular, or, as one of the most popular slogans in this campaign stated, "The people want a change." This civil discontent with the government's performance and inattentiveness, fueled by last-minute official exposures of some incidents of official corruption, like those highlighted in the state comptroller's annual report, steadily gained momentum. However, unlike earlier waves of dissatisfaction, this one was accompanied by a significant rise of grassroots, participatory orientations. This powerful combination of acute discontent and the readiness to act to remedy its cause had already been manifested years before this election by less institutional means than voting, such as the fervent protest of homeless couples in 1990–91. However, it was formulated and manifested in its most clear and structured form in the reform campaign.

In various aspects the 1988–92 reform campaign was not a great success: it failed to sustain active public support for long, the legislative proposals it tried to promote were slowly and even then only partly implemented, and it fell short of maintaining internal harmony. Some would even say that it was frequently manipulated by specific interest groups to serve their particular concerns. Nevertheless, it clearly reflected the Israeli voters' new perception of their position vis-à-vis the political establishment; this in turn influenced their voting. It is quite obvious that this campaign did not create the citizens' reservations about the establishment and how it functioned. However, it helped to give these reservations a clear shape, and, unlike former protest endeavors, it also offered a solution that was likely to bring some relief to the grievances felt nationwide, without the risk of shattering the political order.

To sum up, the establishment's legitimization of the reform campaign, achieved by cooperation among the campaign's leadership and top-level politicians and the central parties, intensive though intermittent activity at the grassroots level, and the intensive public relations effort that sustained them—all together opened the door for the consolidation of two basic democratic ideas: politicians' accountability and active citizenship. The outcome of this process, as indicated by the results of the 1992 elections, suggests the introduction of instrumental voting along with the formerly dominant ideology-based voting.

Appendix: Major Events and Dates

July 1984 Elections for eleventh Knesset end in deadlock. After prolonged inter-party negotiations, the first national unity government is constituted. Situation draws renewed attention to deficiencies of proportional representation electoral system.

Spring 1986 First phase of activity. A group of TAU Law School professors begins drafting of a constitution which includes a new, mixed electoral system and a Bill of Rights. Draft presented to public in September 1987.

January 1988 Second phase of activity. Sixteen thousand people attend establishing rally of the Movement for a Constitution for the State of Israel in Tel Aviv.

June 1988 New elections bill passes first reading in the Knesset.

November 1988 Elections for twelfth Knesset again end in parliamentary deadlock, and a public sense of "political paralysis" mounts. One hundred thousand people attend a demonstration for governance reform.

December 1988 through January–February 1989 Four private bills, each including an electoral reform plan, are submitted to Knesset by MKs Linn (Likud), Libai (Labor), Zidon (Tzomet), and Rubinstein (Shinui).

January 1989 The Second Unity Government is formed.

February 1989 A joint bipartisan committee for reform of electoral system nominated.

March 1990 Third phase of activity. The Second Unity Government collapses. Interparty negotiations on formation of new coalition stir up a massive wave of public protest. The Movement for Governance Reform is established. Mayors Lahat, Bar, and Landau demonstrate in front of Knesset demanding a reform. All four private bill proposals pass preliminary readings.

April 1990 Hundreds of thousands of people demanding governance reform attend Tel Aviv rally co-organized by Committee for a Constitution for Israel, Movement for Governance Reform, Organization of IDF Disabled, and a group of mayors.

May 1990 A petition demanding reform signed by 501,234 Israelis is delivered to President of Israel by leaders of the Movement for Governance Reform. President Herzog expresses his support of campaign's causes and methods. Ten thousand people demonstrate for this same purpose in front of Knesset. The four bills pass the first reading and are later combined into one by their initiators. In September, a bill is submitted for deliberation to Knesset Committee for Law, Constitution and Justice.

November 1990 Knesset Committee begins discussing the combined bill, preparing it for second and third readings.

December 1990 Labor's Central Assembly decides to support bill.

January 1991 - Knesset Constitution Law and Justice Committee begins discussing a bill on the direct election of the prime minister.

July 1991 Knesset decision to return to committee for further revisions bill for direct election of prime minister stirs up another wave of mass protest. Fourth phase of activity begins.

November 1991 The Supreme Court orders Speaker of Knesset Dov Shilanski of Likud to bring the bill for direct election of prime minister for second and third readings.

December 1991 Likud Central Assembly decides to reject the bill.

March 1992 The bill for direct election of the prime minister is ratified by the Knesset.

Notes

1. Most electoral reform plans were formulated by professional politicians. However, there were also several pro-reform initiatives of nonestablishment character. In 1957, for example, Shmuel Tamir, Ari Zabotinski, Eliezer Livne, Yeshaayahu Leibowitz, Elyakim Ha'Etzni, and other politically active and well-known Israelis of various parties organized in a group called "The New Regime" (Ha'Mishtar Hachadash), which advocated the adoption of a constitution, including a new electoral system.

2. This hiatus is well explained by the theoretical argument that a phase of latent dissatisfaction often precedes a visible outbreak of protest. See Turner and Killian 1972, 253.

3. In May 1990, only two months after the intensively media-covered demonstration against the inter-party agreements that had followed the collapse of the second unity government, it was observed by certain newspapers that the massive participation had been only an episode (e.g., Galili 1990). A month later, Avi Kadish himself was quoted as saying that the initiative he and his colleagues had headed: "is perhaps dying, although it is not dead yet" (Drori-Wilf 1990). Ten months later, in April 1991 "a requiem for a protest movement" was published in the press after fewer than one thousand people attended what was planned to be a massive pro-reform rally in front of the Knesset in the morning of the Independence Day (Gvirtz 17.4.91).

4. For a sharp criticism of the aspiration of the leaders of the Movement for a Constitution to speak for the people, see Nitzan's (1990) comments: "Their People, and there is nothing to do about it, is not everyone's People. When they say: 'The People will win' they don't mean the textile workers . . . When they say what they say they mean The People as a metaphor . . . "

5. On the differences between inclusive and exclusive strategies of extraparliamentary movements, see Zald and Ash (1966).

6. The notion of a social movement's respectability is analyzed by Turner and Killian (1972, 259).

7. The main struggles were held between four components of the campaign: the two major ones, the Movement for a Constitution and the Movement for Governance Reform, and two numerically and organizationally minor components, the Group of Mayors and the Movement for the Improvement of the Quality of Government. This last group was actually a movement of one person, Eliad Shraga, and it took the legal course of action. Throughout the years it had most impressive achievements, such as obtaining the Supreme Court order to open the coalition agreements to public review.

8. In late 1990, when the ebb in participation became highly visible, one of the activists said in so many words that he hoped very much that "we won't reach such a level of disgust that the people will again be upset enough to get out and demonstrate in order to press the Knesset into action" (Lipkin-Shachak 1990).

9. On the use of the protest-absorbing strategy by the Israeli political establishment, see Etzioni-Halevi (1975).

References

Arian, Asher, and Michal Shamir. 1990. Introduction to *The Elections in Israel— 1988*, ed. Asher Arian and Michal Shamir. Boulder: Westview Press.

Bar, Orna. 1990. "Mr. Prime Minister, We Came Here to Warn You" (in Hebrew). *Hadashot Hedera*, 29 June.

Barnea, Nahum. 1988. "The Professor is Angry" (in Hebrew). *Koteret Rashit*, 3 August.

Brichta, Avraham. 1991. "Proposed Electoral Reform In Israel." *The Jewish Journal of Sociology* 33:83–96.

The Constitution Drafting Committee. 1987. Acknowledgements to *A Constitution for the State of Israel* (in Hebrew). Tel Aviv: The Constitution Drafting Committee.

Drori-Wilf, Neta. 1990. "The Movement for the Protest System Reform" (in Hebrew). *Kolbo Haifa*, 29 June.

Etzioni-Halevy, Eva. 1975. "Protest Politics in the Israeli Democracy." *Political Science Quarterly* 90:497–520.

Galili, Lili. 1990. "The Rose Garden is Deserted" (in Hebrew). *Ha'Aretz*, 11 May.

Gvirtz, Yael. 1991. "A Requiem for a Protest Movement" (in Hebrew). *Yediot Aharonot*, 17 April.

Horwitz, Ronit. 1992. "This Was the Last Battle" (in Hebrew). *Hadashot,* 26 June.

Kadish, Avi. 1991. "The First Step" (in Hebrew). *Ha'Aretz,* 31 December.

Landau, Orna. 1991. "Kadish about the Law" (in Hebrew). *Ha'Aretz,* 14 June.

Lehman-Wilzig, Sam. 1992. *Wildfire—Grassroots Revolt in Israel in the Post-Socialist Era.* Albany: SUNY Press.

Lipkin-Shachak, Tali. 1990. "The Movement is Alive but is Hiding" (in Hebrew). *Davar,* 4 November.

Margalit, Dan. 1987. "A Marathon Discussion over the Bill of Rights" (in Hebrew). *Ha'Aretz,* 10 December.

Melamed, Orly, and Drora Chalfon. 1992. "The Role of the Media in the Development of the Protest for Governance Reform" (in Hebrew). *Patuah: Journal for Politics, Communication and Society* 1992: 102–5.

The Movement for a Constitution for the State of Israel. 1991. *In '92 The Prime Minister Is Directly Elected* (in Hebrew). Tel Aviv: The Movement for a Constitution for the State of Israel.

The Movement for Governance Reform. 1990. *Courses and Objectives.* Tel Aviv: The Movement for Governance Reform.

Nitzan, Gabi. 1990. "Alibi" (in Hebrew). *Hadashot,* 10 January.

Reichman, Uriel. 1992. "A New Democracy" (in Hebrew). *Ha'Aretz,* 29 January.

Turner, Ralph H., and Lewis, M. Killian. 1972. *Collective Behavior.* Englewood Cliffs: Prentice-Hall.

Tzimuki, Tova. 1989. "The Day of the Constitution-Giving" (in Hebrew). *Davar,* 8 June.

Weir, Stuart. 1992. "Waiting for Change: Public Opinion and Electoral Reform." *The Political Quarterly* 63:197–221.

Zald, Mayer, and Roberta Ash. 1966. "Social Movement Organizations: Growth, Decay and Decay." *Social Forces,* 44:327–341.

CHAPTER 14

Reforming Israel's Voting Schemes

GIDEON DORON
Tel Aviv University
and
BARRY KAY
Wilfrid-Laurier University

I. Introduction

Electoral rules are mathematical schemes that aggregate individual preferences and produce collective choices. A change in the definition of the scheme results, of course, in the production of different outcomes. When election outcomes do not favor some political players, or when individuals or groups believe that an alteration in the prevailing method may yield desired results from their perspective, then proposals for changing the way votes are aggregated and offices assigned are often made. Because in democracies there are always winners and losers, a built-in potential for electoral reform exists, and it is usually manifested in actual proposals for change. Electoral reforms—actual or proposed—are thus a common feature of political life in all democracies.

Since the first election to the Constituent Assembly in 1949, the issue of electoral reform has been high on the agenda of certain of the Israeli politicians. Concern with this issue, however, expanded in the mid-1980s. It was intensified during, and due to, the negotiating excesses that occurred in forming and maintaining the government coalition in the twelfth Knesset

The authors would like to thank Rebecca Kook and Avraham Brichta for their comments and helpful suggestions.

following the November 1988 election, and the March 1990 coalition crisis. Several popular movements were formed around this goal, and numerous public demonstrations accompanied it. The spirit of the reform was recognized by the Knesset itself. Agreements to reform the electoral system were signed between Likud and Labor in 1988 and between Likud and Tzomet in 1990.

The intended change consisted of two elements. The first referred to a transformation of the current system, which selects Knesset members from national parties, to one that also includes local (i.e., district) representatives. The other involved direct election of the prime minister. This latter proposal was referred to as a "regime change," distinguishing it from the more commonplace effort to reform the electoral scheme. In March 1992, the Knesset adopted a law that required the direct selection of a prime minister by popular vote. It was decided, however, that the implementation of this law should take place alongside the election to the fourteenth Knesset scheduled to be held in 1996.

This decision to support a system that resembles a presidential-type regime does indeed signify a potential shift in the nature of the Israeli political dynamic. Other changes, however, less significant in their scope and impact, also occurred during the term of the twelfth Knesset. Among these, two have emerged as most important. The first involves a decision to increase the threshold level (e.g., blocking percentage) of votes necessary to qualify for a Knesset seat from 1 percent to 1.5 percent of the popular votes. The second change occurred at the party level. Labor moved to democratize its nominating procedure. Instead of selecting its Knesset list in the party center, party members elected the head of the list and their candidates to the Knesset through a system of primaries.

This chapter explores the reasons and explains the logic underlying the prevailing urge for change that has pervaded the Israeli political system. Its principle thesis is that while proposals for electoral reform may be based on some normative view people hold regarding political affairs, their actual design and practical implementation depends entirely on politicians' self-interest and the power relationships that exist among them.

The second part provides the theoretical orientation upon which this thesis rests for the construction of its reasoning. In the third section the political background of electoral reform in Israel is presented. This is followed by two sections describing and analyzing the two main proposals for electoral reform and the Labor primaries scheme. The evaluation of the political consequences of the actual and proposed reforms appears in the sixth part. We conclude by arguing that electoral changes will not, because they cannot, materially affect the substance and quality of Israeli politics and policy making and that such changes can be obtained only through a long term alteration of the country's political culture and a redefinition of some central elements that currently define the Israeli polity.

II. Theoretical Framework

Democratic schemes are designed to satisfy two basic purposes: (1) to enable an amalgamation of individual values such that the social choice will reflect them as much as possible and (2) to obtain an outcome that will perpetuate the political framework in which individuals specify their preferences. These schemes, which are often called the democratic "rules of the game," should enable society to obtain the values of representation and governability. While representation signifies the internal content of the game, that is, the nature of the relationship between members of society and their political institutions, governability provides for the framework within which the rules are preserved and public policy is made. Representation without the ability to govern and, conversely, governability without representation are two situations foreign to the concept of democracy. Thus, democracy has two dimensions. One dimension involves values such as freedom of association, which enables the grouping of preferences, freedom of speech, which assures an uninterrupted expression of preferences, or universal suffrage which, defines the qualifications needed of all those whose preferences are to be considered relevant for the determination of the social choice. The other dimension is related to procedures: majority rule, district determination, frequency of contests, duration of office terms, and so on.

The extent to which a system may be defined as more or less democratic is a question to be addressed empirically. It can be answered by a separate examination of the two dimensions. For example, various systems define the boundaries of their suffrage differently while permitting freedom of association and other liberties. Likewise, the nature and the relevance of election frequency may vary among political systems. Hence, while it is commonly assumed that representation and governability are two notions defining a single—unidimensional—spectrum and that, therefore, maximization of one must come at the expense of the other, in reality such a conception cannot be supported. Nonetheless, democratic values and procedures should be consistent with and reinforce each other.

The problem is that from both a theoretical point of view and a practical examination of reality, democratic values and procedures are found to be inconsistent. In fact, it has been proven to be impossible theoretically, and hence in practice, to devise a scheme that would accurately reflect the desires of individuals in society. (Arrow 1963; Sen 1970). Therefore, there is always some measure of arbitrariness associated with the choices societies arrive at. Moreover, because cycles of preferences over alternatives are always possible and often ubiquitous, it is difficult to say whether social choices are based upon the expression of individuals preferences or if they result from the particular technique employed to summarize them. Thus, for any prevailing social outcome, a majority of people may prefer some other outcomes. Therefore, public preferences may be in a state of constant flux and political stability is not assured.

This disturbing finding and inference was labeled by William Riker (1980) as the "disequilibrium of preferences" to denote the essence of the democratic dilemma. He writes, "outcomes are the consequences not only of institutions and tastes, but also of the political skill and artistry of those who manipulate agendas, formulate and reformulate questions, generate "false" issues, etc., in order to exploit the disequilibrium of tastes to their advantage" (445). People vote, but the outcome of their choices may, at best, select an alternative that only tangentially represents their position. The fact that voters mostly agree with some position does not imply that at the time of choice they even considered its alternative. Rather, choices depend, among other things, on the particular features of the decision process.

Indeed, it has been shown that each electoral system can be designed such as to produce results that are compatible with the interests of the designers (Gibbrad 1973). This is providing, of course, that the designers understand the underlying logic of the scheme and that they have knowledge, acquired by means of public polls or simulation, of the way people actually vote. The French, for example, seem to make frequent use of the recommendation embodied in the above findings. During the Fourth Republic, to help the Socialists sustain their political dominance they employed two voting schemes at the very same time: one for Paris and the other for the rest of the country (Rae 1967, 33, 36, 42). The frequent alterations of the French voting methods continues in the Fifth Republic.

Short-term equilibria are generated also because people express preferences over outcomes and not necessarily over the decision process in and of itself. That is, it is assumed that voters are mostly outcome oriented and not process oriented. If we assume, however, that people's preferences extend over procedures as well (i.e., "the rules of the game") then it is possible to argue that the ruling institution, or rather the institution of a particular set of rules, is conducive for the generation of long-term, stable equilibria. In essence, this is the argument advanced by proponents of the so-called neo-institutionalism school of social choice theorists (Shepsle and Weingast 1981, 1987; Denzua and Mackay 1981; Laver and Schofield 1990). Accordingly, preferences are, indeed, shaped by the various democratic institutions, and their durability is less a matter of the social consensus they reflect than of the difficulties involved in mobilizing majorities to undermine them. The stability of the institution thus assures the stability of the choice. Hence, institutions such as constitutions, political parties, unions, or systems of legal directives affect and shape preferences and are therefore conducive to the production of some measures of stability that could persist for a long time.

Perhaps the ongoing theoretical debate between the neo-institutionalists and the more traditionally oriented social choice theorists need not be settled. For if stability of choices can be defined, it must include manifestations of these choices in the form of the so-defined stability-inducing institutions. Therefore, myopic-type choices may result in the formation of institutions that persist over long periods of time, but their mere persistence may also imply that they produce a type of information that at times affects the nature of peoples' preferences and at other times constitute an obstacle to be removed or ignored. One cannot infer therefore, from the relative stability of say, the U.S. Constitution, that constitutions everywhere, as institutions, will induce stability. In fact, it can be said that *only* the U.S. Constitution is stable, perhaps because its principles are internalized by most Americans or because there are several highly limiting mechanisms and ideological underpinnings that guard it from frequent change. Nonetheless, even in the United States, major economic interests or social crises have induced major constitutional changes. In the first case the constitution could not preserve the unity of the nation and led to a civil war, and in the second, occurring in the early 1960s, its framework had to be enlarged to include Afro-Americans in the definition of the American corporate national identity (Kook 1992).

To recapitulate: new institutions embodying voting methods may induce stability because they may affect and even stop cycles of preferences. But the prevailing new reality in and of itself is transformed into information that breeds various interpretations. Hence, the institution itself becomes a variable affecting individual preferences, and these in turn may resume their cyclical pattern on a different plateau. Stability is thus temporary, and if at all desired by policy makers, it would be enhanced by other mechanisms not related to voters' preferences or even to the democratic rules of the game.

Thus we conclude that preservation of institutionalized or noninstitutionalized induced social states, or their alterations, is mostly dependent on the interests of the people involved in the production and maintenance of these states. Short of changes caused by social revolutions, it is usually the politicians who are the effective guardians of the status quo or the promoters of change. When their interests so dictate, and they are able to mobilize enough people to support these interests—change may occur, otherwise it does not.

Changes in general and in the electoral arena in particular are, of course, empirical events. Some are small, and others are larger in scope. To differentiate between these two types of changes we follow the strategy offered by Braybrooke and Lindblom (1963). Accordingly, small changes occur within the prevailing structures, while larger changes apply to the alterations of the structures themselves. Likewise, while predictions of the consequences of small incremental changes are possible, they become much more difficult and problematic when changes are large. Hence, changing the threshold from 1 percent to 1.5 percent is a small change, and its consequences can fairly be anticipated. A requirement to directly elect the prime minister, however, is a large structural change whose implications are not clear. This latter change qualifies for the label "electoral reform." Small changes in the rules that guide electoral competition are common in Israel. Large changes—electoral reforms, the focus of this article—were demanded and implemented during the tenure of the twelfth Knesset.

III. Electoral Reform: Political Background

The Israeli political system offers an extreme case of representative democracy that often faces problems of governability. Every four years, citizens are asked to elect their candidates to the one-house 120-member Knesset. Each party constructs and presents to the public its list of nominated candidates asking for a popular support. The votes of all parties able to obtain more than 1.5 percent of the popular vote are then tabulated. Seats are assigned in accordance with the proportion of votes each party is able to obtain. Specifically, two methods for seat assignment have been employed: until 1973 the "Largest Remainder" formula and since then the "Highest Average" (d'Hondt) formula. This latter one favors the large parties at the expense of the small ones (Rae 1967).

The combined affect of the low threshold and the fact that the entire country constitutes one voting zone creates a general impression that it is relatively easy to capture at least one seat in the Knesset. As a result of this impression, as many as thirty parties competed for seats in 1981 and no fewer than fourteen parties did so in 1961. Since 1973, at least twenty parties have competed in each election. Not all have been successful, of course. The number of parties able to acquire at least one seat in the Knesset has been no larger than fifteen (in 1951 and in 1988) but no smaller than ten (in 1973 and in 1992). Furthermore, since 1949 no party has been able to obtain a majority of popular votes. Therefore, to rule, governments rely on coalitions of parties.

Why did Israel adopt this particular political system? This question, which is often asked by academic and laymen alike, may have a simple answer: the political system employed in Israel was adopted from the one used in the prestate era by the World Zionist Organization. Put differently, politicians who were favored by the old system continued to use it after the state obtained its independence.

During the latter part of the nineteenth century, the Jewish national movement (which was formed in Eastern and Central Europe) faced severe recruitment problems. Only a minority chose to get involved in a movement that promoted a "national solution" to the so-called Jewish problem. Many of the early Zionists were young people, characterized, like most young people, by a high propensity to take risks and adopt changes in their personal lives (Arian 1985, 13–20; Eisenstadt 1969, 7–12). To be able to obtain political gains in the international arena, leaders of the movement needed to create the impression that they represented a greater body of people than they really did, that they were speaking for all the Jews (Galnor 1985). For that purpose they adopted a very generous proportional representation system that is in its essence inclusive. It permitted the inclusion of many groups and individuals from small and large places where Jews resided, thus creating the image that the movement represented and spoke for the majority of world Jewry. The real Zionist interests were, however, generally carried out by a small group of executives. Thus, representation that was made possible through the electoral system was not usually associated with much political leverage.

In a sovereign state, however, representation also means the selection of those individuals who get to decide "who gets what"—who makes policies, controls and distributes national resources. Electoral systems, thus, are used as means to exclude individuals and groups from effectively sharing the goods and the services that are made available through the control of governments. This is accomplished by instituting an effective set of structural and legal barriers to the entry of small and new parties into politics (Doron and Maor 1989). The Israeli system, however, continued to be inclusive, because no decision was ever made concerning the electoral method that should be used in the new state. As a matter of fact, no election was ever held to the first Knesset, which began its tenure in 1949. The election that was held in that year was for the Constituent Assembly, a body that was expected to decide upon a constitution and a proper electoral method for the new state. Once elected, the representatives decided to transform the assembly into a parliament. In parliament, for reasons which will be presented later, it became very difficult for the parties in power to acquire a majority for a significant change in the electoral method.

David Ben-Gurion, the first prime minister who stood behind the decision to transform the assembly into the Knesset, soon became a proponent of electoral change, a change that would enable him to rule without the need to rely on a coalition with small parties. The model he had in mind was the two-party British system (Ben-Gurion 1969). He could not, however, get enough support outside of, and even within, his own party for this idea. The closest he came was in 1952, when together with the General Zionists, then the second largest party in the Knesset, he planned to set a 10 percent threshold. This would have excluded from the Knesset almost all other parties. Nonetheless, threats to deny future political support, coming from the small Progressive Party, on the one hand, and the inability to predict electoral results after the proposed change would be enacted, on the other hand, were presumably the reasons he abandoned his plan (Brichta 1977).

But the urge to change the laws that guide electoral competition continued. Many small changes, in the Braybrooke and Lindblom sense, were enacted over the years. On the national level, they included alterations in party financing laws, specification of the allocation of free time in the electronic media, determination of the legitimacy of the parties' platform, and so on. In 1973 the Labor Alignment (which, counting the automatic support it obtained from its affiliated Arab parties, had sixty seats in the Knesset) colluded with Gahal, then the second largest party, and adopted the "Highest Average" formula. This adaptation is better known in Israel as the "Bader-Ofer formula" after its two designers. Other changes on the municipal and the party levels also took place in Israel over the years.

The historical presentation thus far leaves two interesting questions unanswered. The first is why the public urge to reform the electoral system became salient in the eleventh Knesset and was so intensified during the twelfth Knesset. The second question is why Labor and Likud, the two largest parties, which hold the majority of Knesset members, find it so difficult to collude on electoral reform matters (following the 1973 example) and design a system that could favor them at the expense of the small parties.

Many explanations have been provided to the first question. Most stress the ineffectiveness of the government decision-making process, the long period of bargaining that elapsed before coalitions were formed, the unresponsiveness of the politicians to public demands, the substandard behavior of politicians, and so on. Electoral reform would remedy, so it has been argued, some of the main problems of the Israeli polity; the new structure would breed new political behavior and policy substance. We propose a different, coalition-based explanation for this desire for change phenomenon.

The multiparty situation necessitates the formation of coalition government. Until 1977, Labor (Mapai) was the dominant party (Arian 1985, 96–103). It governed by forming coalitions with parties that were located both to its left (e.g., Mapam) and to its right (General Zionists and/or the Progressive Party). It also relied on the "traditional alliance" with the National Religious Party. From 1977 and until 1992, however, when Likud became the largest party, coalition formation was relatively more difficult. In 1981, the political system was transformed into a two-headed structure. Likud and Labor were almost equal in size. Likewise, the political camps consisting of small parties that aligned themselves with one or the other major parties were similar in size. In 1984 the Likud and Labor camps tied in size, and, instead of calling for new elections to break the tie, the leaders of the two parties decided to form a grand coalition between them and the other small parties. The posts of prime minister and foreign minister rotated between Shimon Peres of Labor and Yitzhak Shamir of the Likud. Because the Likud and Labor blocs tied again in 1988, a similar grand coalition was formed without, however, the rotation arrangement. This grand coalition dissipated in 1990.

In his seminal book, *The Theory of Political Coalitions*, Riker (1962, chap. 3) provides an elaborate explanation as to why one should expect all grand coalitions (especially those that operate in a political environment that is not facing a real crisis or threat to the survival of the system) to encounter severe governability problems. This is because the larger formation requires a greater degree of compromise from its members on basic ideological positions and material payoffs than is required in a smaller size coalition. The distance between the ideal positions of the partner-parties may be too far, and because of its size members receive less of the spoils as reward for their participation. In Israel's case, there was an additional problem: the public was not comfortable with the performance of its political representatives. Leaders of each of the two big parties continuously undermined policy initiatives taken by the leaders of the ideological rival-turned-partner of the other party. The government was locked in a stalemate. Policy decisions were made with great difficulty, and only when indecision could not serve as a feasible option.

There was no surprise that the public was looking for ways to ensure a more effective policy-making process. Two "villains" were identified: the electoral system, which permits the selection of small parties (especially religious ones) upon whose support government has to rely, and the legal requirement imposed on the government and the prime minister to recruit Knesset support for policy initiatives. Lack of political accountability and responsiveness to citizens' desires, high politicization of public administration, government involvement in various aspects of social and economic life, intolerable interference in personal life by government-supported institutions, and the inability to bring peace to the country or ensure the lives of the citizens were issues which were usually identified as by-products of a deficient political system. Consequently, proposals were made and public actions were taken to reform the system.

Before turning to the presentation and analysis of the essence of these proposals, it is appropriate to offer an answer to the second question. Again, there may be many explanations to the fact that Likud and Labor, in spite of their size advantage in the Knesset and their legally unrestricted ability to institute any desired change, do not readily exploit the said advantage and reform the system. We propose one interpretation, which should be accredited to Moshe Arens.[1] The reason the two big parties do not collude on matters of electoral reform is the prevailing mistrust that exists among their leaders. A mutual agreement may be rendered temporary and may be exploited by either one of the big parties to show the small parties that the other has betrayed them and hence cannot be considered as a potential coalition partner. This lack of trust induces defection on the reform issue and prevents voluntary cooperation among Labor and the Likud, which is exactly the situation predicted by the game known as "prisoners' dilemma" (Poundstone 1992).

IV. Two Routes to Electoral Reform

In many ways the mid-1980s renewed ambition to reform the electoral system continued the line that was first presented by Ben-Gurion. Among the many individuals who called publicly for a reform, two served as a propelling force, Gad Ya'acobi and Uriel Reichman. Ya'acobi, a prominent Labor MK until 1992, and a government minister at times, began lobbying for electoral change as early as 1975. (Ya'acobi and Gera 1975). Reichman, one-time dean of the law school at Tel Aviv University, began working on his own design about ten years later (Reichman et al. 1987). While the Ya'acobi proposal introduced the notion of local districts in addition to the prevailing national party lists, the Reichman initiative was more ambitious. It offered a modified version of the German two-tier electoral system, a method that was once used but abandoned by the Danish electorate. It also proposed the concept of direct popular election of the prime minister. These suggestions were included in the framework of a larger proposal for a formal constitution for Israel.

Changing the Electoral Method to the Knesset

Problems encountered by the coalition and the public campaign that followed encouraged the formation of several other groups of reformers. Reichman's group, "Constitution for Israel," was, however, the most successful one. Together with Ya'acobi, the group was able to recruit enough support from MKs to pass both of their proposals through the first reading of the bill (three readings are necessary to transform a proposed bill into a law). The vote took place just before the Knesset ended its term in 1988, but it left open the question of which of the two proposals should be adopted as a law. During the bargaining that preceded the formation of the grand coalition in 1988, Labor and Likud agreed to form a committee that would examine the two proposals and suggest a design to be implemented.

Ya'acobi was nominated to head the committee consisting of members of the two big parties. After a long period of deliberation the committee proposed in 1990 a design that combined elements of the two proposals into a single system. Its general features were as follows: the country was to be divided into twenty voting zones, each selecting three members. The other sixty members were to be elected nationally in the same manner they were elected to the twelfth Knesset. Only parties able to obtain at least 3.3 percent of the national votes (or four seats) would be qualified to send their representatives from the district to the Knesset. Thus, for example, if a party were to win two district seats and 5 percent of the national votes, it would get six seats in the Knesset. The two representatives from the district would replace two members from the national list. And if the same party were to win six district seats, all the local representatives would replace the national ones. This design, of course, favored the districts, but the proportion of representation in the Knesset would be determined by the success of parties in the national level. Hence, while the local layer of Reichman's sixty single-member districts was changed in favor of twenty three-member districts, the essence of his proposal, in which the upper national-layer indicated the strength of the parties in parliament, was preserved.

Understanding well the relative advantage local politicians have over national ones in the proposed design, members of the Ya'acobi committee included a provision that national politicians would be permitted to compete in local contests as well. They also accepted as a matter of fact the technical flaw that exists in Reichman's adaptation of the German system: What happens when the number of district seats exceeds the number of seats obtained by the national election? The committee's solution was: the size of the Knesset must become a variable to correct for such possibility. Because of the March 1990 coalition crisis, the Ya'acobi committee dissolved, and its product was not brought up for confirmation by the entire Knesset.

The Prime Minister Regime

Efforts to reform the system progressed via a different route: direct election to the prime minister. This idea became salient during the three months (March–June 1990) in which both Labor and Likud each tried to form its own minimum winning coalition. This time initiation came from four MKs who proposed similar schemes. Most interesting among them was the idea proposed by Yoash Zidon, a member of the two-man Tzomet Party, which conditioned its coalition agreement with the Likud upon the adoption of a law for direct popular election of the prime minister. Indeed, Zidon had effective political leverage in Shamir's minimum winning coalition. Shamir's refusal to support a call for a direct election of the prime minister led Tzomet to leave the coalition briefly in 1991 and then again in 1992.

Essentially, the reform calls for a separation of the office of prime minister from the Knesset. Under the current structure the public elects MKs, and they elect the government. The prime minister is usually the head of the largest party that is able to sign a coalition agreement with a majority of Knesset members. The prime minister is thus dependent upon a coalition of parties, each pulling in its own direction, and when they are in a "pivot" position each can potentially use its leverage to "blackmail" the government. The regular pressure imposed by small religious parties on the government to obtain "uniquely" appropriated state funds for their learning institutions had the appearance of a political ritual in Israel. Direct popular election of the prime minister would free him or her from such and similar coalition pressures. It would enable the selection of a government of professionals and the pursuit of uncompromising policies. For that, the prime minister would need, of course, a majority base of support in the Knesset.

The four proposals differed in several technical points, especially in those concerning the specification of the size of the majority of Knesset members needed for a vote of no-confidence in the government's policies. Such votes set legal limits to the prime minister's powers and can bring the government down if widely based disagreement develops against its policies and actions. This design of a "prime ministerial regime" borrows some important elements from both the American and French political structures, including the two-stage majority rule and the limitation of tenure in office. It also legally restricts the number of ministries that are permitted to form after the election.

As it happened, Yitzhak Shamir and his people opposed the proposed reform. They presumably feared—and public polls taken during the last months of 1991 reinforced these fears—that in a personal popular contest with Yitzhak Rabin, then challenger to the position of Labor leader, Shamir would lose. Instead, they proposed the idea of a "constructive no-confidence" method advanced some years earlier by scholars of the Carmon team, one of the public groups that supported electoral changes (Peri 1989, 21). Accordingly, to bring the government down opposition must show that it controls a viable majority-based parliamentary support. Lack of such presentation of an alternative government would result in the persistence of the present one and would ensure stability. This idea, however, was not supported by people outside of the Likud. Shamir then reneged on early commitments by having the reform proposal returned to the Knesset committee for further study in January 1992. However, such delay tactics could not be prolonged. Electoral reform became a major political issue and a weapon in the hands of Labor against the Likud, and because it became so salient it threatened to provide Labor with a significant advantage during the electoral campaign. Thus, on the final day of the twelfth Knesset, 18 March

1992, the legislation was returned from the committee and passed in an amended form (Book of Laws 1992).

The adopted law replaced the earlier Basic Law: Government (Rubinstein 1980). It has several new interesting features: The prime minister derives his authority directly from the citizens, who are asked (except in special elections) to vote for both him or her while also casting their votes for the Knesset. The duration of the prime minister's term is thus defined by the duration of corresponding Knesset tenures. A candidate may enter the race for the post of prime minister only if proposed by ten MKs or fifty thousand voters. The prime minister will be selected by a two-stage majority rule, but if only one person is proposed for the post, the election would still take place. In such cases a "winner" well be declared only if the number of votes in his favor is greater than the number of votes cast against him. When the prime minister is absent for some reason (death, impeachment, inability to function, or visit abroad) one of the ministers (who must be an MK) will serve as an acting prime minister. The number of ministers in the cabinet will be no more than eighteen but no fewer than eight, half of whom must be MKs. Most significant among this law's amendments is the time framework for its application: a delay until the election of the fourteenth Knesset (scheduled to be held in 1996). This decision, it was hypothesized, would not affect the then seventy-seven-year old Shamir, who announced his plans to retire from politics after the 1992 election.

As we show in the next section, Labor, headed by Yitzhak Rabin, exploited this public urge for reform and utilized an electoral campaign strategy that placed its leader as if he were competing, de facto, directly and personally with Shamir for the post of prime minister.

V. Adaptation of the Primaries Scheme

In section three above, the March 1990 government crisis was identified as a crucial political event that fueled and intensified the public desire for electoral reform. This, coupled with growing understanding among Labor politicians that their leader Shimon Peres, the four-time electoral loser against Likud, needed to be replaced led to the institution of the primaries scheme.

The idea of conducting American-style primaries to select Labor front-runners and candidates to the Knesset was seriously introduced after the 1988 election when the party studied the reasons for the recurring failure to secure electoral victory. Some alternative designs were proposed, but because the party participated in the grand coalition with the Likud, the adaptation of a final version was postponed. The March 1990 crisis, however, changed matters dramatically. Peres's reliance on promises made by a small religious party, Shas, initiated the crisis. However, after three months of negotiations, it was Shamir who together with extreme right-wing and religious parties formed the winning coalition in June 1990. Stripped of actual power, Labor MKs decided to replace Peres as the leader of the party. Failing to identify an agreed-upon front-runner among the second generation of MKs, they turned to Rabin as their consensual choice.

Rabin, who served as prime minister (1974–77) and defense minister (1984–90) had little to gain from Peres's initiation of the March crisis. He was already positioned as second to Shamir and to Peres, and hence he could not have improved upon his political position in the government or in his party. His attitude changed after Shamir succeeded in forming a coalition. He then agreed to spearhead the opposition to Peres. The challengers, however, underestimated Peres's strength among members of the party's Center, the broad-based decision making forum of the party. In the confrontation that took place in the Center in July 1990, Peres was able to defeat the opposition to his leadership.

During 1991, when Shamir's government gained success on several important issues including immigration, decision (or indecision) to participate in the Gulf War, and initiation of the peace process with the Arab states and the Palestinians, public approval of Labor was at its lowest. Several polls conducted at the end of that year showed a considerable margin in favor of Likud if the election were to be held at that time. Relatively speaking, they also showed that, indeed, Rabin was the only Labor electoral asset. Micha Harish, the general secretary of labor, aided by several of Rabin's supporters, decided to bypass Peres's domination of the Center by appealing to a larger body of voters—party members. The working assumption was that Rabin was more popular than Peres among party members and the general electorate.

Indeed, the actual design of the primaries scheme was supposed to reflect and capitalize on Rabin's strength among party members. The scheme was structured in two stages. The first called for a run-off to select the front runner of the party. The first one to pass the forty percent post would be declared the winner. If more than one passed this threshold, then the one who held plurality would win. If no one passed, than a second round between the two candidates who obtained most votes in the first round would be called for a few days later. The second stage, to be enacted several days after the completion of the first, utilized a simple plurality scheme. However, the final ranking of candidates on the Knesset list was predetermined. Thus, candidates could choose to compete on the "national list" or on a "districts list." Winning a first or second position in the district would automatically place them in a fixed spot on the Knesset list. Determination of the exact spot on this combined list was calculated in accordance with the size of the district, its weight in the party's power structure, and other political considerations.

The primaries for the party's front runner were held on 19 February 1992. Seventy-one percent of the 152,176 registered party members cast their votes for one of the four competing candidates. They were Peres, and Rabin, and two "spoilers"—Israel Kiesar and Ora Namir. Rabin received 40.6 percent of the votes, barely passing the designated threshold. The percentage of votes cast for the other candidates were: Peres, 34.5; Kiesar, 19.3; and Namir, 5.6. So a second round was not required. Registration of party members continued and reached 164,163 people by 31 February 1992, the date designated for the second stage of the primaries. At this stage Peres came first, capturing more than 83 percent of the 113,727 party members who participated. Only two of his loyal supporters were able to secure positions among the first ten people on the Knesset list. Thus, Rabin's victory was complete. No less importantly, however, the primaries focused public and media attention for an extended period of time on Labor's democratization process, which was in tune with the general urge to reform the political system.

Likud's failure to follow suit and the tension that erupted in March 1992, when the Likud Party Center convened to choose its Knesset list, reinforced this positive image of Labor (and especially of Rabin) gained during the primaries. Perhaps this was why Shamir decided to remove his opposition to the "direct election to the prime minister" bill.

But Likud support of the said bill came too late. By March Rabin's political strategists were already laying the foundations for a campaign that would position their leader as if he were running directly for the prime minister post. Such a design was based on survey findings which showed Rabin as a winner of a head-to-head competition with each and every member of the Likud leadership. These polls also showed that the Likud had a good chance to defeat Labor if the election would be publicly perceived as a competition between parties. The inference Labor strategists drew from this information was simple: emphasize Rabin and deemphasize his party, especially the role of Peres and his people. For that purpose several tactical moves were taken: the party changed its name to "Labor headed by Rabin"; blue replaced the traditional red as the party's color; Rabin altered his lingo from the collective *we* to the charismatic *I*; in media commercials Peres was "permitted" to appear only once, while Rabin appeared several times a day, and so forth. This and more, for the creation of a desired "presidential-like" image, Rabin addressed the public by talking of "my government of professionals," "my responsibility to the voters," "my order of priorities," and so forth, all of the same ingredients that make for a personal direct election to the prime minister post. As election results were tabulated during the night of 23 June, it became evident that this strategy was effective. Immediately, several of the defeated Likud MKs were proposing that their party, too, adopt the primaries scheme for the selection of their leader(s).

VI. Evaluation of the Actual and Proposed Reforms

Labor's victory in the election can only partly be accredited to a clever exploitation of the reform issue. Likud's inability—and perhaps some of its leaders' unwillingness—to bridge intrafactional tension and to effectively mobilize all its forces to counter the Labor challenge is a major factor responsible for its electoral defeat. It is proper, therefore, to analyze and evaluate the potential consequences the changes presented in sections IV and V above may have on the Israeli political system.

Arrow's (1963) general finding, which underlies the theoretical discussion in section II, that electoral systems are not reflective of individual preferences, is well understood, albeit intuitively, by Israeli politicians. In fact, Ben-Gurion, a major proponent of electoral reform admits: "the truth is that no representative body can reliably and accurately reflect the opinion of the voters" (1969, 577). His proposed design and that of his future fellow reformers, was supposed to maximize the potential for governability. This, Ben-Gurion believed, could be achieved by imposing several structural restrictions on the electoral system, thus transforming it into a two-party, British-style system.

The expectation that active politicians, especially members of small parties but also backbenchers of the big parties, would support a design that in effect decreased their chances of reelection is realistically quiet remote. After all, as Mayhew (1974) argued, politicians function everywhere so as to maximize the probability of their reelection; and because many of them have vested interests in the prevailing system, most would oppose proposed changes. Except for a few ambitious politicians (who presumably believe that the new electoral method could enhance their mobility upward) and leaders of the parties (whose positions are secured under any electoral system), most are either opposed or are ambivalent regarding the proposed reform of the electoral method to the Knesset. Even among supporters of the reform, it is not easy to distinguish between those who sincerely believe in its utility for the improvement of political life in Israel and those who simply favor it as a product of their personal political calculations. It is "relatively easy for those in doubt or opposition within the [large] parties to obey the discipline that guides them to support something [whose outcomes] they do not favor if it is clear to them that the undesirable outcome will not materialize" (Ya'acobi and Gera 1975, 52). Perhaps, this "hidden" opposition explains, at least partly, the lack of support encountered by Ya'acobi, Linn, and Zidon, three of the most prominent proponents of the reform, during the period when their respective parties selected their candidates to the thirteenth Knesset.

This "risk averse" tendency that everywhere characterizes politicians— holders of real power—presumably would have lesser personal ramifications when reform is directed toward the selection of a prime minister. At the top there could be only one person, who actually has been there anyway, and hence formalizing his position carries no or minimal spillover effects to the positions and power relations that exist among others. By determining the identity of the prime minister on election night, much of the friction created in building a government coalition would seemingly be obviated. The elected prime minister therefore would need not be overly concerned with gaining favor from other parties when putting together a cabinet. Instead, in selecting ministers, competence and harmony could be emphasized more extensively than the case has been in the past. This at least has been the hope and the explicit intention among advocates of this reform.

Can such novel expectations be met in reality? Fearing that the prime minister will gain too much power over the policy and legislative processes and even worse—over the extent of their tenure in Knesset, the "regret-mini-mizer" politicians have devise a scheme of checks that will make it very difficult for the prime minister to function independently. This scheme has a couple of interesting controls. First, under the new system both the executive and the legislative branches have control over each other's term of office. Either branch can dissolve the other and call for a new election (Book of Laws 1992, pars. 19, 22). However, such an action must be accompanied by the dissolution of the requesting branch. Hence election for both branches must be simultaneous. Thus, the uncertainty involved in obtaining desired outcomes in the future is supposed to check retaliatory action of one branch against the other, induce stability, and prevent, prolonged paralysis. The second control, which is perhaps even more important, refers to the requirement that the government must have a majority endorsement of the Knesset for conformation of its ministers (para. 3[c]), initiation of laws, especially the Budget Law (par. 20), and enacting of public regulation (pars. 47 and 48). To overcome these obstacles would require, as it does in the current system, a formation of winning coalitions in the Knesset and in its committees. Interparty bargaining (some call it "political extortion") would not be avoided.

This last inference rests, of course, on the extrapolation of the present highly fragmented political situation into the future. Indeed, if the prime minister's party were able to obtain a majority among MKs, then he or she would be in a position to operate in relative freedom. The following four points question the likelihood of the occurrence of such a development:

First, the proposal to reform the voting scheme to the Knesset, if ever enacted, is not designed to do away with small parties. As explained before, the system preserves the proportional strength of the parties in the Knesset; it permits them, as the current system does, to run, if so they wish, only in the national contest. So, if a party obtains 5 percent popular support, then all its six MKs will come from the national list, and none from the district list. In such a case fragmentation will not be alleviated, and formation of coalitions will be required.

Second, to counter such an effect, proponents of the reform have suggested a further increase of the vote threshold. Accordingly, the cutoff point would gradually move from 1.5 to 2.5 and then to 3.3 percent as proposed by the Ya'acobi committee. This too may not change matters much. Small parties would band together with like-minded groups and form "technical blocs"—an arrangement that would help them pass the post but not require discipline in Knesset. In fact, the change from 1 to 1.5 percent, which occurred in the twelfth Knesset, has already led to such a form of collusion. The two-man parties Shinui and Degel Hatora joined forces with left and religious parties, respectively, so as to be able to secure their political future. Hence, instead of having ten parties in the Knesset, a higher cutoff may generate say, only five or six parties, but these would be equipped with similar bargaining powers and may include several undisciplined members.

Third, the interrelation between the two types of electoral reforms may produce the common phenomenon (e.g., as manifested in the election to the American presidency and Congress or to the mayor and city council in Israel) of "split voting": a voter may support a candidate from one party for prime minister but at the same time vote for an opposition party member in the election for the Knesset. Here again "regret-minimizing" voters may reduce the risk of making wrong choices by balancing the tickets.

Potential for paralysis and even further extended political fragmentation may be generated from another source of voters' calculus: voters who usually vote for big parties for strategic reasons (i.e., to prevent victory from the opposition) may choose under the "prime ministerial regime" to follow their sincere preferences and support smaller parties.[2] Consequently, small parties would gain power at the expense of the big ones, and bargaining for support for government programs may become even more difficult. It must be noted, however, following Laver and Schofield (1990, 145–63), that such a diffusion and a potential equalization of the size and the bargaining powers of the parties may be rather conducive to long-term political stability if certain parameters are met. It is not clear if such potential stability may also permit a dynamic and innovative public policy.

Finally, the ramifications of the connection between reform of the party nomination process—the primaries and the other national level reforms—are also not clear. This vagueness is caused by the expansion of the organ that selects the candidates from party centers to the entire body of the party's members. Such an expansion necessarily reduces the control leaders have over their own party MKs (Doron and Goldberg 1990). Representatives become less accountable to their leaders and more accountable to the average party voter.

Similarly, in the proposed scheme for the election to the Knesset, traditional party control may further be dissipated because representatives may decide to be attuned only to the desires of their voters and not to the wishes of their parties. Consequently, the task of forming Knesset coalitions based on small parties and relatively independent politicians may became a task as difficult as is that of creating coalitions in the current Israeli political system.

VII. Conclusion

It is quite healthy for a political system to reevaluate its performance and reform itself. It is another thing to try, through a major reform of the electoral process, to achieve outcomes that cannot be obtained by small incremental alterations of the way votes are counted. As argued in section VI, large changes may produce unpredictable results, but even the political consequences of small changes may not always be anticipated. A case in point is the 1973 Bader-Ofer formula. Indeed, in the election that was held at the end of 1973 this small change adopted several months earlier favored, as expected, the two large parties at the expense of the small ones. But a careful simulation of the votes casted for the Israeli parties in 1977 shows that had Labor, the initiator of the 1973 change, benefited from the old "larger remainder" scheme, it would have been in a position to block the formation of a Likud minimal winning coalition (Doron 1988). As a result, the political history of Israel might had taken quite a different route.

Advocates of electoral reform want political stability, accountability, better qualified politicians, more effective public policy, and so on. Many of them believe that structural changes in the electoral schemes will bring about such objectives by reducing the number of parties. Beliefs, even if they are most noble, cannot, however, replace scientific knowledge, reasoning, and findings. Based on the accumulated knowledge of the political phenomenon, it is doubtful if such objectives could be met by the proposed reforms.

We know, for example, that political stability is related not necessarily to the number of parties in a given system but rather to the presence of parties in and outside of the formal boundaries of the system that have an interest in changing the prevailing status quo (Powell 1982). As in the free market, where no one buyer or seller can by himself upset the prevailing equilibrium, so it may be in politics too: the more parties there are in a system the higher the likelihood that the system will remain stable. This is perhaps the reason for the remarkable stability of the American Congress, stability that is enhanced by the activities of 535 relatively independent "parties" consisting of one member each.

Reliable political accountability is more a function of political culture (even if this term is not clearly defined) and of the internalization, through socialization and long-term learning processes, of democratic values than of a formal legal requirement. Here again, the legal requirement or structural change may have a short-term desired affect, but in the long-run other, more substantive factors may affect the outcomes: groupings according to ethnic, religious, or national characteristics; economic interests; and social stratifications are but some of these factors.

The ability to attract qualified politicians sensitive to the desires of the people and able to make decisions is also a function of political culture, the status of politics in a given society, and the interpretation of the payoffs awarded by those active in the *res publica.* A more effective public policy is dependent upon a specific action deduced from a clear set of goals and national priorities.

Thus, political culture, interests of parties (economic and other types of interests), political manipulation, specification of goals, random events, and so on are all parts of an unspecified formula that, next to the legislative and structural changes, affect voters' preferences and social choices. "The system is much too complex and the interrelations too many to use a simple mechanistic model to expect change in the political system as a result of legislation" (Arian 1985, 124). Nonetheless, a change may occur in the system; it may, however, produce outcomes in the form not desired by the reformers.

When the grand coalition ruled Israel for six years it was very difficult— other than to reach agreement on the basic goal of survival (as individuals and as a nation)—to obtain public consent over fundamental national dilemmas: religion versus state, religion versus nationality, communitarism versus individualism, the nature of the economy, and so on. These issues affect individual and group preferences and can only partly be addressed by the prevailing electoral system or the proposed ones. Because they cannot be avoided, they will continue to affect social choices in Israel one way or another.

Notes

1. Moshe Arens, Israel's defense minister from 1990 to 1992, suggested the following explanation as an answer to a question asked in the framework of a conference, "Coalitions and Bargaining," that was held at Tel Aviv University in May 1992.

2. This possibility was expressed to us in private conversations with several MKs of the left-wing small parties during January 1992. It explains why they support the direct election to the prime minister even though they covertly opposed changes in the method of election to the Knesset. On the difference between strategic ("sophisticated") and sincere voting, see Brams 1985, 70–73 and Riker 1982, 160–68.

References

Arian, Asher. 1985. *Politics in Israel: The Second Generation.* Chatham, N.J.: Chatham House.

Arrow, Kenneth. 1963. *Social Choice and Individual Values.* 2nd ed. New Haven: Yale University Press.

Ben-Gurion, David. 1969. *Renewed Eretz Israel.* Tel Aviv: Am Oved.

Book of Laws. 1992. Basic Law: The Government. Pp. 214–28. Faculty of Law: Tel Aviv University, 14 April.

Brams, Steven. 1985. *Rational Politics: Decisions, Games and Strategy.* Washington D.C.: Congressional Quarterly Press.

Braybrooke, David, and Charles Lindblom. 1963. *A Strategy of Decision.* New York: Free Press.

Brichta, Avraham. 1977. *Democracy and Election.* Tel Aviv: Am Oved.

Denzua, Arthur, and Robert Mackay. 1981. "Structure Induced Equilibrium and Perfect Foresight Expectations." *American Journal of Political Science,* 25:762–79.

Doron, Gideon. 1988. *Rational Politics in Israel.* Tel Aviv: Ramot.

Doron, Gideon, and Giora Goldberg. 1990. "No Big Deal: Democratization of the Nominating Process." In *The Election in Israel—1988,* ed. Arian Asher and Michal Shamir, 155–71. Boulder: Westview Press.

Doron, Gideon, and Moshe Maor. 1989. *Barriers to Entry into Israeli Politics.* Tel Aviv: Papyrus.

Eisenstadt, S. N. 1969. *The Israeli Society.* Jerusalem: Magnes.

Galnor, Itzhak. 1985. *The Origins of Israeli Democracy.* Tel Aviv: Am Oved.

Gibbrad, Alan. 1973. "The Manipulation of Voting Schemes: A General Result." *Econometrica* 41 (July):587–601.

Kook, Rebecca. 1992. "The Politics and Production of Corporate National Identity within Democratic Regimes." Ph.D. diss. Columbia University, New York.

Laver, Michael, and Norman Schofield. 1990. *Multiparty Government.* New York: Oxford University Press.

Mayhew, David. 1974. *Congress: The Electoral Connection.* New Haven: Yale University Press.

Peri, Yoram, ed. 1989. *Electoral Reform in Israel.* Tel Aviv: Israel Diaspora Institute.

Powell, G. Bingham, Jr. 1982. *Contemporary Democracies.* Cambridge: Harvard University Press.

Poundstone, William. 1992. *Prisoner's Dilemma.* New York: Doubleday.

Rae, Douglas. 1967. *The Political Consequences of Electoral Laws.* New Haven: Yale University Press.

Reichman, Uriel, et. al. 1987. *A Proposal for a Constitution for the State of Israel.* Tel Aviv: Tel Aviv University.

Riker, William. 1962. *The Theory of Political Coalitions.* New Haven: Yale University Press.

———. 1980. "Implications of the Disequilibrium of Majority Rule for the Study of Institutions." *American Political Review* 74:432–46.

———. 1982. *Liberalism against Populism.* San Francisco: Freeman.

Rubinstein, Amnon. 1980. *The Constitutional Law of Israel.* Tel Aviv: Schocken.

Sen, Amartya. 1970. *Collective Choice and Social Welfare.* San Francisco: Holden-Day.

Shepsle, Kenneth, and Barry Weingast. 1981. "Structure Induced Equilibrium and Legislative Choice." *Public Choice* 37:503–19.

———. 1987. "The Institutional Foundations of Committee Power." *American Political Science Review* 81:85–1204.

Ya'acobi, Gad, and Ehoud Gera. 1975. *The Freedom to Choose.* Tel Aviv: Am Oved.

Index